The ETHICS *of IDENTITY*

The ETHICS *of IDENTITY*

KWAME ANTHONY APPIAH

Library of Congress Cataloging-in-Publication Data

Appiah, Anthony.
The ethics of identity / Kwame Anthony Appiah.
p.   cm.
Includes bibliographical references and index.
ISBN 0-691-12036-6 (alk. paper)
1. Ethics. 2. Group identity—Moral and ethical aspects.
3. Identity (Psychology)—Moral and ethical aspects. I. Title.
BJ1031.A64 2005
170—dc22   2004044535

British Library Cataloging-in-Publication Data is available

This book has been composed in Minion

Printed on acid-free paper.∞

pupress.princeton.edu

Printed in the United States of America

10   9   8   7   6   5   4   3

∾ For Henry Finder

"totum muneris hoc tui est . . ."
—HORACE, *Odes* 4.3

Contents

~

Preface

~

IN CONTEMPORARY philosophical discussion in the English-speaking world, there is a broad consensus on the outlines and the history of a liberal political tradition. It is conventional, for example, to suppose that this tradition owes much to Locke's conception of religious toleration *and* to his theory of property; that the language of human equality and human rights, which was developed in the French and American Revolutions, is central to the heritage; that it is natural for a liberal to speak of human dignity and to suppose that it is (*ceteris*, as usual, *paribus*) equally a possession of each human being. It is also regularly assumed that the tradition is ethically *individualist*—in the sense that it assumes that, in the end, everything that matters morally, matters because of its impact on individuals—so that if nations, or religious communities, or families matter, they matter because they make a difference to the people who compose them.[1] We may have learned to think of these core elements of the liberal tradition as contested: so that, to put it crudely, liberals are not people who *agree* about the meaning of dignity, liberty, equality, individuality, toleration, and the rest, but are, rather, people who *argue* about their significance for political life. We may have learned, that is, that the liberal tradition—like all intellectual traditions—is not so much a body of doctrine as a set of debates. Still, it is widely agreed that there *is* such a tradition.

It is an interesting question whether we can, in fact, identify a tradition of thought that includes these elements; and it is, of course, a question that would require serious historical inquiry. My own suspicion is that if you began such an inquiry, the intellectual antecedents of Mill or Hobhouse or Berlin or Rawls would turn out to be more multifarious than singular, and that what we now call the liberal tradition would look less like a body of ideas that developed through time and more like a collection of sources and interpretations of sources that we now find useful, looking backward, in articulating one influential philosophical view of politics: yet another instance of the Owl of Minerva's taking wing as the light fades. One reason—a shallow one, perhaps, but it has impressed me—for thinking that liberalism is a creation of hindsight is that the use of the word "liberalism," as the name for a political faith, is a nineteenth-century development; it occurs nowhere in the writings of Locke or the American Founders, in whose absence the history of liberalism we now tell would be sorely depleted.[2]

So you might try to identify liberalism with traditions of practice, instead of thought. Taking a feet-first rather than headfirst approach, you could point to the development over the last few centuries, but especially since the American and French Revolutions, of a new form of political life. This form of life finds expression in certain political institutions: among them elected rather than hereditary rulers, and, more generally, some sort of appeal to the consent of the governed, but also limitations on the power of those who govern—even in the name of a majority—expressed in a legal system that respects certain fundamental rights. These civil or political rights carve out for citizens a corresponding sphere of freedoms, including freedom of political expression and freedom of religion. To be sure, each of these elements can come on its own: there were republics in Europe as far back as Athens; the first German emperors were elected;[3] and freedom of the press and religious toleration developed in England within a monarchical scheme. What characterizes the beginnings of liberalism, then, would seem to be a *combination* of political institutions: constitutions, rights, elections, and safeguards for private property. In the twentieth century, across both Europe and North America, these things were supplemented by a public concern to guarantee certain minimum conditions of welfare for every citizen.

Still, talk of practice won't protect you from the perplexities of principle, and you won't get very far with the attempt to draw a line between the two. For theories of politics aren't like theories of celestial mechanics: in the realm of the political, theories have a tendency to become a part of what they theorize. If there is a liberal form of life, it was always characterized not only by institutions but also by a rhetoric, a body of ideas and arguments. When the American colonists declared it to be "self-evident" that they had inalienable rights to life, liberty, and the pursuit of happiness, they sought to *make* it so. It's possible, though, that an emphasis on practices rather than principles can be helpful in showing just how heterogeneous those principles can be. For example, historians have debated the importance, for America's Founders, of classical republicanism—of a politics founded upon ideals of citizenship, rather than upon notions of individual rights. But once you accept that liberal democracy has been informed by talk of civic virtues as well as talk of rights, than you might well conclude that liberalism should be taken to subsume such putatively contending traditions. Not only does liberalism, taken in this loose and baggy sense, encompass nearly all members of nearly all of the mainstream political parties in Europe and North America; it also encompasses theorists who, in criticizing "atomism" or deontology, say, regard themselves as hostile to the liberal tradition rather than part of it. Letting "liberalism" absorb many of its ostensible rivals may invite charges of lexical imperialism. But it will at least forestall those grindingly familiar arguments about whether this or that putatively liberal position is or isn't really liberal. Such arguments are often illuminating in their substance, but not, I think, as arguments over a word.

So why ride that swaybacked steed, weighed down with its multifarious semantic baggage, in the first place? That's a good question. I should admit I'd once hoped to be able to write this book without recourse to it. That I didn't get very far is a reminder that *all* of our political terms are shopsoiled by history; to talk about autonomy or toleration or dignity is to join a conversation that has been ongoing long before you arrived and will continue long after you've departed. The problems I'll be exploring have arisen for those of us who find ourselves broadly convinced that certain values, now associated by anglophone philosophers with the word "liberal," matter to the lives we lead, and to the politics we wish to fashion. At the same time, the problems I want to discuss are of significance whether or not "liberalism" is the right name for the project within which they arise. Indeed, I hope to persuade you that they are significant even if, mirabile dictu, you do not find yourself disposed to think of yourself as a liberal at all.

∾

Let me sketch out a picture within which the problems I want to talk about arise. Each of us has one life to live; and although there are many moral constraints on how we live our lives—prominent among them being constraints that derive from our obligations to other persons—these constraints do not determine which particular life we must live. We must not live lives of cruelty and dishonesty, for example, but there are many lives we can live without these vices. There are also constraints on how we may live that derive from our historical circumstances and our physical and mental endowments: I was born into the wrong family to be a Yoruba chief and with the wrong body for motherhood; I am too short to be a successful professional basketball player, insufficiently dexterous to be a concert pianist. But even when we have taken these things into account, we know that each human life starts out with many possibilities. Some people have a wider and more interesting range of options than others. I once had a conversation with the late Nobel laureate Jacques Monod—one of the founding fathers of molecular biology—who told me he had had to choose, at a certain point in his life, among being (as I recall) a concert cellist, a philosopher, and a scientist. But everybody has, or should have, a variety of decisions to make in shaping a life. And for a person of a liberal disposition these choices belong, in the end, to the person whose life it is.

This means at least two things. First, the measure of my life, the standard by which it is to be assessed as more or less successful, depends, if only in part, on my life's aims as specified by me. Second, my life's shape is up to me (provided that I have done my duty toward others), even if I make a life that is less good than a life I could have made. All of us could, no doubt, have made better lives than we have: but that is no reason for others to attempt to force those better lives upon us. Thoughtful friends, benevolent sages, anxious relatives will rightly offer us both assistance and advice as to how to proceed. But it will *be* advice, not coercion, that they justly offer. And, just as coercion will be wrong in these private circumstances, it will be wrong when it is undertaken by governments interested in the perfection of their citizens. That is what it means to say that—once I have done my duties—the shaping of my life is up to me. What Mill taught us to call individuality is one term for this task. But it doesn't take place in a vacuum; rather, it is itself shaped by the available social forms. And it can involve obligations that seem to go beyond my voluntary undertakings, and beyond the basic requirements of morality.

So far, I can assume what I've been saying is fairly unexceptionable—a recitation of common sense even among my academic tribe. The fact that it *is* common sense reflects important changes in the climate of metaethical reflection over the past few decades. In particular, we philosophers—whatever position we take on "value pluralism" or "moral realism"—have become increasingly conscious that moral obligation represents only a subset of our normative concerns. In just this spirit, T. M. Scanlon has distinguished a rump morality—morality in the sense of "what we owe to each other"—from "morality in the wider sense," which involves things like being a good parent or friend, or striving to meet high standards in your profession. And Bernard Williams similarly identified morality as a "narrower system"—indeed, in his view, a "peculiar institution"—within the broader tradition of what he called the ethical. But then this basic intuition, and the nomenclatural worries it presents, is scarcely new. In the 1930s, the English translators of Henri Bergson's *The Two Sources of Morality and Religion* warned readers, as a matter "of the utmost importance," that they'd used the word "morality" to translate "the word 'morale,' which has a wider meaning in French than in English, conveying both morality and ethics." And an insistence upon some such distinction can be pushed further back, certainly to Hegel, and arguably much further still. You might suppose that morality, in this narrow sense, is a concoction of philosophers; you might blame it on Kant, or take it to be an outgrowth of liberal toleration. But I think Williams is right to insist that, on the contrary, it is "the outlook, or, incoherently, part of the outlook, of almost all of us." As we've seen, there's no settled convention for how to mark the distinction; or, indeed, for exactly what such a distinction would distinguish. For the most part, though, I shall find it convenient to follow Ronald Dworkin's stipulative lexicon, whereby ethics "includes convictions about which kinds of lives are good or bad for a person to lead, and morality includes principles about how a person should treat other people."[4]

In moving from the realm of moral obligation to that of ethical flourishing, philosophical reflection among the moderns has returned to questions that absorbed the ancients: questions about what lives we should lead, defining the well-lived life as something more than a life in which our preferences are well satisfied. Once we take such questions seriously, we are bound to acknowledge that the tools with which we make our lives include many socially provided resources and forms: among them, most obviously, language, but also countless other private and public institutions. What has proved especially vexatious, though, is the effort to take account of those social forms we now call *identities*: genders and sexual orientations, ethnicities and nationalities, professions and vocations. Identities make ethical claims because—and this is just a fact about the world we human beings have created—we make our lives *as* men and *as* women, *as* gay and *as* straight people, *as* Ghanaians and *as* Americans, *as* blacks and *as* whites. Immediately, conundrums start to assemble. Do identities represent a curb on autonomy, or do they provide its contours? What claims, if any, can identity groups as such justly make upon the state? These are concerns that have gained a certain measure of salience in recent political philosophy, but, as I hope to show, they are anything but newfangled. What's modern is that we conceptualize identity in particular ways. What's age-old is that when we are asked—and ask ourselves—*who* we are, we are being asked *what* we are as well.

～

In the pages that follow, I plan to explore the ethics of identity in our personal and political lives; but I want to do so in an account that takes seriously Mill's notion of individuality. Indeed, Mill, who has become a central figure in modern political thought for many good reasons, and a few bad ones, will serve us as something of a traveling companion in the pages ahead. What will make him an agreeable traveling companion—as opposed to a traveling icon, dangling from the rearview mirror—isn't that we will agree with all his analyses; it's that he cared about so many of the issues we care about, and, in a day when talk of "identity" can sound merely modish, he reminds us that the issues it presents are scarcely alien to the high canon of political philosophy.

I said that the problems I would be discussing have arisen in the general arena of liberal thought (taking it to be a *very* general arena indeed). But, of course, many theorists who have been engaged by these problems are inclined to view them as *challenges* to liberalism. They're worried that liberalism has given us a picture of the world that leaves too much out; that the founders of the liberal canon, as we've assembled it, were oblivious to, or uninterested in, the differences among forms of life. In particular, we have been urged to distrust the habit of abstraction, of uninflected talk of individuals, rather than singular, situated selves. Thus it has sometimes been said that John Locke and the other founding theorists of something like liberal democracy lived in a deeply homogeneous world; that their notions weren't appropriate for our multiethnic modernity. Now, much can be learned from the contemporary clash between the Leavers Out and the Putters In; there is such a thing as the clarity of the battlefield. But there is also such a thing as the fog of war. My own suspicion is that the conceptual resources of conventional liberal theory really aren't so very impoverished; and that, in any case, not every omission is a sin.

For, of course, Locke was writing in the wake of protracted and bloody sectarian strife; his abstraction did not arise from inadvertence or obliviousness or mere ethnic vanity. The matter of diversity, far from being marginal to the origins of modern political philosophy, was central to it. The leaving-out was purposeful; and the purpose was not a negligible one. It was to make possible something that liberals talk about a good deal—respect for persons. And the ambit of "respect" is precisely where the habit of liberal abstraction shows its strength. The encumbered self, laden with all the specificity of its manifold allegiances, is not something we can, as a rule, be bound to respect. I am not alone is doubting the imperative to respect cultures, as opposed to persons; and I believe we can respect persons only inasmuch as we consider them as abstract rights-holders. Much of our moral advancement has depended on such a tendency toward abstraction. As Peter Railton observes, "broad historical trends have pushed the development of generalization in moral thought," and what promoted such generalization was precisely the challenges of internal diversity. "Religious tolerance, for example, requires that we see the views of others as religions, rather than mere heresies. This requires adopting some critical distance not only on their convictions, but on ours as well."[5] To say all this is decidedly not to doubt the value of putting-in: it is only to say that putting-in should be done with caution, and that more isn't necessarily better. If the leaving-out was strategic, the putting-in must be as well.

And so I write neither as identity's friend nor as its foe. Either posture is likely to call to mind that full-hearted avowal, by the American transcendentalist Margaret Fuller, "I accept the universe!"—and Carlyle's storied rejoinder, "Gad! She'd better!" As with gravity, you might as well be on good terms with it, but there's no point in buttering it up. Indeed, in the spirit of those side-effects warnings you find in drug advertisements—those blocks of microscopic type that cause the blurred vision they warn about—I should offer a disclaimer. I have often found it helpful to supplant talk of "race" or "culture" with talk of identity; but I should admit, preemptively, that talk of identity, too, can have reifying tendencies. As it is mobilized within the discourse of psychology, it can be compromised by the spurious notion of psychological wholeness (echoed in those bromides about "identity crisis," "finding oneself," and so forth). As it is mobilized within the discourse of ethnography, it can harden into something fixed and determinate, a homogeneity of Difference.[6] But I don't know what to do about such perils, aside from pointing them out, and trying to avoid them.

You will have to judge for yourself whether I've succeeded. In these pages, I've tried to pull together my thinking and writing over the past decade on ethics and identity. The *together* part has inevitably entailed a considerable amount of revision: protraction, contraction, retraction. The first, introductory chapter maps out the terrain, with particular reference to Millian individuality. It is, by design, the least contentious part of the book, a marshaling of what I take to be common sense, before it is put to the test. (And, like many philosophers, I am of the school that what goes without saying often goes even better *with* saying.) The subsequent chapters carry the discussion into a number of areas—the contested domain of "autonomy," the debates surrounding citizenship and identity; the proper role of the state with respect to our ethical flourishing; the negotiations between partiality and morality; the prospects for conversations across ethical communities. In focusing on these normative questions, I have largely tried to abstain from meta-

physical commitment on the grand questions of moral realism, the issues about the ontological significance of the fact-value distinction. I
have therefore also tried to stay away from explicit discussion of moral
epistemology, although, of course, you cannot proceed without metaphysical or epistemological presuppositions altogether. If there is something distinctive in my approach, it is that I start always from the perspective of the individual engaged in making his or her life, recognizing
that others are engaged in the same project, and concerned to ask what
social and political life means for this ethical project we share. This is,
then, I want to emphasize, a work of ethics, in the special sense I have
picked out, and not of political theory, because it does not start with
an interest in the state. Rather, the political questions it addresses are
those that arise inevitably once we recognize that the ethical task each
of us has—our life making—is inevitably bound up with the ethical
lives of others. That is why I discuss some of our wider social, as well
as our more narrowly political, relationships. And that is also why I
end with an exploration of questions that take us beyond the issues
that arise about national politics into wider global concerns: the others
whose ethical projects matter are not only our fellow citizens, they are
also the citizens of every other nation on the planet. I began with a
discussion of liberalism, a political tradition: but that is because I believe that some of the ethical presuppositions of that tradition are profoundly correct, not because I am mostly concerned with politics.

My last and most forceful disclaimer, however, is addressed to those
who are looking for practical guidance, for specific recommendations
about precisely what laws or institutions will best heal our social and
political ills. Alas, I am a poor physician: I'm interested in diagnosis—
in etiology and nosology—but not in cures. If an agenda, a set of action
items, is what you're after, my one bit of practical advice is that you
look elsewhere.

What's on offer here, indeed, is more in the spirit of exploration
than of conclusion. One of the great figures of early twentieth-century
economics—was it Arthur Cecil Pigou?—avowed that the purpose of
his discipline was to provide heat, not light. He meant that it should
be useful rather than merely illuminating. Though I'd like to start an
argument or two, the explorations that follow can be relied upon to
provide very little heat, if any; my hope has been to shed some light,

even if dim, even if flickering. Philosophy is invariably more helpful in framing questions than in framing policies. My aim isn't to win converts, and I scarcely care whether you agree with every view I have ventured; I couldn't say for sure that *I* do. How we are to make sense of the relations between identity and individuality—between the *what* and the *who*—is, as I say, the subject of a conversation half as old as time. Whether or not you find my approach sympathetic, I hope that I can at least persuade you that the conversation is worth joining.

The ETHICS *of IDENTITY*

Chapter One

∿ The Ethics of Individuality

THE GREAT EXPERIMENT—LIBERTY AND INDIVIDUALITY—
PLANS OF LIFE—THE SOUL OF THE SERVITOR—SOCIAL
CHOICES—INVENTION AND AUTHENTICITY—THE SOCIAL
SCRIPTORIUM—ETHICS IN IDENTITY—INDIVIDUALITY AND
THE STATE—THE COMMON PURSUIT

THE GREAT EXPERIMENT

Depending upon how you look at it, John Stuart Mill's celebrated education was either a case study in individuality or a vigorous attempt to erase it. He himself seems to have been unable to decide which. He called his education "the experiment," and the account he provided in his *Autobiography* ensured that it would become the stuff of legend. He was learning Greek at three, and by the time he was twelve, he had read the whole of Herodotus, a fair amount of Xenophon, Virgil's *Eclogues* and the first six books of the *Aeneid*, most of Horace, and major works by Sophocles, Euripides, Polybius, Plato, and Aristotle, among others. After studying Pope's Homer, he set about composing a "continuation of the Iliad," at first on whim and then on command. He had also made serious forays into geometry, algebra, and differential calculus.

The young Mill was kept away as much as possible from the corrupting influence of other boys ("the contagion," as he put it, "of vulgar modes of thought and feeling"); and so, in his fourteenth year, when John Stuart was about to meet some new people beyond the range of his father's supervision, James Mill took his son for a walk in Hyde Park to prepare him for what he might expect to encounter. If he found that he was ahead of other children, he must attribute it not to his own superiority, but to the particular rigors of his intellectual upbringing: "it was no matter of praise to me, if I knew more than those who had not had a similar advantage, but the deepest disgrace to me if I did not." This was the first inkling he had that he was precocious, and Mill had every reason to be astonished. "If I thought anything about myself, it was that I was rather backward in my studies," he recounts, "since I always found myself so, in comparison with what my father expected from me."[1]

But James Mill was a man with a mission, and it was his eldest son's appointed role to carry forward that mission. James, as Jeremy Bentham's foremost disciple, was molding yet another disciple—someone who, trained in accordance with Benthamite principles, would extend and promulgate the grand *raisonneur*'s creed for a new era. He was, so to speak, the samurai's son. In the event, self-development was to be a central theme of Mill's thought and, indeed, a main element of his complaint against his intellectual patrimony. When he was twenty-four, he wrote to his friend John Sterling about the loneliness that had come to overwhelm him: "There is now no human being (with whom I can associate on terms of equality) who acknowledges a common object with me, or with whom I can cooperate even in any practical undertaking, without feeling that I am only using a man, whose purposes are different, as an instrument for the furtherance of my own."[2] And his sensitivity about using another in this way surely flows from his sense that he himself had been thus used—that he had been conscripted into a master plan that was not his own.

Mill memorably wrote about the great crisis in his life—a sort of midlife crisis, which, as befitted his precocity, visited when he was twenty—and the spiral of anomie into which he descended, during the winter of 1826.

> In this frame of mind it occurred to me to put the question directly to myself: "Suppose that all your objects in life were realized; that all the changes in institution and opinions which you are looking forward to, could be completely effected at this very instant: would this be a great joy and happiness to you?" And an irrepressible self-consciousness distinctly answered, "No!" At this my heart sank within me: the whole foundation on which my life was constructed fell down.[3]

He pulled out of it, stepped blinking into the light; but for a long while thereafter found himself dazed and adrift. Intent on deprogramming himself from the cult of Bentham, he plunged into an uncritical eclecticism, unwilling to exercise his perhaps overdeveloped faculties of discrimination. He was determinedly, even perversely, receptive to the arguments of those he would once have considered the embodiment of Error, whether the breathless utopianism of the Saint-Simonians or the murky Teutonic mysticisms of Coleridge and Carlyle. When intellectual direction returned to his life, it was through the agency of his new friend and soul mate, Mrs. Harriet Hardy Taylor. "My great readiness and eagerness to learn from everybody, and to make room in my opinions for every new acquisition by adjusting the old and the new to one another, might, but for her steadying influence, have seduced me into modifying my early opinions too much," he would write.[4]

It was a relationship that was greeted with considerable censure, not least by James Mill. So there is some irony that it was she, more than anyone, who seems to have returned the rudderless craft he had become to the tenets of the patrimonial cause. His love for her was at once rebellion and restoration—and the beginning of an intellectual partnership that spanned almost three decades. Only when Mrs. Taylor was widowed, in 1851, could she and Mill live together as man and wife, and in the mid-1850s their collaboration bore its greatest fruit: *On Liberty*, surely the most widely read work of political philosophy in the English language.

I retell this familiar story because so many of the themes that preoccupied Mill's social and political thought wend their way through his life. It is a rare convenience. Buridan's ass did not itself tap out any contributions to decision theory before succumbing to starvation. Paul Gauguin, the emblem and avatar of Bernard Williams's famous analysis of "moral luck," was not himself a moral philosopher. Yet Mill's concern with self-development and experimentation was a matter of both philosophical inquiry and personal experience. *On Liberty* is an impasto of influences—ranging from German romanticism, by way of Wilhelm von Humboldt and Coleridge, to the sturdy, each-person-counts-for-one equality and tolerance that were Mill's intellectual birthright. But my interest in Mill's work is essentially and tendentiously presentist, for it adumbrates the main themes of this book, as it does so many topics in liberal theory.

Consider his emphasis on the importance of diversity; his recognition of the irreducibly plural nature of human values; his insistence that the state has a role in promoting human flourishing, broadly construed; his effort to elaborate a notion of well-being that was at once individualist and (in ways that are sometimes overlooked) profoundly social. Finally, his robust ideal of individuality mobilizes, as we'll see, the critical notions of autonomy and identity. My focus on Mill isn't by way of *argumentum ad verecundiam*; I don't suppose (nor did he) that his opinions represented the last word. But none before him—and, I am inclined to add, none since—charted out the terrain as clearly and as carefully as he did. We may cultivate a different garden, but we do so on soil that he fenced in and terraced.

Liberty and Individuality

"If it were felt that the free development of individuality is one of the leading essentials of well-being; that it is not only a coordinate element with all that is designated by the terms civilization, instruction, education, culture, but is itself a necessary part and condition of all those things; there would be no danger that liberty should be undervalued, and the adjustment of the boundaries between it and social control would present no extraordinary difficulty."[5] So Mill wrote in the book's celebrated third chapter, "On Individuality, as One of the Elements of Wellbeing," and it is a powerful proposal. For it seems to suggest that individuality could be taken as prior even to the book's titular subject, liberty itself. Our capacity to use all our faculties in our individual ways was, at least in part, what made liberty valuable to us. In Mill's accounting, individuality doesn't merely conduce to, it is constitutive of, the social good. And he returns to the point, lest anyone miss it: "Having said that Individuality is the same thing with development, and that it is only the cultivation of individuality which produces, or can produce, well-developed human beings, I might here close the argument: for what more or better can be said of any condition of human affairs, than that it brings human beings themselves nearer to the best thing they can be? or what worse can be said of any obstruction to good, than that it prevents this?"[6]

To be sure, Mill does offer conventionally consequentialist arguments for liberty—arguments that liberty is likely to have good effects. His most famous arguments for freedom of expression assume that we will find the truth more often and more easily if we allow our opinions to be tested in public debate, in what we all now call the marketplace of ideas. But he argued with especial fervor that the cultivation of one's individuality is itself a part of well-being, something good *in se*, and here liberty is not a means to an end but part of the end. For individuality means, among other things, choosing for myself instead of merely being shaped by the constraint of political or social sanction. It was part of Mill's view, in other words, that freedom mattered not just because it enabled other things—such as the discovery of truth—but also because without it people could not develop the individuality that is an essential element of human good.[7] As he writes,

> He who lets the world, or his own portion of it, choose his plan of life for him, has no need for any other faculty than the ape-like one of imitation. He who chooses his plan for himself, employs all his faculties. He must use observation to see, reasoning and judgment to foresee, activity to gather materials for decision, discrimination to decide, and when he has decided, firmness and self-control to hold to his deliberate decision. And these qualities he requires and exercises exactly in proportion as the part of his conduct which he determines according to his own judgment and feelings is a large one. It is possible that he might be guided in some good path, and kept out of harm's way, without any of these things. But what will be his comparative worth as a human being? It really is of importance, not only what men do, but also what manner of men they are that do it.[8]

Individuality is not so much a state to be achieved as a mode of life to be pursued. Mill says that it is important that one choose one's own plan of life, and liberty consists, at least in part, in providing the conditions under which a choice among acceptable options is possible. But one must choose one's own plan of life not because one will necessarily make the wisest choices; indeed, one might make poor choices. What matters most about a plan of life (Mill's insistence on the point is especially plangent coming from the subject of James and Jeremy's great experiment) is simply that it be chosen by the person whose life it is: "If a person possesses any tolerable amount of common sense and experience, his own mode of laying out his existence is best, not because it is the best in itself, but because it is his own mode." Not only is exercising one's autonomy valuable in itself, but such exercise leads to self-development, to the cultivation of one's faculties of observation, reason, and judgment.[9] Developing the *capacity* for autonomy is necessary for human well-being, which is why it matters not just what people choose but "what manner of men they are that do it." So Mill invokes "individuality" to refer both to the precondition and to the result of such deliberative choice making.[10]

The account of individuality that Mill offers in chapter 3 of *On Liberty* does not distinguish consistently between the idea that it is good to be different from other people and the idea that it is good to be, in some measure, self-created, to be someone who "chooses his plan for himself."[11] Still, I think it is best to read Mill as finding inherent value not in diversity—being different—but in the enterprise of self-creation. For I might choose a plan of life that was, as it happened, very like other people's and still not be merely aping them, following them blindly as a model. I wouldn't, then, be contributing to diversity (so, in one sense, I wouldn't be very individual), but I would still be constructing my own—in another sense, individual—plan of life. *On Liberty* defends freedom because only free people can take full command of their own lives.

PLANS OF LIFE

Why does Mill insist that individuality is something that develops in coordination with a "plan of life"? His training as a utilitarian means that he wouldn't have separated well-being from the satisfaction of wants; but he was well aware that to make sense of such wants, we had to see them as structured in particular ways. Our immediate desires and preferences so often run contrary to other, longer-term ones. We wish to have written a book, but we don't wish to write one. We wish to ace our gross anatomy exam, but don't wish to study for it on this sunny afternoon. It's for this reason that we devise all manner of mechanisms to bind ourselves (in chapter 5, we'll see that much of "culture" comprises institutions of self-binding), so that, as we often say, we "force ourselves" to do what our interest requires. Moreover, many of our goals are clearly intermediate in nature, subordinate to more comprehensive goals. You want to ace your gross anatomy exam because you want to be a surgeon; you want to be a surgeon because you want to mend cleft palates in Burkina Faso or, as the case may be, carve retroussé noses in Beverly Hills; and these ambitions may be in the service of still other ambitions. For reasons I'll explore more fully in chapter 5, it's worth bearing in mind that for Mill the activity of choosing freely had a *rational* dimension, was bound up in observation, reason, judgment, and deliberation. In *A System of Logic*, Mill even suggests that the consolidation of fleeting preferences into steadier purposes is what constitutes maturity:

> A habit of willing is commonly called a purpose; and among the causes of our volitions, and of the actions which flow from them, must be reckoned not only likings and aversions, but also purposes. It is only when our purposes have become independent of the feelings of pain or pleasure from which they originally took their rise, that we are said to have a confirmed character. "A character," says Novalis, "is a completely fashioned will", and the will, once so fashioned, may be steady and constant, when the passive susceptibilities of pleasure and pain are greatly weakened, or materially changed.[12]

Precisely this notion became central to a subsequent theorist of "life plans," Josiah Royce, who essentially defined a person as someone in possession of one. Rawls, too, was working within this Millian discourse when he stipulated that "a person's plan of life is rational if, and only if, (1) it is one of the plans that is consistent with the principles of rational choice when these are applied to all the relevant features of his situation, and (2) it is that plan among those meeting this condition which would be chosen by him with full deliberative rationality, that is, with full awareness of the relevant facts and after a careful consideration of the consequences."[13]

The currency such talk of "plans" has acquired in contemporary liberal theory has invited some gimlet-eyed scrutiny. "In general, people do not and cannot make an overall choice of a total plan of life," J. L. Mackie observes. "They choose successively to pursue various activities from time to time, not once and for all." Daniel A. Bell, in a critique of the sort of liberal individualism associated with Rawls, maintains that "people do not necessarily have a 'highest-order interest' in ratio-

nally choosing their career and marriage partner, as opposed to following their instincts, striving for ends and goals set for them by others
(family, friends, community groups, the government, God), and letting
fate do the rest of the work. . . . This, combined with an awareness of
the unchosen nature of most of our social attachments, undermines
those justifications for a liberal form of social organization founded on
the value of reflective choice." And Michael Slote has raised concerns
about the ways in which such "plans of life" mobilize preferences across
time. Sometimes, given certain future uncertainties, we will be better
served if we cultivate a measure of passivity, of watchful waiting. It's
also the case that, as he puts it, "rational life-planfulness is a virtue with
a temporal aspect"—it's not advisable for children to arrive at hard-
and-fast decisions about their careers, because the activity requires the
sort of prudence they're unlikely to possess. What's more, there are
important human goods, like love or friendship, that we don't exactly
"plan" for.[14]

The critics have a point. No doubt such talk of plans can be misleading if we imagine that people stride around with a neatly folded
blueprint of their lives tucked into their back pocket—if we imagine
life plans to be singular and fixed, rather than multiple and constantly
shifting.[15] Dickens hardly needed to underscore the irony when he had
Mr. Dombey announce, of his doomed young heir, "There is nothing
of chance or doubt in the course before my son. His way in life was
clear and prepared, and marked out before he existed."[16] Plans can
evolve, reverse course, be derailed by contingencies large and small; and
to speak of them should not commit us to the notion that there's one
optimal plan for an individual. (It's noteworthy that even the great
embodiments of ambition in European fiction—Stendhal's Julien Sorel,
say, or Trollope's Phineas Finn—stumble into their careers through a
succession of fortuities. Sorel's choice of the black over the red reflects
not inner conviction, but the particular positions of the army and the
church during the French restoration.) Mill himself did not labor under
any such illusions. Nobody would have planned to fall in love with
another man's wife and spend the next two decades in a nerve-racking
ménage à trois.[17] Precisely because of his temperamental constancy, he
was acutely aware of the ways in which his thought and goals shifted
over time. That's one reason he came to think that the exploration of

the ends of life would yield to "experiments in living," although he had reason to know that conducting an experiment and having one conducted upon you were two different things.

The Soul of the Servitor

Though talk of plans can sound overly determinate, Mill's rhetorical excesses were frequently in the opposite direction—suggesting not too much structure but too little. The way he wrote about individuality, the product (and condition) of the freely chosen life plan, occasionally makes it sound like a weirdly exalted affair—an existence of ceaseless nonconformity, de novo judgments, poeticizing flights. It may conjure the whirling, willowy performance artist the cartoonist Jules Pfeiffer likes to draw, a character who perpetually expresses her every velleity in dance. This is not Mill's view,[18] any more than the engineering-schematic view is, but because Mill speaks abstractly, it may help to imagine a more concrete example. Consider, then, Mr. Stevens, the butler in Kazuo Ishiguro's celebrated novel *The Remains of the Day*. Mr. Stevens has spent a whole life in service in a "great house," and his aim has been to perform his task to the very best of his ability. He sees himself as part of the machinery that made the life of his master, Lord Darlington, possible. Since his master has acted on the stage of public history, he sees Lord Darlington's public acts as part of what gives meaning to his own life. As he puts it: "Let us establish this quite clearly: a butler's duty is to provide good service. It is not to meddle in the great affairs of the nation. The fact is, such great affairs will always be beyond the understanding of those such as you and I, and those of us who wish to make our mark must realize that we best do so by concentrating on what *is* within our realm."[19]

Mr. Stevens takes what is "within our realm" extremely seriously; for example, he feels, as he says, "uplifted" by a "sense of triumph" when he manages to pursue his duties unflustered on the evening that the woman he barely realizes he loves has announced to him that she is going to marry somebody else.[20] By the time he tells us about this fateful day, we know him well enough to understand how such a sentiment is possible.

At the end of the book, Mr. Stevens is returning to Darlington Hall from the holiday during which he has reviewed his life with us, and he tells us he is going back to work on what he calls his "bantering skills" in order to satisfy his new American master.

> I have of course already devoted much time to developing my bantering skills, but it is possible I have never previously approached the task with the commitment I might have done. Perhaps, then, when I return to Darlington Hall tomorrow ... I will begin practising with renewed effort. I should hope, then, by the time of my employer's return, I shall be in a position to pleasantly surprise him.[21]

Few readers of Ishiguro's novel will aspire to be a butler, least of all the sort of butler that Mr. Stevens aimed to be. And there is, indeed, something mildly ridiculous in the thought of an elderly man working on his skills at light conversation in order to entertain his young "master." Ishiguro specializes in starchy, self-deceived narrators, and readers are likely to feel when they come to these last words a tremendous sadness at what is missing from Mr. Stevens's life.

Nevertheless, Mr. Stevens is continuing to live out the life he has chosen. And it does seem to me that we can understand part of what Mill is suggesting by saying that bantering is something of value to Mr. Stevens because he has chosen to be the best butler he can be. This is not a life *we* would have chosen; but for someone who *has* chosen it, it is intelligible that improving one's bantering skills is a good. Mill isn't very clear in *On Liberty* about how "individuality" might relate to other kinds of goods. But he recognized that sometimes a thing matters because a person has chosen to make a life in which it matters, and that it would not matter if he or she had not chosen to make such a life. To say that bantering is of value to Mr. Stevens is not just to say that he wants to be able to do it well, as he might want to be good at bridge or bowling. It is to say that, given his aims, his "plan of life," bantering matters to him; we, for whom bantering does not matter in this way, can still see that it is a value for him within the life he has chosen.

You may think that this is not a life that anyone who had other reasonable options should have chosen, and that even someone who was forced into it should not have taken to it with the enthusiasm and commitment that Mr. Stevens manifests. You might even explain this by saying that the life of the perfect servant is not one of great dignity. But the fact is that Mr. Stevens did choose this mode of life, in the full awareness of alternatives, and pursued it with focused ambition: among other things, he clearly sought to surpass his father's own considerable achievement in the profession. It is because of his commitment that he has engaged in such vigorous self-development, cultivating and improving his various skills. And the seriousness with which he takes the imperative of self-development is one that Mill could only have applauded. As Mill wrote in an emphatic letter to his friend David Barclay, "there is only one plain rule of life eternally binding, and independent of all variations in creeds, and in the interpretation of creeds, embracing equally the greatest moralities and the smallest; it is this: try thyself unweariedly till thou findest the highest thing thou art capable of doing, faculties and outward circumstances being both duly considered, and then DO IT."[22] Mill also says that "a sense of dignity" is something that "all human beings possess in one form or another,"[23] and dignity is something that Mr. Stevens himself knows a good deal about. He even offers a definition of it in response to the questioning of a doctor he meets on his travels.

> 'What do *you* think dignity's all about?'
> The directness of the inquiry did, I admit, take me rather by surprise. 'It's rather a hard thing to explain in a few words, sir,' I said. 'But I suspect it comes down to not removing one's clothing in public.'[24]

This is more than a joke. Mr. Stevens *believes* in decorum, good manners, formality. These compose the world that he has chosen to inhabit and make it the world that it is. Once again, these may not be values for us, but they *are* values for him, given his plan of life. When he is serious, when he is explaining to a room full of villagers what makes the difference between a gentleman and someone who is not, he says: "one would suspect that the quality . . . might be most usefully termed 'dignity.' " This is a quality that he, like many conservatives, believes to be far from equally distributed. "Dignity's not just something for gentlemen," says a character called Harry Smith. And Mr. Stevens observes in his narrative voice, "I perceived, of course, that Mr. Harry Smith and I were rather at cross purposes on this matter."[25]

If Mr. Stevens is a helpful illustration of individuality—of the values of self-development and autonomy—it is in part because he must seem an unlikely representative of such things; to cite him as such is to read Ishiguro's novel against the grain. Ishiguro is like you and me, a modern person, and his novel is sad (and comic) because Mr. Stevens's life seems, in ways he does not recognize, a failure. Mr. Stevens is also a contentious example because—for reasons I'll be discussing further in the next chapter—some philosophers would want to deny that he was fully autonomous, and so to ascribe autonomy to him is to challenge a certain conception of what autonomy requires. At first blush, Mr. Stevens represents precisely the dead hand of convention and custom that Mill railed against in *On Liberty*. Yet Mill's view of convention and custom was rather more complicated than such denunciations suggest. In a somewhat wistful passage in *A System of Logic*, he writes:

> The longer our species lasts, and the more civilized it becomes, the more, as Comte remarks, does the influence of past generations over the present, and of mankind en masse over every individual in it, predominate over other forces; and though the course of affairs never ceases to be susceptible of alteration both by accidents and by personal qualities, the increasing preponderance of the collective agency of the species over all minor causes, is constantly bringing the general evolution of the race into something which deviates less from a certain and preappointed track.[26]

At the same time, Stevens's rather circumscribed conception of what belongs in his "realm" of interest and expertise does make him especially vulnerable to the vagaries of moral luck. For Lord Darlington turns out to be a weak man, an easy mark for the National Socialist Joachim von Ribbentrop, Germany's prewar ambassador to London. The result is that (at least in the novel's apparent accounting) Mr. Stevens's life is a failure because his master's life has proved one, not because service is, in fact, bound to lead to failure. After all, if Mr. Stevens had been working for Winston Churchill, he, at least, could deny that he had failed; he could claim to have been the faithful servant of a great man, just as he set out to be.[27] Instead, Mr. Stevens's pursuit of his vocation robs him both of his dignity and of a love life, since the only woman he might have married works in the same household and he believes a relationship with her would most likely have compromised their professional relations. Though Mr. Stevens makes a mess of this, there is, as I say, no reason to think that these losses are the fault of his vocation.[28]

Then again, perhaps the reason his life seems a failure is that he is servile. Servility, as Thomas E. Hill has suggested we understand the term, isn't just happily earning your living by working for another; it's acting as an unfree person, a person whose will is somehow subjected to another's—a person who, in Hill's formulation, disavows his own moral rights.[29] And yet Mr. Stevens might be defended even from this charge. Has he, in fact, disavowed his own moral rights? His sense of duty to his employer seems derivative from his sense of duty to himself and his own amour propre, for we have no doubt that he could let standards slip without his employer's being any the wiser. Mr. Stevens, who holds to his sense of what is proper despite the caviling of his peers and the inattentiveness of his employer, is conscious that he represents a way of life that is endangered; his conservatism is decidedly not that of conformity. What makes Mr. Stevens a useful example of the moral power of individuality, then, is that he exemplifies it even though he himself doesn't much believe in liberty, equality, or fraternity. Even someone as illiberal as Mr. Stevens, that is, demonstrates the power of individuality as an ideal.

SOCIAL CHOICES

For Mill, Royce, and others, as we've seen, a plan of life serves as a way of integrating one's purposes over time, of fitting together the different things one values. The fulfillment of goals that flow from such a plan—or what we might prefer to call our ground projects and commitments[30]—has more value than the satisfaction of a fleeting desire. In particular, Mill says that it matters because, in effect, the life plan is an expression of my individuality, of who I am: and, in this sense, a desire that flows from a value that itself derives from a life plan is more important than a desire (such as an appetite) that I just happen to have; for it flows from my reflective choices, my commitments, not just from passing fancy.

The ideal of self-authorship strikes a popular chord: we all know the sentiment in the form that Frank Sinatra made famous. In a song in which a person reviews his life toward its end, Mr. Sinatra sings: "I've lived a life that's full. / I've traveled each and ev'ry highway; / But more, much more than this, / I did it my way."[31] If my choosing it is part of what makes my life plan good, then imposing on me a plan of life—even one that is, in other respects, an enviable one—is depriving me of a certain kind of good. For a person of a liberal disposition, my life's shape is up to me, even if I make a life that is objectively less good than a life I could have made, provided that I have done my duty toward others.[32] All of us could, no doubt, have made better lives than we have: but that, Mill says, is no reason for others to attempt to force those better lives upon us.

And yet this scenario of self-chosen individuality invites a couple of worries. First, it is hard to accept the idea that certain values derive from my choices if those choices themselves are just arbitrary. Why should the mere fact that I have laid out my existence mean that it is the best, especially if it is not the best "in itself"?

Suppose, for example, I adopt a life as a solitary traveler around the world, free of entanglements with family and community, settling for a few months here and there, making what little money I need by giving English lessons to businesspeople. My parents tell me that I am wasting my life as a Scholar Gypsy, that I have a good education, talent as a musician, and a wonderful gift for friendship, all of which are being put to no use. You don't have to be a communitarian to wonder whether it is a satisfactory response to say only that I have considered the options and this is the way I have chosen. Don't I need to say something about what this way makes possible for me and for those I meet? Or about what other talents of mine it makes use of? It is one thing to say that the government or society or your parents ought not to stop you from wasting your life if you choose to; but it is another to say that wasting your life in your own way is good just because it *is* your way, just because you have chosen to waste your life.

This may be why Mill seesaws between arguing that I am in the optimal position to decide what plan of life is best for me, given "the mental, moral, and aesthetic stature" of which I am capable, and the more radical view that the mere fact that I have chosen a plan of life recommends it. For on the former view, my choice is *not* arbitrary. It reflects the facts of my capacities, and, given that I have enough "common sense and experience," I am likely to do a better job than anybody else of judging how to make a life that fits those capacities. On this view, I discover a life for myself, based in the facts of my nature and my place in the world. But on the latter, my role is as originator of value, not as discoverer of it. Here the charge against individuality is that it is *arbitrary*.

Let me raise a second worry with the picture of self-chosen individuality we've been examining. At times, Mill's way of talking can suggest a rather unattractive form of individualism, in which the aim is to make a life in which you yourself matter most. This conception has sometimes been prettified with a particular account of the unfettered human soul. The result finds memorable expression in the misty-eyed antinomianism of Oscar Wilde's "Soul of Man under Socialism," in which, once the shackles of convention are thrown off, some sort of dewy and flower-strewn Pre-Raphaelitism will reign: "It will be a marvellous thing—the true personality of man—when we see it. It will grow naturally and simply, flowerlike, or as a dispute. It will not prove things. It will know everything. And yet it will not busy itself about knowledge." And so breathlessly on.[33] This is the sort of moral kitsch that gives individuality a bad name.

And Mill does argue for a view of one's self as a project, in a way that might be read as suggesting that self-cultivation and sociability are competing values, though each has its place.[34] This can lead us to think that the good of individuality is reined in by or traded off against the goods of sociability so that there is an intrinsic opposition between the self and society. It can lead us to think that political institutions, which develop and reflect the value of sociability, are always a source of constraint on our individuality. Here is a second charge against individuality: that it is *unsociable*.

Now, to show that individuality, or, more baldly, self-creation, doesn't necessarily succumb to these pitfalls is not to show that it isn't susceptible to them; but, right away, we can establish that it *needn't* involve either arbitrariness or unsociability. A plan of life for Mill was likely to include family and friends and might include (as his did) public service. Mr. Stevens's individuality, too, is far from unsociable because what he has chosen to be is a butler, which is something you can be only if there are other people to play other roles in the social world; a butler needs a master or mistress, cooks, housekeepers, maids. It is an intrinsically social role, a station with its public duties, not just an opportunity to follow one's private tastes. And Mr. Stevens's individuality is far from arbitrary because it is a role that has developed within a tradition, a role that makes sense within a certain social world: a social world that no longer exists, as it happens, which is one of many reasons why none of us wants to be a butler in the way Mr. Stevens was. We don't want to be butlers in that way because—without a social world of "great houses," house parties, and the rest—one *can't* be a butler in that way. (This is a point that Bernard Williams has made by noting that, relative to a particular historical position, certain forms of life are not "real options.")[35] Mr. Stevens is an individual, and he has made his own plan of life: but he hasn't made it arbitrarily. The butler elements in his plan, for example, make sense—to give but two reasons—because there is, first, a career available with that role, a way of making a living; and, second, because his father was a butler before him. (Once again, I don't expect you to find these reasons attractive; but you should find them intelligible.)

As we've seen, a plan of life is not like an engineer's plan. It doesn't map out all the important (and many unimportant) features of our life in advance. These plans are, rather, mutable sets of organizing aims, aims within which you can fit both daily choices and a longer-term vision. Still, there remains a certain lack of clarity to talk of Mr. Stevens's plan of life: what precisely is his plan? Forced to speak in that way, we should say that his plan is to be the best butler he can be, to follow in his father's footsteps, to be a man. But I think it is more natural to say that he plans to live *as* a butler, his father's son, a man, a loyal Englishman. What structures his sense of his life, then, is something less like a blueprint and more like what we nowadays call an "identity."[36] For to speak of *living-as* here is to speak of identities.[37]

Mr. Stevens has constructed for himself an identity as a butler: more specifically as the butler to Lord Darlington and of Darlington Hall and as his father's son. It is an identity in which his gender plays a role (butlers must be men) and in which his nationality is important, too, because in the late 1930s Lord Darlington meddles (rather incompetently, it turns out) in the "great affairs" of the British nation, and it is his service to a man who is serving that nation that gives Mr. Stevens part of his satisfaction.[38] But Ishiguro's character has put these more generic identities—butler, son, man, Englishman—together with other skills and capacities that are more particular, and, in so doing, he has fashioned a self. And, as we shall see in chapter 3, the idea of identity already has built into it a recognition of the complex interdependence of self-creation and sociability.

INVENTION AND AUTHENTICITY

At this point, it may be helpful to consider two rival pictures of what is involved in shaping one's individuality. One, a picture that comes from romanticism, is the idea of finding one's self—of discovering, by means of reflection or a careful attention to the world, a meaning for one's life that is already there, waiting to be found. This is the vision we can call *authenticity*: it is a matter of being true to who you already really are, or would be if it weren't for distorting influences. "The Soul of Man under Socialism" is one locus classicus of this vision. ("The personality of man . . . will be as wonderful as the personality of a child.") The other picture, the *existentialist* picture, let's call it, is one in which, as the doctrine goes, existence precedes essence: that is, you exist first and then have to decide what to exist *as*, who to be, afterward. On an extreme version of this view, we have to make a self up, as it were out of nothing, like God at the Creation, and individuality is valuable because only a person who has made a self has a life worth living.[39]

But neither of these pictures is right.

The authenticity picture is wrong because it suggests that there is no role for creativity in making a self, that the self is already and in its totality fixed by our natures. Mill was rightly emphatic that we do have such a role, however constrained we are by our nature and circumstances. Man "has, to a certain extent, a power to alter his character," he writes in *A System of Logic*:

> His character is formed by his circumstances (including among these his particular organization); but his own desire to mould it in a particular way, is one of those circumstances, and by no means one of the least influential.

We can not, indeed, directly will to be different from what we are. But neither did those who are supposed to have formed our character directly will that we should be what we are. Their will had no direct power except over their own actions. They made us what they did make us, by willing, not the end, but the requisite means; and we, when our habits are not too inveterate, can, by similarly willing the requisite means, make ourselves different. If they could place us under the influence of certain circumstances, we, in like manner, can place ourselves under the influence of other circumstances. We are exactly as capable of making our own character, if we will, as others are of making it for us.[40]

By the same token, the existentialist picture is wrong because it suggests that there is *only* creativity, that there is nothing for us to respond to, nothing out of which to do the construction. "Human nature is not a machine to be built after a model, and set to do exactly the work prescribed for it, but a tree, which requires to grow ... according to the tendency of the inward forces which make it a living thing," Mill told us. His metaphor makes the constraints apparent: a tree, whatever the circumstances, does not become a legume, a vine, or a cow. The reasonable middle view is that constructing an identity is a good thing (if self-authorship is a good thing) but that the identity must make some kind of sense. And for it to make sense, it must be an identity constructed in response to facts outside oneself, things that are beyond one's own choices.

Some philosophers—Sartre among them—have tried to combine both the romantic and the existentialist views, as Michel Foucault suggested some years ago: "Sartre avoids the idea of the self as something that is given to us, but through the moral notion of authenticity, he turns back to the idea that we have to be ourselves—to be truly our true self. I think the only acceptable practical consequence of what Sartre has said is to link his theoretical insight to the practice of creativity—and not to that of authenticity. From the idea that the self is not given to us, I think there is only one practical consequence: we have to create ourselves as a work of art."[41]

Now Foucault, in this passage, speaks of creativity without, perhaps, sufficiently acknowledging the role of the materials on which our creativity is exercised. As Charles Taylor notes, "I can define my identity only against the background of things that matter. But to bracket out history, nature, society, the demands of solidarity, everything but what I find in myself, would be to eliminate all candidates for what matters."[42]

Let me propose a thought experiment that might dissuade those who speak of self-choice as the ultimate value. Suppose it were possible, through some sort of instantaneous genetic engineering, to change any aspect of your nature, so that you could have any combination of capacities that has ever been within the range of human possibility: you could have Michael Jordan's fade-away shot, Mozart's musicality, Groucho Marx's comic gifts, Proust's delicate way with language. Suppose you could put these together with any desires you wanted—homo- or hetero-, a taste for Wagner or Eminem. (You might saunter into the metamorphosis chamber whistling the overture to *Die Meistersinger* and strut out murmuring "Will the Real Slim Shady Please Stand Up?") Suppose, further, that there were no careers or professions in this world because all material needs and services were met by intelligent machines. Far from being a utopia, so it seems to me, this would be a kind of hell. There would be no reason to choose any of these options, because there would be no achievement in putting together a life. One way of explaining why this life would be meaningless comes from Nietzsche:

> *One thing is needful.*—To "give style" to one's character—a great and rare art! It is practiced by those who survey all the strengths and weaknesses of their nature and then fit them into an artistic plan until every one of them appears as art and reason and even weaknesses delight the eye. Here a large mass of second nature has been added; there a piece of original nature has been removed—both times through long practice and daily work at it. Here the ugly that could not be removed is concealed; there it has been reinterpreted and made sublime.[43]

To create a life is to create a life out of the materials that history has given you. As we saw, Mill's rhetoric juxtaposes the value of self-authorship with the value of achieving our capacities, perhaps because the former can seem arbitrary; but once it is tied to something out of our control, once our self-construction is seen as a creative response to our capacities and our circumstances, then the accusation of arbitrariness loses its power.

Thinking about the capacities and circumstances that history has, in fact, given each of us will also allow us to address the worry about the unsociability of the individuated self, further elaborating on the social dependence we ascribed to Mr. Stevens. The language of identity reminds us to what extent we are, in Charles Taylor's formulation, "dialogically" constituted. Beginning in infancy, it is in dialogue with other people's understandings of who I am that I develop a conception of my own identity. We come into the world "mewling and puking in the nurse's arms" (as Shakespeare so genially put it), capable of human individuality but only if we have the chance to develop it in interaction with others. An identity is always articulated through concepts (and practices) made available to you by religion, society, school, and state, mediated by family, peers, friends. Indeed, the very material out of which our identities are shaped is provided, in part, by what Taylor has called our language in "a broad sense," comprising "not only the words we speak, but also other modes of expression whereby we define ourselves, including the 'languages' of art, of gesture, of love, and the like."[44] It follows that the self whose choices liberalism celebrates is not a presocial thing—not some authentic inner essence independent of the human world into which we have grown—but rather the product of our interaction from our earliest years with others.

As a result, individuality presupposes sociability, not just a grudging respect for the individuality of others. A free self is a human self, and we are, as Aristotle long ago insisted, creatures of the πολις, social beings. We are social in many ways and for many reasons: because we desire company, because we depend on one another for survival, because so much that we care about is collectively created. And the prospect of such sociability was basic to Mill's own ethical vision. "The social feeling of mankind" was, he thought, "a powerful natural sentiment," and one that formed a basis for morality:

> The social state is at once so natural, so necessary, and so habitual to man, that, except in some unusual circumstances or by an effort of voluntary abstraction, he never conceives himself otherwise than as a member of a body; and this association is riveted more and more, as mankind are further removed from the state of savage independence. Any condition, therefore, which is essential to a state of society, becomes more and more an inseparable part of every person's conception of the state of things which he is born

into, and which is the destiny of a human being. . . . The deeply-rooted conception which every individual even now has of himself as a social being, tends to make him feel it one of his natural wants that there should be harmony between his feelings and aims and those of his fellow creatures. . . . To those who have it, it possesses all the characters of a natural feeling. It does not present itself to their minds as a superstition of education, or a law despotically imposed by the power of society, but as an attribute which it would not be well for them to be without. This conviction is the ultimate sanction of the greatest happiness morality.[45]

And it's worth returning to the point that Mill's conception of happiness or well-being included individuality, freedom, autonomy; that these had a constitutive, not just an instrumental, relation to it.[46] To value individuality properly just *is* to acknowledge the dependence of the good for each of us on relationships with others. Without these bonds, as I say, we could not come to be free selves, not least because we could not come to be selves at all. Throughout our lives part of the material that we are responding to in shaping our selves is not within us but outside us, out there in the social world. Most people shape their identities as partners of lovers who become spouses and fellow parents; these aspects of our identities, though in a sense social, are peculiar to who we are as individuals, and so represent a *personal* dimension of our identities. But we are all, as well, members of broader collectivities. To say that *collective* identities—that is, the collective dimensions of our individual identities—are responses to something outside our selves is to say that they are the products of histories, and our engagement with them invokes capacities that are not under our control. Yet they are social not just because they involve others, but because they are constituted in part by socially transmitted conceptions of how a person of that identity properly behaves.

THE SOCIAL SCRIPTORIUM

In constructing an identity, one draws, among other things, on the kinds of person available in one's society. Of course, there is not just *one* way that gay or straight people or blacks or whites or men or women are to behave, but there are ideas around (contested, many of them, but all sides in these contests shape our options) about how gay, straight, black, white, male, or female people ought to conduct themselves.[47] These notions provide loose norms or models, which play a role in shaping our plans of life. Collective identities, in short, provide what we might call scripts: narratives that people can use in shaping their projects and in telling their life stories. (We'll explore this matter further in chapter 3.)

To be sure, an emphasis on how we make sense of our lives, our selves, through narrative is shared by a number of philosophers—Charles Taylor and Alasdair MacIntyre among them—who worry that conventional versions of liberal theory scant the social matrix in which our identities take shape. At the same time, the Millian language of life plans resonates with their insistence that to live our lives as agents requires that we see our actions and experiences as belonging to something like a story.[48] For Charles Taylor, it is "a basic condition of making sense of ourselves" that "we grasp our lives in a narrative"; narrative, then, is not "an optional extra." For Alasdair MacIntyre, it is "because we understand our own lives in terms of the narratives that we live out that the form of narrative is appropriate for understanding the actions of others." As he argues, each of our "shorter-term intentions is, and can only be made, intelligible by reference to some longer-term intentions," and so "behavior is only characterized adequately when we know what the longer and longest term intentions are and how the shorter-term intentions are related to the longer. Once again we are involved in writing a narrative history."[49] Such concerns, as I hope I've established, aren't foreign to the sort of liberalism that Mill, at least, sought to promulgate.

So we should acknowledge how much our personal histories, the stories we tell of where we have been and where we are going, are constructed, like novels and movies, short stories and folktales, within narrative conventions. Indeed, one of the things that popular narratives (whether filmed or televised, spoken or written) do for us is to provide models for telling our lives.[50] At the same time, part of the function of our collective identities—of the whole repertory of them that a society makes available to its members—is to structure possible narratives of the individual self.

Thus, for example, the rites of passage that many societies associate with the identities male and female provide shape to the transition to adulthood; gay identities may organize lives around the narrative of coming out; Pentecostalists are born again; and black identities in America often engage oppositional narratives of self-construction in the face of racism. One thing that matters to people across many socie-ties is a certain narrative unity, the ability to tell a story of one's life that hangs together. The story—my story—should cohere in the way appropriate to a person in my society.[51] It need not be the exact same story, from week to week, or year to year, but how it fits into the wider story of various collectivities matters for most of us. It is not just that, say, gender identities give shape to one's life; it is also that ethnic and national identities fit a personal narrative into a larger narrative. For modern people, the narrative form entails seeing one's life as having a certain arc, as making sense through a life story that expresses who one is through one's own project of self-making. That narrative arc is yet another way in which an individual's life depends deeply on something socially created and transmitted.

I made a distinction earlier between a personal and a collective di-mension of identity. Both play a role in these stories of the self. But only the collective identities have scripts, and only they count as what Ian Hacking meant by "kinds of person."[52] There is a logical category but no social category of the witty, or the clever, or the charming, or the greedy. People who share these properties do not constitute a social group. In the relevant sense, they are not a kind of person. In our society (though not, perhaps, in the England of Addison and Steele) being witty does not, for example, suggest the life-script of "the wit." And the main reason why the personal dimensions are different is that they are not dependent on labeling: while intelligence, in our society, is of the first social importance, people could be intelligent even if no one had the concept. To say that race is socially constructed, that an African American is, in Hacking's sense, a "kind of person," is, in part, to say that there are no African Americans independent of social prac-tices associated with the racial label; by contrast, there could certainly be clever people even if we did not have the concept of cleverness.[53] I shall pursue these issues in more detail in chapter 3.

ETHICS IN IDENTITY

How does identity fit into our broader moral projects? One view is this: there are many things of value in the world. Their value is objective; they are important whether or not anybody recognizes they are important. But there is no way of ranking these many goods or trading them off against one another, so there is not always, all things considered, a best thing to do. As a result, there are many morally permissible options. One thing identity provides is another source of value, one that helps us make our way among those options. To adopt an identity, to make it mine, is to see it as structuring my way through life. That is, my identity has patterns built into it (so Mill is wrong when he implies that it is always better to be different from others), patterns that help me think about my life; one such simple pattern, for example, is the pattern of a career, which ends, if we live long enough, with retirement.[54] But identities also create forms of solidarity: if I think of myself as an X, then, sometimes, the mere fact that somebody else is an X, too, may incline me to do something with or for them; where X might be "woman," "black," or "American." Now solidarity with those who share your identity might be thought of as, other things being equal, a good thing. As such there is a universal value of solidarity, but it works out in different ways for different people because different people have different identities. Or it might be thought to be a good thing because we enjoy it and, other things being equal, it is good for people to have and to do what they enjoy having and doing.

As we have seen, however, many values are internal to an identity: they are among the values someone who has that identity must take into account, but are not values for people who do not have that identity. Take the value of ritual purity, as conceived of by many orthodox Jews. They think they should keep kosher because they are Jewish; they don't expect anyone who is not a Jew to do so, and they may not even think it would be a good thing if non-Jews did. It is a good thing only for those who are or those who become Jewish: and they do not think that it would be a better world if everybody did become Jewish. The Covenant, after all, is only with the Children of Israel.

Similarly, we might think that your identity as a nationalist in a struggle against colonial domination made it valuable for you to risk your life for the liberation of your country, as Nathan Hale did, regretting that he had only one of them to give. If you were not a nationalist, you might still die advancing a country's cause; and then, while some good might come of it, that good would not be, so to speak, a good for you. We might regard your life as wasted, just because you did not identify with the nation you had died for.

There are thus various ways that identity might be a source of value, rather than being something that realizes other values. First, if an identity is yours, it may determine certain acts of solidarity as valuable, or be an internal part of the specification of your satisfactions and enjoyments, or motivate and give meaning to acts of supererogatory kindness. Indeed, the presence of an identity concept in the specification of my aim—as helping a fellow bearer of some identity—may be part of what explains why I have the aim at all. Someone may gain satisfaction from giving money to the Red Cross after a hurricane in Florida as an act of solidarity with other Cuban Americans. Here the fact of the shared identity is part of why he or she has the aim. By the same token, a shared identity may give certain acts or achievements a value for me they would not otherwise have had. When a Ghanaian team wins the African Cup of Nations in soccer, that is of value to me by virtue of my identity as a Ghanaian. If I were a Catholic, a wedding in a Catholic church might be of value to me in a special way because I was a Catholic.

There are still other ways in which the success of our projects (not to mention our having those projects in the first place) might derive from a social identity. Since human beings are social creatures, Mill writes, they are "familiar with the fact of cooperating with others and proposing to themselves a collective, not an individual interest as the aim (at least for the time being) of their actions. So long as they are cooperating, their ends are identified with those of others; there is at least a temporary feeling that the interests of others are their own interests."[55] Projects and commitments may involve collective intentions, as with a religious ritual that requires the coordinated involvement of one's fellow worshipers for its realization.[56] A social project may involve the creation or re-creation of an identity, in the way that Elijah Muhammad sought to redefine the American Negro's collective self-understanding, or the way that Deaf activists seek to construct a group identity that supervenes upon the condition of deafness. For Theodor Herzl, success depended on creating a sense of national consciousness among a people who might never have conceived themselves (at least in his terms) as belonging to a common nation. But a common pursuit may involve much smaller-scale groups—of twenty, or ten, or two. "When two persons have their thoughts and speculations completely in common; when all subjects of intellectual or moral interest are discussed between them in daily life ... when they set out from the same principles, and arrive at their conclusions by processes pursued jointly," Mill wrote of the composition of *On Liberty,* "it is of little consequence in respect to the question of originality, which of them holds the pen."[57]

INDIVIDUALITY AND THE STATE

The picture of self-development we've been tracing puts identity at the heart of human life. A theory of politics, I am suggesting, ought to take this picture seriously. That alone doesn't settle much in the way of practicalities, but the picture is one that we can develop and explore in trying to negotiate the political world we share. Self-development, as Wendy Donner has shown, is a theme that bridges Mill's ethical, social, and political contributions; but his view that the state has a role to play in such development brings him into conflict with some powerful currents of modern political thought, which insist that the public sphere be neutral among different conceptions of the good.[58] Unlike many contemporary liberals—Rawls, Dworkin, and Nagel, say—Mill made no claim to be a neutralist. "The first element of good government," Mill wrote in *Considerations on Representative Government,* "being the virtue and intelligence of the human beings composing the community, the most important point of excellence which any form of government can possess is to promote the virtue and intelligence of the people themselves."[59]

This is not, to be sure, a terribly *confining* conception of the good and, in Mill's construction of it, was bound to encourage diversity rather than inhibit it. Still, as we'll see in chapter 4, Mill has been charged with playing favorites among religions, because of his emphasis on the fostering of personal autonomy as an appropriate goal of the state: does this not suggest that strong forms of Calvinism, say, will be contemned?[60]

And so *On Liberty* has had a curious legacy among liberal theorists. On the one hand, it has been taken to advocate a sort of nightwatchman state—a strong, my-freedom-ends-at-your-nose form of antipaternalism. On the other, as we've seen, it has been taken to espouse a sectarian conception of the good, and so a vision of the state that was excessively paternalist, intrusive, intolerant. (In Rawlsian terms, it is guilty of advocating a comprehensive, rather than a strictly political, liberalism.) What Isaiah Berlin called "negative liberty"—protection from government intervention in certain areas of our lives—can obviously be an aid in the development of a life of one's own, as Mill believed. But Mill's view of individuality also led him to suppose that we might need not only liberty from the state and society, but also help from state and society to achieve our selves. Isaiah Berlin taught us to call this "positive liberty," and he was deeply (and thoughtfully) skeptical about it: skeptical because, among other things, he thought that in the name of positive liberty, governments had been—and would continue to be—tempted to set out to shape people in the name of the better selves they might become.[61] It is hard to deny that terrible things have been done in the name of freedom, and that some bad arguments have led people from the ideal of emancipation down the path to the Gulag. But, pace Berlin, enabling people to construct and live out an identity does not have to go awry.[62]

Recall those words of Mill: "What more or better can be said of any condition of human affairs, than that it brings human beings themselves nearer to the best thing they can be? or what worse can be said of any obstruction to good, than that it prevents this?"[63] He took this to be a goal for governance, not merely a brake on governance. Certainly the author of *On Liberty* wasn't any kind of libertarian; he thought the state should sponsor scientific inquiry, regulate child labor, and restrict the working day for factory workers; require that children be educated; provide poor relief, and so forth.[64] At the same time, it was anathema to him that the government should seek to entrench a single form of life. "If it were only that people have diversities of taste that is reason enough for not attempting to shape them all after one model," he writes. "But different persons also require different conditions for their spiritual development; and can no more exist healthily in the same moral, than all variety of plants can exist in the same physical atmosphere and climate. The same things which are helps to one person towards the cultivation of his higher nature, are hindrances to another." And such are the differences among people that "unless there is a corresponding diversity in their modes of life, they neither obtain their fair share of happiness, nor grow up to the mental, moral, and aesthetic stature of which their nature is capable."[65] Here the idea is that freedom allows people to make the best of themselves. In such passages, it looks as though making the best of oneself entails becoming a kind of person that it is objectively valuable to be—a person of high mental or moral or aesthetic stature—whatever one's chosen plan of life.[66]

In truth, it's not obvious that Mill's "comprehensive" ideals (and I'll have more to say on the subject, under the rubric of "perfectionism," in chapter 5) should estrange him from the standard-bearers of modern liberal theory. The ideal of self-cultivation you find in Mill has enjoyed widespread currency; Matthew Arnold enunciated it in *Culture and Anarchy* when he quoted Epictetus's view that "the formation of the spirit and character must be our real concern."[67] But it is most commonly associated with Aristotle, and it remains a powerful strand in political philosophy today. Indeed, what Rawls famously endorsed as "the Aristotelian Principle" was the notion that "other things being equal, human beings enjoy the exercise of their realized capacities, and this enjoyment increases the more the capacity is realized, or the greater its complexity."[68] At the same time, Mill's insistence that self-development should take diversity into account finds kinship with Amartya Sen's "capabilities" approach to equality. "Investigations of equality—theoretical as well as practical—that proceed with the assumption of antecedent uniformity (including the presumption that 'all men are created equal') thus miss out on a major aspect of the problem," Sen has written. "Human diversity is no secondary complication (to be ignored, or to be introduced 'later on'); it is a fundamental aspect of our interest in equality."[69] And—in ways we'll explore later—Dworkin's "challenge model" of human life, too, has deep affinities with Mill's picture of individuality. In each of these formulations is a version of the ethical idea: that there are things we owe to ourselves.

What my duties to *others* are, of course, remains one of the central questions for liberalism. Making a life as a social being requires making commitments to others. If these are voluntary, it may be proper to enforce them even against my (later) will. But how much does what I owe go beyond my voluntary undertakings? One of Mill's suggestions was, roughly, that what we owed to others, in addition to what we had committed ourselves to, was that we should not harm them; and that leads to interesting discussions about what counts as harm.[70] But it was critical to his vision that the mere fact that I do something you do not want me to do does not *eo ipso* count as my harming you:

> There are many who consider as an injury to themselves any conduct which they have a distaste for, and resent it as an outrage to their feelings. . . . But there is no parity between the feeling of a person for his own opinion, and the feeling of another who is offended at his holding it; no more than between the desire of a thief to take a purse, and the desire of the right owner to keep it. And a person's taste is as much his peculiar concern as his opinion or his purse.[71]

Accordingly, the view that I should be permitted to make whatever life flows from my choices, provided that I give you what I owe you and do you no harm, seems to leave me a wide range of freedom, which is as you'd expect. And yet Mill could appeal to the ideals of both self-authorship and self-development in order to justify state action.

Governments do, for example, provide public education in many countries that helps children who do not yet have any settled identity or projects, hopes, and dreams. This is more than negative liberty, more than government's getting out of the way. You may say that parents could do this; in principle, they could. But suppose they won't or can't? Shouldn't society step in, in the name of individuality, to insist that children be prepared for life as free adults? And, in our society, won't that require them to be able to read? To know the language or languages of their community? To be able to assess arguments, interpret traditions? And even if the parents are trying to provide all these things, isn't there a case to be made that society, through the state, should offer them positive support?[72]

Or take welfare provision. If individuality is a matter of developing a life in response to the materials provided by your capacities and your social world (including the social identities embedded in it), then liberalism seeks a politics that allows people to do this. But there can be obstacles to the realization of our individuality other than the limitations of law. Can people really construct dignified individual lives in a modern world where there is no frontier to conquer, no empty land to cultivate, unless they have certain basic material resources? Can people be said to be free to develop their individuality if they are ill and unable to afford treatment that will, as we say, "free them" from disease?

What holds together the desire to educate children, provide welfare for the poor, and give physical assistance to the handicapped who need it is the idea that assistance of these sorts enables people to develop lives worth living. Berlin wondered who would decide what a life worth living was. As we have seen, Mill had an answer to that question: "If a person possesses any tolerable amount of common sense and experience, his own mode of laying out his existence is best." But can communal institutions really afford to accommodate everyone's "own mode"? We'll return to this question in chapter 5.

I mentioned just now Mill's celebrated "harm principle"—according to which the only justification for coercion is to prevent someone from harming another—and, though it is often given a libertarian construction, it may actually invite an appreciable amount of governmental intervention. To have autonomy, we must have acceptable choices. We are harmed when deprived of such choices. For Joseph Raz, accordingly, the "autonomy-based principle of freedom is best regarded as providing the moral foundation for the harm principle," and that tenet leads him to a rather expansive interpretation. "To harm a person is to diminish his prospects, to affect adversely his possibilities," Raz maintains. "It is a mistake to think that the harm principle recognizes only the duty of government to prevent loss of autonomy. Sometimes failing to improve the situation of another is harming him"—as when we deny someone what is due him, by, for example, discriminating against a potential employee.[73] Here his position is quite in keeping with Mill's stipulation: "The most marked cases of injustice . . . are acts of wrongful aggression, or wrongful exercise of power over some one; the next are those which consist in wrongfully withholding from him something which is his due; in both cases, inflicting on him a positive hurt, either in the form of direct suffering, or of the privation of some good which he had reasonable ground, either of a physical or of a social kind, for counting upon."[74] More generally, if (as Raz suggests) we harm someone by undermining the conditions necessary for the exercise of his or her autonomy (including the social forms in which it takes shape), then the state has considerable, perhaps excessive, latitude for interference.

Mill himself, though he thought the cultivation of individual excellence was central to the role of the state, was hardly impetuous about enlisting state power in the service of this good. He famously held that "there is a circle around every individual which no government . . . ought to be permitted to overstep."[75] And he took seriously the roles played by social approbation and opprobrium as alternate mechanisms for the regulation of behavior. In his essay "Thornton on Labour and Its Claims," he wrote that, outside the realm of moral duty, which must be enforced "compulsively," "there is the innumerable variety of modes in which the acts of human beings are either a cause, or a hindrance, of good to their fellow-creatures, but to which it is, on the whole, for the general interest that they should be left free; being merely encouraged, by praise and honour, to the performance of such beneficial actions as are not sufficiently stimulated by benefits flowing from them to the agent himself. This larger sphere is that of Merit or Virtue."[76]

And though Mill seems to celebrate an ideal of personal autonomy, he did not generally seek to enlist the coercive powers of the state to foster it, perhaps sensitive to the paradox of relying on an outside power to increase self-reliance. He thought the Mormon polygamous way of life inferior, particularly because of the subordinate role of women in a polygamous system, but so long as the marriages were predicated on consent, he thought they should not be unlawful. As Mill wrote in *On Liberty*, "I am not aware that any community has the right to force another to be civilized."[77]

But state action is not restricted to acts that take the form of prohibitions, of course. In *Principles of Political Economy*, Mill distinguishes "authoritative interference by government"—encompassing the realm of crimes and punishment—from another mode of involvement, in which

> a government, instead of issuing a command and enforcing it by penalties, adopts the course so seldom reverted to by governments, and of which such important use might be made, that of giving advice or promulgating information; and when, leaving individuals free to use their own means of pursuing any object of general interest, the government, not meddling

with them, but not trusting the object solely to their care, establishes, side by side with their arrangements, an agency of its own for a like purpose.[78]

And he returned to the point in the fourth chapter of *On Liberty,* when he again abjures the notion that "human beings have no business with each other's conduct in life, and that they should not concern themselves about the well-doing or well-being of one another, unless their own interest is involved." On the contrary, Mill says, "Instead of any diminution, there is need of a great increase of disinterested exertion to promote the good of others.... Human beings owe to each other help to distinguish the better from the worse, and encouragement to choose the former and avoid the latter. They should be forever stimulating each other to increased exercise of their higher faculties."[79] But this obligation may not be restricted to individual citizens, and toward the end of *On Liberty,* he acknowledges "a large class of questions respecting to limits of government interference, which, though closely connected with the subject of this Essay, do not, in strictness, belong to it. These are cases in which the reasons against interference do not turn upon the principle of liberty: the question is not about restraining the actions of individuals, but about helping them: it is asked whether the government should do, or cause to be done, something for their benefit, instead of leaving it to be done by themselves, individually, or in voluntary combination."[80] This class of "interferences" has proved equally problematic for recent political philosophy, for reasons we'll explore in chapter 5.

The Common Pursuit

"As Brutus was called the last of the Romans," Mill wrote of his father, "so was he the last of the eighteenth century."[81] John Stuart himself sought a careful equipoise among the various climates of thought through which he lived: it is what made him both deeply constant and deeply wayward. And yet this very equipoise, this sense of balance, ensured that *On Liberty* would not immediately enjoy the reception that Mill might have hoped for his and Harriet's *grand projet.* "None of my writings have been either so carefully composed, or so

sedulously corrected as this," Mill recounted in his *Autobiography.*
"After it had been written as usual twice over, we kept going through
it *de novo*, reading, weighing, and criticizing every sentence. Its final
revision was to have been a work of the winter of 1858–9, the first after
my retirement, which we had arranged to pass in the South of Europe.
That hope and every other were frustrated by the most unexpected and
bitter calamity of her death—at Avignon, on our way to Montpellier,
from a sudden attack of pulmonary congestion."[82] A few weeks later,
Mill sent the manuscript of *On Liberty* to his publisher.

For various reasons, as his biographer points out, the timing of its
publication was less than opportune. There were causes both for dis-
traction and for resistance. *The Origin of Species* appeared in the same
year, to be enlisted in causes progressive and reactionary; the Oxford
movement was in full flower; and various forms of collectivism—
whether promulgated by trade unionists or by Christian socialists—
were gathering force. Many radicals found Mill's vision disabling; conservatives found it irresponsible and destructive. Sir James Fitzjames
Stephen famously took after it with a cudgel: "To attack opinions on
which the framework of society rests is a proceeding which both is and
ought to be dangerous," he concluded, and he did his part to make it
so. The book sent Thomas Carlyle into a choleric lather (though few
things did not). "As if it were a sin to control, or coerce into better
methods, human swine in any way; Ach Gott in Himmel!"[83]

For the recently bereaved author, of course, the book was as much a
mortuary as a monument. "To us who have known what it is to be with
her and to belong to her, this silly phantasmagoria of human life, devoid
of her, would be utterly meaningless and unendurably wearisome, were
there not still some things to do in it which she wished done, and some
public and other objects which she cared for, and in which therefore it
is still possible to keep up some degree of interest," he wrote to a friend.
"I have been publishing some of her opinions, and I hope to employ
what remains to me of life (if I am able to retain my health) in continuing to work for them and to spread them, though with sadly diminished
powers now that I no longer have her to prompt and guide me."[84] In
his *Autobiography*, too, he wrote of Harriet's role in his life—of their
common pursuit—in terms that are almost the reciprocal of the robust
individuality he endorsed.

My objects in life are solely those which were hers; my pursuits and occupations those in which she shared, or sympathized, and which are indissolubly associated with her. Her memory is to me a religion, and her approbation the standard by which, summing up as it does all worthiness, I endeavor to regulate my life.[85]

It is the language of religious devotion, abjection, heteronomy, self-abnegation; and yet it does not cut against his commitment to individuality so much as it attests to its profoundly social nature. He was attentive to just those forms of collective intention that were omitted from his father's agent-centered view of politics; deprived of the company of his peers as a child, he tirelessly established societies and reviews as a young man, fraternal associations of politics and culture. And the associations that mattered to him, that gave meaning to his endeavors, were not just fraternal. What had been diminished, on his own account, by the loss of his life companion and of their common pursuits was precisely his individuality.

It did not still his pen. The ends of life may have been revisable; they were not, for him, perishable. And Mill himself—object and subject of so many bold experiments, a man whom all manner of visionary, from Bentham to Carlyle to Comte, sought and failed to enlist as a disciple—had a keen sense that influence went only so far, and communion was always incomplete. If no person was whole author of himself, neither could a person be wholly authored by another. "We can not, indeed, directly will to be different from what we are," as he wrote. "But neither did those who are supposed to have formed our character directly will that we should be what we are." Nobody knew better than Mill how one's life plans could be elevated when fused into a common pursuit. Yet at the same time nobody knew better how readily the attempt to promote another's excellence could become an oppression. As he wrote, in words of peculiar resonance: "Let any man call to mind what he himself felt on emerging from boyhood—from the tutelage and control of even loved and affectionate elders—and entering upon the responsibilities of manhood. Was it not like the physical effect of taking off a heavy weight, or releasing him from obstructive, even if not otherwise painful bonds? Did he not feel twice as much alive, twice as much a human being, as before?"[86]

Mill famously celebrated freedom from government and from public opinion: but what we see here is how much he also believed that in the business of making a life—in shaping your individuality—however many common pursuits you have, you must, in the end, find freedom even from the good intentions of those who love you. However social the individuality that Mill prized was, it was, first and last, still individuality: the final responsibility for each life is always the responsibility of the person whose life it is.

Chapter Two

~ Autonomy and Its Critics

WHAT AUTONOMY DEMANDS

Anna Karenina's dissolute brother has a weakness for oysters, and cigars, and unmarried governesses, but what a recent generation of ethicists has found most worrying is how totally he lacks a proper independence of mind. Here is Tolstoy's often-quoted description:

> Stepan Arkadyich subscribed to and read a liberal newspaper, not an extreme one, but one with the tendency to which the majority held. And though neither science, nor art, nor politics itself interested him, he firmly held the same views on all these subjects as the majority and his newspaper did, and changed them only when the majority did, or, rather, he did not change them, but they themselves changed imperceptibly in him.[1]

You can see why theorists of autonomy have pounced. For Gerald Dworkin, "the beliefs are not his because they are borrowed; and they are borrowed without even being aware of their source; and, it is implied, he is not capable of giving some account of their validity—not even an account which, say, stresses the likelihood of the majority being correct, or the necessity for moral consensus."[2] For Joel Feinberg, Stepan is a portrait of inauthenticity, in that he "can construct no rationale for his beliefs other than that they are the beliefs held by those to whom he responds (if he even knows who *they* are), and can give no reason for thinking that *their* beliefs (like those of some reasonably selected authority) might be correct."[3]

And, of course, Mill voiced congruent concerns: we know he viewed with disfavor the person "who lets the world . . . choose his plan of life for him," rather than choosing it himself. Yet a question immediately arises: what is required to choose freely? It's customary to mention the absence of coercion and the availability of options, but Mill (like contemporary theorists of autonomy) also worries about deformations of the will: about preferences that are unreflectively bequeathed by custom, about "likings in groups." So personal autonomy seems to entail a lot more than just being left to your own devices; it sounds like a capacity we need to cultivate, or perhaps one of those virtues, like courage or integrity, that people are likely to honor in the breach. Just how autonomous do you have to be to have true autonomy?

There's reason to take the question seriously. What we can call "autonomism"—following Lawrence Haworth and wresting the term from a few superannuated Italian radicals—undergirds a great deal of liberal thought; the notion is central to a range of normative theories of politics, including the ones that will be of particular interest to us in the context of what I'll be calling "soul making": the so-called liberal perfectionism associated with Joseph Raz and others.[4] Unfortunately, in making a case for the value of autonomy (in some instances as a primary value; in some instances just as a very fine thing indeed), many of its proponents have succumbed to the temptation to make it seem not just necessary but admirable—not so much a poured-concrete foundation on which to build as a shimmering jade mountain toward which to journey.

And so personal autonomy is promoted from value to ideal, one that directs us to do what Stepan does not—winnow the contents of our souls. In Robert Young's view, autonomy is a kind of self-direction that imposes a shape on the "principles of thought and action" that guide one's life: "To the extent that an individual is self-directed he (or she) brings the entire course of his life into a unified order. This suggests that a person who is free of external constraints and who has the capacity to pursue a particular pattern of living may fail to be autonomous . . . because he is not able to organize these principles in a unified way."[5] Stanley Benn, emphasizing the importance of critical reflection on one's norms and practices, sets the bar almost as high: "the autonomous person has realized the potentialities of his autarchic status to a higher degree than someone who merely falls in with the projects of others and assesses his performance by standards thrust on him by his environment."[6] It has, indeed, become commonplace to stipulate that the autonomous agent has distanced himself from social influences and conventions, and conducts himself according to principles that he has himself ratified through critical reflection.[7] Behold the citizen as a one-person ethics committee, tasked with from-the-ground-up axiology; how this leaves time for the humbler pursuits of getting and spending is anyone's guess.

There's a pattern here. Advocates of strong autonomy (as I'll call it) are responding to those who point out the ways in which our values and convictions and habits are often anything but autochthonous. Their solution has been to define autonomy *up*: to make it more exalted, more demanding. In short, faced with on-the-ground resistance, they have fallen victim to conceptual mission creep. The consequence has been to make autonomy look outlandishly exigent. Its devotees want it to be as common as crabgrass; but they talk as if it is a rare orchid, and just as particular about soil and climate.

The result is to bring autonomy some unearned adversaries. David Johnston's *The Idea of a Liberal Theory*, for example, worries that personal autonomy is something of a luxury item. Johnston starts by distinguishing personal autonomy from what he variously calls "agent autonomy" or, simply, agency. To have agency is just to be able to conceive and pursue projects, plans, values. By contrast, to have personal autonomy is actively to choose the values and projects you wish to pursue— to be a subject of self-authorship. (If this seems, as he anticipates, a too-stringent construction, he suggests "reflective self-direction" as a milder alternative.) What's an example of an agent who lacks personal autonomy? Johnston introduces us to Michael, who's born in a provincial town and attends public school and a local college, goes to work for his father's chain of drugstores, and marries his high-school sweetheart. Because Michael "never gives serious consideration to any pattern of life other than the one he actually pursues," Johnston says that, though he has agency, he "is not personally autonomous."[8] He concludes that a good society should create the conditions by which its members can become agents, and foster a sense of justice (that is, *moral* autonomy), but that personal autonomy, contrary to Joseph Raz, is not essential. Given Johnston's overextended construction of personal autonomy, it's hard to disagree.

Yet this is not, one might point out, precisely Raz's construction. Raz, in *The Morality of Freedom,* says that the "autonomous person is part author of his life," but immediately goes on to issue a series of deflating caveats. The notion is "not to be identified with the ideal of giving one's life a unity"; and, he says, "a person who frequently changes his tastes can be as autonomous as one who never shakes off his adolescent preferences." The autonomous person

> must be aware of his life as stretching over time. He must be capable of understanding how various choices will have considerable and lasting impact on his life. He may always prefer to avoid long-term commitments. But he must be aware of their availability. This has led to some over-intellectualized conceptions of personal autonomy. I know of nothing wrong with the intellectual life, just as I know of nothing wrong with people who consciously endow their lives with great unity. But the ideal of personal autonomy is meant to be wider and compatible with other styles of life, including those which are very unintellectual.[9]

As Raz goes on to stress, awareness of one's opportunities and abilities "does not mean premeditation or a very deliberate style of life, nor does it necessitate any high degree of self-awareness or rationality All it requires is the awareness of one's options and the knowledge that one's actions amount to charting a course that could have been otherwise."[10] Michael passes this test easily. For him, large issues about how else he might live his life don't arise, Johnston says. But what of it? He knows that his "actions amount to charting a course that could have been otherwise." Indeed, the capacity to form and execute plans, as Raz also points out, is a necessary feature of having practical reason.[11] George Sher has similarly elaborated a view of autonomy as "responsiveness to reasons," again centering the notion on the prerequisites of practical rationality.[12] So it would seem that what Johnston calls "agent autonomy"—along with the correlative requirement that society provide conditions under which people are able to formulate and pursue projects and values—is all that's necessary.

Yet even in this blandly tempered version, autonomy remains a fighting word. In this chapter, I want to defend what I take to be the core idea of autonomy against both those who worry it isn't strong enough and those who worry that it's too strong—both those who want to promote it to the status of unattainable ideal and those who want to demote it to the realm of parochial values. My aim is to protect it from its enthusiasts and its detractors alike. And yet, as we'll see, even a more modest version of autonomy can become easily ensnared in ambiguities and antinomies. And the real debates can't be dissolved by definitional refinements. In the end, I'll try to connect the debates over autonomy to the venerable opposition between structure and agency—and suggest that this opposition, too, has been wrongly framed in the first place.

Autonomy as Intolerance

The controversy over how to formulate autonomy— over what set of criteria best captures our intuition, or best expresses our ideal; or over the precise content of the ideal (the debate has both conceptual and normative dimensions)—immediately lets on to another: whether autonomy, even putting aside the details of its specification, is or ought to be a value in the first place, at least outside of the liberal democracies of the West. An availability of options, an endowment with minimum rationality, an absence of coercion: if this is the core of personal autonomy, what could be more anodyne and unexceptionable? And yet, perhaps goaded by the sort of autonomist overstretch we've seen, many political theorists write about it as if it were an industrial effluent, something generated by Western modernity and exported, willy-nilly, to hapless denizens of the non-Western world. In autonomism, they descry the tyranny of the *hypermarché*, paving over rooted, unglamorous ways of life that do not, themselves, embody the value of autonomy. By insisting that each person should have the ability to choose his own conception of the good, are we, paradoxically, truncating the available range of such conceptions? For Mill, as we saw, autonomy and diversity were plaited together in his ideal of individuality. For many critics, however, the language of autonomy reflects an arrogant insularity; all that talk of self-fashioning, self-direction, self-authorship suggests a bid to create the Performance Art Republic, elbowing aside Grandma Walton in order to make the world safe for Karen Finley.

The apparent discord between autonomy and diversity has been variously framed; William Galston diagnoses a conflict between the Enlightenment and the post-Reformation projects—between the contrary ideals of self-directed reason and of tolerance.[13] As he says, a tension between tolerance and autonomy has surely been a part of liberalism since its origins. And yet autonomist overreach raises these tensions to the point where some theorists have sought their divorce on the grounds of irreconcilable differences.

The political theorist John Gray, rather hastily conflating Isaiah Berlin's critique of positive liberty with his strictures about the ideal of self-direction—states the critique forcefully, and with an interesting twist:

> Such autonomy-based liberalism, from Berlin's standpoint, elevates a controversial and questionable ideal of life uncritically and unduly. There are many excellent lives that are not especially autonomous, and which liberal societies can shelter: the life of a nun, of the professional soldier, or the artist passionately devoted to his work, may be lives in which rare and precious goods are embodied, and yet lives that are, in very different ways, far from autonomous. The idea which the 'basic freedom' of choice-making supports is not that of autonomy, but of self-creation, where the self that is created may very well not be that of an autonomous agent. To demand of self-creation that it conform with an ideal of rational autonomy is . . . an unacceptably and necessarily restrictive requirement. It excludes the life of the traditionalist, whose choices confirm a self-identity that has been inherited, as much as those of the mystic, or the playful hedonist, for whom a fixed identity may be a useless encumbrance, and the reflective deliberation that is involved in autonomous agency a burdensome distraction.[14]

In pitting autonomy against diversity—in painting autonomism as the bigotry of liberals—his voice is one of a chorus. "Autonomy-based liberalism ultimately contains no commitment to the value of diversity in and of itself," writes Susan Mendus. "It justifies only those diverse forms of life which themselves value autonomy and thus makes toleration a pragmatic device—a temporary expedient—not a matter of principle." Charles Larmore says, "liberals such as Kant and Mill, who have coupled their political theory with a corresponding notion of what in general ought to be our personal ideal, have betrayed in fact the liberal spirit." According to Chandran Kukathas, many cultures don't "place such value on the *individual's* freedom to choose his ends. Often, the individual and his interest are subordinated to the community." Bhikhu Parekh joins this point to a larger critique of "monism" among moral and political philosophers, and Mill, despite his diversitarian rhetoric, is among the culprits: "Since Mill's theory of diversity was embedded in an individualist vision of life, he cherished individual but not cultural diversity, that is diversity of views and lifestyles within a shared individualist culture but not diversity of cultures including the nonindividualist."[15] And these are weaknesses that Mill, in Parekh's view, shares with his contemporary heirs.

Amid this enfilade of objections, some things can be clearly made out. There's a widespread anxiety that autonomism is predicated upon the notion of a "true self" that Berlin associated with the dangerous ideal of positive liberty. In this way, Gray wishes to separate Berlin from the "autonomist liberalism" he identifies with Raz: but the result is a persuasive reading neither of Berlin nor of Raz. One might note that the traditionalist whom Gray seeks to protect is precisely someone who rejects the voluntaristic model of self-choice or self-creation that Gray evidently plumps for, and it is a curious suggestion that "self-creation" is less (rather than more) burdensome an ideal than autonomy. For that matter, the ethic of autonomy shouldn't, on its face, pose any problems for the self-chosen life of the nun, or playboy, or artist.[16] To assume that a passionately committed artist fails to be autonomous implies that the autonomous must be only lightly committed to their projects; whereas some conceptions of autonomy, as we've seen, insist on precisely the opposite—they require that we embrace our norms and preferences.

As for Susan Mendus's worry that liberalism "ultimately contains no commitment to the value of diversity in and of itself," the autonomist might plead nolo contendere. Earlier, we saw—in Mill and such later theorists as Sen—an insistence that the *fact* of diversity be recognized and incorporated in the way we think about liberty (for Mill) and equality (for Sen); this was part of the doctrine of individuality, as it is part of the doctrine of autonomism. But to say that diversity in and of itself is a value, a primordial good, is to say something altogether different and less obvious, and I will explore this controversial claim in chapter

4. Mendus's additional charge of cultural cronyism—the charge that autonomism "justifies" only autonomist forms of life—invites a number of confusions. Autonomy-based liberalism, or any doctrine of social ordering, need not "justify" diverse forms of life in any strong sense; it need only accommodate them and extend equal respect to their members. Further, such toleration or accommodation, far from being a "temporary expedient," can plausibly be considered a precondition for the exercise of autonomy. It is true that associations that encroach on the autonomy of their members pose hard questions—and we will take these up later—but then, for a liberal society that seeks to guarantee the rights of its members, these groups *should* pose hard problems. The autonomist can consistently reject what Nancy L. Rosenblum has criticized as the "logic of congruence," according to which civic associations in a democracy must themselves be internally democratic.[17] At a minimum, as I've suggested, it's not obvious that autonomism must rule out voluntary membership in autonomy-scanting forms of life. "One cannot be, at one and the same time, a fully autonomous liberal individual and a dutifully obedient member of a traditional community," Gray says.[18] That can't be right. Notwithstanding Thomas Merton's elective membership in a faith-based community that valued obedience and self-abnegation, it would be very strange to say that Merton lacked autonomy; on the contrary, his intensely self-reflective attitude toward his own values seems to manifest autonomy of an extremely robust form.

Gray levels another charge against autonomy, one at odds with his charge that autonomy is ethnocentric: it is that autonomy is indeterminate. "There are many rival autonomies," Gray argues. "When pursued by people with differing views of what makes human lives worthwhile, the liberal project of promoting autonomy can have very different outcomes. . . . When we judge that choice is greater in one context than it is in another, we do so on the basis of an evaluation of the options that they contain. We have no value-free measure of relative autonomy."[19] His insistence that there is no "value-free" measure of relative autonomy is then used to justify a politics of retreat, the failure of nerve that he would ennoble as *modus vivendi*.

> If diversity comes into conflict with liberty, and the diversity is that of worthwhile forms of life expressive of genuine human needs and embodying

authentic varieties of human flourishing, why should liberty always trump diversity—especially if one is a value pluralist? To claim that it must do so is to say that no form of life deserves to survive if it cannot withstand the force of the exercise of free choice by its members. But this is precisely the pure philosophy of rights that Berlinian value-pluralism undercuts.[20]

So Gray maintains, appealing to what we might call the Argument from Other Cultures; and yet it remains unclear by what value-free measure those forms are deemed "worthwhile" examples of human flourishing.[21] His doctrine of *modus vivendi* asks that we cater to authoritarian groups while maintaining some sort of exquisite impartiality among them. (Gray, it should be noted, rejects liberal neutrality—rejects both "political liberalism" and "comprehensive liberalism"—because, as he sees it, the workings of value pluralism apply to the Right, as well as the Good.) Liberty isn't an ultimate value, for Gray; harmony seems to be. And in his zeal to give peace offerings to *les coutumes étrangères*, we're offered a liberalism of bound feet, barely able to totter across the room to settle a dispute.

"We cannot agree on what most advances autonomy, because our views of the good diverge in precisely the ways of which value-pluralism speaks," he says, in an influential line of argument. "Autonomy is not a still point in the turning world of values. It is a point of intersection for all their conflicts." The error is to suppose that liberalism should *want* to remove such debates from the realm of politics, or that agreement on what best serves the purposes of autonomy should be reached in advance; on the contrary, the hard cases are meet subject for the rough-and-tumble of political debate and deliberation. Nobody promised that a liberal politics would be "a refuge from conflict."[22] Here, virtue is miscast as vice.

Gray finds it telling that in most "late modern societies . . . the liberal discourse of rights and personal autonomy is deployed in a continuing conflict to gain and hold power by communities and ways of life having highly diverse values. Where it exists, the hegemony of liberal discourse is often skin deep." Yet, from the perspective of conventional liberal theory, the thinness of liberal discourse is a considerable recommendation. American fundamentalism, he continues darkly, "appropriates [liberal values] for its own purposes."[23] But, again, politically speaking that's what talk of values is *for*—to be appropriated by political actors for their "own purposes." This is not the subversion of liberal language so much as its vindication. (I'll be saying more about this, in the context of "incompletely theorized agreement," in chapter 6.) It is not a small service to provide a shared vocabulary through which people and groups may contend for the exercise of power. So when Gray warns that even the United States "is not hegemonically liberal but morally pluralist," this will not trouble the post-Rawlsian liberal, who regards its moral pluralism as a tribute to its political liberalism. A political liberalism that functioned only for comprehensive liberals, let us agree, would be a poor and shrunken thing. Once again, a virtue has been miscast as vice.

AUTONOMY AGONISTES

It should be obvious, in any case, that the Argument from Other Cultures is a bit of a red herring. Indeed, what has been dramatized in terms of Us and Them, the West and the Rest, really plays out familiar conflicts between liberals and communitarians, between "atomistic" and "holistic" conceptions of society, conflicts that are *internal* to the West. We're like the astronomer who mistakes the fly on the other end of the telescope for a planet a good deal farther away.

After all, it can be disputed whether it makes sense, in *any* society, to speak of individuals' choosing their ends. "Can we imagine individuals without any involuntary ties at all, unbound, utterly free?" Michael Walzer writes. "The thought experiment is especially useful now, when postmodern theorists are writing so excitedly about 'self-fashioning,' an enterprise undertaken not exactly in a social vacuum but rather—so we are told—amid the ruins of conventional social forms. I suspect that the effort to describe a society of self-fashioning individuals is necessarily self-defeating." Charles Taylor makes a similar point when he says that a "self exists only within what I call 'webs of interlocution,'" that "living within such strongly qualified horizons is constitutive of human agency, that stepping outside these limits would be tantamount to stepping outside what we recognize as integral, that is, undamaged human personhood." Likewise Sandel's skepticism toward the "volun-

taristic" relation between ourselves and our ends which Rawls is said
to posit: "we cannot regard ourselves as independent in this way without great cost to those loyalties and convictions whose moral force consists partly in the fact that living by them is inseparable from understanding ourselves as the particular persons we are—as members of this
family or community or nation or people, as bearers of this history. To
imagine a person incapable of constitutive attachments such as these is
not to conceive an ideally free and rational agent, but to imagine a
person wholly without character." Or Daniel A. Bell's insistence that
"one's social world supplies more than trivial norm-government practices—it also sets the authoritative moral horizons within which we
determine" what's worth striving for.[24]

There's a Wittgensteinian thread that runs through some of these
considerations. Wittgenstein, of course, urged us to accept that the
"form of life" might be explanatory bedrock in social thought. So, in
an example of his, when children have learned how to proceed with the
number-series, following 1,000 by 1,001 and 1,002, there's no content
to saying they've "grasped the principle of adding 1": talk of "principles"
puts a shiny top hat on the bald truth—that they have simply acquired
a "way of going on." It is an easy step from here to the thought that
there really is no place outside the practice of using numerals in the
way we do from which to assess that practice: to understand elementary
arithmetic is to participate in the practice; what is available outside the
practice is not a review of arithmetical practice but only no arithmetical
understanding at all. Wittgenstein (at least in one influential construction) wants us to stop simply with the recognition that it is part of the
natural history of our species that most of us can count. This has led
many people to stress that issues of value and rationality always arise
within a form of life, and that it is only within the practices of a certain
community—against a background in which these practices are taken
as given—that we can ask the questions "Is this so?" and "Is that reasonable?" They might doubt whether it even makes sense to "reflect criti-
cally" upon our views, values, and preferences. We *are* our ends, the
communitarians urge in a consonant spirit: we can't imagine ourselves
as independent from our loyalties or convictions because, Sandel says,
"living by them is inseparable from understanding ourselves as the particular persons we are."[25]

One needn't be a card-carrying communitarian to accept that these considerations aren't without substance. As we saw in the previous chapter—in defending individuality from the charges of unsociability and arbitrariness—to give people a conceptual vocabulary is to influence them; but to deprive them of it is to cripple them, not to empower them. As we also conceded in that chapter, liberal talk about the role of critical reflection in arriving at one's life plan, or one's conception of the good life, can sometimes seem remote from lived experience. But these aren't considerations that cut against autonomism as such; they're considerations that our understanding of autonomy must accommodate.

So it's important to note that one needn't subscribe to autonomism to have autonomy. Now, there are many activities that must be conducted under a certain description; you can get married only under the description of getting married. To get married, that is, you have to recognize that this is what you're doing. By contrast, the exercise of autonomy—of what passes for uncoerced, unmanipulated choice making; of "reason-responsive" behavior—doesn't require an ethic of autonomy. To be autonomous you don't need the concept of autonomy at all. You might well exercise your capacity for practical rationality under the label, say, of Recognizing the Truth. People don't, as a rule, imagine themselves as having arrived at their own conception of the good life: their conception of the good or well-lived life would be undermined by their imagining it to be a wholly volitional affair, chosen among equally qualified candidates. Consider the religious believer who has decided to follow the One True Path: to him, what's crucial is that he has been guided by the truth, by the nature of the universe. He has (he may insist) no more "decided" to walk this path than he "decided" to view the sky as blue. And what's true of the zealot is true, as well, of the slacker. Neither sees himself as being in the plan-formulating business. Both can be plausibly credited with autonomy.

And so, for that matter, can poor old Stepan Arkadyich. His choice of his liberal paper isn't, after all, arbitrary: a conservative tendency was "also held to by many in his circle," Tolstoy assures us. But Stepan's paper was more consistent with his own everyday experiences—it "more closely suited his manner of life." (And in that sense he has "come to identify" with these beliefs and preferences, just as Gerald Dworkin asks.)

The liberal party said that everything was bad in Russia, and indeed Stepan Arkadyich had many debts and decidedly too little money. The liberal party said that marriage was an obsolete institution and was in need of reform, and indeed family life gave Stepan Arkadyich little pleasure and forced him to lie and pretend, which was so contrary to his nature. The liberal party said, or rather implied, that religion was just a bridle for the barbarous parts of the population, and indeed Stepan Arkadyich could not even stand through a short prayer service without aching feet and could not grasp the point of all these fearsome and high-flown words about the other world, when life in this one could be so merry.[26]

His putative failure to be independent, then, seems really a deliberate policy of what we might call "intellectual outsourcing." And surely it counts in his favor that he seems to be a fan of Mill's, at least at second hand. (He reads with particular enjoyment an article "in which mention was made of Bentham and Mill and fine barbs were shot at the ministry," Tolstoy recounts.)[27] Since Stepan's name has been so besmirched, it may be worth pointing out that this is not his only appealing trait. Stepan, we're told, was "liked by all who knew him" for, among other things, "his kind, cheerful temper and unquestionable honesty." He commanded the respect of his colleagues, superiors, and subordinates, owing to such qualities as "an extreme indulgence toward people, based on his awareness of his own shortcomings," and "a perfect liberalism, not the sort he read about in the newspapers, but the sort he had in his blood, which made him treat all people, whatever their rank or status, in a perfectly equal and identical way." Elsewhere, Tolstoy stresses that he was "incapable of self-deception," which would suggest that his penchant for secondhand opinions is predicated upon something more complicated than bad faith.[28] Now, Stepan is a less than admirable character in lots of ways; he's a faithless husband, for one thing, and so, in the wake of his sister's ostracism, serves as an emblem of his class's sexual hypocrisy. But he stays loyal to the beleaguered Anna, and his unabashed enjoyment of luxury is unmarred by pretense or cruelty. There is nothing small or stunted about him. He enjoys the good life, has a sort of hedonistic full-heartedness—there are virtues here, too.

I'm not defending this wayward Millian just to be mischievous; the bigger point is that, in falling back upon the (congenial) cognitive authority of others, we are all Stepan. Certainly this is true in the rudimentary elms-and-experts way that Hilary Putnam has written about.[29] Our cognitive division of labor is as useful and as widespread as the economic division of labor. It would be stultifying to abjure words we cannot fully explain or claims we cannot ourselves adequately defend. But it's also the case that, as a body of empirical research into the nature of political identity suggests, few of us acquire our political convictions with any greater rigor than Stepan does. Among the many reasons that autonomy (or authenticity or the other character ideals sometimes allied with it) cannot require a very high degree of self-scrutiny, the most persuasive is that we would be hard put to describe *ourselves* that way. What the psychologist John Bargh has dubbed the "automaticity of being" characterizes vast swaths of our waking existence.[30] (The phenomenon Stepan in fact demonstrates is rather more interesting: how a disapproving attitude toward the prevailing norms can be as reflexive as a blinkered adherence to those norms. For, as we saw, it is a liberal paper to which he subscribes, and the liberal paper is constantly calling this or that convention to the bar of rational scrutiny and finding it wanting.) In general, proponents of strong autonomy have moved too quickly from the fact that we sentient creatures have the ability to step back and evaluate our beliefs to the mandate that we actively do so. They confuse a capacity and its exercise. This much should certainly be conceded to some of autonomy's critics; but, as I say, it is not an objection to autonomy properly understood.

In arguing against ultrademanding conceptions of autonomy, I have been concerned that autonomy not price itself out of the market. But it must not sell itself too cheaply either. Though a more modest conception of autonomy sidesteps many difficulties, plenty of perplexities cannot be sidestepped, some of which, but only some, I've already touched on. Raz himself says that the autonomous agent, in addition to having minimum rationality and adequate options, has to be "free from coercion and manipulation by others, he must be independent."[31] And, of course, much depends on how aggressively the latter desiderata are specified. For the philosophical literature on autonomy has turned up countless puzzles: sometimes we are more autonomous than we might appear, and sometimes we are less.

Consider a particularly grueling day in the life of a store owner—David Johnston's incurious provincial, perhaps. In the morning, let's say, Michael reluctantly gives his assistant manager a raise; she's made it clear that she'll quit the drugstore otherwise, and he can't afford the disruption just now. At midday, a blackmailer tells him that if he doesn't give him five hundred dollars, he'll inform Michael's wife that he's been having an affair. In the afternoon, he decides to open another drugstore downtown—based on misleading information supplied by his bookkeeper, who's looking to land her sister a job there. In the evening, a robber enters his store and demands that he open the vault where the cash is held. He weighs various options (should he pretend that the vault is on a timer, and that he can't open it? should he pretend that the key is with someone else, activate the silent alarm, and stall for time?) and decides to open the vault.

In short, it has been a day crammed with conundrums. Michael has twice had to pay dearly to prevent a person—the assistant manager; the blackmailer—from doing something that would harm him. Yet most people would classify only the second instance as involving coercion. During the robbery, Michael formed the intention to open the vault after considering all the options; although he wouldn't have made his decision without coercion, he could have done otherwise. Did he form his intention autonomously? Reasonable people may differ.[32] Michael's decision to open the store downtown is a pretty straightforward result of informational manipulation. But the information and opinion that any executive gets from his advisers will be affected by their biases, and so, just as you'd suppose, it's hard to demarcate manipulation from persuasion. Certainly, freedom from manipulation can't mean freedom from social pressure. As we saw, those who would insist on a heavy task of critical reflection are worried that such pressures may compromise our independence of mind. But there's no way to distinguish, even in principle, between such propagation of norms, on the one hand, and, on the other, the establishment of those "horizons of choice" that are necessary to choosing in the first place.

Mill himself stepped carefully here, and his celebration of diversity and nonconformity shouldn't distract us from his many concessions to both custom and "natural sentiment." People who identify autonomy with critical reflection often trace the position back to Mill.[33] And yet to dwell on deformations of will is to leave out the other half of the Millian picture. He did indeed deplore "liking in groups"; he also upheld the importance of moral consensus. Thus, for example, Mill, in his *Utilitarianism*, raised a worry about the potentially corrosive effects of analysis on moral sentiment—and allayed it by suggesting that the crucial ethical norms would not be forever the object of such analysis. With the "strengthening of social ties, and all healthy growth of society," Mill says, an individual

> comes, as though instinctively, to be conscious of himself as a being who of course pays regard to others. The good of others becomes to him a thing naturally and necessarily to be attended to, like any of the physical conditions of our existence.... Consequently the smallest germs of the feeling are laid hold of and nourished by the contagion of sympathy and the influences of education; and a complete web of corroborative association is woven round it, by the powerful agency of the external sanction.... This mode of conceiving ourselves and human life, as civilisation goes on, is felt to be more and more natural.[34]

Note the organicist language here—the way Mill speaks of what comes "instinctively," "naturally," "necessarily." The putatively natural basis of these sentiments (which society is directed to amplify) guarantees that they will be proof against "the dissolving force of analysis" that, Mill says, "intellectual culture" must pose to moral associations that are artificial in character. Nor was Mill generally dismissive of received wisdom, the norms and conventions one is bequeathed by society; he just thought this wisdom was more likely to be accurate about common things, and that when it came to things that were distinctively one's own, one should prefer one's own perspective. As we saw in the previous chapter, Mill's position flows, in part, from his ideal of self-development, but in part, too, from his belief that individuals were likely to be the best judges of their own interests. Unlike many theorists of autonomy today, who would assign us all to undertake a comprehensive assessment of norms and values, Mill never confused the job description of the citizen with that of the moral theorist.

THE TWO STANDPOINTS

So what are we to make of that putative tension between, on the one hand, the theme of reflective self-direction as it runs through Locke, and Kant, and, indeed, Mill—as well as through much recent liberal thought—and, on the other hand, the communitarian emphasis on a social matrix that not only constrains but constitutes our selves? By way of reconciling the two, it's natural to speak of "partial autonomy," and "partial authorship." In Raz's words, "All three conditions, mental abilities, adequacy of options, and independence admit of degree. Autonomy in both its primary and secondary senses is a matter of degree."[35] The partitive rhetoric, unexceptionable though it sounds, papers over a deeper divide.

When you stare at the language of autonomy for any length of time, you can start to wonder not whether it's good or bad, a basic need or a luxury item, but whether it's even coherent. The notion of partial autonomy suggests the conceptual possibility of "full" autonomy: if we have difficulty making sense of the latter, we should find the former equally elusive. In fact, *both* sides of the liberal-communitarian debate have trouble with autonomy. Here we can follow Samuel Scheffler, who, in an important essay on contemporary liberalism as a politics and as a theory, points out that it largely scants the notion of desert, and offers the following diagnosis: "The widespread reluctance among political philosophers to defend a robust notion of preinstitutional desert is due in part to the power in contemporary philosophy of the idea that human thought and action may be wholly subsumable within a broadly naturalistic view of the world. The reticence of these philosophers . . . testifies in part to the prevalence of the often unstated conviction that a thoroughgoing naturalism leaves no room for a conception of individual agency substantial enough to sustain such a notion."[36]

If this is right, talking about "partial authorship," or "partial autonomy," will sound like a bit of a dodge. In fact, there's a duck-rabbit oscillation between a perspective in which autonomy is salient and one in which it disappears entirely. Man makes history, Marx famously averred, but under circumstances and conditions not of his own choosing. That's a natural gloss to place upon the stricture that our autonomy is always only partial. Yet from the perspective that sees us as the product of history, society, culture—and, a fortiori, from the grandly scientific perspective that sees us enmeshed in causal chains that stretch from starfish to the stars—what really remains of autonomy? You, the putatively autonomous individual, are confined to the options that are available to you; and those options themselves represent substantial fixities, a nexus of institutions and practices you did not create yourself. If your values represent what you desire to desire (in David K. Lewis's elegant formulation), what you desire to desire may not be up to you, in the sense that your "will" is the product of forces external to it. Even sticking to the social realm, we know that, for example, the phenomenon that Jon Elster taught us to call "adaptive preference formation" tends to align what people want with what they can get—to conform their desires to their options. And your choices are further limited by your capacities. And those capacities are bequeathed by your natural endowments and your training, neither of which you chose.

The familiar determinist conclusion is that a really complete specification of your conditions and circumstances, internal and external, would permit one to infer your preferences, plans, and actions. From this highly granular perspective, the concept of autonomy simply has no role to play. You are not author; you are authored.

Recall Raz's caveat: "All three conditions, mental abilities, adequacy of options, and independence admit of degree. Autonomy in both its primary and secondary senses is a matter of degree." This suggests (among other things) that there can be better and worse arrays of options. Given that, as Gerald Dworkin has observed, more options aren't necessarily better, how are we to say what sort of option set would advance our autonomy?[37] Does the pianist who also had the skills to be a violinist have more autonomy than the pianist who lacked that second option? Does the rich bachelor idler have more autonomy than the family man with a full-time job? Is Levin more autonomous than Stepan Arkadyich? Such are the imponderables posed by talk of options. And the independence-function is even more vexing. What would complete independence of mind look like? Surely it would mean (as Walzer and others warned) not to be "minded" at all: to have no fixtures, no horizons of decision making, no pregiven ends or values or interests or goals. Such a creature starts to look distinctively inhuman.

And yet without such strictures, aren't we in danger of ascribing autonomy to automatons—to people in whom desires seem to be implanted, like a foreign body? To people who couldn't really want what they seem to want, but are subordinate to the will of others, or blinded by inadequate knowledge of the world? So we find our way back to the quandary. As we saw, from certain perspectives, autonomy is a thing that most people have; from other perspectives, one has reason to wonder whether such an exalted state is achievable, or even intelligible.

How, then, to reconcile subject-centered and social-centered accounts? Perhaps the most persuasive attempt is the one made by Charles Taylor, who has elaborated a notion of social practices wherein our actions belong to the practices that give them shape and meaning. "A great deal of human action only happens insofar as the agent understands and constitutes himself as integrally part of a 'we,' " he writes.[38] And he invokes Bourdieu's notion of the "habitus," a "system of durable and transposable dispositions," to flesh out the essentially social nature of the self. Taylor is intent on giving human agency its full glory—he does not want to reduce us to epiphenomena—but insists that we see agency as constituted by the web of practices and collectivities in which it emerges and to which it belongs. It's a perspective, he says, that "runs against the grain of much modern thought and culture, in particular our scientific culture and its associated epistemology"—the kind of naturalism that has, in his view, deformed "our contemporary sense of self." In its place, he urges us to see the agent "as engaged in practices, as a being who acts in and on a world." What we should take from Bourdieu's notion of the habitus, he says, is that "practice is, as it were, a continual interpretation and reinterpretation of what the rule really means," that the relation between rule and practice is richly reciprocal.[39]

And yet the thesis can seem at odds with its Wittgensteinian underpinnings. "When I obey a rule, I do not choose," Wittgenstein says, in a passage Taylor cites; "I obey the rule *blindly*." Taylor's vision has thus been criticized—not least by Taylor's colleague James Tully—for being inadequately Wittgensteinian. Doesn't Taylor's emphasis on interpretation—the notion that "we must speak of man as a self-interpreting being, because this kind of interpretation is not an optional extra, but is an essential part of our existence"—invoke the sort of critical reflection and evaluation that Wittgenstein was at pains to call into question? To understand a sign is not to interpret it; to grasp it is "*nicht eine Deutung*," not an interpretation, but merely a "way of going on." The core of Wittgenstein's remarks on rule following was a line of reasoning aimed to eliminate precisely that interim step—interpretation—that Taylor would exalt.[40]

There have been numerous other attempts to reconcile agency and structure, subject and society, dancer and dance. Typically these insist upon their mutually constitutive character, or—as in Anthony Giddens's talk of "the duality of structure"—the recursive nature of their interactions. I will not dwell on the details of these accounts: for it cannot be said that Taylor has failed where others have succeeded. But then maybe it's no wonder that the matter should give us so much trouble.

There's an old urban legend about a couple who, during a trip to India, adopt an adorable stray kitten and return home with it to Cincinnati—only to watch, with mounting horror, as it turns into a child-mauling tiger. At this point, we might as well state something crashingly obvious. The problem of autonomy in political theory—like the "problem of agency" in the social sciences[41]—has a whiskers-to-stripes resemblance to one of the fiercest problems in all philosophy, that of free will.

The literature on the subject—as Providence has no doubt decreed—is immense, and immensely intricate. But I will find it useful to enlist one of the most familiar responses to the most familiar of problems. It is the "two standpoints" response associated with Kant. For some purposes, we must acknowledge that we are natural beings and regard ourselves and others as part of the natural realm, subject to theoretical explanations in terms of natural causes. From this standpoint, we belong to the so-called sensible world, the *Sinnenwelt*. But that is not a standpoint we can adopt when we ourselves act as rational agents: "All men think of themselves as having a free will," he noted. Accordingly, "for *purposes of action* the footpath of freedom is the only one on which we can make use of reason in our conduct." Here we situate ourselves in the so-called intelligible world, the *Verstandeswelt*. As he writes in the *Groundwork of the Metaphysic of Morals*, "We can enquire whether we do not take one standpoint when by means of freedom we conceive ourselves as causes acting a priori, and another standpoint when we contemplate ourselves with reference to our actions as effects which we see before our eyes. . . . [W]hen we think of ourselves as free, we transfer ourselves into the intelligible world as members and recognize the autonomy of the will together with its consequence—morality."[42]

And these worlds of Kant's are indeed standpoints, not planes of reality. "The concept of the intelligible world is," for him, "only a *point of view* which reason finds itself constrained to adopt outside appearances *in order to conceive itself as practical.*"[43] We have to act as if freedom is possible even though we can't provide any theoretical justification for it; in that sense, he says, it can't be explained, only defended. Let me arrest the argument, and close the *Groundwork*, right here. Kant's *zwei Standpunkte*, which derive, in some sense, from two kinds of purposes or interests, is the basic move I want to borrow.

For notice that the whole debate over agency and structure—between autonomists and their critics—has tended to suppose an opposition between them in which they compete, so to speak, for the same causal space. In simpler times, the case for structure might have been exemplified by the claim that in *Native Son*, Bigger Thomas acts as he does because of his social conditioning. (So Mr. Max, Bigger's lawyer, believed, and argued lengthily at his trial.) The case for agency, posed in terms of the same simplicity, is the case for the individual: the figure whose escape from society makes the romantic subject its most obvious epitome. (So Bigger himself seems to have believed: "I didn't know I was really alive in this world until I felt things hard enough to kill for 'em.")[44] To resolve this supposed tension, as I say, various dialectics have been proposed, in which structure is taken as enabling agency while structure is itself constituted by social practices.[45] What the two-standpoints doctrine suggests, by contrast, is that we give up trying to see structure and agency as competing for the same causal space. Instead, the logic of structure (which yields *causes* for action) and the logic of agency (which yields *reasons* for action) belong to two distinct standpoints. To act *as if*, to regard oneself *as if*: this notion of the *als ob* is central to Kant's way of arguing; it is the hallmark of his "critical" philosophy. And so is the allied notion of interests and purposes that select which *als ob* comes into play. (An "interest," Kant says, "is that in virtue of which reason becomes practical—that is, becomes a cause determining the will.")[46]

You hear echoes of this tradition, I think, when Habermas accounts for the distinction that Dilthey had sought to establish between the *Naturwissenschaften* and the *Geisteswissenschaften* by arguing that each kind of theory is constituted by a distinct kind of interest. The natural sciences, Habermas says, are rooted in a "knowledge-constitutive interest in possible technical control," while the knowledge-constitutive interest of the *Geisteswissenschaften* is "practical." There's plenty to quibble with here, but the basic idea that *interests* play a role in the constitution of areas of inquiry seems plausible enough.[47] Many philosophers (Donald Davidson and Daniel Dennett among them) have held, for example, that in understanding people as intentional systems—as having the beliefs, desires, intentions, and other propositional attitudes of commonsense psychology—we make a certain *projection* of rationality. We ascribe beliefs and desires to people in such a way as to "make rational" their acts, even though we know that people aren't fully rational. At this point, it is usual to mention "idealization." As Jerry Fodor has often insisted, we should not make methodological demands of psychology that cannot be met by chemistry and physics: and both in "bench science" and in scientific theory idealization is ubiquitous. Whether we count a theory as false *simpliciter* or approximately true turns out to be a question of judgment, a judgment that may legitimately depend on what we're interested in. A chemistry whose practical focus is on the development of industrial dyes might accept the idealizing assumption that filtered river water is H_2O; a chemistry interested in energy regulation at the cellular level could not. An idealization is a useful falsehood: and useful always means "useful for some purpose." Depending on our practical purposes, we may need to proceed as if planes were frictionless and firms were profit maximizers. We may suppose that, from the point of view of the universe, everything observable could be reduced to particle physics; but this is not a point of view available to us, and our theories, like all our products, are imperfect things. Indeed, the history of science is a catalog of the errors that flow from premature attempts to constrain theories of one level by the demand that they postulate only phenomena that can be understood in terms of theories at a lower level. Since we do not have perfect theories, we proceed with the best theories we can muster: and the best theory for some purposes may be better—for *those* purposes—than the best theory that meets this demand for methodological reductionism. We wouldn't want to jettison whatever useful insights we might get from economics or meteorology, say, just because we can't give an account of those disciplines in terms of the movement of molecules.

I say all this in order to soften up the target. If we get accustomed to the fact that there's plenty of *as-if*-ing even within the realm of naturalistic explanation (by way of interest-guided "idealizations"), we might worry less about the bigger Kantian *as if* that we've been entertaining. And surely the basic notion that our theories are guided by our pragmatic purposes, our *praktischer Absicht*, has a Kantian taproot. The two-standpoints doctrine suggests, then, that talk of agency is guided by different interests or intentions from talk of structure; and we go only a little further when we say that these different interests make different idealizations appropriate, different *as if*s useful.

AGENCY AND THE INTERESTS OF THEORY

"All men think of themselves as having a free will," Kant told us, which is to say that we are ourselves agents. To regard others as ends in themselves—to recognize their human dignity—is to regard them in this way, too. The standpoint of agency is connected, in the most direct possible way, to our concern to live intelligible lives in community with other people who are, first of all, lovers, families, and friends, and then colleagues, officers, checkout-counter assistants, garage mechanics, doctors, congressional representatives, strangers, and so on. This practical interest requires us to be able to articulate our own behavior in relation to theirs, and this we do through our understanding of them as having beliefs and intentions—in short, as reasoning—and also as having passions and prejudices: in short, as always potentially unreasonable. We have (in that phrase of Strawson's) "reactive attitudes"—we respond to others with gratitude and anger, praise and blame, and so forth—and we wish to hold on to and make sense of these attitudes. It's in this realm that we conceive our goals and aims, our decisions large and small, the life we want to make.

As you will have noticed, to adopt a third-person perspective on agency is already, as Kant says, to "contemplate ourselves with reference to our actions as effects which we see before our eyes." To theorize about the standpoint of agency is not to inhabit that standpoint; the autonomist's standpoint is a second-order one. But the model of standpoints and purposes is still helpful in parsing purely theoretical disagreement. Clashes between, say, traditionalist and libertarian perspectives express clashes about what people care about more—social stability or expressive freedom; the management of society or individual liberty. They're not over what the world is like but what the world ought to be like. Yet sometimes the clash is really more basic: it concerns what we want to talk about. Taylor has diagnosed the old liberalism-communitarianism debates as involving "cross-purposes," and the notion that different agendas—cross-purposes rather than conflicting ones—might be involved seems right. If, like Rawls, you want to foreground distributive justice against an autonomist background, you may find it useful to be able to regard individuals in one way. If, like Sandel, you want to foreground the value of community, you need to conceive them in another way. In social thought, talk of "structure" has a specific historical trajectory, too, which passes through Saint-Simon and Marx and is guided by an active political interest in achieving a sweeping egalitarianism. To insist on agency within the discourse of structure—or vice versa—is simply, so to speak, to change the subject.

The two-standpoints approach ought to shed light on some of the other conundrums and indeterminacies that propelled us down this road as well. Recall, for example, Michael and his Bad Day at the Office. Whether we say he had autonomy when he opened the vault at gunpoint may indeed depend on what account of autonomy we're peddling. But rather than demand that our account supply an answer, we might instead attend to what we're interested in. The answer we give, as a matter of everyday intuition, will depend on what story we're telling, and what its constitutive interests are. It depends, *in fine*, on what we're trying to make sense of. If we're interested in the conditions that make people act a certain way—if we're interested, say, in "situationist" psychology—we tell one narrative: here's how Michael acts under these conditions. If we're interested in retribution and blame, we tell another: look what that villain did to poor Michael! What we should resist is the temptation to qualify and subtilize our accounts, to say that Michael had partial autonomy or (an even further remove) the potential of partial autonomy. When is something a condition of choosing and when is it a constraint upon choice? Inevitably, how we answer is a matter of interest-guided judgment, of what standpoint we adopt. As freedom and necessity can be decoupled and assigned to two different explanatory registers, so it is with debates in political theory.[48]

That is why—to return to my point of departure—talk of partial autonomy is an ill-fated attempt to split the difference between two standpoints: one in which I have autonomy and one in which I do not. Just as, in the specific debates over free will and compatibilism, it's not a way out to say that my actions are partly caused, so here, the language of partitive autonomy misguidedly seeks a midpoint between first-person and third-person perspectives, oblivious of the distinct purposes served by each of the two standpoints. To the contrary, as I say, there is something to be gained by disconnecting these concepts from each other analytically; by proceeding with the discourse of structure without always seeking an agent-based reduction. In fact, there is much to be said more generally for the noncoherence of our different theoretical practices, for the existence of theories that illuminate certain projects in ways that simply say, "So what?" to the fact that they contradict other theories that belong to other projects. Game theorists can legitimately make assumptions that differ from those of ethnographers; economists may need to idealize differently from psychologists. More grandly still: explanations in terms of reasons and explanations in terms of causes needn't proceed in lockstep. Once motivated, this noncoherence can be seen as both necessary and desirable; what we ask of a theory is that it be adequate to its own constitutive project—that it earn its *as ifs*.

This is all, I'll admit, a little too quick. The various standpoints can't be made to converge, but they will sometimes be superimposed. You, as a theorist, can take account of agency; and I, as an agent, will be responsive to whatever "structural" or naturalistic theories of society I happen to have. And sometimes we do want to see ourselves as belonging to the *Sinnenwelt*. It's true that we fail to treat others with dignity when we insist on regarding what they take to be free actions as *caused*. Tell somebody, "Adjust your meds," in the course of a disagreement, and you'll rarely find your suggestion taken as benevolent. (This is a thought experiment only; do not attempt at home.) And yet one reason people go to shrinks—or, elsewhere in the world, to oracles and witch doctors—is to uncover supposedly hidden causes of their actions. Which is just to say that, in our actual lives, we aren't confined to any one standpoint, any one purpose.[49]

Kant said that freedom couldn't be explained, only defended. If we ought to defend the discourse of personal autonomy, it's chiefly because of what this vocabulary allows us to see, and to say. To take autonomy seriously—even in the unaggressive form that poor old Stepan enjoyed—is not without consequences. It proposes a politics that regards persons as ends, as possessing dignity and inherent worth. It proposes a social order conducive to some version of individuality.

In the next chapter, we'll take up the seeming tension between those who view the entrenchment of social identities as a precondition for autonomy and those who view it as a threat to autonomy. Distinguishing between a road and a rut, between a citadel and cell, surely involves judgments of the interest-guided sort we've explored, judgments that are not just about politics but—precisely because, from the standpoint of our interest in social life, autonomy matters—part of politics, too. These judgments won't, in Tolstoy's formulation, "make themselves in us"; we have to make them.

Chapter Three

∼ The Demands of Identity

LEARNING HOW TO CURSE

In the summer of 1953, a team of researchers assembled two groups of eleven-year-old boys at adjoining but separate campsites in the Sans Bois Mountains, part of Oklahoma's Robbers Cave State Park. The boys were drawn from the Oklahoma City area and, though previously unacquainted, came from a fairly homogeneous background—they were Protestant, white, middle-class. All this was by careful design. The researchers sought to study the formation of in-groups and out-groups—the way that tension developed between them and the way it might be alleviated—and the Robbers Cave experiment has justly become something of a classic in the social sciences.

The camp area was heavily wooded and completely isolated. At first, each group was unaware of the other's existence. Only after the boys were allowed to settle in on their own for a couple of days did the staff members tell each group that there was another camp of boys nearby. The two groups of boys promptly challenged each other in competitive sports, like baseball and tug-of-war, as well as the less obviously appealing activity of "tent pitching." Soon—and this was perhaps the study's most dramatic finding—tempers flared and a violent enmity developed between the two groups, the Rattlers and the Eagles (as they came to dub themselves). Flags weren't just captured but burned and shredded. Raids were staged on the other group's cabin; property was disarrayed, trophies stolen. Staff members had to intervene when one group of boys prepared themselves for a retaliatory raid by arming themselves with rocks.[1]

A less dramatic, but, for our purposes, equally intriguing, development was also recorded. It starts with the self-assigned labels of the two groups: the Rattlers and the Eagles. The groups did not arrive with these names; nor did it occur to group members that they needed a name, until they learned about the presence of another group on the campgrounds.[2] Among the Rattlers, an ethic of "toughness" had arisen, after it emerged that one of the higher-status boys in the group had stoically endured a minor injury without telling anyone about it. Cursing, for equally contingent reasons, also became commonplace in this group. When the Eagles won a baseball game against the Rattlers, they came, during a postgame conversation, to attribute the victory to a group prayer they'd offered before the game. After further deliberation, the Eagles decided that the Rattlers' tendency to curse had contributed to their defeat as well. "Hey, you guys, let's not do any more cussing, and I'm serious, too," one Eagle said to the others, and the proposal won general approval.[3] In the course of a subsequent football game, the Rattlers (who won narrowly) engaged in clamorous jeering and boasting. Rather than respond in kind, the Eagles decided that yelling in front of the Rattlers would bring bad luck: they came to refrain not only from cussing but from bragging. These differences were reflected in the way the groups described each other. To the Rattlers (in their internal discussions), the Eagles were "sissies," "cowards," "little babies." To the Eagles, the Rattlers were a "bunch of cussers," "poor losers," and "bums."[4] One group saw itself, and was seen, as prayerful, pious, and clean-living; the other as boisterous, tough, and scrappy.

And all this arose in just four days.

The Robbers Cave study, for a student of identity, is a bit like those origins-of-life experiments where scientists direct a bolt of artificial lightning at a solution meant to represent the earth's primordial ocean. It's a long way from those simple amino acids to Noah's ark. Nor would one want to claim that the nascent trait divergence between the Rattlers and the Eagles does justice to the welter of deep social and linguistic diversity human beings have evolved over the millennia. But as a snap-

shot of "ethnogenesis," there is clarity in its lack of complication, starting with the priority of identity to culture. We often treat cultural differentia as if they give rise to collective identities; what happened at
Robbers Cave suggests we might think of it the other way around.

Comparative scholars of ethnicity have certainly provided no shortage of confirming examples; their reports suggest a similar dynamic of
antagonism, lumping even as it splits. The Malay came to know one
another as such only after, and in opposition to, the arrival of the Chinese; the Hindu became Hindu only when the British created the class
in the early nineteenth century, to take in those who weren't members
of the famous monotheisms, and the identity gained salience only in
opposition to South Asian Muslims.[5] As Jean-Loup Amselle, the French
anthropologist, says (in his French way), cultural identities arise, in the
first place, from a "structured field of relations," which is to say that
they might be seen, in the first instance, as the consequence, not the
cause, of conflicts. "Culture is important in the making of ethnic
groups," Donald Horowitz says, less grandly, "but it is more important
for providing post facto content to group identity than it is for providing some ineluctable prerequisite for an identity to come into being."[6]
And so I'll be proceeding in this chapter on the not-uncontroversial
assumption that differences of identity are, in various ways, prior to
those of culture (a view I've argued elsewhere and will defend further
in chapter 4).

Among the things we may take from the story of the Robbers Cave
experiment is that identity allegiances can be easily conjured into being;
and that (if we needed reminding) the Other may not be very other at
all. We also know that identity as a social form is no less powerful for
all that. Though we may be a society of individuals, in classical liberal
terms, the abstraction of that term omits a great deal that matters to
us, as individuals and as members of identity groups. Does the liberal
goal of equal concern rule out, or require, the acknowledgment of people as the bearers of identities? If identity may be acknowledged, what
sort of political demands can we validly make as members of a collective
identity, as opposed to members of a polity? These are the sorts of
questions I want to pursue in this chapter. But before exploring what
identity demands, I shall say something about what identity *means*.

THE STRUCTURE OF SOCIAL IDENTITIES

The contemporary use of "identity" to refer to such features of people as their race, ethnicity, nationality, gender, religion, or sexuality first achieved prominence in the social psychology of the 1950s—particularly in the work of Erik Erikson and Alvin Gouldner. This use of the term reflects the conviction that each person's identity—in the older sense of who he or she truly is—is deeply inflected by such social features.[7] And it is a fact of contemporary life that this conviction is increasingly prevalent. In political and moral thinking nowadays it has become commonplace to suppose that a person's projects can be expected to be shaped by such features of his or her identity and that this is, if not morally required, then at least morally permissible.

To be sure, not every aspect of the collective dimension of someone's identity will have the general power of sex or gender, sexuality or nationality, ethnicity or religion. What the collective dimensions have in common, as I mentioned in chapter 1, is that they are what Ian Hacking has dubbed *kinds of person*: men, gays, Americans, Catholics, but also butlers, hairdressers, and philosophers.[8]

Hacking relies on a crucial insight about "kinds of person," which is that they are brought into being by the creation of labels for them. So he defends what he calls a "dynamic nominalism," arguing that "numerous kinds of human beings and human acts come into being hand in hand with our invention of the categories labeling them."[9] (It is not incidental that the Rattlers and the Eagles came into being along with their designations.)

Hacking begins from a philosophical truism that finds its most influential formulation in Elizabeth Anscombe's work on intention: actions are intentional "under descriptions"; in other words, action is conceptually shaped.[10] What I do intentionally is dependent on what I think I am doing. To use a simple example, I have to have a wide range of concepts for my writing my name in a certain way to count specifically as "signing a contract." It follows that what I can do intentionally depends on what concepts I have available to me; and among the concepts that may shape my action is the concept of a certain kind of person and the behavior appropriate to a person of that kind.

Hacking himself offers as an example Sartre's brilliant evocation in *Being and Nothingness* of the Parisian *garçon de café*, with his studied air of alertness and solicitude.[11] Our own Mr. Stevens, for his part, was driven, in thinking about whether he should develop his bantering skills, by the thought that he is a butler and that banter is a butler's sort of skill.

The idea of the butler lacks the sort of theoretical commitments that are trailed by many of our social identities: black and white, gay and straight, man and woman. So it makes no sense to ask of someone who is employed as a butler whether that is what he really is. Because we have expectations of the butler, it is a recognizable identity. Those expectations are, however, about the performance of the role; they depend on our assumption of intentional conformity to the expectations.

But with other identities—and here the familiar collectives of race, ethnicity, gender, and the rest come back into view—the expectations we have are not based simply on the idea that those who have these identities are playing out a role. Rightly or wrongly, we do not think of the expectations we have of men or of women as being simply the result of the fact that there are conventions about how men and women behave.

Once labels are applied to people, ideas about people who fit the label come to have social and psychological effects. In particular, these ideas shape the ways people conceive of themselves and their projects. So the labels operate to mold what we may call *identification*, the process through which individuals shape their projects—including their plans for their own lives and their conceptions of the good life—by reference to available labels, available identities. In identification, I shape my life by the thought that something is an appropriate aim or an appropriate way of acting for an American, a black man, a philosopher. It seems right to call this "identification" because the label plays a role in shaping the way the agent makes decisions about how to conduct a life, in the process of the construction of one's identity.

We can describe the relation between identification and identity with a little more precision. In particular, every collective identity seems to have the following sort of structure.[12]

First, it requires the availability of terms in public discourse that are used to pick out the bearers of the identity by way of criteria of ascription, so that some people are recognized *as* members of the group—women, men; blacks, whites; straights, gays. The availability of these terms in public discourse requires both that it be mutually known among most members of the society that the labels exist and that there be some degree of consensus on how to identify those to whom they should be applied. Let us call a typical label for a group "L."[13] This consensus is usually organized around a set of stereotypes (which may be true or false) concerning Ls, beliefs about what typical Ls are like, how they behave, how they may be detected. Some elements of a stereotype are normatively derived: they are views about how Ls will probably behave, rooted in their conformity to norms about how they should behave. We can say, in a convenient shorthand, that there must first be a *social conception* of Ls. Stereotypes are rough-and-ready things, and there may be different conceptions of Ls associated with different individuals or groups within the society. For a social conception to exist, it is enough that there be a rough overlap in the classes picked out by the term "L," so there need be no precisely agreed boundaries, no determinate extension; nor is it necessary that the stereotypes or criteria of ascription be identical for all users of the term. We need not worry that the exact boundary between women and men is not agreed upon (do F-to-M transgendered folk count as men all along, or only after surgery, or never?), or that, even given a full specification of his affectional life and sexual habits, it might well not be universally agreed whether or not Shakespeare was what we now call "straight." One cannot, therefore, always speak of *the* content of a social conception: sketching a social conception requires an ethnography of ways of conceiving of Ls, one that recognizes especially that different stereotypes of Ls may tend to be held by people with different social positions. African Americans, for example, may well have characteristically different social conceptions of a black identity from others in the United States; and homosexuals may tend to conceive gay identity differently from heterosexuals. Now, many people have the idea that the normative content of an identity should be determined essentially by its bearers. Even if that is true—which I doubt, since recognition by people of other identities is often a proper source of their meaning—this would still mean that some people would have the content of their identities determined in part by others; namely, those of the same identity.

A second element of a social identity is the internalization of those labels as parts of the individual identities of at least some of those who bear the label. If the label in question is, once more, "L," we can call this *identification as an L*. Identification as an L, as I've suggested, means thinking of yourself as an L in ways that make a difference: perhaps thinking of yourself as an L shapes your feelings (so that you respond with pride as an L when an L triumphs); perhaps it shapes your actions, so that you sometimes do something as an L (offering a helping hand to another L, perhaps, who is otherwise a stranger; or restraining your public conduct by the thought that misbehavior will reflect badly on Ls). Often, then, being an L carries ethical and moral weight: the notion, say, that Jews ought to help other Jews and should avoid behaving in ways that discredit the Jewish community. And often, too, there are behavioral norms associated with identities that it seems wrong to dignify with the epithets "ethical" or "moral": men (sometimes we say *real* men) walk this way, hold their hands that way, don't cover their mouths when they laugh. Eagles refrain from cursing and braggadocio.

Identification, in ways we touched upon in chapter 1, typically has a strong narrative dimension. By way of my identity I fit my life story into certain patterns—confirmation at puberty for a religious identity, tenure in your mid-thirties for a professorial one—and I also fit that story into larger stories; for example, of a people, a religious tradition, or a race. Nor is this narrative element simply a feature of Western modernity. Around the world, it matters to people that they can tell a story of their lives that meshes with larger narratives. This may involve rites of passage into womanhood and manhood; or a sense of national identity that fits one's life into a larger saga.[14] Such collective identifications can also confer significance upon very individual achievements: by way of them, you can think of yourself as the first person of African descent to gain a Harvard doctorate in history, or the first Jewish president of the United States.

The final element of a social identity is the existence of patterns of behavior toward Ls, such that Ls are sometimes *treated as Ls*. To treat someone as an L is to do something to her in part, at least, because she is an L (where "because she is an L" figures in the agent's internal specification of her reasons for the act).[15] In the current landscape of identity, the treatment-as that is often in focus is invidious discrimina-

tion: gender, sexuality, and racial and ethnic identity have all been profoundly shaped (even, in a sense, produced) by histories of sexism,
homophobia, racism, and ethnic hatred. But it is as well to recall that
not all treatment-as is negative or morally troublesome: sexuality requires responding to people as women and as men, and this means that
there are patterns of action toward men and toward women that are
constitutive of the standard range of sexual orientations.[16] Many benevolent forms of "treatment-as" are meant to counter malevolent forms
of "treatment-as." (Consider the person who, in the late 1930s, urged
her German Jewish friends to leave the Third Reich.) Indeed, that identity-based responses can be morally positive should be uncontroversial:
many of the world's acts of supererogatory benevolence involve treating
people as fellow Ls—generosity, then, is often a form of treatment-as.

Where a classification of people as Ls is associated with a *social conception* of Ls, some people *identify as* Ls, and people are sometimes
treated as Ls, we have a paradigm of a social identity that matters for
ethical and political life. That it matters for ethical life—in the sense I
have stipulated—flows from the fact that it figures in identification, in
people's shaping and evaluation of their own lives; that it might matter
for politics flows from the fact that it figures in treatment by others,
and that how others treat one will help determine one's success and
failure in living one's life.

In the case of the butler, conventions of behavior associated with a
role are explicitly central: the ascriptions are based on the simple idea
that someone who works in grand houses of a certain sort will conform
to certain expectations; the expectations are based on the conventions
that govern the role of the butler; because of those conventions, acting
as a butler means constructing a particular performance; and how you
are treated may depend on how well you perform the role (even if there
are aspects of butlering that are likely to be appreciated only by your
fellow butlers). But for some other identities—as a gay man, for example—there is more than convention.

For being a gay man is, in part, a matter of having certain desires,
and those desires are not something that the gay man has himself chosen. You can choose whether or not to play a certain conventional role,
and, if all there is to an identity is a conventional set of behaviors, and
you are capable of them, then you can chose whether to adopt the iden-

tity. But when the criteria for ascribing a certain identity include things over which you have no control—as is the case with gender, race, and sexual orientation—then whether you identify with that identity, whether, for example, you think of yourself as gay and act sometimes as a gay person, is not only up to you.[17] As we saw in chapter 1, while someone who has a gay identity is doing more than simply acknowledging the fact that he has homosexual desires, and someone who has an identity as a black person, identifying with his or her African American identity, is doing more than simply acknowledging an African ancestry, it is nevertheless true that they are responding to a fact (about desire or ancestry) that is independent of their choices, a fact that comes, so to speak, from outside the self. Even Sartre's *garçon de café* takes up an identity that has a function outside himself: he is taking up a profession that provides a service; he is finding, as Mr. Stevens did in butlering, a way of making a life. (Moreover, the profession that he is taking up, with its intricate conventions and protocols, is not one of his own devising.)

For a long time—since the Enlightenment, we might say—the great liberal struggle was to get the state to treat its members as individuals only, without favoring or disfavoring particular ethnic or religious or gender identities. And many people continue to argue that state acknowledgment of such identities is intrinsically illiberal: precisely because the shaping of my life is up to me, the government should seek to constrain my acts independent of my identities. Otherwise the state will be in the business of advantaging and disadvantaging particular identities in ways that encroach upon the individual's freedom to shape his or her own life. Such skepticism draws some of its appeal from the historical arguments for tolerance; and from the apparent clash between the constraining nature of identities and the liberal ideal of the self-directed individual, of the autarky of the soul.

Others, including many so-called multiculturalists, have argued, to the contrary, that the state *must* recognize these identities because without them individuals will lack what they need for making a life. To the extent that social identities allow people options for making their lives, these theorists argue, they are a positive part of that process. And their recognition by the state is part of what makes them available for this purpose.

As we'll see, those who think that the political acknowledgment of identity groups is important have produced various arguments for how

it should matter. Some focus on the state provision of goods and benefits; some focus on the suspension of certain rules or obligations that
unduly burden members of certain identity groups. Some people go
further and—particularly when these identity groups are associated
with "societal cultures"[18]—embrace the principle of cultural sovereignty. Multiculturalism, perhaps appropriately, comes in many hues.
In the past decade or so, the slogans and rallying cries have multiplied:
terms like "differential citizenship" (Iris M. Young); the "politics of
recognition" (Charles Taylor); and *modus vivendi* (John Gray) are each
associated with distinct approaches toward the matter.

And there are many who occupy an intermediate position. They
think that the sorts of social identities I have mentioned are, indeed,
ethically central to our lives, but also that this is an argument for toleration of identities, not for their recognition. That is, they are inclined to
a view about these social identities that is analogous to the position on
religious toleration popularly associated with the American Founders:
so far as is possible, no establishment of identities, on the one hand;
but, on the other, free exercise (subject to the constraints of duty and
harm) as well.[19] This position, too, courts its share of perplexities. What
would it mean to allow (the analogue of) free exercise of them while
avoiding (the analogue of) establishment? The answer, as we'll see, is
far from obvious.

In the next section, I'll be discussing a relatively uncompromised
approach toward the acknowledgment of identities—an approach that
sees the state as a federation of identity groups, each to be ceded a
high degree of autonomy. Group autonomy, as an ideal, comes in many
forms, and I cannot do justice to them all; I have largely confined my
attention to those forms that arise in the context of liberal political
theory (as opposed to, say, Stalinist ethnic engineering). Still, I hope at
least to give a flavor both of what its proponents find appealing in this
approach and of what others of us find worrying.

MILLET MULTICULTURALISM

Before proceeding with those questions, however, I
think it will be helpful to make two distinctions: one about individual-

ism and one about group rights. The distinction about individualism in the sphere of rights is between what we can call *ethical* individualism, on the one hand, and *substantive* individualism, on the other. Ethical individualism about rights is a liberal assumption I identified in the preface. It is the view that we should defend rights by showing what they do for individuals—social individuals, to be sure, living in families and communities, usually, but still individuals. Substantive individualism about rights is the view that rights must always attach to individuals: that human rights, as framed in our conventions and in law, should always be the rights of persons, not of groups.

The second useful distinction is between two ways of thinking of group rights. One way sees them as exercised collectively: for this to work in practice, there have to be mechanisms by which the groups can be legally identified and institutions through which their interests can be asserted. If an American Indian tribe has the collective right to run a gaming casino, it must be decided both who belongs to that tribe, and how they should decide whether to exercise it. The right of self-determination is a group right of this sort: and it raises both kinds of questions. Who is a Palestinian, a Kurd, a Tibetan? And how should they decide to exercise their rights? Call group rights of this sort *collective rights*. A second conception of group rights is the idea that the law, whether national or international, might treat each member of certain groups as being individually entitled to certain claims qua member of the group. For instance, members of the English hereditary peerage used each to be able to exercise their right to a trial by the House of Lords. Call group rights of this sort *membership rights*.

Membership rights are individual rights in a certain sense: they belong to individuals. But those who say they are skeptical of group rights often mean to be challenging membership rights. What they are objecting to is the idea that a state should relate to any citizen in virtue of his or her membership of a group rather than simply as a citizen. It was an objection to the membership rights of whites (and the membership burdens of blacks) that underlay much of the opposition to American Jim Crow and to apartheid. Among the membership rights that have a large body of support are the membership rights of citizens of democratic states: it is widely thought to be fine to treat citizens and noncitizens differently before the law; for example in deciding who may take jobs where. Collective rights tend to have more friends, however. Most people think that it is just fine that Utah or the city of Cambridge or the Catholic Church can exercise rights, through the ballot box or (in the case of churches) through whatever consensual internal mechanisms they agree upon.

It should be admitted at once that ethical individualism is not, on its face, quite so strong a constraint as one might suppose. If our selves are embedded in social forms—the most commonplace of communitarian commonplaces—it might be impossible to treat individuals with equal respect without somehow coming to terms with those social forms. That's a thought that can be given various formulations, some more exigent than others. It might seem that human flourishing—our individual well-being—demands the flourishing of the identity groups within which the meaning of our lives takes its shape. Perhaps, then, a state cannot treat us with equal respect without striving to respect equally the communities in which we are embedded, and which give our choices their context and content.[20] Thus we move swiftly from the equal standing of individuals to the equal standing of identity groups, and, indeed, a homology between identity groups and persons is a staple of certain forms of multiculturalism, those sponsored by what we might dub *hard pluralism*. (Here, "pluralism" is used in something like Horace Kallen's sense of the term, which promoted the ideal of multiethnic coexistence.) As we shall see, it can be hard to keep clear, in such arguments, whether ethical individualism has been breached.

Hard pluralism is a tendency; I do not use the phrase to delimit a single, coherent doctrine. Many hard pluralists object to the automatic elevation of personal autonomy over group autonomy; some are inclined to suspect even the attempt to draw a distinction between the two. These pluralists are quick to point out the ascriptive and involuntary nature of those identity groups with which they are concerned.[21] Other hard pluralists find their rationale within the traditional vocabulary of liberalism; in particular, they judge the freedom of association to be trumps. And there are those hard pluralists who take liberalism to be discredited by the existence of different ways of life, and, in particular, by staunchly illiberal ones: gazing among the various communities in their midst, these pluralists judge nothing to be trumps, save the need to abjure judgment itself.

To speak of "autonomy" is, of course, to map a term that originally described polities—self-governing city-states like ancient Athens—onto persons. But that Kantian move of treating persons as polities can be reversed; many hard pluralists essentially treat polities as persons. They may suggest that identity groups are entitled to all the rights and protections owed a citizen, and so must be indulged on their own terms, without worrying overmuch about how it affects the individuals involved. You can get here by various routes. You can, as David Ingram does, make the case for group rights; you can, like Chandran Kukathas, mobilize the freedom of association; you can, with John Gray, appeal to an overriding principle of *modus vivendi*, thereby raising a strategy of coexistence to an ideal.[22] None of these three consistently respects ethical individualism. Drawing upon these approaches, sometimes in combination, theorists have sought to honor the sovereignty of the group, and to minimize outside interference with its affairs, in a way that has sometimes called to mind the millet system of the Ottoman Empire.[23]

Thus for hard pluralists, personal autonomy is a good the way Marmite on toast is: perfectly fine if you happen to have a taste for it, but no more than a local preference aggrandized by the legacy of empire. Toleration—conceived as a relation between the state and its constituent groups—is what matters. They are especially concerned that the state not interfere with groups that don't accept the value of critical reflection and so force the minority group to become more liberal, a concern that is, as we saw in the previous chapter, widely shared by critics of autonomism. William Galston, urging a policy of "maximum feasible accommodation," recoils at a suggestion made by Will Kymlicka that a state may have the task of liberalizing certain illiberal communities while helping to sustain them. "What Kymlicka calls liberalization," he writes, "will in many cases amount to a forced shift of basic group identity; it turns out to be the cultural equivalent of the Vietnam-era principle of destroying the village in order to save it."[24]

Hard pluralism would avoid such enormities by leaving groups free to do just about anything to their members short of physical coercion.[25] Kukathas argues, for instance, that parents should be able to do what they want with their kids' education, so long as it has cultural warrant: "because gypsy custom does not value school, the parents believing that they can educate a child satisfactorily through informal instruction in the ways of their culture, only a minority of children receive any formal primary education. Their freedom to associate and live by their own ways, however, would, by my argument, make this permissible."[26] And, as we've seen, John Gray has made similar arguments for insulating cultural communities from the encroachments of autonomism. Like the millet system of yore, their approach respects the sovereignty of the cultural constituents, imposing external constraints of orderliness but few internal restrictions on how the members of these communities are to be treated.

Yet this elaborate vision is perched upon a very slender plinth. For the proponents of millet multiculturalism have it as an object of faith that *personal* autonomy is a (usually "Western") parochialism while *group* autonomy (often as a "non-Western" demand) is sacrosanct. Why the latter is any less provincial than the former is never explained. And the matter of "cultural warrant" becomes hugely important, requiring a close scrutiny of the habits of strangers. Suppose that, as members of certain religious or ethnic communities sometimes do, you wish to withhold blood transfusions for your injured son, or subject your daughter to female genital mutilation. The main question, for Kukathas, is whether your behavior has the sanction of your group—whether it is licensed by the freedom of association.

Now, one kind of situation where the practices of a group are likely to attract interference (as with the examples I've cited) has to do with the young, who do not yet enjoy full autonomy. Kukathas, it seems, doesn't mind a state that imposes compulsory education upon its Scots-Irish families; it's the Gypsies (or, as they might prefer to call themselves, the Roma) who may be exempt. But compulsory education arises as an issue of interference only when someone wants to resist it. And who is to tell the Scots-Irish family that doesn't see the point to schooling its children that education is part of its culture—that it is, for them, a value? The fact that the family doesn't want to school its children, you might suppose, is sufficient proof to the contrary.

A second type of situation where the state is likely to interfere with the affairs of a group arises when a member of that group feels that his or her autonomy is under attack. (The doctrine would have no teeth if it only discouraged the state from doing what ordinary scruples about individual autonomy would discourage the state from doing anyway.)

Suppose a Bengali family in England wants to compel its grown daughter to enter into an arranged marriage. If she declines, she has, *eo ipso*, rejected her parent's values, at least in some measure. The state cannot immediately decline to uphold her rights on the principle of her parents' cultural autonomy, for what about *her* culture? Or, if you doubt (reasonably enough) that an individual, by herself, can have a distinct culture, the culture of her cohort? For upon investigation, you may learn that her attitudes are shared by various young women in the community. How, in short, are we to establish the boundaries of the group deserving deference? One imagines a vast brigade of state-employed ethnographers, tasked with certifying this or that practice as legitimized by this or that social group.

And, practically speaking, even if you wanted to leave members of some group to themselves, to preserve their autochthonous form of life, you'd find it was too late: the nature and shape of the leadership structure of a substate polity—a Pueblo tribal council, in the United States, to take an example I'll be returning to—will have been profoundly shaped by the policies of the state in question. When leadership is contested within the tribe, the state will recognize some bids for authority and not others. In this and other respects, the state can't not take sides.

Even aside from such concerns, you can be forgiven if you do not find the social picture drawn by the strong pluralists to be terribly appealing. A free assembly of small sovereign entities doesn't resemble a liberal society; it's a society modeled on the UN Security Council— its plebiscites open to despot and democrat alike. To explain why the approach has the appeal it does among liberals, one must mention a crucial escape hatch it provides: the right of exit. For those who seek to reconcile group and individual autonomy—who seek to exalt the freedom of association without utterly scanting conventional autonomist considerations—the right of exit has become a veritable workhorse. As long as a group permits members to leave, a great deal is permitted: if you haven't exercised that right, you have, in some sense, consented to whatever is likely to befall you. Exit thus promises to dissolve any number of difficulties. Rather than fussing about how internally democratic a cultural community should be—about balancing this interest against that interest, that right against this right—why not simply require the right of exit, and have done with it? Do what you like to your own members, we can then say, so long as you let them leave if they want to. That may appear to comport with ethical individualism, because it means that group choices that are bad for the individual member cannot be imposed without her consent. Unfortunately, this right is not so straightforward an affair.

Is Exit Enough?

For one thing, the right of exit is actually rejected by some hard pluralists. It may sound like a pretty minimal condition, but those who have no time for autonomism regard even this right as too exacting. Gray, for example, sees exit as yet another corrosive liberal imposition. How can you eliminate any form of life that can't withstand the exercise of free choice by its members, he asks, and still call yourself a pluralist? What if the exit of a few would ruin a community for the majority who endorse it? Then wouldn't the infringement on individual autonomy be justified, as in the case of the fire-shouting theatergoer? Nor are these merely abstract concerns. It should be admitted that there are social formations that couldn't survive an opt-out clause; history has seen one or another leisure class that depended upon the services of a class of serfs or slaves: once the slaves opt out, the aristocratic charms of Southern plantation culture are imperiled. Those of us who love the literature of Augustan Rome must recognize its dependence on the resources of an involuntary empire. Or consider Athenian democracy: the golden age of Pericles, and the role of involuntary servitude in sustaining it.[27] The right of exit is certainly inconsistent with radical tolerance of groups; and how you feel about that depends on what sort of priority you give that form of tolerance.

But a more widely shared concern is that, conversely, the formal right of exit is too weak to do the work assigned it. Indeed, once you start thinking about such mechanisms of escape, you can start to wonder whether the "freedom of association" model doesn't lump together some terribly disparate phenomena. Can a nationality fairly be seen as analogous to a private club? Is an identity group something you can simply resign from?

Consider a situation where there's a dramatic collision between group and personal autonomy. The Pueblo tribal council doesn't permit religious freedom among members of the Pueblo tribe. It also has control over communal property, which is, for the Pueblo, essentially all property. Now, to take an example that has occasioned litigation: does the Pueblo who is expelled for converting to Protestantism fully enjoy the privilege of exit, when exit entails the loss of all his earthly goods? You may wish to construe the Pueblo community as analogous to any old voluntary community; but it plainly has power over its members that, say, the Knickerbocker Club or the Park Slope Food Coop does not.[28]

And barriers to exit needn't take the form of property deprivation to be formidable. The philosopher and legal scholar Leslie Green points out, "It is risky, wrenching, and disorienting to have to tear oneself from one's religion or culture; the fact that it is possible to do so does not suffice to show that those who do not manage to achieve the task have stayed voluntarily, at least not in any sense strong enough to undercut any rights they might otherwise have."[29] And, as he sees, the identity groups we're most likely to take seriously as "experiments in living" are ones in which belonging is an ascriptive, organic affair, the furthest thing from the voluntarist model. "Everything about a culture is an exit barrier," Jacob T. Levy persuasively observes. "To have a culture where exit is entirely costless . . . is to have no culture at all."[30]

Indeed, you may ask what sense it really makes to say you can exit an identity group. As ex-Mormons like to point out, being an ex-Mormon has itself become a kind of ethnicity; and something like that condition seems to hold for other ascriptive groups. More to the point, if the unencumbered self is a myth, how can you extricate yourself from the context that confers meaning? After all, it would make little sense to speak of "exiting" your language, especially when it is the only one you have.

But if the mere existence of an exit isn't enough to justify a policy of millet-like laissez-faire, we're left without this shortcut and must take the long way around. In particular, we have to take seriously an approach we might call liberal multiculturalism, or soft pluralism. Here the aim is to balance external rights and internal constraints. If strong autonomists are apt to suspect substate groups of restricting freedom, and hard pluralists, contrarily, are apt to celebrate them as sites where state authority is kept at bay, soft pluralists try to salvage something of both group and personal autonomy. To what extent the approach succeeds is something I want to consider now.

AUTONOMISM, PLURALISM, NEUTRALISM

In soft, or liberal, pluralism, the individual remains both the terminus a quo and the terminus ad quem: its concern for identity groups is not only motivated by but ultimately subordinated to the well-being of the individual and the bundle of rights and protections that traditional liberalism would accord her. Ethical individualism is meant to have its way. In contrast to the kind of millet multiculturalism we've considered—where state power is made to recede as far as possible, and substate autocracy is indulged, at least short of outright coercion—soft pluralists try to find a point of equilibrium between the rights of individuals and the integrity of intermediate associations. For many of them, moreover, that ideal of balancing has a name: neutrality.

People who share this goal can differ widely in how willing they are to accommodate identity groups. Will Kymlicka, an exemplary soft pluralist, is the most eloquent of those who would justify group autonomy as a means to the end of individual liberty. He is one of those who doubt that the right of exit is sufficient protection for the individuals involved. Accordingly, he is concerned to strike a balance between two desiderata. On the one hand, he wants to ensure external rights (the rights of the group against the state, and against the incursion of outsiders; but also the rights of the group to procure, from the state, certain group-specific benefits). On the other hand, he wants to limit the internal restrictions a group may impose upon the autonomy of the group's members. In balancing these things, though, he would deny that he is trading off individual interests against collective ones. The flourishing of individuals, in his view, requires the stability and security of their social forms.

And yet the contrast between internal restrictions and external protections quickly breaks down. A group wishes to educate its members only in the minority language: is this external protection from the linguistic hegemony of the overlords? Or is it internal restriction, inasmuch as it constrains the opportunities of the younger generations, impedes their right of exit, and so infringes on the autonomy of their future selves? Kymlicka regards the *Wisconsin v. Yoder* case—in which the Old Order Amish asked for (and received) an exemption from the state of Wisconsin's requirement that they send their children to school until the age of sixteen—as involving an instance of internal restriction; and yet it could as easily be presented, and doubtless strikes the Old Order Amish themselves, as a matter of external protection of their agrarian way of life. In another familiar type of case, an aboriginal group imposes restrictions on who may buy members' land: again, this is a safeguard against the encroachments of the outside world that constrains the autonomy of the group's members. As Kymlicka admits, the distinction "is not always easy to draw."[31]

I mentioned that the American conception of religious tolerance provided one obvious model for how the state should respond to identity groups. Indeed, as the Yoder case should remind us, the project of reconciling the two desiderata of our associational affairs—freedom *of* and freedom *from*—is most prominently represented by the tradition of First Amendment jurisprudence, by which the U.S. Supreme Court has tried to work out a systematic approach to religious freedom. The challenge starts with the very first sentence of the Bill of Rights: "Congress shall pass no law respecting an establishment of religion or prohibiting the free exercise thereof." Constitutional interpretation bifurcates along that "or." In modern jurisprudence, the "free exercise" clause has been taken to require the state to extend special deference to religionists; the "establishment" clause has been taken to forbid it. Now, our moral modernity naturally takes the prohibition of "establishment" as an expression of a larger ideal, namely, that the state should be neutral— neutral among competing conceptions of the good, neutral among the competing interests of identity groups. It is the ideal at the heart of Rawls's famous, and famously vexed, distinction between "political liberalism" and "comprehensive liberalism."

Famously vexed: skeptics have argued at length that such neutrality is incoherent or undesirable or, in a manner of speaking, both— that such neutrality is bad because it favors neutralists over others and so isn't really neutral at all. Thus, in the context of the First Amendment, religious advocates accuse neutralists of elevating a controversial conception to the level of procedure; and they feel oppressed by neutralist strictures that (as they interpret them) exclude religion from the public square.

In one widely discussed version of the argument, Michael Perry has taken aim at the suggestion advanced by theorists such as Thomas Nagel, Robert Audi, and Bruce Ackerman that ideal political discourse should appeal, as much as possible, to shared and publicly accessible forms of reason. To the extent that expressly religious appeals—appeals, for instance, to the "revealed truth" of God—shut out and do not seek to engage nonbelievers, they are not ideal specimens of political deliberation, of what John Rawls calls "public reason." What Michael Perry maintains is that to ask one to check one's religious convictions at the town-hall door is to ask one to "bracket—to annihilate—essential aspects of one's very self." Conversational strictures that purport to be neutral are really anything but: they condemn one's spiritual self to be "marginalized or privatized," leaving the devout unable to participate in the political realm on an equal footing with their secular compatriots. Perry, accordingly, seeks to establish that a duly pluralistic conception of the public realm should leave space for "religious-moral discourse."[32]

In truth, the adherents of "political liberalism" have never been quite so coercively monistic as their critics often represent them. Certainly the *right* of the zealous to say what they like is not disputed by neutralists; at issue is merely what ideal political discourse ought to sound like. As Rawls insists, public reason, far from requiring citizens to suspend or withdraw their religious convictions, in fact presupposes that citizens have a variety of comprehensive conceptions, including religious ones, whose "overlapping consensus" is consistent with the institutions of liberal democracy.[33] Indeed, those Rawlsian strictures about the ideal of public reason are perhaps best interpreted as debating tips: as rhetorical advice about how best, within a plural polity, to win adherents and influence policies. There's nothing coercive about such counsel. Sectarians may speak however they prefer, but if they seek to win over those who do not already share their sectarian convictions, they will be well advised to appeal, as much as possible, to those norms and premises that are most generally accepted. So the spirit behind these liberal strictures is less Madalyn Murray O'Hair than Dale Carnegie.

If the neutralist ethic is less invidious than some religionists would claim, it does face some rather daunting problems all the same. Thus

Will Kymlicka objects to the notion that the diversity of social forms ought simply to be treated with "benign neglect" by an assiduously impartial state. "In the areas of official languages, political boundaries, and the division of powers, there is no way to avoid supporting this or that societal culture, or deciding which groups will form a majority in political units that control culture-affecting decisions regarding language, education, and immigration," he points out. As he elsewhere elaborates: "It is quite possible for a state not to have an established church. But the state cannot help but give at least partial establishment to a culture when it decides which language is to be used in public schooling, or in the provision of state services. The state can (and should) replace religious oaths in court with secular oaths, but it cannot replace the use of English in courts with no language."[34]

And, of course, the government—at least in anything resembling an actually existing liberal democracy—is not neutral, cannot be neutral, over a vast range of things. A government science agency bestows grants to avenues of research it thinks are promising and not to others; the language of governance is not Esperanto; decisions are made, and rules are interpreted, in ways that favor some interests and disfavor others: competing rights and interests are balanced, and the balance typically comes out in the favor of one party over another. In such cases, facts and values come together in a theory-saturated mélange, so that one cannot say that a finding of fact was not also a finding of value.

But perhaps this sort of neutrality isn't the sort that neutralism is really concerned with. In an influential line of argument, Raz and (in more detail) Kymlicka have proposed that the ideal of "neutrality" applies not to effects but to justifications. State actions can never achieve anything like neutrality of consequences; but states *can* strive toward neutrality of rationale. That is, liberal neutralists realize that the state will act in ways that have nonneutral effects, but want to be assured that such acts have a motivation other than (say) reshaping our religious identities. And there is a range of examples where the neutrality-of-justification test can provide some conceptual purchase. A law regulating the slaughtering of animals will not pass muster if it clearly has no real purpose except to target practitioners of Santeria, as the Supreme Court found of certain ordinances passed by the city of Hialeah, Florida.[35] A case like that seems straightforward. But, as we'll see, most cases aren't.

What First Amendment jurisprudence offers isn't so much wisdom as an illustration of the perplexities that arise from all efforts to honor both state neutrality and group autonomy. At the same time, religious groups are among the more salient buttresses of identity in the West; this isn't merely an analogy but an example—indeed, for many, a paradigm.

A First Amendment Example:
The Accommodationist Program

A little background may be helpful. Over the past couple of decades, a diverse and influential group of so-called accommodationist scholars (among them Michael McConnell, Frederick Gedicks, W. Cole Durham, Harold Berman, David Smolin, and Stephen L. Carter) have sought to strengthen the free exercise clause; many have, accordingly, sought to reverse what they see as a grave misinterpretation of the establishment clause that took root in the Warren Court years. It is a cause that has enjoyed impressive, though partial, success.

As the accommodationists like to point out, the notion of a strict separation between church and government is a recent one. Although Jefferson spoke of a "wall of separation between church and state" in his 1802 letter to the Danbury Baptists, the First Amendment, speaking only of what laws Congress could pass, left the states to determine their own church-state relations. Only in 1947, with *Everson v. Board of Education*, did the Supreme Court pronounce nonestablishment to be binding upon the states as well as the federal government. And it is with *Everson* that modern "separationist" jurisprudence originates. In words quoted as often with opprobrium as approval, Justice Hugo Black's opinion declared not only that the First Amendment "has erected a wall between church and state," but also that this wall "must be kept high and impregnable. We could not approve the slightest breach." In fact, the Court has long since retired Justice Black's rhetoric of separation. Since 1971, Black's high and impregnable wall between church and state has been replaced with what the Burger Court called a "blurred, indistinct, and variable barrier depending on all the circumstances of a particular relationship." In a doctrine first introduced in *Lemon v. Kurtzman* in that year, and still apparently in effect, disputed legislation would be submitted to a three-pronged test. First, the legislation must have a secular purpose; second, its primary effect must neither promote nor inhibit religion; and third, it must not foster excessive entanglement of government with religion. Violation of any of these conditions would render a statute unconstitutional under the establishment clause.

The *Lemon* test seems an earnest effort to achieve justificatory neutrality, but, across a surprising swath of the political spectrum, its defects are widely agreed upon and widely bemoaned. Consider the "secular purpose" proviso. As subsequent decisions have interpreted it, that "purpose" refers to the subjective motivation of the legislators. But if religious scruple motivates a legislator to introduce funding to shelter the homeless or feed the hungry, should the resultant statute really be declared unconstitutional? Next, consider the "neither promote nor inhibit" proviso. If a government refuses to provide the sort of assistance to religious schools that it provides to other private schools, is it not inhibiting religion? But if it does provide such assistance, is it not promoting religion? Here the state is in a no-win situation.[36] Finally, consider the "no excessive entanglement" proviso. To ensure the religious neutrality and secular intent required of the first two prongs, state funding for church-run social services may require that the services be monitored to ensure they do not involve religious inculcation; but such monitoring, even if the church acceded to it, may be forbidden as "excessive entanglement." Here the church is in a no-win situation. So it's little wonder that the *Lemon* doctrine has pleased neither accommodationists nor separationists. Until a majority can agree upon a replacement, however, it persists, as Justice Scalia once complained, like "some ghoul in a late-night horror movie" that won't stay dead.

What *Everson* did for the establishment clause, *Sherbert v. Verner* did for the free exercise clause in 1963. It propounded the doctrine that the application of a law that burdened an important religious practice was permissible only if justified by compelling state interest. The offer of religious exemptions from generally applicable laws was not new: much "temperance" legislation, for example, accommodated Catholics and Jews by exempting the sacramental use of wine; selective service legislation made similar allowances for religious objectors. What was new in *Sherbert* was the notion that the Constitution might *require* such a religious exemption. In this case, a Seventh-Day Adventist, discharged for failing to work on Saturday, his day of Sabbath, sued the state for unemployment benefits and won on free exercise grounds. Unfortunately for the vitality of the principle, almost all subsequent applications of the mandatory exemption rule involved dissident Sabbatarians pursuing unemployment compensation cases.

To complicate matters further, the two religion clauses have often been pitted against each other, and without any accepted techniques of mediation. On the one hand, the Court has continued to declare unconstitutional, on free exercise grounds, the denial of state unemployment benefits to religionists who lost work because they refused to work on their Sabbath. On the other hand, in *Thornton v. Caldor* (1985), the Court ruled against a Presbyterian petitioner in declaring unconstitutional, on establishment grounds, a Connecticut statute that wrote this evident principle of Sabbatarian accommodation into law.

As it happens, the real cause for accommodationist alarm isn't establishment clause jurisprudence, where the religionists have generally had their way. The real cause for alarm has been the abandonment of the doctrine of free exercise exemptions—the end of the old *Sherbert* test requiring exemptions, in the absence of a compelling state interest to the contrary, from laws that interfere with a central aspect of religious practice. And here civil libertarians and religious accommodationists alike stand united in opposition. It might be said that a conservative fusillade cut the establishment clause down to size, and the free exercise clause was an accidental casualty.

The contrast Galston and others assert between autonomism and diversitarian tolerance is perhaps visible here. What many accommodationists argue *against* is the tradition—John Locke's *Letter Concerning Toleration* is its touchstone—that sees the primary value enshrined in the doctrine of religious freedom to be the autonomy of the individual conscience. On the contrary, they argue, religious freedom must further the autonomy not of the individual but of the church, the collective entity, which is much more than the sum of its parts.[37] The claims of the religious institution against the state, rather than the claims of the individual religious dissenter as such, must be taken as primary.

Such religious communitarianism is often buttressed by a frankly Madisonian rationale. The state that accommodates religion has accepted an important check on its own power. Rather than being mere aggregations of individuals, religions should be seen as communities often engaged in "interposing the group judgment against the judgment of a larger society" (in Stephen L. Carter's words); because they provide a potential alternative source of authority, religions function as a bulwark against state tyranny.[38] That, in the relevant sense, is what religion is for: and, consequently, what free exercise accommodations are for.

This communitarian perspective asks us to give the widest berth to the autonomy of religions as self-regulating institutions. (And let me stress that this is not a view shared by all accommodationists: it is one strain of thought among others.) It asks us to accommodate, *ceteris paribus*, the demands of corporate worship over the demands of the individual religious dissident. It asks us to be wary about interposing secular judgments about racial or sexual equality upon dissenting belief communities. The result is a sort of jurisprudence of group autonomy.[39] No doubt one could often arrive at the same place through resolutely individualist considerations (traveling by routes we've explored); free exercise for me might require a corporate body with authority over its members. But there will surely be cases in which it matters whether one takes the robustness of the religious community to be the prior objective.

Many accommodationists are also concerned that courts often fail to respect religious beliefs—fail to respect what Carter terms the "alternative epistemology" of the church. What we haven't understood, we're told, is that religion demands "an epistemology of its own"—that it is "really an alien way of knowing the world—alien, at least, in a political and legal culture in which reason supposedly rules."[40] And yet the attempt to protect the church not merely politically but epistemologically may tend to undermine the call for greater inclusion of religion within the public sphere.

Consider the conflict that has sometimes arisen between Jehovah's Witnesses and the courts on the subject of blood transfusions. Jehovah's Witnesses believe that such transfusions violate the Divine injunction against ingesting blood and—even if received unknowingly—will forever doom their souls to perdition.[41] As accommodationists have reprovingly noted, the courts do not take these convictions into account. Although courts generally respect the expressed wishes of an adult to refuse a potentially lifesaving transfusion, they do so on general grounds of individual autonomy, irrespective of the religious nature of the request. Consequently, the courts are inclined to make no such allowances for a member of the sect who has arrived at the hospital unconscious, or who has not reached the age of majority.

Now then: can the law, in failing to take religion into account, be accused of discriminating religiously? Apparently so. This is Carter's analysis: "By forcing the Witness to live and be damned rather than permitting her to die and be saved, the state is necessarily treating her religious claim not as irrelevant, but as false." And that, he stresses, is a crucial distinction. Liberal epistemology, captive to empiricism, cannot take seriously a very serious truth-claim indeed. Once again, liberalism's vaunted neutrality reveals itself to be anything but. "Liberal neutrality," Michael McConnell writes, "is of a very peculiar sort," for it proceeds "as if agnosticism about the theistic foundations of the universe were common ground among believers and nonbelievers alike."[42]

We are thus invited to see things from the religionists' viewpoint, respect their version of reality, and defer to their "alternative epistemology": the temporal authority of the medical practitioner may thus be trumped by the spiritual authority of the sect. The ultimate result of such epistemic forbearance, however, goes beyond protecting the sectarian from unwelcome interference; the ultimate result is to erase the legal distinction between spiritual and temporal considerations. If the judge and the medical practitioner can be compelled to act as if the sectarian's beliefs are true, on what grounds can we deprive belief communities of—or, conversely, exempt them from—the agencies of temporal adjudication?

To see where this leads, consider another example. In the early eighties, as Carter reports, New York State passed "legislation that, in effect, requires an Orthodox Jewish husband seeking a civil divorce to give his wife a *get*—a religious divorce—without which she cannot remarry under Jewish law."[43] The accommodationists show us how such a statute is to be defended. Requiring the granting of a *get* in such cases can now be seen as a humane provision, and an instance of the state treating religion seriously, rather than as a hobby, as a matter of conviction, rather than velleity. As such, it exemplifies the sort of jurisprudence of relativism that guided us through the Jehovah's Witness case.

The trouble is that this jurisprudence of relativism is on a collision course with the jurisprudence of group autonomy. Under the former, what the *Lemon* test calls "excessive entanglement" is positively required. If the courts have the authority to enjoin *gets* from reluctant religionists, why stop there? Why not review excommunication decisions made by Mormons, or the dreaded commands to shun apostates issued by Jehovah's Witnesses? Did the preacher wrongly damn your soul to hell everlasting? The state, by this logic, should be able to offer at least the injunctive remedy of preacherly recantation. In short, there's a clash between the proposed politics of religion and the proposed epistemology of religion. The ideal of regarding religious truth-claims as self-validating cannot be squared with the ideal of protecting institutional autonomy. One directs insulation; the other forbids it.[44]

Indeed, every state is constantly taking sides on creedal matters, a point Kent Greenawalt makes with marvelous concision: "A court orders a state to desegregate its schools, the country goes to war, educational funds are made available equally to men and women. The government has implicitly rejected religious notions that (1) God wishes rigid racial separation, (2) all killing in war violates God's commandments, (3) all women should occupy themselves with domestic tasks. A vast array of laws and policies similarly imply the incorrectness of particular religious views."[45] And the most vigorous efforts to eliminate such disagreement between church and state seem to disserve both.

Neutrality Reconsidered

To make progress here we need, I think, to see what is right and what is wrong about talk of liberal "neutrality." The ideal, put negatively, is that governmental action, including but by no means limited to legislation, should not exhibit partiality toward some subgroup of the nation; put affirmatively, then, states should be neutral among identities. We have already seen that state action cannot be neutral in its effects; necessarily, many state acts will have differential impacts on people of different identities, including religious identities. Once we turn to the other obvious alternative—neutrality of aim or justification—however, we face immediately the question of how to identify a state's aims or justifications. What is it for a state act to be undertaken for this or that reason or to be guided by this or that intent?

American courts regularly appeal to the intent of legislators in guiding statutory interpretation and in scrutinizing statutes to see whether they pass constitutional muster, and there is a tradition of thought as to how to carry out this task. Such notions of legislative intent may be useful legal fictions. But it does not in general make sense to suppose that a legislature has *an* intent in passing a law. Legislation is a political process, in which deals are cut and compromises made. In both the public and the private deliberations about any statute many inconsistent reasons will be offered for framing a clause one way or another; many suggestions, not all of them consonant with one another, will be offered as to what the overall aims of the statute are. To extract from this mishmash of mixed motives a singular coherent intention will usually be impossible.[46]

You might think that the problem is easier when you are inquiring into just those intentions relevant to establishing neutrality, for these fall into a relatively focused domain. A law should not be aimed to advantage or disadvantage people of a certain identity (narrower than the whole political community) as such: that a legislator is or is not individually motivated in this way might be something we could assess. We could propose, for example, that the presence of such motives in a majority of those enacting the measure established it as nonneutral.

This principle seems, however, to be both too strong in some respects and too weak in others. It is too strong because the mere presence of such a motive does not seem by itself to be enough to discredit an official act. We saw this when we discussed the "secular purpose" proviso of the *Lemon* test. If there is a good impartial, unbiased, reason for a legislative act (or, indeed, for any act of a state official) why should we deny that the act is neutral? If there is a good neutral reason operative, the fact that there is a biased one as well seems to discredit the actor, not the act.

We can see this both in the legislative case and in judicial and executive action. Let's call a set of reasons for an official act that, taken together, would be strong enough to motivate that act a set of *sufficient reasons*. It might be that every member of some legislature has a private grudge against a group and knows that a law will tend to affect them adversely. But if each of them is also motivated by a set of neutral suffi- cient reasons, and the neutral reasons would have led them to vote that way without the extra element of bias, then there seems no reason to impugn the law that they enact. We might think the law was unobjection- able, even if they were not motivated by such a neutral set of sufficient reasons, so long as there *were* such a set of reasons; that is, so long as there were good enough neutral reasons to motivate the law, even though they did not in fact motivate it. The same applies, mutatis mutandis, to other official acts. If a judge dislikes Catholics and takes pleasure in sentencing a Catholic for a crime, this surely reflects badly on her. But provided there are adequate grounds for the sentence that do not reflect that bias—and especially if those are the grounds she gives for her sen- tence—there seems no reason to claim that the sentence reflects state bias; just as a law that would have been passed if there had been no such biased motives is not vitiated by the presence of subjective bias.[47]

On the other hand, as I say, the proposal that we count as nonneutral only those acts that are motivated in part by bias seems too weak. For one kind of state nonneutrality consists in passing laws that negatively affect some subcommunity not because legislators intend to do so, but because they have not taken the trouble to examine what the impact of the law will be on them. Sometimes nonneutrality shows up, in other words, in negligence. This is evident in the case of religion. Suppose that, motivated by the desire to protect both husbands and wives from the possibility that their partners would will them too little of the mari- tal property (in order, say, to provide for a secret lover), a state were to require that people must provide for their spouses in a certain way. Suppose that, unbeknownst to the legislators, that rule was in some way inconsistent with the rather specific commands of the Koran. (I should make it plain that the Koran is itself concerned that husbands make adequate provision for their widows.) It would be reasonable, I think, for an American Muslim to object that such a law offended against the idea of neutrality, on the grounds that it would be possible to achieve its stated aim without offending against (at least this aspect of) sharia. (If, per contra, there were a compelling state interest that did not admit of accommodation, a state could legitimately ignore such an objection.) Something like this notion lies behind the idea, in Ameri- can antidiscrimination law, of "disparate impact." Where a policy with a certain express aim tends to disadvantage a historically disadvantaged racial minority—and thus has a "disparate" racial impact—and an alternative policy that would achieve the same aim and would not so disadvantage them is available, the Court has sometimes held that the policy may be legally barred as discriminatory, even without any showing of an intent to discriminate.[48]

You might think that, in speaking of legislators' aims, we should address ourselves to a bill's rationale—what it ostensibly aims to do— rather than to the subjective motivations behind its support. But, as the matter of disparate impact makes clear, a law can fail to be neutral even if its stated rationale is scrupulously so. And sometimes public acts that profess neutrality are nonneutral out of intent, not merely inadvertence. A city council might, in promulgating a rule, proclaim a concern about cruelty to animals but really seek to rein in an unpopular form of religious worship. So a law could be facially neutral—neutral in its rationale and its declared justification—but, in both motivation and effect, be discriminatory. Distinguishing between aims and intent, or justification and motivation, doesn't seem to clear things up.

In the face of these objections, there might still, I think, be a way to salvage something of the idea of neutrality among identities. It is to insist that state acts should treat people of diverse social identities with equal respect. Where an act disadvantages people of identity L, they can reasonably ask whether they could have been treated better and whether they would have been, had they not been regarded as Ls. In all the cases I have just considered, if the answer to that question is yes, we were inclined to treat the case as one of nonneutrality; where it was no, we were not. I shall call the ideal implicit in this test—that state acts shouldn't disadvantage anyone in virtue of his identity—*neutrality as equal respect.*

(Given the aims of this book, it is worth underlining here how differently identity works, on this liberal conception, for the state and for the individual. For the individual, as we have seen, that someone is an L can be a perfectly proper reason for treating him differently from others. Because identification constitutively makes being-an-L figure among our reasons for action, neutrality among identities, far from being an attractive moral ideal, is barely intelligible for us as individuals. That it may be required of the state is a reflection of something special about public reasons: that they address us all equally as citizens. I have called this notion of neutrality "neutrality as equal respect" in part to indicate how close it is in substance to the ideal of equality that is a long-established part of the practice of liberalism. It is the equality that traveled with liberty and fraternity in the French Revolution; the equality of the American Founding Fathers. I shall have more to say about the ways in which our private reasons are free from the obligations of this sort of neutrality in chapter 6.)

I have expressed skepticism about identifying the aims of state acts: you might, therefore, think the right question to ask is not whether someone would have been treated better if she hadn't been *regarded as* an L, but whether she would have been treated better if she hadn't *been* an L. So let me spell out why, on our test, the fact that someone is regarded as an L must explain her disadvantage. Consider a particular case where the treatment of a minority disadvantages them in relation to a majority. Left-handed people live in a public world where many things—scissors, door handles, cabinet doors—are configured in a way that suits the right-handed. They are disadvantaged by this fact; and the fact that they are left-handed plays a role in the explanation why. But the fact that they are *regarded as left-handed* plays no such role, at least most places in the industrialized world, where there is nowadays little prejudice against the left-handed. The reason they are disadvantaged is that some things have to be done in either a left-handed or a right-handed way, and right-handed people are in the majority.[49] Similarly, when it comes to Sabbatarian issues, the fact that our weekend coincides with the religious requirements of the Christian majority doesn't display a failure of neutrality as equal respect, provided that what accounts for the fact is that it suits a majority (and that, for coordination reasons, people cannot be permitted to take their two days in seven on whichever days they choose) and not that some minorities are disadvantaged by it. If a majority of Americans became Muslims and Friday mosque became a majority institution, it would not reflect a lack of regard for Christians if we shifted the days when government offices were closed to Friday and Saturday.

This formulation allows us to see something important in the defenses of liberal neutrality that focus on there being neutral reasons for a state policy. Thomas Nagel, in an influential paper titled "Moral Conflict and Political Legitimacy," argued that questions of neutrality arise where the state exercises its coercive power against the will of a citizen. He suggested that in these circumstances, the citizen is entitled to a reason (or a set of reasons) for the act that legitimated it: by which he meant a reason the coerced citizen should accept as a ground for the act.[50] (Nagel rightly insisted that we need not be bound by whether the citizen in fact accepts our reason, for otherwise people could, in effect, veto policies simply by being unreasonable; he required only that there be a reason that the coerced citizen should accept, or, equivalently, that she would accept if she were reasonable.)

There are three immediate problems with this proposal as it stands, none of which is a problem for neutrality as equal respect. The first is that citizen and reason-giver may disagree about what is reasonable. In these circumstances—especially, for example, in matters of religious belief—even if the state's view is in fact reasonable, ignoring the citizen's objections may not adequately display equal respect for all religions, given our ordinary understanding of liberal religious toleration. In the sphere of religion, one of the issues in dispute is often what it is reasonable to think and do. Neutrality as equal respect is not open to this objection. Under neutrality as equal respect, we can make sure that we don't treat people of one religion (as such) worse than others, even if we believe their views are unreasonable—even if they are, in fact, unreasonable. Many Jehovah's Witnesses, as I mentioned, believe that having a blood transfusion will lead to their damnation. Even knowing this, we might pass a law that required the provision of blood transfusions to unconscious persons who needed them, because a policy requiring us to establish consent would endanger the lives of many. Of course, if we thought blood transfusions would in fact lead to damnation, we would have a decisive reason not to adopt this policy. But we do not believe this. We mostly do not think it is even reasonable to believe this. On the account of neutrality in terms of reasonable acceptance, if we are coercing people who are unreasonable, we have no obligation to provide justifications that satisfy them. We must merely offer reasons that they would accept if they were reasonable. Here, so it seems to me, Nagel's neutrality demands too little. Under neutrality as equal respect, Jehovah's Witnesses will also sometimes be coerced into doing what we think is best for them, even though, because their beliefs are unreasonable, they think we are doing them great harm: but we will be thwarting their wills for some good reason, having reflected on whether we could adopt a policy that did not thwart their aims, and so the fact that they are Witnesses does not explain why we went against their aims.[51] Neutrality as equal respect doesn't require us to feign agnosticism about the beliefs of our fellow citizens or avoid relying on controversial claims: it merely asks us to avoid offending the beliefs of minorities as much as we can.

A second problem becomes clear when we realize that the existence of a reason that the citizen should accept—a neutral reason—can be construed in two different ways. It might mean that there was a neutral *all-things-considered* reason: a reason strong enough, in the light of all the countervailing considerations, to justify the policy. But to insist on this would mean that we could never legally proscribe an act where there were citizens who rejected our reasons for proscribing it. For otherwise the law would be coercing some people (whether by punishment or the mere threat of punishment) who did not recognize our grounds for legislating as adequate. Given the fact of pluralism, this would make legislation in many areas impossible. Nagel's argument construed the existence of a neutral reason for a policy in the other way—as meaning only that there are considerations shared by the state and by the person coerced that favor that policy; but this makes neutrality too easy to achieve. We could, for example, prohibit the wearing of turbans, on the grounds that anti-Sikh sentiment leads to some acts of violence. This is certainly *a* reason for the policy, and, since Sikhs obviously have reasons to want Sikhs protected from the assaults of bigots, it is a reason a reasonable Sikh would accept. But he would go on to say that the wearing of turbans was too important a matter to be banned for this reason. Why, he might ask, shouldn't we beef up policing of bigots instead?

Now, the reasons Sikhs have for wearing turbans are not reasons that most of the rest of us recognize. And that, of course, is the point. Even if we had sufficient nonreligious reasons to support a policy that coerced members of a religious group, absent consideration of their religious reasons, and even if they took those nonreligious reasons to be valid, they might still believe that these reasons were overridden by religious considerations. Nagel's proposal would count us as neutral because we had sufficient reasons, shared with the Sikhs, for the policy: but that is only because we do not share the reasons that they would take to be dispositive. If the Sikh asks whether his religious duty (to wear a turban) was ignored because he belonged to a religious group with which others have little sympathy, I think a fair answer might sometimes be yes. Neutrality as equal respect might then lead us to take the fact that the wearing of turbans is central to Sikh life as grounds for carving out an exception for them, as we would carve out exceptions, where practicable, for other religious practices. Sikhs, the principle is, are entitled to the same concern for their religious beliefs (true or false, reasonable or unreasonable) as all others. We cannot ignore their concerns because we think of them as "just Sikhs."

A third problem is that state acts need justifying to all citizens, not just to those whose actions are directly affected by them. One kind of disadvantage in a democracy is not having what you take to be the best policy enacted into law. On many topics, there are opposed views on what the best policy is. Abortions cannot be both permitted and banned: but some people think that, all things considered, they should be banned and others think that, at the end of the day, they should be permitted. Nagel's view is that a pro-life policy is not neutral because under it pro-choice women will sometimes be coerced into not having abortions; and we cannot offer them reasons they should accept for our coercion. (Pro-choice policies leave the decision up to the mother: so no one is coerced and so the state need not offer anyone reasons.) The thought, presumably, is that justifying pro-life legislation involves an appeal to religious grounds that are controversial, and so reasonable pro-choice women can deny that they have been offered neutral reasons. But many pro-life people will rightly feel that there is something fishy here. It is true that a pro-choice regime coerces no one into having an abortion; but it is also true that a pro-choice regime is possible only if we put aside the admittedly controversial considerations that are offered by those who are pro-life. Nagel thinks that questions about the justification of state action arise with especial intensity when people are being coerced. This seems to me right. But, as I said, laws need justifying to all citizens, not only to those who are coerced by them. And the pro-life person is likely to feel that ignoring her appeal to the sanctity of the life of the unborn fetus is not a way of being neutral between her religious views and others, but a way of taking sides against them. She can reasonably ask, "Would my views have been ruled out as a basis of state action if they had not been the views of an evangelical Christian (or a Catholic)?" And unless the answer is no, the policy will not count as neutral by the standard of equal respect, even though it satisfies Nagel. (I think the answer *is* no, by the way; so I don't think our current regime does in fact violate neutrality as equal respect.)

But there are perplexities here we'd better not skate over. Under neutrality as equal respect, the right question to ask in deciding whether a state act is neutral, in the way that matters, is, Would this person have been treated better had he or she not been regarded as an L? In some cases, it's easy to make sense of this question. If the San Antonio Spurs are playing the Chicago Bulls and suspect the referee is biased against their team, it would be natural for a Spurs point guard to ask himself, Would that foul have been called if I had been playing for the Bulls? The legal scholar David A. Strauss, with cases of racial and sexual discrimination in mind, recommends the test of "reversing the groups."[52] In many cases, though, it's difficult to know what to reverse—to know what counterfactual we ought to be considering, let alone how we should evaluate it. Consider *Thomas v. Review Board*, in which the U.S. Supreme Court considered the case of Mr. Thomas, a Jehovah's Witness who quit his job after being transferred by his employer from a foundry, where steel was prepared for a variety of uses, into a job manufacturing turrets for military tanks. (I owe this example to my colleague Chris Eisgruber.) He decided, after some struggle with his conscience, that his religion required him to be a pacifist and that his new job offended one of his deeply held religious convictions. So he quit. He then applied for unemployment benefits from the state of Indiana and was denied. The Supreme Court, however, invoking *Sherbert*, sustained his claim for compensation. Writing for the majority, Chief Justice Burger said: "The mere fact that the petitioner's religious practice is burdened by a governmental program does not mean that an exemption accommodating his practice must be granted. The state may justify an inroad on religious liberty by showing that it is the least restrictive means of achieving some compelling state interest." Burger then rejected the state of Indiana's claims that there was such an interest and went on to argue that, provided that granting Thomas his unemployment pay did not amount to establishment (which, he briskly, and correctly, maintained, it did not), he should therefore have been paid.[53]

Does neutrality as equal respect offer guidance here? As Chris Eisgruber points out, had Thomas been a secular pacifist, he isn't likely to have fared better—on the contrary. On the other hand, Eisgruber observes, "Thomas might have been treated better if he had been a mainstream religious worshiper, forced to quit his job because of a mainstream Christian conviction (e.g., don't work on Sunday)—or if he had to quit his job because he was transferred to some division (say, textiles) that triggered serious allergic reactions."

There are two important points raised here. One is a logical point. Evaluating a counterfactual about what would have happened *if P* is different from evaluating a counterfactual about what would have happened *if both P and Q*. If it had rained yesterday, I would have stayed home. But not if my mother had needed visiting in the hospital. The question about Thomas should, I think, be whether he would have been granted unemployment pay if he had quit his job for a reason of conscience other than a Jehovah's Witness's. The only circumstance we are required to alter in the counterfactual situation is the religious identity under which the relevant state actors conceived of him.

But this raises the second real difficulty, which is that it can be hard in many cases to answer this question. As Eisgruber's question (and Strauss's test) suggest, we naturally explore this issue by asking how he would have been treated not if he had been just *not-a-Jehovah's-Witness*, but if he had been something else specifically: an atheist, a member of a mainstream denomination, a person allergic to something in the tank division. The answer will then be sometimes better (for a mainstream denomination), sometimes worse (for a conscientious atheist). This does not mean it is indeterminate whether he would have fared better had he not been a Jehovah's Witness.[54] But it does mean that we have to be careful to ask the right question; it is also true that, once we have asked the right question, we may still not be able to answer it clearly.

On the face of the necessarily caricatural account of the facts of the *Thomas* case given in the Supreme Court's decision, I think it is very hard to say whether or not the initial finding of the Indiana review board was consistent with neutrality as equal respect. There does not seem, on the face of the record, to be any evidence that Thomas's religious scruples were treated with anything other than respect because they were seen as the scruples of a Jehovah's Witness. When the Indiana Court of Appeals reversed, they did so, in essence, because they thought of his case as being like the Sabbatarian cases: and when the Supreme Court of Indiana reversed *them* (by 3 to 2) the majority seems to have thought that the fact that other Jehovah's Witnesses regarded work on armaments as permissible was grounds for seeing his decision to quit as "personal" rather than religious. Though these various bodies reached different conclusions, Thomas's faith as a Jehovah's Witness does not seem to be why he lost before the two tribunals that rejected his claim.

From the fact that the Indiana board was behaving consistently with neutrality as equal respect, it does not follow, of course, that we should defend the outcome. Their job was to interpret a law in a nonprejudicial way. But we can also ask whether the law itself was well conceived and, in particular, whether the law itself displayed neutrality as equal respect. If you are going to give people unemployment benefits when they lose their jobs or have to give them up for a serious reason—such as a threat to their health—should you also do so when that serious reason is, like Thomas's, a reason of conscience? To this question I am inclined to say, Yes, absent a compelling state interest to the contrary. But is this required by neutrality as equal respect? Here I think the answer is that what is required is only that you treat equally conscientious reasons equally. More precisely, if you grant an exemption to a member of one denomination who has a reason of conscience substantial enough to make her leave a job, then you should grant it to those whose consciences are driven by other identities. Of course, it can be hard to compare burdens across religions: is a Muslim or Jew who must eat pork in prison more burdened than a secular vegetarian convinced of the rights of animals? There are, I think, no easy answers here. If, however, a state denies (as it might) that leaving a job for a reason of conscience should entitle you to unemployment compensation, I don't think it offends against equal respect, or against neutrality among identities properly understood. Whether such a decision is wise is a different question.[55]

There might still be a good liberal reason for framing and interpreting the law so as to grant Mr. Thomas compensation: namely, that to do so is to help him sustain his individuality. To give up your job is often a substantial loss, and finding a new one requires that you be able to put bread on the table while you search. Unemployment payments to those who leave for reasons of conscience are a way of removing one obstacle to their acting in conformity with their deepest beliefs; one barrier to their sustaining their individualities. Of course, as the state of Indiana observed, there are moral hazards in allowing people to claim conscience. No doubt lazy people could invent all kinds of "conscientious" objections. But the rate of unemployment pay in Indiana is surely not sufficiently attractive for this to be a major problem. And there is, as I say, a problem facing us if we do *not* allow conscientious objection to working on certain projects: namely, that it can require people to choose between remaining in an occupation that betrays their legitimate sense of who they are and putting their families on the street.

To be sure, you should not suppose that you will readily end up with America's First Amendment regime without reference to the specific history of state and sects that has made the subject so charged. Some liberals, in their theorizing, still try to subsume religious accommodation under a general concern for personal autonomy, say, and avoid special treatment of claims that issue from religious conviction. (The Sikh who wanted an exemption from a helmet law would simply be treated as someone who really, really wanted to keep his turban on.) It's just that this way of proceeding will not get you to where we are today. You'd come a little closer if you took special account of religious practices as likely to represent deeply constitutive aspects of people's identity, rather than something like a taste for one candy over another. We can make distinctions between the Mr. Thomases who, with Luther, declare, *Ich kann nicht anders*, and the Mr. Bartlebys who simply "prefer not to." We can, even if we are the stoniest of secularists, make distinctions between Communion wafers and Necco wafers.

THE LANGUAGE OF RECOGNITION

Talk of neutrality among identities, in ways we've seen, helps flesh out what happens when we try to generalize the First Amendment paradigm to deal with identity groups *tout court*. A state that "established" a certain identity might be taken to have betrayed the aim of neutrality as equal respect, and so might a state that unnecessarily burdened members of a certain identity group, thus infringing on "free exercise" or its identitarian analogue.[56] Of course, the state is constantly imposing differential burdens on this or that identity: the heir to the duke of Omnium will rightly see estate taxes as constraining his life as a scion of a landed aristocracy. But we might say (in the spirit of equal-respect neutrality) that government should not aim, in taxing him, to constrain his identity *as such*. As this example suggests, the accommodation of identity quickly runs into the problem of the enormous scope of that term "identity": identities are multiple and overlapping and context-sensitive, and some are relatively trivial or transient. That's why those who want to secure state deference (whether affirmative or exemptive) toward nonreligious identities take pains to distinguish the sort worth attention, and the rigorous tests they've had to meet: so it is, as we shall see, with Margalit and Raz's notion of the "encompassing group," and with Kymlicka's "societal culture."

As it happens, at least one generalization of the accommodationist movement has been argued for, in some detail. It proceeds under the rubric of "recognition."[57] It is among the most influential developments in recent political theory, and so perhaps deserving of extended consideration. What Charles Taylor has called "the politics of recognition" has little time for either neutralism or autonomy as such: his value term is "authenticity." And yet the proposal does occupy the same political space, so to speak, as other efforts at brokering a relationship between identities and the state.

The concept of recognition, as it is found in much recent multiculturalist discussion, is at root a Hegelian one, drawing on the now too familiar discussion of lordship and bondage in *The Phenomenology of Spirit*. There the thought is that my identity as master is constituted in part by the acknowledgment of my status by the bondsman (and, of course, if less interestingly, vice versa). I cannot be a master, act as and think of myself as a master, unless the bondsman acts toward me as bondsman to master and treats me as a master. It will be uncontroversial among those who have normal human relations that the responses of other people play a crucial role in shaping one's sense of who one is. As Charles Taylor has put it: "On the intimate level, we can see how much an original identity needs and is vulnerable to the recognition given or withheld by significant others. . . . Love relationships are not just important because of the general emphasis in modern culture on the fulfillment of ordinary needs. They are also crucial because they are crucibles of inwardly generated identity."[58]

But to grasp all this is not yet to say what role the state should have in the regulation of such acts of Hegelian recognition and misrecognition. On the one side lies the individual oppressor whose expressions of contempt may be part of who he or she is, and whose rights of free expression are presumably grounded, at least in part, in the connection between individuality and self-expression. On the other, the oppressed individual, whose life can go best only if his or her identity is consistent with self-respect. How, if at all, is the state to intervene? Some writers, Charles Taylor among them, seem to hold that the state itself, through government recognition, can sustain identities that face the danger of self-contempt imposed by the social contempt of others.

"Policies aimed at survival actively seek to create members of the community, for instance, in their assuring that future generations continue to identify as French-speakers," Taylor writes, reflecting on the language policies of Quebec. And he insists that the desire for survival is not simply the desire that the social forms that give meaning to the lives of currently existing individuals should continue for them, but requires the continued existence of a way of life through "indefinite future generations." Yet, though the desire that an identity shall be maintained is not a negligible one, it has to be conditioned and contoured by other considerations, including the requirements of participation in a larger polity. A politics of recognition, in short, must be buffered by a recognition of politics.

If we are reluctant to accept, as a rationale for Quebec's language policy, an overriding value of survival, how else might one negotiate the issue of language politics raised by multilingual societies? Let me sketch a way to think about language and schooling in this context, putting to one side the merits of the actual practice that Taylor was interpreting. (Here as elsewhere, I'm happy to put myself in the position of the proverbial philosopher who demands, "That's all very well in practice, but will it work in theory?") Citizenship, we can agree, is one of the primary means for the making of lives in the modern world. The exercise of citizenship requires the capacity to participate in the public discussion of the polity, and so there needs to be a language that is one of the instruments of citizenship. We can call this the political language. Some states may elect to try to manage more than one political language, and there are complications, to which I will return, that follow from this. But let me pursue the issue first in terms of a single political language.

Public education should aim to give the political language to all citizens—and where private education is permitted, it should be required, for the sake of the child who will become a citizen, that mastery of the political language be one of its elements. Such mastery is, of course, consistent with another language's being the medium of instruction and with learning yet other languages. Our real concern here is what languages the school's students end up knowing.

Language minorities have an interest in their children's mastery of the political language; but typically they also have a concern, rooted in the connection between language and identity, that their children should master their "own" language, too. The availability of the minority language is to a great degree a condition for the exercise of one possible identity option, namely, to live a life in which one's experience as a member of the group is shaped, interpreted, mediated by *its* language. This means that children of the minority group for whom this option is to remain open must acquire their language, which might best be accomplished as part of their schooling: and, provided they are also learning the political language, they can thus retain the option without being trapped in a minority identity they cannot escape. So in a country with language minorities, the state should make such options available to parents and children who seek them, if it can. I say "if it can," because there are resource issues involved in such provision, and trade-offs to be made among many competing desiderata. If the group is very small or the costs would be very high, we may well leave it to the group to sustain the language. The crucial point is that there is a legitimate identity-derived interest here in maintaining the language; the sort of interest that a state that cares for its citizens will certainly bear in mind.

There is then, in my view, nothing wrong in the insistence of a state, like Quebec, that all its schools produce competence in the political language. It is, in fact, the right thing to do. This means, however, that the right of anglophone parents to send their children to English-medium schools is reasonable only if those schools also teach the political language, i.e., French; and, equally, in francophone schools generally, anglophone children (like speakers of other minority languages) should be able—within the limits set by resource constraints that I mentioned earlier—to learn literate mastery of their own language as well.

The complication, of course, is that Quebec is not an independent sovereign but a province of the Canadian nation. That nation has not one but two political languages. As citizens of the Canadian state (and not just of Quebec) francophones are entitled to access to its political language. The question, then, is whether, in states that are officially multilingual, speakers of one of the languages need fluency in the others to achieve equal citizenship. The history of Switzerland suggests that, as an empirical matter, this is not necessary, and in South Africa, for example, with eleven political languages, it would not even be possible. The answer will depend on many historical contingencies (such as what degree of trust between communities exists in view of their past relations), and on questions of political structure (such as the degree to which there is—as in Canada, Belgium, or Switzerland—a decentralized politics of regions with different political languages).

And so, whatever the practical merits or difficulties of the current political resolution of these issue in Quebec, the way that it has been *conceptualized*, via a politics of recognition, gets things exactly the wrong way round. Taylor says, with approval, that "restrictions have been placed on Quebeckers by their government, in the name of the collective goal of survival."[59] But the right issue in deciding the primary language of instruction in state schools is not the maintenance of a francophone ethnic identity—not *survivance*—but equality of citizenship in a francophone state. Under Quebec law, "le français est la langue officielle du Québec." Once a democratic process has made French the political language, access to French is the right of all citizens and so must be made available to them; access to minority languages is a central enough interest that children of minority communities should have access to their minority language as well. (And a wise and cosmopolitan community will also encourage children to learn languages that are not, in this sense, theirs.)

Survivance is aided by the choice of French as the political language, of course; that is part of why it was democratically chosen as the political language. Such an aim is a perfectly acceptable consideration in democratic politics. But such aims must be managed within the framework of equal citizenship and a concern for the personal autonomy of citizens, not by notions of compulsory identities. Allowing for the existence of a minority without proper access to the political language offends against equality; placing obstacles in the way of learning other languages offends against autonomy.

If English were the sole political language of Canada, it would be clear, too, that Quebeckers had a right to be taught it as well. But it isn't; and, given that the country is bilingual, so long as monolinguals are able to exercise full citizenship—a question that is, by its nature, not one that admits of resolutions with sharp boundaries—there is no obvious reason why Quebeckers whose parents don't want them to learn English should be forced to do so. Of course, they will have wider opportunities if they learn English; they might have even wider ones, however, if they learned Chinese, Hindi, or Spanish. Were it unnecessary to learn English for adequate political participation, the fact that it provides opportunity would be no more reason to force it on them than the fact that Chinese does. If Quebec officials would be wrong to allow anglophone children to escape French altogether, they would also be wrong to discourage a child from learning English in order to deprive him or her of access to an anglophone identity. Where people can gain access to an identity by learning a language and they wish for that access, it is not the state's business to stop them.

The general point is this: there are two ways to bring full citizenship to minority-language communities. One is to make their language one of the political languages, and entitle them to access to official communications in it. (Here you want to be sure that the practicalities of this process will produce real equality of political participation.) The other way is to teach them the political language, while allowing them, if they choose, to maintain their own, which is the route that has been followed in India and the multilingual countries of Africa. The Canadian case makes clear that where political participation is layered and the different levels have different political languages, these principles may lead to complex outcomes: given the enormously variegated patterns in which languages are distributed across states, however, any solution is going to have to be complex.

The politics of language is a central and difficult issue in the management of many modern multilingual states, states whose plurality of languages result from histories of migration, both voluntary and involuntary, and of conquest.[60] I hope I've indicated a plausible way to frame this issue. But after even this crayon-on-a-napkin discussion of policy it is worth repeating a point I made in the preface: this book aims to pick out and explore certain key concepts in our thinking about the ethics of identity. It is not—it does not aim to be—a book of political prescriptions or policy proposals. If what I have said about Quebec is wrong, I hope it is wrong because I have misunderstood the political history or the facts on the ground. What I am committed to is not the policy I have gestured toward, with all its factual predicates, but rather the claims about the way in which considerations of language as a material for identity and as a tool of citizenship should be brought to bear in the construction of a policy. Here, as everywhere, my aim is to begin with the interests of individuals and to show how identities give individuals complex interests that ethics—and, therefore, a satisfactory politics—must bear in mind.

THE MEDUSA SYNDROME

Ethical individualism, it may be worth spelling out, has no simple friend-or-foe relation to "recognition"; and careful readers of Hegel, such as Charles Taylor and Axel Honneth, are surely right that much of modern social and political life turns on such questions of recognition. In our liberal tradition, of course, we see recognition largely as a matter of acknowledging individuals and their identities: and we have the notion, which comes (as Taylor says) from the ethics of authenticity, that, other things being equal, people have the right to be acknowledged publicly as what they already really are. It is because someone is already authentically Jewish or gay that we deny him something in requiring him to hide this fact, to "pass," as we say, for something that he is not. As has often been observed, though, the way much discussion of recognition proceeds is at odds with the individualistic thrust of talk of authenticity.[61] In particular, attending to the oppositional aspects of authenticity would complicate the picture, because it would bring sharply into focus the difference between two levels of authenticity that the contemporary politics of recognition seems to conflate.

To bring out the problem, let me start with a point Taylor has made about Herder—that Herder "applied his conception of originality at two levels, not only to the individual person among other persons, but also to the culture-bearing people among other peoples. Just like individuals, a Volk should be true to itself, that is, its own culture."[62] After all, in many places nowadays, as I suggested earlier, the individual identity, whose authenticity cries out for recognition, is likely to have what Herder would have seen as a national identity as a component of its collective dimension. It is, among other things, your being, say, an African American that shapes the authentic self that you seek to express. And it is, in part, because you seek to express your self that you seek recognition of an African American identity. This is what makes problems for Lionel Trilling's notion of the "opposing self": for recognition as an African American means social acknowledgment of that collective identity, which requires not just recognizing its existence but actually demonstrating respect for it. If, in understanding yourself as African American, you see yourself as resisting white norms, mainstream American conventions, the racism (and, perhaps, the materialism or the individualism) of "white culture," why should you at the same time seek recognition from these white others? (I will have more to say about such paradoxes of support in the next chapter.)

There is, in other words, at least an irony in the way that an ideal of authenticity—you will recognize it if I call it the Bohemian ideal—requiring us to reject much that is conventional in our society, is turned around and made the basis of a "politics of recognition."[63] Now, you may be skeptical of the Bohemian ideal, or see it as a mere indulgence or affectation; but the notion that identities are founded in antagonism—recall the Rattlers and the Eagles—should by now be an unsurprising one.

I used the example of African Americans just now, and it might seem that this complaint cannot be lodged against an American black nationalism: African American identity, it might be said, is shaped by African American society, culture, and religion. Here is how the argument might be framed: "It is dialogue with these black others that shapes the black self; it is from these black contexts that the concepts through which African-Americans shape themselves are derived. The white society, the white culture, over against which an African-American nationalism of the counter-conventional kind poses itself, is therefore not part of what shapes the collective dimension of the individual identities of black people in the United States."

This claim seems to me to be simply false. What shows that it is false is the fact that it is in part a recognition of a black identity by "white society" that is demanded by nationalism of this form. And "recognition" here means what Taylor means by it, not mere acknowledgment of one's existence. African American identity (like all other American ethnoracial identities) is centrally shaped by American society and institutions: it cannot be seen as constructed solely within African American communities, any more than whiteness is made only by whites.

There is another error in the standard framing of authenticity as an ideal, and that is the philosophical realism (which is nowadays usually called "essentialism") that seems inherent in the way questions of authenticity are normally posed. Authenticity speaks of the real self buried in there, the self one has to dig out and express. It is only later, after romanticism, that the idea develops that one's self is something that one creates, makes up, like a work of art. For reasons touched on in chapter 1, neither the picture in which there is just an authentic nugget of selfhood, the core that is distinctively me, waiting to be dug out, nor the notion that I can simply make up any self I choose, should tempt us. As we saw, we make up selves from a tool kit of options made available by our culture and society. We do make choices, but we don't, individually, determine the options among which we choose. To neglect this fact is to ignore Taylor's "webs of interlocution," to fail to recognize the dialogical construction of the self, and thus to commit what Taylor calls the "monological" fallacy.

If you agree with this, you will wonder to what extent we should acknowledge authenticity in our political morality: and that will depend, surely, on whether an account of it can be developed that isn't monological. It would be too large a claim that the identities that cry out for recognition in the multicultural chorus *must* be monological. But it seems to me that one reasonable ground for suspicion of much contemporary multicultural talk is that the conceptions of collective identity they presuppose are indeed remarkably unsubtle in their understandings of the processes by which identities, both individual and collective, develop. And I am not sure whether Taylor would agree with me that collective identities disciplined by historical knowledge and philosophical reflection would be radically unlike the identities that now parade before us for recognition, and would raise, as a result, questions different from the ones he addresses. In a rather unphilosophical nutshell: my suspicion is that Taylor is happier with the collective identities that actually inhabit our globe than I am: and that may be one of the reasons why I am more hesitant to make the concessions to them that he does. For an ethics of identity (to anticipate my discussion in chapter 5) must confront two distinct though not wholly separable questions: how existing identities should be treated; and what sort of identities there should be.

As we saw, the large collective identities that call for recognition come with notions of how a proper person of that kind behaves: it is not that there is *one* way that gay people or blacks should behave, but that there are gay and black modes of behavior. These notions provide loose norms or models, which play a role in shaping the ground projects of those for whom these collective identities are central to their individual identities. Collective identities, again, provide what I have been calling scripts: narratives that people use in shaping their pursuits and in telling their life stories. And that is why, as we've seen, the personal dimensions of identity work differently from the collective ones.

How does this general idea apply to our current situation in the West? We live in societies in which certain individuals have not been treated with equal dignity because they were, for example, women, homosexuals, blacks, Catholics. Because, as Taylor observes, our identities are dialogically shaped, people who have these characteristics find them central—often, negatively central—to their identities. Nowadays there is widespread agreement that the insults to their dignity and the limitations of their autonomy imposed in the name of these collective identities are seriously wrong. One way the stigmatized have responded has been to uphold these collective identities not as sources of limitation and insult but as a central and valuable part of what they are. Because the ethics of authenticity requires us to express what we centrally are, they move, next, to the demand that they be recognized in social life *as* women, homosexuals, blacks, Catholics. Because there was no good reason to treat people of these sorts badly, and because society continues to provide degrading images of them nevertheless, they demand

THE DEMANDS OF IDENTITY ~ 109

that we work to resist the stereotypes, to challenge the insults, to lift the restrictions.

These old restrictions suggested life-scripts for the bearers of these identities, but they were, in substantial part, negative ones. I need hardly repeat that one does not construct a social identity ab ovo, that our choices are at once constrained and enabled by existing practices and beliefs; but neither do we always "play it as it lays." And there have been historical moments where we see groups contesting and transforming the meaning of their identities with seismic vigor. Certainly this has been a notable dimension of the grand identity movements of the late twentieth century. In order to construct a life with dignity, it has seemed natural to take the collective identity and construct positive life-scripts instead. An African American after the Black Power movement takes the old script of self-hatred, the script in which he or she is a nigger, and works, in community with others, to construct a series of positive black life-scripts. In these life-scripts, being a Negro is recoded as being black: and for some this may entrain, among other things, refusing to assimilate to white norms of speech and behavior. And if one is to be black in a society that is racist, then one has constantly to deal with assaults on one's dignity. In this context, insisting on the right to live a dignified life will not be enough. It will not even be enough to require that one be treated with equal dignity despite being black: for that would suggest that being black counts to some degree against one's dignity. And so one will end up asking to be respected *as a black*.

Let me rewrite this paragraph as a paragraph about gay identity: An American homosexual after Stonewall and gay liberation takes the old script of self-hatred, the script of the closet, and works, in community with others, to construct a series of positive gay life-scripts. In these life-scripts, being a faggot is recoded as being gay: and this requires, among other things, refusing to stay in the closet. And if one is to be out of the closet in a society that deprives homosexuals of equal dignity and respect, then one has constantly to deal with assaults on one's dignity. In this context, the right to live as an "open homosexual" will not be enough. It will not even be enough to be treated with equal dignity despite being homosexual: for that would suggest that being homosexual counts to some degree against one's dignity. And so one will end up asking to be respected *as a homosexual*.

I hope I seem sympathetic to the stories of gay and black identity I have just told, distilling those identity movements of the 1960s and 1970s. I see how the story goes. It may even be historically, strategically necessary for the story to go this way. But I think we need to go on to the next step, which is to ask whether the identities constructed in this way are ones we can be happy with in the longer run. Demanding respect for people *as blacks* and *as gays* can go along with notably rigid strictures as to how one is to be an African American or a person with same-sex desires. In a particularly fraught and emphatic way, there will be proper modes of being black and gay: there will be demands that are made; expectations to be met; battles lines to be drawn. It is at this point that someone who takes autonomy seriously may worry whether we have replaced one kind of tyranny with another. We know that acts of recognition, and the civil apparatus of such recognition, can sometimes ossify the identities that are their object. Because here a gaze can turn to stone, we can call this the Medusa Syndrome. The politics of recognition, if pursued with excessive zeal, can seem to require that one's skin color, one's sexual body, should be politically acknowledged in ways that make it hard for those who want to treat their skin and their sexual body as personal dimensions of the self. And personal, here, does not mean secret or (*per impossible*) wholly unscripted or innocent of social meanings; it means, rather, something that is not too tightly scripted, not too resistant to our individual vagaries. Even though my race and my sexuality may be elements of my individuality, someone who demands that I organize my life around these things is not an ally of individuality. Because identities are constituted in part by social conceptions and by treatment-as, in the realm of identity there is no bright line between recognition and imposition.

LIMITS AND PARAMETERS

In a well-known essay, "Equality and the Good Life," Ronald Dworkin takes up Aristotle's view that "a good life has the inherent value of a skillful performance," and proposes what he calls "the model of challenge." The model "holds that living a life is *itself* a perfor-

mance that demands skill, that it is the most comprehensive and important challenge we face, and that our critical interests consist in the
achievements, events, and experiences that mean that we have met the
challenge well." Now, the notion I want to borrow from Dworkin is a
useful distinction between different ways in which our circumstances
figure in the evaluation of how well we have met the challenge. Some
of our circumstances (including our own physical, mental, and social
attributes) act as *parameters*, he says, defining what it is for us to have
lived a successful life. They are, so to speak, part of the challenge that
we must meet. Others are *limits*—obstacles that get in the way of our
making the ideal life that the parameters help define.

Each person, in thinking about her own life, must decide how to
allocate her circumstances between these categories, just as an artist
must decide which aspects of the tradition she inherits define what her
art is and which are barriers to or instruments for her creativity. Dworkin writes: "We have no settled template for that decision, in art or in
ethics, and no philosophical model can provide one, for the circumstances in which each of us lives are enormously complex. . . . Anyone
who reflects seriously on the question which of the various lives he
might lead is right for him will consciously or unconsciously discriminate among these, treating some as limits and others as parameters."[64]

Among the circumstances Dworkin regards as his own parameters is
his being American. His American-ness is, he says, "a condition of the
good life for" him.[65] So, for example, even though he has long taught
jurisprudence in England and has no doubt influenced the development of English legal thinking, there surely is, for him, a special significance to his contributions to American constitutional jurisprudence, a
significance that derives from the fact that America—and not England—is *his* country. So when we're describing the parameters of our
lives, social identities are one obvious class of candidates.

To refer back to the discussion of *identification* with which I started,
you might think that to identify as an L is to treat one's being an L as
a parameter. But just as with identities there is no bright line between
recognition and imposition, the relation between parameters and limits
is a fluid and shifting affair. Consider homosexuality once more. For
some people, homosexuality is a parameter: they are openly gay, and—

happy or unhappy, rich or poor—the life they seek to make will be a life in which relationships with members of their own sex will be central. Others think of their sexuality as a limitation: they want desperately to be rid of homosexual desires, and, if they cannot be rid of them, they would at least like to succeed in not acting on them. At the same time, circumstances that one might assume would be merely impediments may be transmuted into a positive way of being. Thus for many deaf people deafness is not a limit but a parameter: they are not trying to overcome a disability; they are trying to live successful lives as the hard-of-hearing people that they are. A condition becomes an identity—the deaf become the Deaf.

I think the limit-parameter distinction helps us see why "identity" has become a locus of such warring political intuitions. Black, woman, gay, aboriginal—so many of the identity categories that are politically salient are precisely ones that have functioned as limits, the result of the attitudes and acts of hostile or contemptuous others. Each of these categories has served as an instrument of subordination, as a constraint upon autonomy, as, indeed, a proxy for misfortune. Some identities, we can show, were *created* as part of a classificatory system for oppression. And in the context of antidiscrimination law, say, these identities are treated as a sort of handicap, to be disregarded or remedied. Yet the reversible-raincoat nature of these terms is demonstrated by the fact that categories designed for subordination can also be used to mobilize and empower people as members of a self-affirmative identity. (The disconcerting ease with which limits become parameters recalls the duck-rabbit oscillation between structure and agency we explored in the previous chapter, and it may help explain the ambivalence commonly occasioned by talk of "identity politics.") As a parameter, identities provide a context for choosing, for defining the shape of our lives, but they also provide a basis for community, for positive forms of solidarity. And it is perfectly consistent to consider your membership in an identity group as both parameter and limit: the Black Nationalist who deplores white supremacy is keenly aware of color as constraint, even as he seeks to make it the basis of a political mode of resistance. There is a two-way traffic between limits and parameters, then.

Yet to say all this is not to lose sight of other aspirations and other ideals, among them what Peter Singer has called the "expanding circle" of our moral sympathies. The contours of identity are profoundly real: and yet no more imperishable, unchanging, or transcendent than other things that men and women make. Indeed, talk of division and disharmony can lead us to neglect the powerful countervailing forces: conflict may be productive of identities, but conflict can also be a powerful unifying force across identity groups. It is not a new thought—and in some ways not an entirely heartening one—that the two world wars had a powerful effect in forging an American identity that lessened the social salience of small social divisions; that the Second World War, in particular, did as much as anything to make the civil rights era inevitable.

What happened at Robbers Cave State Park confirms this intuition with almost comic schematism: the intergroup bloodlust that was so easily conjured into being finally subsided before what the researchers called "shared superordinate goals." As the animosity between the groups and solidarity within them was beginning to boil over, the ingenious researchers devised a series of communal crises. Necessity was the mother of amity.

To start with, the researchers sabotaged the camp's water system. Two groups of increasingly thirsty boys worked together to identify the problem and repair it. And then a truck, which was to have fetched food for them, broke down, or gave every appearance of having done so. It would have to be pulled up with a rope; and only the collective force of both groups—the raffish Rattlers and the high-minded Eagles—would suffice. By the by, banners were set down, putative differences set aside. Shoulder to shoulder, tugging on their tug-of-war rope (the experimenters had an appreciative eye for symbolism), the kids winched the stalled truck uphill.

No single crisis was enough to erase the poisonous animosity between the Rattlers and the Eagles; a series of them, however, produced genuine confraternity and the dissolution of social boundaries. The truck started up, food was brought back, and a meal was collaboratively prepared. "After supper a good-natured water fight started at the edge of the lake," the researchers dutifully noted; but, as they were careful to add, "the throwing and splashing was not along group lines."[66]

Chapter Four

∼ The Trouble with Culture

MAKING UP THE DIFFERENCE—IS CULTURE A GOOD?—THE
PRESERVATIONIST ETHIC—NEGATION AS AFFIRMATION—
THE DIVERSITY PRINCIPLE

MAKING UP THE DIFFERENCE

It hasn't escaped notice that "culture"—the word—has been getting a hefty workout in recent years. The notion seems to be that everything from anorexia to zydeco is illuminated by being displayed as the product of some group's culture.[1] It has reached the point that when you hear the word "culture," you reach for your dictionary.

Culture's major rival in its kudzu-like progression is "diversity," a favorite now of corporate CEOs and educational administrators, politicians and pundits. And "cultural diversity" brings these two trends together. It has become one of the most pious of the pieties of our age that the United States is a society of enormous cultural diversity. American diversity is indeed easily granted, and so is the need of a response to that diversity. What isn't so clear is that it is our *cultural* diversity that deserves attention.

Let's begin with a place where the idea of somebody's culture really does appear to explain something. When Jews from the *shtetl* and Italians from the *villagio* arrived at Ellis Island, they brought with them a rich brew of what we call culture. They brought a language and stories and songs and sayings in it; they transplanted a religion with specific rituals, beliefs, and traditions, a cuisine of a certain hearty peasant quality, and distinctive modes of dress; and they came with particular ideas about family life. It was often reasonable for their new neighbors to ask what these first-generation immigrants were doing, and why; and a sensible answer would frequently have been, "It's an Italian thing," "It's a Jewish thing," or, simply, "It's their culture."

In America, it is striking how much of this form of difference has vanished. The proportion of foreign-born Americans is far less than it was seventy years ago; rates of exogamy among immigrant groups have soared just in the past few decades; fewer and fewer Americans live in neighborhoods with a concentration of people who share their "national" origins. The rhetoric of diversity has risen as its demographic reality has declined. The sociologist Mary Waters has argued persuasively that the cultural residue of that rich immigrant gumbo has become thin gruel.[2] There are still seders and nuptial masses, still gefilte fish and spaghetti. But how much does an Italian name tell you, these days, about church attendance, or knowledge of Italian, or tastes in food or spouses? Even Jews, who, given their status as a small non-Christian group in an overwhelmingly Christian society, might have been expected to keep their "difference" in focus, are getting harder to identify as a cultural group.

The usual story of immigration doesn't apply to the descendants of African slaves, who have not had the privilege of becoming "white." Yet the striking contrast between black and white stories can lead us to neglect what they have in common. There are, indeed, forms of English speech that are black: even if there are also large regional and class variations in black, as in white, speech. But what we are talking about here are all forms of *English*. Indeed, despite the vast waves of immigration of the last few decades, something like 97 percent of adult Americans, whatever their color, speak English "like a native"; and, with the occasional adjustment for an accent here and there, those 97 percent can all understand one other. Leave out recent immigrants and the number gets close to 100 percent.

Not only blacks and whites, but Asians and Native Americans share the English language. Even Hispanics, the one American ethnic group *defined* by language, prove no exception. People talk a great deal nowadays about the Hispanization of America, and you can indeed hear Spanish spoken in stores and on street corners in places you wouldn't have heard it thirty years ago. But, as the linguist Geoffrey Nunberg has pointed out, the proportion of non-English-speaking residents is just a quarter of what it was in 1890, in the midst of the last great period of immigration. He cites a Florida poll that shows that 98 percent of Hispanics want their children to speak English well; and a RAND Corpora-

tion study showing that in California the vast majority of first-generation Hispanics have native fluency in English, and only half of their
children speak Spanish at all.[3] If being American means understanding
English, then U.S.-born Hispanics overwhelmingly (and increasingly)
pass the test. Rates of English fluency run equally high among the children of immigrants from Asia.

Language is only one of many things most Americans share. This is
also, for example, a country where almost every citizen knows something about baseball and basketball. And Americans share a familiarity
with our consumer culture. They shop American style and know a good
deal about the same consumer goods: Coca-Cola, Nike, Levi-Strauss,
Ford, Nissan, GE. They have mostly seen Hollywood movies and know
the names of some stars; and even the few who watch little or no television can probably tell you the names of some of its "personalities."

The supposedly persistent differences of religion, too, turn out to
be shallower than you might think. Indeed, the often-remarked-upon
growth of certain orthodox and fundamentalist sects seems to attest to
the pervasion of the civic creed, if only by reaction. In the main, American Judaism is, as is often observed, extraordinarily American. Catholics in this country are a nuisance for Rome just because they are . . .
well, so Protestant. They typically claim individual freedom of conscience, for example—so they don't simply take the church's line on
contraception or divorce.[4] Above all, most Americans who claim a religion (which means pretty much most Americans) regard it as essentially private, something for which they desire neither help nor hindrance from the government. Even Christian Coalition parents who
want prayer in the schools generally just want their own children sustained in their faith; they don't want the public school to set about
converting the children of others. In these key respects—the sovereignty
of the individual conscience within the confession, and the privacy of
religious belief—American religion, whatever its formal sectarian designation, tends to be decidedly Protestant. Many of the religious traditions from Asia that have increased in significance in the present wave
of immigration are also quickly Americanizing: much of American
Islam, for example, is as happy with the separation of church and state
as most Muslims elsewhere are resistant to it.

Coming, as I do, from Ghana, I find the contrast with a nation of a
more substantial diversity of folkways to be striking. Take language.

When I was a child, we lived in a household where you could hear at least three mother tongues spoken every day. Ghana, with a population close to that of New York State, has several dozen languages in active use and no one language that is spoken at home—or even fluently understood—by a majority of the population.

So why, in America, which seems so much less diverse than most other societies, are we so preoccupied with diversity and so inclined to conceive of it as cultural? By now, it will come as no surprise when I say that the diversity that preoccupies us is really a matter not so much of cultures as of identities.

As we've seen, the social identities that clamor for recognition are extremely multifarious. Some groups have the names of the earlier ethnicities: Italian, Jewish, Polish. Some correspond to the old races (black, Asian, Indian); or to religions (Baptist, Catholic, Jewish, again). Some are basically regional (Southern, Western, Puerto Rican). Yet others are new groups that meld together people of particular geographic origins (Hispanic, Asian American) or are social categories (woman, gay, bisexual, disabled, Deaf) that are none of these. And, nowadays, we are not the slightest bit surprised when someone remarks upon the "culture" of such groups. Gay culture, Deaf culture, Chicano culture, Jewish culture: see how these phrases trip off the tongue. But if you ask what distinctively marks off gay people or Deaf people or Jews from others, it is not obviously the fact that to each identity there corresponds a distinct culture. "Hispanic" sounds like the name of a cultural group defined by sharing the cultural trait of speaking Spanish; but, as I've already pointed out, half the second-generation Hispanics in California don't speak Spanish fluently, and in the next generation the proportion will fall. "Hispanic" is, of course, a category that's as made-in-the-U.S.A. as black and white, a product of immigration, an artifact of the U.S. census. Whatever "culture" Guatemalan peasants and Cuban professionals have in common, the loss of Spanish confirms that Hispanic, as a category, is thinning out culturally in the way that white ethnicity has already done.

You might wonder, in fact, whether there isn't a connection between the thinning of the cultural content of identities and the rising stridency of their claims. Those European immigrants, with their richly distinct customs, were busy demanding the linguistic Americanization of their children, making sure they learned America's official culture. One suspects they didn't need to insist on the public recognition of their culture, because they simply took it for granted. Their middle-class descendants, whose domestic lives are conducted in English and extend eclectically from MTV to Chinese takeout, are discomfited by a sense that their identities are somehow shallow by comparison with those of their *nonnas* and *bubbehs*; and so they are busy demanding we all acknowledge the importance of their difference.

Something similar has happened with African Americans. When there were still legal barriers to full citizenship, before the judicial decisions from *Brown* to *Loving* and the civil rights legislation of the sixties, the public recognition of a unique black culture was not exactly the major item on the black political agenda. Black people wanted recognition by state and society of things they had in common with white people: their humanity and those famous "inalienable rights." In part as a result of these legal changes, middle-class African Americans, who were always quite close in language and religion to their white Protestant neighbors, are now in many cultural and economic respects even closer. And just at this moment, many of them have been attracted to an Afrocentrism that demands the recognition in public life of the cultural distinctness of African Americans.

I am not denying—who could?—that there are significant differences between the average experiences of blacks and whites in the United States. We all know of the concentration of the poorest blacks in inner cities with terrible schools and no jobs; the persistence of discrimination in housing, employment, and the legal system; the tendency of whites to flee neighborhoods whose black populations rise beyond a "tipping point." Many poor urban blacks (like just as many poor rural whites) are doing badly in an economy that is supposed to be doing well. All this I grant. But the fact is that the black middle class is also larger and doing better than it ever has; and it is primarily they, not the poor, who have led the fight for the recognition of a distinctive African American cultural heritage, just in a moment when cultural differences are diminishing.

None of this is to say that we shouldn't take seriously the many claims made on culture's behalf; but it does suggest a measure of wariness as we approach a singularly boggy terrain. The culture concept has, of course, been historicized and anatomized within an inch of its life.

These days, in the context of globalization, people have been inclined to fret about the export of Western culture; but among the most successful Western cultural imports has been the concept of culture itself—a concept that has then been mobilized against "cultural imperialism." All over the world, Marshall Sahlins has pointed out, some variant of the Western term has been appropriated by other peoples: this Amazonian and that Solomon Islander find that they have a "culture." As he concludes, "The cultural self-consciousness developing among imperialism's erstwhile victims is one of the more remarkable phenomena of world history in the later twentieth century."[5] When I was a child, in my hometown of Kumasi, the "Cultural Center" was a place where you could go and listen—and dance—to drumming, and watch our *kĕntĕ* cloth being woven and our goldweights being cast in brass. You could visit a model of a "traditional compound" and see how our ancestors cooked for our chiefs. The idea was that it was *our* culture being celebrated and represented; and when we were setting off there we would say, in Asante-Twi, *yĕkō kōkya*, "we are going to culture"—"*kōkya*" (pronounced "ko-cha") being the way the word "culture" has passed into our language. Many years later I was setting out with a friend who works at the palace of the Asante Queen Mother for some celebration about which he was greatly excited, and I asked him why it mattered so. He looked at me in puzzlement for a moment and replied: "*Ēyĕ yĕ kōkya.*" It is our culture.

I don't want to reprise a genealogy that has been traced with a good deal of careful scholarship elsewhere, but it's fair to say that our word derives much of its energy from eighteenth- and nineteenth-century German romanticism, a formidable Counter-Enlightenment unto itself. At least since Norbert Elias's *The Civilizing Process*, which appeared in German in 1939, it has been customary to contrast the German notion of *Kultur* (which is the possession of a *Volk*, and which aspires to authenticity) to the French ideal of *civilisation* (which is meant to be a universal ideal, and which aspires to progressive rationality).[6] Yet while "civilization" would fall into conceptual disrepute, "culture" would gain extraordinary intellectual traction. Before long, it came to be taken as a disciplinary subject by ethnologists, notably Sir Edward Burnett Tylor, whose 1871 definition of the word is widely quoted: Culture, he wrote, "is that complex whole which includes knowledge, belief, arts, morals, law, customs, and any other capabilities and habits acquired by man as a member of society." In the twentieth century, especially after Franz Boas, this social-scientific notion becomes attended by a rapidly proliferating profession of "cultural anthropologists." In the postwar era, it became common to think of culture as something like a language, something whose codes might admit of systematic explication. Or, perhaps (and this was the postmodern turn), interpretation would always itself remain just another cultural practice: perhaps, then, cultures were more like linguistic expressions, like poems, made things.[7] But then, nearly every conceivable position has been adopted and critiqued in the course of a century's debate. So much so that the question arises whether culture, having allowed us an expansive view, should finally, like Wittgenstein's ladder, be thrown away. The notion has now, as I say, attained ubiquity: but at a cost of conceptual purchase. It is a nearly biblical predicament. What shall it profit a word if it shall gain the whole world and lose its own soul?

Is Culture a Good?

My particular interest in this chapter, of course, will be the roles it has been assigned in political theory, where, as we'll see, it has occasioned no shortage of confusion. There are many ways in which culture might matter to political theory—and, in particular, to social justice—but surely the simplest way of bringing the two together has been to categorize culture as a resource, or good. Where this categorizing is defended, rather than simply assumed, you find several lines of argument, and more than one interpretation of "good." Let me take up two leading approaches in turn.

Culture as Primary Good

For Rawls, of course, goods represent the "satisfaction of rational desire," and primary goods "are things which it is supposed a rational man wants whatever else he wants." As "broad categories," Rawls cites "rights and liberties, opportunities and powers, income and wealth," but also "a sense of one's own worth."[8] This deliberately sketchy formulation appears to leave the door open to many other candidates—not least among them, Will Kymlicka says, being *culture*. Indeed, he thinks Rawls has not just left the door open to it but sat it down and served it tea. "Rawls's own argument for the importance of liberty as a primary good is also an argument for the importance of cultural membership as a primary good," he writes in *Liberalism, Community, and Culture*. That's because autonomy requires choosing, and culture provides "the context of choice": it is "only through having a rich and secure cultural structure that people can become aware, in a vivid way, of the options available to them, and intelligently examine their value." Thus the concern to shore up our culture "accords with, rather than conflicts with, the liberal concern for our ability and freedom to judge the value of our life-plans."[9]

There are variants of the basic idea to which Kymlicka is also sympathetic. He follows Ronald Dworkin (who invites us to see culture as a public good, like parks and bridges) in the view that culture "provides the spectacles through which we identify experiences as valuable";[10] and Margalit and Raz (in their paper "National Self-Determination") in the view that "familiarity with a culture determines the boundaries of the imaginable."[11] Note, again, that Kymlicka's approach is avowedly individualist, inasmuch as the good involved is ultimately a good to persons, rather than peoples. And this is important to bear in mind because in Kymlicka's arguments, as in those of so many other writers on the subject, "culture" sometimes refers to the Tylorian package and sometimes refers to membership in a "cultural group" (in other words, to what I have been calling an identity), and the shifting usages tend to be poorly marked.

What follows, politically, from the notion that culture is a primary good? Group rights, of course, are frequently taken to violate the core of liberalism. Isaiah Berlin famously warned against the dangers of expanding the "self" to mean the tribe, race, and other superindividual entities.[12] Certainly the basic move in much "liberal multiculturalism" has been to assign groups the sorts of liberties and protections that are ordinarily understood to be the province of the citizen. But, for all the reasons we've seen, Kymlicka believes that the conflict between individualism and group rights is a mirage, and that those rights, at least if they are properly titrated, really serve the ends of liberal individualism.

It's no more illiberal for a society to protect my culture, in his view, than it is for a society to protect my property. Hence his endorsement of what Iris Young calls "differentiated citizenship," of the notion that "some forms of group difference can only be accommodated if their members have certain group-specific rights."[13] Or as William Blake would have it, "One Law for the Lion & Ox is Oppression."

Kymlicka has worked out, in commendable detail, a culture-friendly approach that aims to be consistent with the mainstream of liberal thought (which he identifies with Rawls, Dworkin, and Nagel). His paradigm cases center on the aboriginal communities in Canada, to whom he would extend "cultural rights." (For example, these communities would be able to impose residency requirements, regulations as to land sale, and the like.)[14] It might appear that the autonomy of the individual aboriginal is thereby sacrificed, at least in some degree, for the sake of the autonomy of the aboriginal group: but Kymlicka wants us to resist just this conclusion, and to see that, culture being a primary good, the autonomy of the individual indigene depends upon the sustenance of the "societal culture" to which he or she belongs. In the case of immigrants, particularly where they are present in sizable numbers, Kymlicka would provide weaker "polyethnic" measures. These might include positive steps to prevent discrimination, public funding of their "cultural practices," exemption from differentially burdensome regulations, and so forth. "If it is acceptable for immigrants to maintain pride in their ethnic identity," he asserts, "then it is natural to expect that public institutions will be adapted to accommodate this diversity."[15] But here the primary aim is to enable integration. And the sparser the representation of the immigrant group, the lesser its claim to such polyethnic privileges.

It's worth emphasizing that his expressed rationale for such accommodations rests on the conventional liberal values of equality and autonomy. If an individual needs access to his culture to make meaningful choices (and to enjoy self-respect), these sorts of protections are simply in the service of garden-variety liberal individualism. To guarantee citizens some basic level of a primary good is a prerequisite for being a just society. Kymlicka has thus taken great pains to show that his practical suggestions and the points of principle are neatly aligned.

So much so, in fact, that to see the problems in this account, we may find it helpful to start with a peculiar feature of the policy recommendations. Say I am a villager from Kokora, Estonia, who has decided to move to Terril, Iowa, where there are cows and cornfields but nobody else from my part of the world. If "culture" denotes the usual anthropological bundle—encompassing everything from language to nuptial and culinary practices—I shall be hard-pressed to "practice" it. Perhaps this does not strike you as a difficulty: I can practice *your* culture. This will not do: when Kymlicka maintains that an individual, in order to make meaningful choices, needs "access to societal culture," he stresses that what's needed isn't just any culture: it must be "one's *own* culture."[16] Yet if I and my "culture" are Kokoran, and I cannot practice my culture on my own, what will Kymlickan "multicultural citizenship" offer me? Is the state to provide me with others from my hometown? Nobody would suggest such a thing, and not merely because of administrative costs. Only if there were a significant contingent of Kokorans (or, calibrating less finely, of Estonians), with a complement of cooks and priests and other cultural laborers, would he propose those "polyethnic measures"—external protections of my ethnic ways. And only if there were a large and long-settled Kokoran contingent would I be entitled to those stronger measures he calls "cultural rights." Insofar as you take seriously his notion of culture as a resource, though, that's a strange outcome: if culture is a resource, why are remedial measures greatest, as if by some reverse–Robin Hood logic, when I'm least in need? Why, when I am most deprived, am I entitled to the least support? The paradox suggests there is something wrong in the picture of culture as a resource.[17] (Let me be clear that my target is not the particulars of the policy but its rationale. There can be all sorts of reasons—some democratic and responsive to voting power; some prudential and responsive to administrative efficiency—to make greater provisions for sizable ethnic minorities: for having, in a Florida election, bilingual ballots designed for Spanish speakers, but none for Occitan speakers. The Robin Hood *reductio* arises only if you insist that culture is a resource.)

This suspicion is confirmed when we notice that resources, including primary goods, are, in the Rawlsian tradition, things you can have more of or less of; the details of their distribution are something that a just society is deeply concerned with. And yet (aside from a few highly anomalous instances) I doubt that it makes much sense to speak in terms of the unequal distribution of culture. It is relatively straightforward to compare your household's net worth to mine; I cannot see that our respective "cultures" admit of such ordinal assessment. To refer back to a discussion in the previous chapter, culture, in Kymlicka's account, sounds very much like what Dworkin called a parameter; and parameters, in his scheme, are not among the things that it is proper for the government to equalize. For they are, by stipulation, not resources; they define, rather, the person whose resources are to be equalized. The resource model, *in fine*, raises more conundrums than it resolves.

Kymlicka tries to make headway here by invoking a term that had been used by Margalit and Raz: "decayed culture." Some unfortunates are possessors of decayed cultures, he says, and we ought to try to rejuvenate them. I confess I am not sure how to make sense of this notion.[18] If what we have in mind is a troubled period of cultural transition, though, it isn't obvious that such conditions diminish our liberty or autonomy—our ability to choose among a wide range of options. Indeed, as John Tomasi suggests, a greater degree of personal autonomy may be afforded by a less rigid "choosing context," where there are fewer constraints on what counts as an acceptable life plan than there would be in a more stable cultural community.[19] That culture changes is a commonplace. What's not easy to imagine is a person, or people, bereft of culture. (Culture-as-resource talk is surely not motivated by the freak occurrence of a raised-by-wolves wild child.) "Taken existentially," Tomasi observes, "cultural membership is a primary good only in the same uninteresting sense as is, say, oxygen: since (practically) no one is differentially advantaged with respect to that good, it generates no special rights."[20] Indeed, the problem with grand claims for the necessity of culture is that we can't readily imagine an alternative. It's like *form*: you can't not have it.

Now, we could take Kymlicka's defense of culture as a "choosing context" to entail not just that you have a culture but that you have this or that particular culture, in which case the claim goes from being trivial to being untenable. For if what's meant is that the character of a culture—the norms and values and regalia of some configuration of social forms—must be arrested, laminated, and protected from change, then this is a position that few would wish to endorse (Kymlicka least of all, it should be said). Liberals tend to be sympathetic to a Millian notion of experimentation and social progress; the prospect of freezing existing prejudices and inequities and bigotries—the edict that "whatever is, is right"—is hardly a palatable one.

As we saw, multicultural liberals often speak of culture as an ethico-epistemological lens—a way of seeing, of acting, of being; as something that provides a framework of concepts and values, something that "determines the boundaries of the imaginable." But, as I warned, there is often a slippage between the idea of "culture" *simpliciter* and the idea of "cultural membership." It might be objected that we have focused too much on this first conception, and that the argument for culture as a good gains plausibility if we give proper emphasis to the notion of membership—of *belonging*.

Claims about belonging, I suspect, derive their plausibility from the basic notion that it's good to be socialized, good to have social ties; it's hard to imagine such pleasures of association without a shared social context that looks like a shared Tylorian "culture." Raz, in a 1994 essay on multiculturalism, seems to be upholding something unexceptionable when he states, "It is in the interest of every person to be fully integrated in a cultural group."[21] Yet if the value we're honoring is ultimately that of sociality, of being integrated into a group, one might fairly ask what work is being done by the "cultural" predicate. More to the point: what's meant by being "fully integrated" in a cultural group?

Much depends on how you construe this requirement. Was Rimbaud—scandalizing *tout le monde* before he went hopscotching through Africa—fully integrated into a cultural group? What about the Sudanese Islamic scholar Mahmoud Mohamed Taha, who was executed for heresy in 1985 because of his opposition to traditional sharia? Some people, it appears, actively resist being fully integrated into a group, so that they may gain some measure of distance from its reflexive assumptions; to them, "integration" can sound like regulation, even restraint—especially to liberals who, by tradition, favor *Freiheit* over *Einheit*. Nor is this merely an affectation of the vauntedly cosmopolitan. One may find this theme memorably expressed by that least cosmopolitan of poets (to go by self-description, anyway), Philip Larkin. In "The Importance of Elsewhere," Larkin writes of the strangeness of Ireland, at once forbidding and inviting ("the salt rebuff of speech, / Insisting so on difference, made me welcome"), its effect of showing him to be "separate, not unworkable"; and the poet concludes:

> Living in England has no such excuse:
> These are my customs and establishments
> It would be much more serious to refuse.
> Here no elsewhere underwrites my existence.

But perhaps all such people—whether poet *maudit* or religious dissident—really are integrated into their cultural group, so long as we delimit that group correctly, on the every-church-is-orthodox-to-itself principle. The itinerant Cynics of fourth-century Greece, on this interpretation, may have sought to hold themselves aloof from all creed and custom but were fully integrated into the cultural group of their fellow Cynics. Perhaps the seemingly marginalized figure is really integrated into his own cultural cohort, correctly defined, his culture being whatever his culture is. But then the "integration" requirement becomes largely emptied of content. "Most people live in groups of these kinds, so that those who belong to none are denied full access to the opportunities that are shaped in part by the group's culture," Margalit and Raz maintain.[22] Only, who are these people who belong to none? We should be hard-pressed to find them, even in the squalor of the refugee camp. "The same is true of people who grow up among members of a group so that they absorb its culture but are then denied access to it because they are denied full membership of the group," they continue. But one is again hard-pressed to think of people who fit the bill. The Jews of Admiral Horthy's Budapest—to consider some apparent candidates almost at random—are poorly described in these terms, for the exclusion they faced wasn't cultural, in the first instance (what they lacked proper access to were things like jobs and legal protection, not the national culture); the same holds for Israeli Arabs or Turkish Kurds. We might think of the "half-caste" aboriginal children taken from their homes and adopted by "white" families, or raised in orphanages, in a program that Australian government officials conducted for more than six decades. The enormities are real, but I doubt that they are best seen as "cultural" ones. People are wronged when they are decisively excluded from the exercise of power, when they are dispossessed and deprived of equal standing under the law. (Also, to state the obvious: when they are kidnapped and taken from loving families.) But what is at issue is, in the first instance, political, not cultural, exclusion. There are perils in mistaking one form of injury for the other. You may indeed ensure that the dispossessed enjoy a stable and distinctive cultural community—if you take that to be a priority—by a variety of means; perhaps the most efficient goes by the name segregation.

Of course, nothing could be further from what champions of cultural membership have in mind. But, as I say, what makes it so easy to sign on to the ideal of cultural membership is simply that the alternative seems to be the condition of abject friendlessness. At bottom, the case for membership is just the case against being a hermit. And precious little of the misfortune in our world has to do with that uncommon condition.

Culture as Social Good

So far we've been exploring an individualist approach to the subject of culture, in which it figures as a resource available (in the way of Rawlsian resources) to individuals. Maybe we've been wrong-footed by that individualism. There's an orthogonal approach to the subject, which centers on the notion that culture is an irreducibly *social* good. And what's meant by a "social good" is something different from a merely public good, like a bridge or a dam, which is justified in terms of the individuals who benefit. Rather, it is a good whose value cannot be reduced to the satisfaction of a collection of individuals' desires. Charles Taylor, who is the most persuasive exponent of this vision of culture, is a vigilant antireductionist. He objects strenuously to the de-composable conception of such goods, in which (as he lampoons it) "a certain proportion of Quebeckers have a 'taste' for the preservation of the French language, and so this is a good, just like chocolate-chip ice cream and transistor radios." To think this way is to think ourselves outside of culture and estrange ourselves from what matters about it. "The spokesmen for nationalism, or republican rule, don't see its value as contingent on its popularity," he urges. "They think that these are goods whether we recognize them or not, goods we ought to recognize."[23] Others have registered consonant concerns. "Group interests cannot be reduced to individual interests," Margalit and Raz have argued, in their essay on national self-determination. "It makes sense to talk of a group's prospering or declining, of actions and policies as serving the group's interest or of harming it, without having to cash this in terms of individual interests. The group may flourish if its culture prospers, but this need not mean that the lot of its members or of anyone else has improved."[24]

For Charles Taylor, the argument is a simple one. "As individuals we value certain things; we find certain fulfillments good, certain experiences satisfying, certain outcomes positive," he observes. "But these things can only be good in that certain way, or satisfying after their particular fashion, because of the background understanding developed in our culture." A conclusion follows swiftly: "If these things are goods, then other things being equal so is the culture that makes them possible. If I want to maximize these goods, then I must want to preserve and strengthen this culture. But culture as a good, or more cautiously as a locus of some goods (for there might be much that is reprehensible as well), is not an individual good."[25]

Taylor's caution serves us well, for the difference between being a good and being a locus of goods is not a negligible one. The existence of a monetary system is, in the relevant sense, a locus of wealth; it is not a form of wealth. And your wealth can still be an individual good even if the monetary system is not.[26] Even if we thought that culture—by which Taylor means "the background of practices, institutions, and understandings" that give meaning to our actions—was a locus of goods, *its* social nature wouldn't vouchsafe that those goods were social.

Indeed, the very existence of irreducibly social goods remains controversial. Some philosophers, notably James Griffin, have argued that there aren't any genuinely communal goods, valuable not just to the individuals in a community but to the community itself, as a distinct entity. On this line of argument, the "value thesis" subsists on borrowed plausibility. The goods that we think of as social (or "communal," in Griffin's nomenclature) are defined in terms of a relationship among persons—they are defined in terms of a group. They are goods an individual cannot enjoy by himself; they depend upon social interactions. Where we go wrong is to move from these unexceptionable definitional and causal propositions to the proposition that this or that value cannot be accounted for by reference to the role it plays in the lives of individuals.[27]

Culture, Taylor writes,

> is not a mere instrument of the individual goods. It can't be distinguished from them as their merely contingent condition, something they could in principle exist without. That makes no sense. It is essentially linked to what we have identified as good. Consequently, it is hard to see how we could deny it the title of good, not just in some weakened, instrumental sense, like the dam, but as intrinsically good. To say that a certain kind of self-giving heroism is good, or a certain quality of aesthetic experience, must be to judge the cultures in which this kind of heroism and that kind of experience are conceivable options as good cultures. If such virtue and experience are worth cultivating, then the cultures have to be worth fostering, not as contingent instruments, but for themselves.[28]

But who is the "we" in this passage? Suppose, first, that it is someone outside the culture in question. And consider, by way of example, the officer-class ethic of honor that underwrote the dueling practices of Arthur Schnitzler's Vienna. Suppose you were brought by reading *Leutnant Gustl* to understand it, to sympathize with the dishonored junior officer and his desire for vindication. (This would be an extremely odd response: but we are engaged in philosophical conjecture.) Does this count as seeing the dueler's heroism as good? If so, then Taylor seems to be just wrong: one *can* recognize something as a good embedded in a certain culture without remotely mourning this culture's passing. If not, then, presumably, to count it as good is to count it as good oneself. But then one's own judgment shows that this culture is not necessary to sustain *this* value. Suppose, then, that the "we" is someone *inside* the culture. The fact that one values what one values isn't an argument for anything, let alone an argument for "fostering" some culture or other. Any form of life would be self-validating in that sense. To belong to a moral culture is to hold this or that as a good; it would be an exercise in narcissism, not to mention *petitio principii*, to declare that your culture is good because it contains things you have identified as good.

Now, a value is like a fax machine: it's not much use if you're the only one who has one. So if one thinks that "a certain kind of self-giving heroism" is a value, one would do well, as Taylor suggests, to try to promote self-giving heroism of that kind. Perhaps, though, the culture that surrounds and sustains it contains lots of things one disapproves of. So we have to proceed cautiously here. For one thing, it's unclear how we are to bound the thing called "culture"; in the holistic Tylorian conception, we'd be required to sustain absolutely everything, which can't be quite right. And so we end up moving between culture writ large (this great sea of practices, conventions, concepts, values) and culture writ small (often denoted by attributive phrases: the "culture of" this or that). Suppose you were an American who valued chastity and worried that, after the sixties, it was no longer generally valued by your compatriots. You might then wish to promote a culture (writ small) of chastity—to spread an abstinence movement, and hope that it acquired adherents. But you wouldn't be promoting the culture (writ large) of 1880—or whenever you thought chastity was last adequately appreciated—because you wouldn't be concerned with the countless other things that it might have come with (such as, well, the particular culture of honor that led to dueling). That a good is embedded in a way of life may suggest a reason to *record* that way of life; it does not suggest a reason to promote it. (Then again, the fact that you are driven to change the culture suggests that an individual can, solitarily, hold to a value no longer in general circulation.) For all these reasons, culture as a social good proves to be a shape-shifting target.

THE PRESERVATIONIST ETHIC

What worries many advocates and activists, a fair number of political theorists among them, isn't culture's conceptual shiftiness; what worries them is the perishability of actual cultures. In their view, we can't take cultures seriously—whether as an individual or a social good—without concerning ourselves with their preservation. Indeed, the words and images with which people speak of cultural destruction—or, more neutrally, cultural change—typically refer to the destruction of human life. Assimilation is figured as annihilation. The

Karens, in Burma, worry about their "gradual extinction as a community"; the Bihar, in India, worry that they may become "extinct like the American Indians"; the Sikhs, if not enabled to live as equals, face "virtual extinction"; Pakistan's Sindhis fear being "turned into Red Indians." Donald Horowitz, in his magisterial study *Ethnic Groups in Conflict*, has had no difficulty in compiling a long list of such descriptions, each equating cultural and physical survival.[29] So perhaps we should not be surprised when William Galston likens the liberalizing of illiberal communities to the My Lai massacre, casting Kymlicka, of all people, as the William Calley of culture. Few issues arouse such strong emotions, and the more abstractly the issue is cast, the stronger those emotions are. As a rule, however, the preservationist ethic is simply posited, not defended.

A rationale might be found in Ronald Dworkin's proposal that we see ourselves as trustees of our culture: "We inherited a cultural structure, and we have some duty, out of simple justice, to leave that structure at least as rich as we found it."[30] But to say this is not to endorse, let alone provide a defense of, the preservationist ethic, which is to say, a concern for the survival of a particular culture. Nothing forbids a responsible trustee to trade the Union Carbide shares in his portfolio for U.S. Steel shares, and nothing in the trusteeship model would forbid us to switch our national language from English to Spanish or Esperanto. Margalit and Raz come closer to a defense when they insist that "encompassing" cultural groups do better when they run themselves. But the winds between political autonomy and cultural differentiation blow in both directions; each is bound to affect the other. And it's perfectly possible that when ethnic groups are submerged into larger entities—when the *Napolitani* start to think of themselves as *Italiani*—individuals may do better. From the point of view of ethical individualism, the question we must pose is, So what if Provençal—or Savoyard or Neapolitan—identity loses its salience as power ascends to a more overarching level? Is it morally troubling that the peoples of the Champa kingdom were long ago absorbed into what's now thought of as Vietnam? That formerly distinct populations of Madi and Bari have coalesced into the Lugbara in northeastern Uganda? Might it not be better if Hutu and Tutsi all became Rwandans or Burundians?

"Most indigenous peoples themselves," Kymlicka writes, understand that "the nature of their cultural identity . . . is dynamic, not static." Indeed, he has argued that societal cultures are "not permanent or immutable," for otherwise "group-specific rights would not be needed to protect them."[31] Yet if cultures are impermanent and mutable, if they are understood by their possessors as dynamic and not static, you may wonder how group-specific rights (whether membership or collective) can be founded on the goal of their preservation.

Often, the issue is resolved through the invocation of a sharp distinction between inside and outside forces. Avishai Margalit and Moshe Habertal, in "Liberalism and the Right to Culture," argue that people have an "overriding interest" that sponsors a right to culture: in particular, a right that it survive, untrammeled by outsiders. Kymlicka, too, seeks to insulate cultures from "outside" forces while permitting them to respond to internal ones. Only in the face of outer-directed change should we speak of "the culture itself being threatened," he says. "It is one thing to learn from the larger world; it is another thing to be swamped by it, and self-government rights may be needed for smaller nations to control the direction and rate of change."[32]

If you're wondering what counts as "swamping," in his account, and how, precisely, it harms, you're on your own. And yet, especially in the context of immigration, we ought to recall that the notion cuts both ways. Mrs. Thatcher favored the term, it will be remembered, in her complaints about the threat represented by the influx of dark-skinned foreigners. It was precisely what Charles Moore, then editor of the *Spectator*, appealed to in his notorious remarks of a decade ago:

> You can be British without speaking English or being Christian or being white, but nevertheless Britain is basically English-speaking and Christian and white, and if one starts to think that it might become Urdu-speaking and Muslim and brown, one gets frightened and angry. Next door to me live a large family of Muslims from the Indian subcontinent. We are friendly enough to one another and they have done us various small acts of kindness. During the Gulf War, however, I heard their morning prayers coming through the wall, and I felt a little uneasy. If such people had outnumbered whites in our square, I should have felt alarmed. Such feelings are not only natural, surely—they are right. You ought to have a sense of your identity, and part of that sense derives from your nation and your race.[33]

Once you elevate protection against swamping to a principle, then, you need to think about who may feel entitled to its protection. I do not say that it's illegitimate to worry about swamping—I can imagine ways of making sense of it, and we rightly abhor policies, like those of the Chinese in Tibet, that are motivated solely by the desire to weaken a way of life.[34] But the argument against it should be laid out, not assumed.

Yet perhaps this is all wrong. Perhaps asking people to make the case for wanting cultural survival is like asking them to make the case for craving bread: it is just because people have these strong desires that we must strive to ensure their fulfillment. The wish is self-validating. This is something like Taylor's perspective when he spells out the situation of Québécois nationalism. "Policies aimed at survival actively seek to *create* members of the community, for instance, in their assuring that future generations continue to identify as French-speakers," Taylor writes.[35] In culturally plural states, such societies—by which he means groups whose continuity through time consists in the transmission, through the generations, of distinctive institutions and values and practices—may legitimately seek to guarantee their own survival. And he claims that the desire for survival is not simply the desire that the culture which gives meaning to the lives of currently existing individuals should continue for them, but requires the continued existence of the culture through "indefinite future generations." As he elsewhere says, once "we're concerned with identity," nothing "is more legitimate than one's aspiration that it never be lost."[36]

And yet the Québécois example reminds us that the political rhetoric of survival is often too modest, for what's involved is creation rather than mere preservation. As the anthropologist Richard Handler shows, in his *Nationalism and the Politics of Culture in Quebec* (1988), the content of Québécois identity is inseparable from the ongoing discourse of Québécois nationalism:

> To be Québécois one must live in Quebec and live as a Québécois. To live as a Québécois means participating in Québécois culture. In discussing this culture people speak vaguely of traditions, typical ways of behaving, and characteristic modes of conceiving the world; yet specific descriptions of these particularities are the business of the historian, ethnologist, or folklorist. Such academic researches would seem to come after the fact: that is,

given the ideological centrality of Québécois culture, it becomes worthwhile to learn about it. But the almost *a priori* belief in the existence of the culture follows inevitably from the belief that a particular human group, the Québécois nation, exists. The existence of the group is in turn predicated upon the existence of a particular culture. . . . the assertion of cultural particularity is another way of proclaiming the existence of a unique collectivity.[37]

This isn't to say that Québécois identity is an empty urn, only that its content is in some sense incidental to the larger task of national self-definition, and that this task is more naturally seen in terms of change than of preservation.

And the same goes for other societal cultures. In the previous chapter, I pointed to the formation of ethnicities through antagonism; it is as easy to point to ethnicities whose existence, at least as distinct, singular entities, is largely the product of concerted state action. Johannes Fabian has explored the way certain ethnicities in the Congo were created precisely by colonial policies of recognition. David Laitin points out that "Hausa-Fulani" was "largely a political claim of the NPC in their battle against the South," and that, only a few decades ago, "Yoruba" would not have been a common predicate of political identity. In Ghana, an Akan political identity arises in opposition to a freshly forged Ewe identity.[38] The colonial-era management of "tribes"—in ways explored in David Cannadine's entertaining study, *Ornamentalism*—often led to the creation of official subject ethnicities sponsored by official "ethnic" leadership elites.

In America, too, the political existence of indigenous groups has an intimate relationship with the mechanisms of government recognition. Contemporary Pequot identity, inasmuch as it exists, or is coming to exist, is a product of federal and state policies of recognition and exemptions, in particular, tax exemptions. For, in addition to the Pequot-owned Foxwoods casino (and allied enterprises, such as the Pequot Pharmaceutical Network), there is now a two-hundred-million-dollar "state-of-the-art" Mashantucket Pequot Museum and Research Center, which has dispatched teams of archaeologists to further deepen our knowledge of a once extinct tribe, advancing the sort of project that Richard Handler referred to. I wrote earlier of the Medusa Syndrome, but sometimes Midas has a hand in things, too. The Ramapough

Mountain tribe, one of about 250 groups in the United States who identify themselves as Indians, has applied to the state of New Jersey for designation as New Jersey Indians, despite the fact that the federal government has rejected the group's claims of origin. (In 1995, the Bureau of Indian Affairs ruled that they were descendants of freed slaves, not, as they maintained, the Munsee. In the 2002–3 session of the New Jersey legislature, bills to recognize the Ramapough, among others, were introduced in the assembly and the senate.) How the state responds may well determine whether the tribe survives as such. Clearly commercial interests have conduced to the revival of once defunct ethnic identities, in a phenomenon that cynics might call casino-culturalism (even if economic motives only amplify the underlying drumbeat of insistence that "culture matters"). But what legal exemptions have called into being can readily come to command heartfelt identitarian allegiances. In the garden of cultural identities, silk flowers quickly grow roots.

Even if you grant cultural nationalism its terms of argument, however, survival can't always be squared with ethical individualism. When, in the Québécois context, Taylor writes of the "indefinite future generations," he refers to descendants of the current population. The desire for the survival of French Canadian culture is not the desire that, for a long time to come, there should be people somewhere or other who speak that Quebec language and practice those Quebec practices. It is the desire that this language and practice should be carried on from one generation to the next. A proposal to solve the problems of Canada by paying a group of unrelated people to carry on French Canadian culture on some island in the South Pacific simply would not meet the need.

Why does this matter? Because it is far from clear that we can always honor such preservationist claims while respecting the autonomy of future individuals. Parents sometimes want their children to persist in some practice that those children resist. This is true for arranged marriage for some women of Indian and Pakistani origin in Britain, to take the example I discussed earlier. In this case, the ethical principles of equal dignity that underlie liberal thinking seem to militate against allowing the parents their way because we care about the autonomy of these young women. If this is true in the individual case, it seems to me equally true where a whole generation of one group wishes to impose a form of life on the next generation—and a fortiori true if they seek to impose it somehow on still later generations.

And once we attend to these vistas of descent, it may strike us that culture talk is not so very far from the race talk that it would supplant in liberal discourse. As I've mentioned, Kymlicka seeks to reconcile the preservationist ethic with what he concedes is the dynamic nature of culture by distinguishing between exogenous and endogenous change. "It is natural, and desirable, for cultures to change as a result of the choices of their members," he says. "We must, therefore, distinguish the existence of a culture from its 'character' at any given moment."[39] But to establish the identity of a culture without reference to the nature of the culture—to speak of its *existence* without recourse to its *character*—leads us toward something conceptually congruent to race. What is left without character is just the fact of descent: and while the significance of descent does not have to be seen in terms of biology, in general, or genes, in particular (as is required for a descent-based account to become a fully racial one), there is a tendency, in our scientistic age, for a biological story (and usually a false one) to take over. Even if descent-based accounts resist the temptations of racialism, there remains something morally arbitrary about basing identities on the scale of thousands or millions on the bare assertion of genealogical relationships. Family rhetoric makes the best moral (and ethical) sense when it is on a family scale.

A similar problem arises when Margalit and Raz stress that membership in an "encompassing culture" is a matter of status, or belonging, rather than accomplishment: "Given that [members] are identified by a common culture, at least in part, they also share a history, for it is through a shared history that cultures develop and are transmitted."[40] But, as I've had occasion to observe in other contexts, we should not want to demarcate the group by reference to this shared history. Just as, to recognize two events at different times as part of the history of a single individual, we have to have a criterion of identity for the individual at each of those times, independent of his or her participation in the two events, so, when we recognize two events as belonging to the history of one group, we have to have a criterion of membership of the group at those two times, independent of the participation of the members in the two events. Sharing a common group history cannot be a *criterion* for being members of the same group, for we need something by which to identify the group in order to identify *its* history; and that something cannot, on pain of circularity, be the history of the group.[41]

In just this vein, Walter Benn Michaels suggests that without some racialized conception of a group, one's culture could only be whatever it was that one actually practiced, and couldn't be lost or retrieved or preserved or betrayed. Thus, when Taylor says that nothing is more legitimate than one's aspiration that identity never be lost, we should ask why we speak of *loss*, rather than change. "Without some way of explaining how what people used to do but no longer do constitutes their real identity, while what they actually do does not, it cannot be said that what the former French-speakers, current English-speakers have lost is their identity," Michaels says. "My point, then, is not that nothing of value is ever lost but that identity is never lost."[42]

Of course, speaking abstractly, a concern for survival is perfectly consistent with respect for autonomy; otherwise every genuinely liberal society would have to die in a generation. If we create a society that our descendants will want to hold on to, our personal and political values will survive in them. But here there is the difficult question of how a respect for autonomy should constrain our ethics of education. (I will explore this matter further in chapter 5.) After all, we have it to some extent in our power to make our children into the kind of people who will want to maintain our values, beliefs, and customs. Precisely because the monological view of identity is incorrect, there is no individual nugget waiting in each child to express itself, if only family and society permit its free development. We have to help children make themselves: and we have to do so according to our values because children do not begin with values of their own. To prize autonomy is to respect the conceptions of others, to weigh their plans for themselves heavily in deciding what is good for them: but children do not start out with plans or conceptions. It follows, therefore, that in education in the broad sense—the sense that is covered by the technical notion of social reproduction—we must appeal to and transmit values more substantial than a respect for liberal procedures. Liberal proceduralism is meant to allow a state to be indifferent among a variety of conceptions of the good: but what conceptions of the good there will be will depend on what goes on in education. Teach children only that they must accept a politics in which other people's conceptions of the good are not ridden over, and there may soon be no substantive conceptions of the good at all.

In most modern societies, the education of most people is conducted by institutions run by the government. Education is, therefore, in the domain of the political. This is not just an accident: social reproduction involves collective goals. Furthermore, as children develop and come to have identities whose autonomy we should respect, the liberal state has a role in protecting the autonomy of children against their parents, churches, and communities. I would be prepared to defend the view that the state in modern society *must* be involved in education on this sort of basis: even if you disagree with this, however, you must admit that it currently does play such a role and that, for the reasons I have been discussing, this means that the state is involved in propagating elements, at least, of a substantive conception of the good. But to say all this is not to say that the state is properly concerned with the survival of specific ethnic subgroups (as opposed to their members) as an end in itself.

Negation as Affirmation

Earlier, I said that the carapace of "cultural preservation" often conceals a project of cultural construction; and that, as a general rule, state recognition does not leave its object untouched. That much can be taken as read. What I wish to focus on now is a special case of the general rule, one that will provide us with an illustrative paradox. What happens when a society undertakes to support a group that defines itself, in no small part, through its opposition to that society? What happens when (with apologies, once more, to Blake's "Marriage of Heaven and Hell") opposition really is true friendship?

Joseph Raz's account of a liberal multiculturalism provides a good starting point, precisely because he's aware that harmony has its limits. "One's culture constitutes (contributes to) one's identity," he writes. "Therefore slighting one's culture, persecuting it, holding it up for ridicule, slighting its value, affects members of that group"—particularly so, he adds, "if it has the imprimatur of one's state." At the same time, Raz acknowledges that some enmity between cultures is inevitable and that "conflict is endemic to multiculturalism."[43]

What this misses is that such enmity may constitute (contribute to) the cultures in question. That's not just a Robbers Cave observation about ethnogenesis. Cultural norms are, after all, constituted not only by what they affirm and revere, but also by what they exclude, reject, scorn, despise, ridicule. To forbid the latter set of social practices is to change the nature of the relevant social forms. Perhaps an Igbo who doesn't find the Yoruba brash and excessively self-assertive will have lost some of his Igbo-ness; certainly a Pentecostalist who found nothing objectionable in contemporary mass culture would be scarcely recognizable to his peers. To favor one thing may entail disfavoring another thing. It isn't strictly incoherent to value modesty and admire grandiosity, but it may be hard in practice to reconcile them. In their paper on national sovereignty, Margalit and Raz say it is "mere common sense" that "individual dignity and self-respect require that the groups, membership of which contributes to one's sense of identity, be generally respected and not be made a subject of ridicule, hatred, discrimination, or persecution."[44] It *is* common sense, but I doubt it is quite correct—I doubt, in such contexts, that we can require "respect," as opposed to simple tolerance. As I said in the preface, the sphere of "respect" is where liberal abstraction shows its strength, for the encumbered self—whom advocates of community would substitute for the abstraction of the liberal individual—is not someone we can, as a rule, be bound to respect.

The Hegelian concept of recognition, as we've seen, looms large in discussions of multiculturalism; and yet to shed light on the paradoxes of cultural support, we might invoke another Hegelian concept, that of internal negation.

> But thou wilt lose the style of conqueror,
> If I, thy conquest, perish by thy hate.
> Then, lest my being nothing lessen thee,
> If thou hate me, take heed of hating me.

So John Donne writes in "The Prohibition," a poem that Jon Elster aptly cites by way of illustrating the dynamic. "A person whose independence requires the destruction of an external object, depends on that object in his very being and hence cannot without contradiction desire its destruction," Elster says. "Once we start thinking about it, the phenomenon is ubiquitous. It explains why militant atheism cannot do without believers, just as a certain kind of communism lives symbiotically with private property"; it explains, he adds, the nostalgia for the Cold War that some anticommunists feel—a yearning not for the stability it provided but for meaning they derived from it.[45]

Imagine, then, a cultural group, the Dyspeptics, that thrives on rejection. Perhaps it had its origins in some sixteenth-century heresy, and ever since the heretics were expelled from the community they once belonged to, they have sought to remain aloof and isolated. Accordingly, the Dyspeptics behave in ways odious to others, ensuring that they will be constantly rejected, gaining strength from the hostility of outsiders, and so keeping their way of life uncorrupted by external influence. Now, however, they find themselves within a regime that welcomes them and lavishes governmental largesse upon them; and as a result the younger members of the group are beginning to question the basic tenets of the Dyspeptic creed. Of course, you might think this was a good thing. You might even take it as a vindication of your hug-a-Dyspeptic-today initiative. But such a policy cannot have as its rationale the *protection* of Dyspeptic culture. You haven't protected it; you've eroded it. The way to preserve its character would have been to encourage your non-Dyspeptic citizens to treat them with contempt. For it was under such conditions that the Dyspeptic culture arose, and under such conditions that it will best perpetuate itself.

Given that ethnic or tribal traditions often arise in adversarial circumstances, there may be no easy way to reconcile the preservationist ethic with the liberal ideal of respect for humanity. Say violin playing is common among some Romani groups because it's one of the few money-making activities a landless, migrant group can maintain: grant them some ethnoterritorial entitlement, and the violins get turned into hoes. Kymlicka dodges the issue when he claims that decayed, weakened cultures can be rejuvenated: "indigenous groups [can] become vibrant and diverse cultures, drawing on their cultural traditions while incorporating the best of the modern world, if given the requisite preconditions." We can't expect much purchase from this decidedly ad hoc, difference-splitting approach. Let me put aside, for a moment, the question whether we should legitimately desire this or that culture to be "diverse" (what it means for a culture to be internally diverse will be the subject of a later discussion). It should be apparent that cultural sustenance and cultural support are not the same. Often one must choose. There is no shortage of liberation movements that call for the erasure, or, anyway, transformation, of the very identities they serve—as appears to be the case with some versions of radical gay politics and, indeed, with some Dalit liberation movements in India.[46] To make sense of such a politics, we must see it as advancing the interests of its constituents as persons, in the first instance, not as identity holders. A movement for poor people does not seek to affirm their identity *as* poor people. Here the object isn't preservation but cultural or socioeconomic change. Of the Devourer and Prolific, Blake says, "these two classes of men are always upon earth, & they should be enemies; whoever tries to reconcile them seeks to destroy existence." Where negation *is* affirmation, in this Blakean sense, one must finally decide whether it is culture or people who are owed respect: and this is one difference that cannot be split.

THE DIVERSITY PRINCIPLE

Here are two touchstones of English political thought:

But the inclinations of men are diverse, according to their diverse Constitutions, Customes, Opinions; as we may see in those things we apprehend by sense, as by tasting, touching, smelling; but much more in those which pertain to the common actions of life, where what this man commends, (that is to say, calls Good) the other undervalues, as being Evil; Nay, very often the same man at diverse times, praises, and dispraises the same thing. Whilst thus they doe, necessary it is there should be discord, and strife: They are therefore so long in the state of War, as by reason of the diversity of the present appetites, they mete Good and Evil by diverse measures.

If it were only that people have diversities of taste, that is reason enough for not attempting to shape them all after one model. But different persons also require different conditions for their spiritual development; and can no more exist healthily in the same moral, than all the variety of plants can exist in the same physical atmosphere and climate. The same things which are helps to one person towards the cultivation of his higher nature, are hindrances to another. . . . unless there is a corresponding diversity in their modes of life, they neither obtain their fair share of happiness, nor grow up to the mental, moral, and aesthetic statures of which their nature is capable.

The first is from Thomas Hobbes's *De Cive*, where we learn that what causes "discord, and strife" is not so much that men fail to seek the good as that they have conflicting notions of it. The second, of course, is a passage I've already invoked from Mill's *On Liberty*.[47] For Mill's precursors—for Hobbes, quite emphatically—diversity was a problem to be solved, not a condition to be promoted. It is only with Mill that a sense of diversity as something that might be of value enters into mainstream Anglo-American political thought. Mill, influenced by the romantic fascination with difference, by Wilhelm von Humboldt's "holistic individualism," celebrates diversity as both a condition and a consequence of individuality.[48] Yet Mill's diversity doctrine really has two faces. Here, diversity is an anterior fact about human beings, which must be accommodated by a society conducive to their well-being. But diversity is also implicated in those "experiments of living" he called for; in this sense, diversity would beget diversity, for a population exposed to a variation of circumstances would grow more various. How we should be treated depends on who we are; but who we will be must be affected by how we are treated. Accordingly, it was not merely the dead hand of custom that Mill feared; there was much in modernity that concerned him, too. Indeed, to a startling degree, he anticipates contemporary complaints about the putatively flattening, homogenizing effect of mass communication and mass culture, of globalization:

The circumstances which surround different classes and individuals, and shape their characters, are daily becoming more assimilated. . . . Comparatively speaking, they now read the same things, listen to the same things, see the same things, go to the same places, have their hopes and fears directed to the same objects, have the same rights and liberties, and the same means of asserting them. . . . And the assimilation is still proceeding. All the political changes of the age promote it, since they all tend to raise the low and to lower the high. Every extension of education promotes it, because education brings people under common influences, and gives them access to the general stock of facts and sentiments. Improvements in the means of communication promote it, by bringing the inhabitants of distant places into personal contact, and keeping up a rapid flow of changes of residence between one place and another. The increase of commerce and manufactures promotes it, by diffusing more widely the advantages of easy circumstances.[49]

And he goes on to denounce the rising role of public opinion in the affairs of state, or what is now familiarly condemned as "poll-driven politics."

The tree Mill planted (we may as well honor his own fondness for arboreal metaphors) has grown up to be mighty indeed. In contemporary political theory, the notion that diversity for its own sake is an important value—what we can call the diversity principle—represents a powerful strain. It has been said that Mill was a transitional figure between an old liberalism, wherein freedom was important because it enabled people to discover truths about morality and metaphysics, and a new liberalism, wherein freedom was important because there were no such truths.[50] The emergent skepticism, needless to say, has itself become a powerful dogma, and some of its adherents have noted with disapproval that Mill's defense of diversity takes fullest form in a book called *On Liberty*: his enthusiasm for diversity was great; it was not boundless. He had no love for theocrats and despots, for ways of life where individuality was stifled. His commitment to diversity did not displace his intertwined ideals of human well-being and self-development. "The progressive principle," he wrote, "is antagonistic to the sway of Custom."[51] Is the progressive principle, then, the ultimate yardstick of success? As far as contemporary diversitarians are concerned, Mill may have led the tribe of political theorists through the deserts of homogeneity, and pointed the way home, but, like Moses, he did not enter the Promised Land.

Menaced by Monism?

Many theorists—among them William Galston, John Gray, Bhikhu Parekh, and Uday Singh Mehta—hold the great enemy to be *monism*, and, in particular, the philosophical monism they associate with the classic texts of liberalism, not excluding Mill himself. The monist tradition that Parekh has painstakingly traced, in his *Rethinking Multiculturalism*, starts with Plato and haunts us still; it is characterized by a belief in the universality of human nature and (in Parekh's rather abstract formulation) an ontological and moral preference for similarities over differences. Rawls is faulted for his metaphysical entanglements, the unacknowledged sectarianism of his liberal commitments; Raz is faulted for his bigoted emphasis on autonomy; Kymlicka is faulted for the requirement that national minorities must, at least in some measure, respect liberal principles of individual liberty. The trail of the monist serpent is over them all. None of these approaches, Parekh complains, takes diversity *simpliciter* to be the value; all see sameness where they ought to recognize difference.

And Mill, naturally, is a chief offender here, with his culpably individualist conception of diversity; indeed, Parekh and others insist, he gives himself away when he intolerantly suggests that the ways of John Knox are not as worthy of admiration as those of Pericles.[52] The gravamen of the indictment, of course, is the familiar point that Mill was an autonomist, and that autonomism is an ethnocentric preference, ruled out by pluralism.

In fact, Mill is truly ethnocentric precisely where he suspends the requirement of autonomy. In the first chapter of *On Liberty*, Mill says: "The only purpose for which power can be exercised over any member of a civilized community, against his will, is to prevent harm to others." So far, so autonomist, you might think—but then he offers this qualification: "It is, perhaps, hardly necessary to say that this doctrine is meant to apply only to human beings in the maturity of their faculties," and so excludes children and "those backward states of society in which the race itself may be considered as in its nonage."[53] In this, Mill anticipates precisely the concessions urged by strong pluralists like John Gray. The Mill who says that even the despotism of an Akbar or a Charlemagne can be beneficial for backward societies cannot be accused of foisting the ethic of autonomy upon cultures for whom autonomy is not a value.[54] It is not the smallest of ironies that these critics of Mill accept his arguments at their weakest—and reject them at their strongest.

For inasmuch as Mill was guilty of "monism," it was expressed in his belief that all humanity should be given the opportunity of self-development. Mill's monism, if we are to call it that, underwrote his fierce opposition to American slavery, that "scourge to humanity." With its insistence on the ultimate similitude of humankind, on the ultimate oneness of human nature, the language of monism stipples his writings on the subject. "I have yet to learn that anything more detestable than this has been done by human beings towards human beings in any part of the earth," he wrote, and the force of his condemnation flows largely from that echo, his insistence upon the essential sameness of victim and victimizer: *by human beings, toward human beings.* In an article published in *Fraser's Magazine,* in 1850—rebutting Carlyle's "Occasional Discourse on the Negro Question"—Mill wrote that had Carlyle less disdain for "the analytical examination of human nature," he would have

> escaped the vulgar error of imputing every difference which he finds among human beings to an original difference of nature. As well might it be said, that of two trees, sprung from the same stock, one cannot be taller than another but from greater vigour in the original seedling. Is nothing to be attributed to soil, nothing to climate, nothing to difference of exposure— has no storm swept over the one and not the other, no lightning scathed it, no beast browsed on it, no insects preyed on it, no passing stranger stript off its leaves or its bark?[55]

Mill's polemic, tellingly, uses the word "human" fully twenty-eight times: it is his argument distilled into a predicate. Slaves are, as he says elsewhere, "human beings, entitled to human rights."[56] The universalizing rhetoric could not be clearer, nor his violation of Parekh's prescriptions more blatant. If this is monism, should we be so quick to cleanse ourselves of it?

Parekh, we saw, denounces those who would assert the universality of human nature, but the adversaries of such universalism are not always the best of company. It hardly needs to be remarked that liberal universalism, or what's sometimes derogated as "essentialist humanism," did not have the field to itself in the Enlightenment. Among the principal dissenters from such universalism were the early theorists of racial difference, and their ideas were inevitably enlisted to justify slavery and colonialism, as they later justified genocide. In the history of ideas, then, one should not assume that it's universalism that has the most to answer for, or that ascriptions of diversity should always command our admiration. Let me go further. Our moral modernity consists chiefly of extending the principle of equal respect to those who had previously been outside the compass of sympathy; in that sense, it has consisted in the ability to see similarity where our predecessors saw only difference. The wisdom was hard-won; it should not be lightly set aside.

Someone might object that it was a contingent fact that the abolitionists operated under the "logic of similarity." Perhaps they could have said that the Negro was radically Other but still should be the subject of liberal rights; or that slavery was wrong because it was a form of domination, corrupting of the master. In truth, many abolitionists did think that that the Negro was inferior to "the white man," and that the two could not live side by side in circumstances of equality. That is, the typical abolitionist didn't look at the black man and see a mirror of himself. But his arguments invariably drew on the basis of some point of similarity: that, like the white man, the Negro was a child of God; or that, like the white man, the Negro was capable of suffering. They saw, and insisted upon, some fundamental resemblance. Had they not done so, it is hard to see how they could have persuaded anyone.[57] And the logic of abolition (as Catherine Gallagher and others have pointed out) would go on to sponsor the campaigns against "wage slavery" during the Industrial Revolution. This is why I say that the progression of our moral modernity is the expansion of what Parekh decries as the logic of similitude. Parekh gives us no reason to suppose that denial of similarity has anything of this sort to recommend it. Is the assumption of a universal human nature (that mainstay of egalitarians, of levelers, of campaigners against slavery) necessarily a malign one? Is it even, properly construed, untrue? If Mill, Raz, Kymlicka, and the others fail to recognize diversity *in se* as an ultimate value, as Parekh alleges, then so much the worse for diversity. Mill's ardent, if not limitless, devotion to diversity requires no further belaboring; nor does the centrality of pluralism to Raz and Kymlicka. Any version of "monism" so weak that they can all be charged with it is surely a version of monism which liberals should happily defend.

Diversity Counted Out

The diversity principle can refer to two different maps, in a manner of speaking. In one, we are charting a *modus vivendi* among various culturally disparate communities, perhaps even sovereign polities; in the other, we're charting the diversity *internal* to a society or a way of life. Although there can be no sharp and stable distinction between them, the first I shall call "external" diversity, the second "internal" diversity. The two versions of diversity can complement each other, as Mill hoped they would; but they are as likely to be at odds. The two versions are at odds when, say, a liberal state takes measures to preserve the authentic character of a subsidiary theocratic community, enabling it to purify itself and reducing its internal diversity. The two versions are at odds, conversely, when such communities are liberalized, becoming more internally diverse, but also more like other communities. Whenever diversity involves not persons but peoples—whenever it carries associational depth—we can expect a conflict between the two ways of talking about diversity.

The case for internal diversity usually echoes the Millian case for diversity in the service of well-being. Bernard Williams has put the matter with elegant simplicity: "if there are many and competing genuine values, then the greater the extent to which a society tends to be single-valued, the more genuine values it neglects or suppresses. More, to this extent, must mean better."[58] Notice that the comparison is not between a world with one culture and a world with many; the comparison is between a rich, variegated culture and a narrow, pinched one. The implication is that persons require real choices, adequate options, in order to achieve their individuality. (The position also dovetails with the notion that "experiments in living" are likely to be valuable.)[59] But how diverse do you have to be to qualify as diverse?

To get the answer to this question right, we must make a distinction among kinds of value. Williams is right, in my view, if by "genuine values," he means those universal values that matter independently of our projects and identities. There is a determinate (if as yet unmapped) list of these, and a society that makes more of them available is, in virtue of that fact, better than one that does not. But I have already suggested that our identities are a further source of value (and in chapter 6 I shall say more about this topic, under the rubric of "project-dependent" values). Once we grasp this, we can see that sometimes we could increase the range of values available in a society by making new projects and identities available; and that this is a process that can proceed effectively without limit. To insist that a society's offering more values *this* way is a good thing is to make a much more controversial claim.[60]

Earlier in this book, I referred to Gerald Dworkin's observation that more options are not necessarily better: we don't necessary want the option to take heroin; we may be grateful for guardrails.[61] "What does have intrinsic value is not having choices but being recognized as the kind of creature who is capable of making choices," Gerald Dworkin says. "But, of course, that it is better intrinsically to be a creature that makes choices does not imply that it is always an improvement to have more."[62] And the same would apply to the notion that more values are necessarily better, understood as a claim about project-dependent values.

But maybe the trouble here is more basic: Can diversity be measured by enumerable features? Does it really make sense to describe societal cultures as having more or fewer values? Recall Charles Taylor's reference to "a certain kind of self-giving heroism"; is that one value, or the intersection of two (an ideal of self-giving plus an ideal of heroism)? Plainly, this isn't a conversation anybody should want to start. If pluralism urges us to see that values are not comparable, common sense surely suggests that values are not countable. We simply don't know how to line up two societies and say that one "contains" (and the key verb here is "contains," not "tolerates") more values; there are no determinate numbers here, no sums that can be stacked against each other in some scalar fashion.[63]

Galston, enlisting Williams's argument, casts his defense of internal diversity in a classical mode. He supposes that the "diversity of human types" exists prior to cultural self-determination. Then "narrow-valued societies"—his example is the Sparta of legend—"will allow only a small fraction of their inhabitants to live their lives in a manner consistent with their flourishing and satisfaction."[64] But how did Sparta get Spartan in the first place? The transition from some prepolitical arrangement of happy diversity to the straitened city-state has to be spelled out if we're to share Galston's concerns. For perhaps it happened that people of Spartan disposition gravitated together and formed Sparta, in which case the claim of general misery becomes implausible. Perhaps, that is, the polity has the character it has because it legitimately reflects and expresses their preferences. Without an additional premise, we can't assume that Sparta denied the diversity of its inhabitants. Even if we suppose that Sparta is not populated by Spartans and only a small fraction of its inhabitants happily accept the Spartan way, then what we have isn't a case for diversity *simpliciter* but a case against the legitimacy of this particular social order, for it is evidently rejected by most of its citizens. Then again, if Sparta isn't populated by Spartans—if it is populated, instead, by Athenians—we can't describe it as a "narrow-valued society." What's hard to imagine is a legitimate, transgenerationally stable Sparta that meets his description.

Now, imagine a region—call it Monomania—in which people assigned themselves into congenial groups: the warriors flocked with the warriors; the lazy pastoralists flocked with lazy pastoralists; the industrious worshipers of Apollo cohabitated with their ilk. We would thus have many narrow-valued societies, perhaps trading goods and services among them, each (let's stipulate) governing itself according to liberal-democratic principles, and each, pace Galston, allowing all their inhabitants to "live their lives in a manner consistent with their flourishing and satisfaction." Lest this sound like a remote fantasy, let me venture that some measure of such value segregation is a familiar feature of liberal polities: there is Main Street and there is Castro Street; there is Greenwich and there is Greenwich Village. Our recognition that people who share values and aspirations will seek each other out is one reason we take freedom of movement and association so seriously.[65]

Spectatorial Diversity

So far I've been discussing the challenges posed by talk of internal diversity; when we fix our gaze upon external diversity, we encounter a separate set of challenges. For one thing, once we have reconfigured the social realm into a confederacy of difference, a grid of communities hewing each to its own customs and creeds, we have to ask for whom diversity is a value. Now, the diversity principle calls for the promotion of diversity for its own sake. To hold that diversity *simpliciter* is of value, you will not need reminding, is a very different thing from saying that a range of social forms is good because people are various, or that the preferences of individuals should be respected, or that the freedom of association among them should be given wide berth, or that different forms of sodality are important in human affairs. Obviously, too, external diversity does not describe a society filled with diversitarians. For whom, then, is the principle a principle? Plainly, its implicit constituency is the tribe of liberals. If the principle is more than a simple peacekeeping expedient, that is, one must conclude that the vista of diversity—the spectacle of the emperor's zoo, so to speak—is essentially there for our appreciation.[66]

Accordingly, the problem with many arguments for "diversity" as an ideal is that they do not respect what Ronald Dworkin calls the "endorsement constraint," which says that you cannot make someone better off by forcing her to do something she does not herself endorse as valuable. In *The Spirit of the Laws*, that charming compendium of cross-cultural commentary, the baron de Montesquieu warned that one must be "careful not to change the general spirit of a nation" because

> If the character is generally good, what difference do a few faults make?
> One could constrain its women, make laws to correct their mores and limit their luxury, but who knows whether one would not lose a certain taste that would be the source of the nation's wealth and a politeness that attracts foreigners to it?[67]

But spectator-sport diversity would seem to have more aesthetic than moral force. I may fervently want there to be Amish driving buggies, Mennonites milking cows, and Shakers shaking on their exquisitely crafted furniture; but it would be a moral error to take measures, therefore, to discourage members of these picturesque communities from leaving and joining ours. *We're* not the ones getting up at four and cleaning the stables, and they're not doing it for our delectation. The decision of whether to uphold "tradition" is for them to make, not for us.

Now, many theorists have cast the diversity principle in terms of biodiversity, taking Mill's analogy of plants and their climates almost literally. Thus David Ingram, after warning us about a "global monoculture of mass-produced and mass-consumed commodities," concludes, "cultural diversity, then, is not simply a spiritual or existential issue but a matter of physical survival." (To illustrate the idea that "emancipation from tradition" may be "unhealthy and destructive of a genuinely human form of existence," he adduces the Ik people, made famous by Colin Turnbull's ethnographic account. For Ingram, the

Ik "represent an extreme example of an individualism that has increasingly come to the fore in our own profit-oriented society.")[68] On a planet afflicted by massive inequality, a planet whose richest country spends only derisory amounts in foreign assistance, you have to wonder about the biodiversity analogy: it seems to call for retreat, a roping-off, when the important struggle is for humanitarian engagement. The larger trouble with the analogy, though, is that it denies agency. Although there are Mennonite farm boys who have elected to become East Village disk jockeys, yellow larkspurs, as a rule, do not decide to become daisies; nor is there any dissent in the social order of the giant sequoia.

It should be said that there are villages that receive government subvention to preserve their quaint cultural differentia. These range from the show villages of the Palóc in Western Hungary to certain Hmong communities in Vietnam, which are allowed to participate in a revenue-generating tourist program so long as they agree to abjure running water, consumer electronics, and other such appurtenances that would spoil the Westerner's enjoyment of their "authenticity." What has been created by this programmatic promotion of diversity is a sort of Epcot ethnicity for the curious traveler.

Uniformly Different

I don't say this by way of condemnation; people have to make a living. But as these instances suggest, upholding differences among groups may entail imposing uniformity within them. As I mentioned earlier, this is one of the ways that internal and external diversity can be in tension. For culture is a Tree of Porphyry: differences and distinctions go all the way down. In the real world, the entrenchment of uniformities happens through the authorization and appointment of elites and "representatives" within the group; through the mobilization of state resources on behalf of such representatives; through the whole apparatus of "cultural autonomy." You will recall that Avishai Margalit and Moshe Habertal, in "Liberalism and the Right to Culture," argue that people have an "overriding interest" that sponsors a right that their culture remain unmolested by outsiders. But much depends on precisely who counts as an outsider. Just because, as Locke said, every church is orthodox to itself, when we accommodate the dissenting church, we may—from the perspective of that church's dissidents—be fortifying another orthodoxy.[69]

Indeed, when multiculturalists like Kymlicka say that there are so many "cultures" in this or that country, what drops out of the picture is that every "culture" represents not only difference but the elimination of difference: the group represents a clump of relative homogeneity, and that homogeneity is perpetuated and enforced by regulative mechanisms designed to marginalize and silence dissent from its basic norms and mores. From a historical perspective, nationalism might be described as imperialism with contiguity. Like treason, tribalism never prospers, as Ernest Gellner dryly noted; else none dare call it tribalism. Hence when a metropolitan *francité* is imposed upon adjoining regions—regions where a little earlier a salient identity might have been Savoyard, Gascon, Burgundian, Provençal—we celebrate the birth of a nation. "While liberal pluralists celebrate legitimate diversity among cultures," Galston notes, "they suspect that diversity will almost always exist within culture as well and that a culture's smoothly homogeneous public face reflects the covert operation of power."[70] The intriguing question, though, is how "legitimate" diversity is to be qualified.

For the erasure of differences within social groups is not necessarily something to be condemned. Rather, it raises the question of whether there are certain norms or uniformities that are useful in preserving a benign social order—whether some measure of homogeneity is a good thing. I began this section by juxtaposing two passages on diversity, one by Hobbes and one by Mill. We make a mistake if we assume that wisdom reposes in only the second.

Hobbes was a conventionalist: he thought we could promulgate a true moral philosophy because the truth, in this realm, was something that human beings made up. It was the responsibility of the polity, the educative state, to rear its citizens with such norms and values that they could together find what he called the "highway to peace." Much on the Hobbesian menu will have little appeal to us; but, as I've said, it seems that we do want our public schools to promulgate some values, some kind of social rationality. I'll have much more to say about this in the context of "soul making" in the next chapter.

Accepting value pluralism means we must set diversity among other values cherished by other communities, including the value of imposing ethical uniformity. "We might argue that richness, variety, and difference are goods in themselves," John Tomlinson points out with his customary clarity, "but then, under other considerations, so are order, uniformity, and universality. Babel and Esperanto both have their enthusiasts."[71]

Certainly, if you care about autonomy—or even, for that matter, about the promulgation of social rationality—you cannot take diversity to be the ultimate good. "Talk of diversity and difference too often proceeds without taking adequate account of the degree of moral convergence it takes to sustain a constitutional order that is liberal, democratic, and characterized by widespread bonds of civic friendship and cooperation," Stephen Macedo writes. "Not every form of cultural and religious diversity is to be celebrated, and not all forms of what can be labeled 'marginalization' and 'exclusion' are to be regretted or apologized for. Profound forms of sameness and convergence should not only be prayed for but planned for without embarrassment."[72] Macedo is surely right, even though the amount of convergence required may be rather less than you might think. But, to circle back to the observation with which this chapter began, the United States has never been less culturally diverse, and never more celebratory of cultural diversity: and these two things are not unrelated. Those who want everyone to embrace diversity have themselves imposed a substantial monism.

Often, when we worry about homogeneity—if I may venture a diagnosis—it's because we take it to be evidence of a previous crime against autonomy, rather as the vistas of a grassy plain may be less pleasing if taken to be the result of recent deforestation. Conversely, it may be that many of us value diversity not because it is a primordial good but because we take it to be a correlative of liberty, of nondomination. But if autonomy is the sponsoring concern, the diversity principle—the value of diversity *simpliciter*—cannot command our loyalty.

The boundaries of Millian diversity—diversity in the service of individual well-being—should cause no embarrassment, then. It is a strength, not a weakness, of Mill's conception of diversity that it did not prevent him from making judgments about cultural practices—

whether those related to his own heritage, like the murderous rampages of John Knox and the subjection of women in Victorian England, or those utterly foreign to him, such as the foot-binding customs of the Chinese. Indeed, nothing more persuasively vindicates Millian diversity than those very moments in his writing that have been castigated by those intolerant of intolerance of intolerance. To insist that liberals, qua liberals, must abstain from judgments of this sort is to exile them from genuine human engagement.

Chapter Five

∼ Soul Making

SOULS AND THE STATE—THE SELF-MANAGEMENT CARD—
RATIONAL WELL-BEING—IRRATIONAL IDENTITIES—SOUL
MAKING AND STEREOTYPES—EDUCATED SOULS—CONFLICTS
OVER IDENTITY CLAIMS

SOULS AND THE STATE

In Mill's view, the excellence of government was to be gauged by the excellence of its citizens—by its success in promoting "the virtue and intelligence of the people themselves."[1] This is one of the themes in his work that seem very old and very new. It was Plato who first taught that politics was the art of caring for souls. But the notion that the state should concern itself with the character of its citizenry could hardly be more current. It is a mainstay of the so-called republican revival, which draws inspiration from a Roman civic humanism that connects Cicero, Machiavelli, and the American Founders, and which holds that society must reproduce itself by producing good citizens. It is a mainstay, too, of the recent accounts of liberal perfectionism that challenge the ideal of liberal neutrality.[2]

But should the state really encroach upon the souls of its citizens? When the question is framed this way, many of us recoil at the prospect; and there are sound reasons for this response. For talk of soul making seems all too redolent of the sort of intrusive government interference that Popper rightly feared, of all those fateful attempts to transform human nature in pursuit of some utopian vision. Hobhouse, in a grandly martial image, called freedom of thought the "inner citadel,"[3] and we do not lightly trespass upon it. But, as a moment's reflection will remind us, this can't be the whole story. There has never been a state without some influence upon the character of its citizens. That inner citadel can feel more like a coffeehouse, alive to every group that bustles through it. Autonomy, we know, is conventionally described as an ideal of self-authorship. But the metaphor should remind us that we write in a language we did not ourselves make. If we are authors of ourselves, it is state and society that provide us with the tools and the contexts of our authorship; we may shape our selves, but others shape our shaping. And so, if the state cannot but affect our souls, we can fairly ask both how it does and how it *should* do so.

That the state's shaping of our souls should seem to need justification at all is a reflection, of course, of our moral modernity. It may be helpful to offer a (highly stylized) genealogy of our current situation to see why. When Plato spoke of the care of souls, it would not have occurred to him that the government needed to consult the citizens' conceptions in order to decide what was best for their souls. When, much later, Saint Thomas defined a law as "nothing other than an ordinance of reason for the common good, made by whoever has the community in its care,"[4] he took it for granted that concern for the common good included care of individual subjects; but he, too, would scarcely have thought it necessary to consult them about what was in their interest. On these premodern views, government might sometimes need to know what citizens wanted in order to treat them as it should. But the mere fact that a citizen wanted something would never have counted in itself as a reason for giving it to her. Sometimes, in fact, it would be necessary to try to tame the citizens' appetites, to curb or correct their desires.

With the Reformation, however, a view begins to take hold in which what is good for us depends at least in part on our own attitudes toward our acts and properties. And this is one source of Kant's notion that we are each entitled to a form of self-governance, which he called "autonomy." It is a significant step from here to the idea that we will ourselves determine what is good for us—from Kantian morality to Rawlsian "political liberalism"; but it is, in some sense (as Rawls, of course, recognized), a working out of an idea that Kant had crystallized. If to be self-governing was to be governed by one's own desires and conceptions of the good, then there was no place for the shaping by others of our ethical desires: they were the given, and the task of political morality was to try to accommodate them. To change what someone wants, then, by any means other than providing him with information will count, on this view, as a wrongful revision of his preferences.

I offer this caricatural genealogy only as an attempt to point to something that is historically quite real: the presence in our culture of two background presumptions. First, that attempts to change what people want, or hold to be valuable, infringe upon a sphere of self-management that is legitimately their own.[5] Second, that we are each equally entitled to the satisfaction of our lawful desires. Someone who sees the flourishing of individuals as a matter of the satisfaction of the desires they happen to have—and this was the view of many utilitarians—has what (after Brian Barry) is sometimes called a purely "want-regarding" understanding of human good. Much modern welfare economics, for example, assumes that the measure of the welfare of a society as a whole is a function (in the mathematical sense) of the individual welfares of each citizen, and that this is measured by the degree to which their preferences are satisfied. Such a conception of human good is consistent with both the background presumptions I have just identified. These presumptions are challenged by any conception of human good that allows that what the government should do cannot be determined solely by attention to what people want. For it will allow that certain desires may legitimately be frustrated in the name of something more than other desires; and it may well allow that your good requires that your desires be changed.

In defense of this notion, a philosophical literature has grown up in the last few decades that characterizes as "perfectionist" (an unhappily misleading term) any conception of the functioning of government that sees it as legitimate for the government (a) to promote the ethical flourishing of its citizens, while (b) relying on a more-than-want-regarding notion of what such flourishing consists in.[6] We need the second condition as well as the first, because no view could be called perfectionist that simply held that government should give us each as much as possible of what we already desire. Perfectionists wish the government to help make our lives go better by making *us* better: deferring to our current desires can only leave us as we are. But the content of the first condition is important too: perfectionism constructs policies whose aim is to make our lives go better, not just to provide a stable context within which we make our own lives. Government, for the perfectionist, ought to help each of us to make a good life, and thus must take a view about the central ethical question: what is it for a life to go well? Any government, perfectionist or not, will help to provide a context in which we can pursue our own answer to this question in our own life. For the security of body and property provided by the law is going to be helpful on (almost) any such conception. But a perfectionist government will take a substantive view about some aspects of what our life's going well consists in and not just about the question what treatment by others—assault, theft, murder—is morally impermissible. Which is why it is appropriate to speak of *ethical* flourishing. Whether or not you find views of this form congenial, perfectionism has been at the center of some arguments that do shed light on the set of issues that will concern me in this chapter.

If perfectionists are riding high, they do so with their heads ducked; the creed remains more often criticized than adopted. Rawls, of course, insisted that governments should be neutral among different reasonable conceptions of the good life, taking the fact of pluralism—the fact that there is a variety of such conceptions—to be an inevitable condition of modern democratic life. This liberal neutralism has become decidedly less fashionable of late; even aside from the perplexities we touched on in chapter 3, it is the umpire's creed, and "kill the ump" has become a rallying cry of postmodernism. But the sort of skepticism that rejects neutralism rejects, even more swiftly, the transcendental certitudes that are (as Rawls thought) implied by perfectionism. Nor does perfectionism sit well with those forms of liberalism that take negative liberty—freedom from coercion—to be the ultimate political value; these encompass a range of political views, but for the purposes at hand, we can group them together under the rubric "negative liberalism."[7]

For negative liberals, there is a reasonable place for government in guaranteeing security of life and property and creating the framework of contract, because these are matters that have to do with how we treat one another; because they are, in this sense, moral matters. But negative liberals claim that the government should not interfere in the ethical dimensions of our lives, should not be guided by notions as to what lives are good and bad for a person to lead, once he or she has met the enforceable demands of moral duty. And so, more specifically, the government should not seek to make me a better person for my own sake. Here, the worry about perfectionism is that it entails a paternalist encroachment upon our personal autonomy: it rides roughshod over, or, worse yet, aims to alter, our desires.

As it happens, the most influential forms of perfectionism in recent years have tended to focus, precisely, upon the promotion of autonomy, which is seen as an element of well-being, both its precondition and its result. In these accounts, no particular sort of life, or set of very specific values—aside from the value of autonomy—is being promoted. None of this, of course, endears such perfectionism to the critics of autonomy. (Having discussed their complaints in chapter 2, I will not dwell on them here.) But it's worth stressing that liberal perfectionists often insist that they are pluralists, too; they consider that human flourishing may take a multiplicity of forms.[8] While they *are* perfecting us, they are seeking only to enable a more effective pursuit of our own conceptions of the good. It is this fact that makes it possible for some liberal perfectionists to deny that they are perfectionists at all: for they can say that while they do indeed favor government promotion of the flourishing of individuals (thus meeting the first condition I laid down), it is in the name of those individuals' own conceptions of the good (thus arguably not meeting the second). "I do not aim, in enhancing your autonomy, to change your desires," the liberal can say, "only to help you carry them out." But while the pursuit by others of my autonomy in this sense certainly can take my conception of the good life as given, it will still count as perfectionist, in the broad sense I have defined, if, first, it rules out certain conceptions of the good life (and thus certain aims) as unreasonable, or if, second, it aspires to enhance my autonomy by getting me to refrain from acting on (or give up altogether) certain of my desires because they are inconsistent with my conception of the good.

So we shouldn't assume that perfectionism is incompatible with a concern for autonomy, or, indeed, for negative liberty. The much misunderstood Thomas Hill Green, to whom we owe the classificatory distinction between positive and negative liberty, affirmed his own creed of perfectionist individualism when he wrote: "Human society indeed is essentially a society of self-determined persons. There can be no progress of society which is not a development of capacities on the part of persons composing it, considered as ends in themselves."[9] But the best illustration of how perfectionism and personal liberty may be reconciled is provided by Mill, who is both a perfectionist and stoutly antipaternalist. In defending something like liberal democracy, Mill is at his most perfectionist, even as he provides an eloquent endorsement of the "endorsement constraint":

> Its superiority in reference to present well-being rests upon two principles, of as universal truth and applicability as any general propositions which can be laid down respecting human affairs. The first is, that the rights and interests of every or any person are only secure from being disregarded when the person interested is himself able, and habitually disposed, to stand up for them. The second is, that the general prosperity attains a greater height, and is more widely diffused, in proportion to the amount and variety of the personal energies enlisted in promoting it.[10]

Here and elsewhere, Mill insists that a government promote the virtues and interests and excellences of its citizens *and* that such things are secured only if the individual is disposed to endorse them, indeed, actively "stand up for them." His critics have sometimes accused him of confusion in this—is he advocating an antipaternalist paternalism?—but the confusion may lie in the minds of his critics. Paternalism itself is something that we rightly have divided feelings about. (Theorists of paternalism tend either to admit the legitimacy of certain forms of paternalism or, by some definitional device or other, declare that the good stuff doesn't count as paternalism.)[11] Most modern citizens are little worried by laws that take aim at self-regarding harm, so long as they do not interfere with our ability to make a life. In the face of human irrationality, then, we have helmet laws and seatbelt laws, and we typically see them as enforcing rational behavior, not promoting any particular conception of the good. In general, someone's ability to create a life isn't eroded by his wearing a helmet when he rides a motorcycle; and where it might be—as with the occasional Sikh complainant—exemptions are common.[12] The state may also launch safety campaigns, exhorting us to take self-protective measures, and so alter our beliefs and desires. As I say, most people accept that such measures to combat irrationality (if this is what they are) lie within the scope of legitimate state involvement. But where does that scope end?

Antiperfectionists as well as perfectionists can have a broad conception of that scope. For example, antiperfectionists can (and often do) advocate the promulgation of civic virtues. The antiperfectionist rationale might be that our liberal democratic state requires citizens who share certain basic values and beliefs. Moreover, having these virtues might be necessary for someone to be able to participate, fully and effectively, in the public sphere. A democracy should promulgate the value of voting, for instance, because if people didn't vote, the polity would falter. Here, you could draw an analogy with the rules of the road. We teach people how to be good drivers (which involves skills, and knowledge, and, perhaps, certain pro-attitudes and con-attitudes toward safe or reckless driving practices) so that the nation's traffic system works *and* so that individuals can be directly advantaged by driving, if they choose to drive. When antiperfectionists inculcate civic virtues, then, they do so for such consequential reasons. The state's principal concern isn't with the ethical success of our lives; it's with the stability and survival of the political order.[13] This is what makes these rationales *anti*perfectionist: I am made virtuous not for my own sake—not so that *I* may flourish—but because it is necessary if I am to serve the commonweal and to treat others as I should.

Yet do these liberals really regard civic virtues—and they can be quite eloquent when they describe the character that is created by, or conduces to, liberal democracy—as goods *only* because they happen to serve such other ends? They may say that they are goods roughly in the way that the national highway system is a good: something the modern state requires to function. But while one could imagine some revolution in transportation that would make the roads superfluous (what happened to those strap-on rocket packs we were promised, anyway?), there are no equivalent scenarios that would obviate character traits such as "a reflective, self-critical attitude, tolerance, openness to change, self-control, a willingness to engage in dialogue with others, and a willingness to revise and shape projects in order to respect the rights of others or in response to fresh insight into one's own character and ideals" (I take this list from Stephen Macedo's *Liberal Virtues*).[14] I think it would be plausible to describe these traits as good in themselves. Yet to accept that they are intrinsically good for those who have them, and to favor their promotion in virtue of that fact, would be to defect from antiperfectionism.

Even liberals who are suspicious of civic-virtue talk often take personal autonomy to be something of inherent value: and, as I have already said, such autonomism (as its critics, and some of its supporters, insist) may be perfectionist. But the distinction between aiming at the virtue of citizens for their own sake, on the one hand, and for the sake of the polity, on the other, can be hard to draw, particularly in the context of education. Consider Amy Gutmann's proposal that "a state of democratic education tries to teach ... what might best be called *democratic* virtue: the ability to deliberate, and hence to participate in conscious social reproduction."[15] Clearly, the proposal combines a concern for the welfare of the polity (the widespread inculcation of this virtue being necessary for its stability and survival) and for the political equality of the individual (who would otherwise be less able to shape, reflectively, his political environment). Yet you might still feel that this gloss left something out. To put it schematically, even if my (internal) deliberations and resultant votes made no difference to the world—and quite aside from the aggregate benefits of having lots of voters—there might still be a sense that it was *good for me* to have participated in this way. The values of citizenship have become part of the ethical dimension of my life, part of who I am.

And these are the issues that I want to explore in this chapter: whether and when the state may intervene to increase the prospects of my ethical success. To get a sense of what's at stake, let me return to the question of the ethical evaluation of one's single human life.[16] Living a life means filling the time between birth (or at any rate adulthood) and death with a pattern of attempts and achievements that may be assessed ethically, in retrospect, as successful or unsuccessful, in whole or in part. And the ethical dimensions of the life include *both* the extent to which a person has created and experienced things—such as relationships, works of art, and institutions—that are objectively significant *and* the degree to which she has lived up to the projects she has set for herself (projects defined in part by way of her identifications). A life has gone well if a person has mostly done for others what she owed them (and is thus morally successful) and has succeeded in creating things of significance and in fulfilling her ambitions (and is thus ethically successful).[17] Your individual identity, your individuality, defines your ambitions, determines what achievements have significance in your own particular life. Your individuality makes certain things a significant part of the measure of your life's success and failure, even though they would not be elements of the measure of success in every life. In my novelist's life—a life that is a novelist's life because I have chosen to make it one—the fact that I have *not* written that witty and intelligent satire of contemporary urban life that I have been struggling toward is a significant failure. My life is diminished by it. In your philosopher's life, the witty and intelligent satire you *have* written is an accidental thing, adding little to your life's value; and its cost was that you failed to complete the thinking-through of metaphysical realism that would have made your life wholly more satisfactory.

To create a life, in other words, is to interpret the materials that history has given you. Your character, your circumstances, your psychological constitution, including the beliefs and preferences generated by the interaction of your innate endowments and your experience: all these need to be taken into account in shaping a life. They are not constraints on that shaping; they are its materials. As we come to maturity, the identities we make, our individualities, are interpretive responses to our talents and disabilities, and the changing social, semantic, and material contexts we enter at birth; and we develop our identities dialectically with our capacities and circumstances, because the latter are in part the product of what our identities lead us to do. A person's shaping of her life flows from her beliefs and from a set of values, tastes, and dispositions of sensibility, all of these influenced by various forms of social identity: let us call all these together a person's ethical self.

Now, I've identified one strain of Mill's liberalism with the view that I should be permitted (in particular, by the state) to make whatever life flows from my choices, provided that I give you what I owe you and do you no harm. But, of course, the fact that each of us has a life to make can at least raise the possibility that others, the state among them, ought to act to help us in that project. And at least some of these possibilities entail some sort of involvement in our *ethical selves*. What complicates matters further is that, as we saw, such involvement has the potential to affect not merely the fulfillment of our ambitions, but the nature of our ambitions. All of which suggests that Platonic notion of politics as the art of caring for souls; which is why I shall be speaking of "soul making."

By "soul making" I mean the project of intervening in the process of interpretation through which each citizen develops an identity—and doing so with the aim of increasing her chances of living an ethically successful life. My particular focus here will be on soul making as a *political* project, something done by the state, and so it will be important to distinguish between different ways in which the state may affect my ethical life. Of course, governments must affect how lives go: for government must enforce contracts and provide the physical security—from assault and the destruction of our property—that is the background to the pursuit of any reasonable life at all. And these acts will certainly affect the circumstances within which I make my life and, thus, the actions I perform, and may well impact my identifications as well. Joseph Raz rightly directs our attention to the role of state-created forms in shaping our lives and identifications: my ambitions might require me to serve my country in the army, and the state, of course, is what makes that option available.[18] Still, providing the option of military service is soul making only if it is done, at least in part, to improve the ethical prospects of those who take it up, by altering their identities, changing the interpretation of their circumstances that guides their lives.

So, obviously, not everything that affects my choices entails soul making. As I say, simply providing people with information (and thus changing their wants and beliefs) isn't soul making, unless it is aimed at reshaping their identities; often it isn't, and doesn't. On the other hand, an action might have a dramatic effect on people's identities, but if the effect is not part of its design, it would not, by my lights, count as soul making. Imagine a municipality that dams a river to make a hydroelectric plant; later it turns out that some group for whom the river was ethically central has changed beyond all recognition. Perhaps they worshiped the river as a powerful god; the putative defeat of this god triggered a sweeping crisis of faith. Still, building the hydroelectric plant wasn't soul making, because these identity effects weren't by design—they had no relation to what the state intended to do. (In many cases, as we'll see, the question of design is not so clear-cut.) This isn't to say that interventions aimed at increasing the ethical success of an individual will not have other aims, as well. With most obvious candidates, the aims are mixed, encompassing both the prudential good of the individual and the civic good of the polity. That a state act has some aim other than shaping my identity does not preclude its having a soul-making goal as well.

In the rest of this chapter, I'll be exploring three large areas where the notion of soul making would seem to have prospects. The first has to do with our defections from rationality: in order to promote our well-being, we may wish the state to help us remedy our incapacities of reason, and these interventions, as we'll see, can have foreseeable, intended consequences for our ethical selves, our social identities. The second has to do with the role of antidiscrimination law in sustaining or reshaping social identities; for these laws forbid only some forms of differential treatment, and in the contours of actual judicial decisions, we can see, for example, how the social meanings of gender have been reconfigured. The third area—which is the most obvious arena of soul making—has to do with social reproduction and the education of the young. Throughout, we should attend to how such soul-making interventions might encroach upon, or, contrarily, reinforce, what Mill called "individuality as an element of well-being."

A final preemptive caveat. To explore the prospects of soul making isn't to say that its bailiwick should be extended; I don't imagine I've written for or against the practice. It is a mistake—that of what Tom Kelly calls "one-way idealization"—to focus only on the imperfections of the governed, ignoring the shortcomings of the governors. We could decide against soul making, in the end, because we thought that actual governments would, in fact, make a mess of it, not because it was theoretically impossible to do justifiably and well. Clearly, human governance can amplify as well as remedy human failure, and the consequences of its actions must be judged empirically. That is why, in liberal polities, such practices are likely to be piecemeal—and why I've largely been speaking of interventions rather than transformations. As Madison says, "In framing a government which is to be administered by men over men, the great difficulty lies in this: you must first enable government to control the governed; and in the next place oblige it to control itself."[19]

THE SELF-MANAGEMENT CARD

"I'm glad I hate peas," says the child in the old sort-of joke, "because if I liked peas, I'd eat peas. And I hate peas." One form of inconsistency in our desires, which is not a logical inconsistency, has to do with the fact that we have second-order preferences, so that, to use the most obvious example, I may both want to smoke a cigarette and want not to have this first-order desire. Work has been done, notably by Harry Frankfurt, that suggests some principles by which we might adjudicate in such cases, between a mere desire and a person's real will. If I not only want to refrain from smoking but also want the first-order desire not to smoke to be effective in my actions, then, Frankfurt says, I have a "second-order volition." Its content is: that I refrain from smoking because I have a first-order desire not to smoke. What I want is not to smoke and not to smoke because I want not to.

There are a lot of ways in which this basic thought can be, and has been, developed. Raz's discussion of "nested" goals—of the ways in which intermediate goals are subsumed by our more character-defining comprehensive ones—reflects another hierarchy among our desires. Not all successful goals, or aims, or desires, or preferences make an equal contribution to well-being. On the contrary, our well-being may entail the defeat of many of our desires. Looking out the window on a high floor of a skyscraper, I may have a wild, sudden impulse to fling myself off the ledge; but I have a powerful second-order desire not to act upon it. The victim of an obsessive-compulsive disorder is happy to take a medication that will relieve him of his felt need to check, repeatedly, whether he turned off the oven. The novelist puts her head down and finishes the chapter, even though the surf outside her window beckons; or perhaps she never does resist the temptation and shudders miserably every time someone asks how the novel is coming along. It's just this sense of hierarchy among desires that sponsored the notion of "life plans" we discussed in the first chapter.

Frankfurt calls a person who has no second-order volitions a "wanton": wantons do not care about why they act. And so Frankfurt says, "When a person acts, the desire by which he is moved is either the will he wants or a will he wants to be without. When a wanton acts, it is neither."[20] Frankfurt has gone on to suggest that a person's second-order volitions reflect the fact that he cares about certain things: "A person who cares about something is, as it were, invested in it. He *identifies* himself with what he cares about in the sense that he makes himself vulnerable to losses and susceptible to benefits depending upon whether what he cares about is diminished or enhanced."

And a further reflection of what one cares about is that one has second-order volitions that derive from one's caring: "The formation of a person's will is most fundamentally a matter of his coming to care about certain things, and of his coming to care about some of them more than about others."[21]

The picture of the person that is implicit in much of what I have been saying in these chapters is of an individual with needs, tastes, values, identities, and dispositions and a capacity for rational deliberation and action. It is, as Kant suggested, because people are capable of reason that we must respect their right to self-management, what we've come to call their autonomy. A creature driven by instinct and appetite, incapable of planning, unguided by commitments, insensitive to reason or to the demands of morality: such a creature would not be entitled to the concern for its autonomy that the liberal ethical perspective entails. Such a creature would not—in the relevant sense—be making a life. We are not that second creature, but we are not unfalteringly that first creature, either. And so I shall be asking whether our pervasive irrationality provides grounds for soul making in order to help us achieve our higher-order desires: call this "the irrationality rationale." But I think it will help to approach the matter indirectly; by sketching, for purposes of contrast, a way in which the state can respond to (some of) our irrationalities that has no such soul-making aspirations.

So let me propose, as a thought experiment, a mechanism that should be congenial to even very minimalist forms of antiperfectionist liberalism—a mechanism by which the state could provide us with a tool for dealing with one form of irrationality: namely, a certain sort of weakness of will, or akrasia.

I am not going to provide an account of what weakness of the will consists in, or even of what is irrational about it.[22] Saint Paul confessed to the Romans, "For the good that I would I do not: but the evil which I would not, that I do."[23] I shall take it for granted only that (a) sometimes, like Saint Paul, we find ourselves not doing what we judge to be all-things-considered best for us to do, even when no one else's interests are at stake, and that (b) this is to breach what I shall call "the demands of reason." All of us have fallen off diets, or bought frivolous things when we had resolved to save, or left tasks to the last minute that we knew we would have done better if we had undertaken them steadily over a longer period of time. In these cases and many like them, it is natural to describe what we are doing as failing to do what reason demands.

Recognizing this, and understanding that every life would go better if we had mechanisms for controlling our akratic tendencies in at least one sphere, a modern government might step in to propose one helpful solution. Each of us will be given a government-authorized Self-Management card. With contemporary technology it would be relatively easy to set it up so that each of us could manage our appetites (whether for calories, for nicotine, for alcohol, or for heroin) in the following way. We could sign in, on the Internet, to the relevant government Web site and list those things that we did not wish to be able to buy. One would be free to bind oneself for up to a certain period in this way, so that a change of mind would be given effect only after due deliberation. By law, all goods would be classified according to categorizations relevant for this purpose, and all purchases would require the presentation of the Self-Management card, which would be swiped and read before any sale. A person who sought to buy anything that was listed as among the items proscribed on the Web site would be told that the store was not able to sell it to her, unless, of course, she went back to the Web site and altered the list. Here, we adopt Ulysses' response to the temptations of the Sirens.[24]

Notice that this is something that would be hard to arrange privately. If there were any shops that did not insist on the card, the device would not work for me. When I am dieting, I should not consume liquor or chocolates or a whole list of other high-calorie foods. I know this. I remove them from my house when I am dieting; I tell my friends not to offer them to me. But if I arrive at the supermarket, tired from work at the end of a long day, I know I will succumb and buy myself a chocolate bar. So, when I go on the diet, I simply enter chocolate onto my Self-Management account as proscribed for the period of the diet, and only a criminal will sell it to me. Since, as it happens, I am fairly law-abiding and my friends are responsible, the fact that it would be a criminal transaction to acquire some actually means that, once the entry on the Web site is done, I will not get chocolates.

Perhaps it is the case that all of us could take heroin once without becoming addicted. In that case, I might be interested in having the experience. So I might sign myself up for one dose of heroin and go out and buy it, knowing that the temptation to do so again would require my reflectively signing on and that I could resist the temptation to do that, even though, faced, in the store, with a second chance at heroin, I might not resist it. The whimsicality of our akratic desires is thus made manageable; and lives that might have failed utterly if heroin had been freely available are in fact lived successfully.

And the Self-Management card could be used to help me live up to commitments that flow from my religious identity. Suppose that, as an observant Jew, I wanted to respect the rules of kashrut, but had a weakness for ham sandwiches; or suppose I were a devout Catholic and had given up ham for Lent. The system keeps me from straying—keeps me faithful to my higher-order dietary desires when my peers are not around to help with baleful glares.

Here, then, is a state-enforced scheme that gives each of us a tool for the management of our lives; nevertheless, it is entirely up to us to decide how to make use of it. You are free to have your Self-Management card declare all goods available to you. The state here takes no view about the question of how we wish to define the challenge of our lives—if you opt for the struggle with heroin addiction (or even drift into it irrationally), this system permits it. It expresses only a second-order commitment to helping us make lives successful by whatever standards we ourselves have defined.

The Self-Management card makes clear, as I say, that the state can respond to our irrationalities—and, in particular, promote our well-being—without soul making. This is important because some people seem to think that there is a direct argument from antiperfectionist premises to the conclusion that the state, though it may play an important role in the equalization of resources or as the guarantor of basic moral obligations, has no proper role in enabling our ethical success. In fact, the state can enable our ethical success in a way that is consistent with the strictures of antiperfectionism—indeed, of negative liberalism. That is, the state can make our lives go better without imposing a conception of the good upon us, without imposing its will upon us at all.[25]

RATIONAL WELL-BEING

When the state provided me with the Self-Management card, it increased my well-being by helping me do what I really desired to do. But perhaps my well-being could be further enhanced by a state that took an interest in what I really desired. It might be, for example, that my second-order desires weren't rational, because they were affected by misinformation or cognitive incapacities.

Now I've said that the ethical evaluation of a life depends, first, on whether one has achieved one's ambitions and, second, on whether one has made or experienced anything of significance. We can call the first dimension the subjective dimension of success—not because it isn't an objective question whether one has achieved one's ambitions, but because each subject determines what her ambitions are. In creating a self—shaping one's identity—one determines the parameters of one's life and thus defines one's ambitions. Let us call the second dimension of ethical success—the creation and experience of significant things—the objective dimension. A plausible account of well-being, as we'll see, is bound to involve both these dimensions. And neither is as straightforward as we might like.

The ethical self I have spoken of requires that, in making our lives, we accumulate evidence, form beliefs, identify options for action, predict and evaluate their outcomes, and act. Ideals of rationality, as they are usually understood, involve both, so to speak, calculation and information—both instrumental and cognitive dimensions. In a variety of ways, we all fall short of these ideals. And so I want to take up some questions about how we should understand the demands of rationality with respect to ethical success, and the broader notion of well-being.

I've referred to well-being without saying much about what it might consist in, but here it will be necessary to rehearse, briskly, some of the many well-explored considerations on the topic. First of all, though well-being may involve an experiential component, it has long been clear that it cannot be reduced to the possession of hedonic mental states. In an example that James Griffin discusses, Freud preferred to end his life in torment rather than experience the addling effect of analgesia, and a well-wisher should have respected his desire.[26] Nor can well-being simply be the subjective sense that our desires have been gratified. In a famous thought experiment, Nozick asked us to imagine an Experience Machine into which we could plug ourselves; the machine would give you the illusion that you had achieved your desires— to have published a successful novel, in one of Nozick's examples— although you'd really be floating ineffectually in a tank. There *are* desires that are reducible to a phenomenology: if you borrowed an Experience Machine to satisfy your desire to hear a Bartók quartet, say, your desire might be truly satisfied. But most desires involve external objects; we decline the machine's enchantments because the desire to have written a novel isn't simply the desire to feel as if one has written a novel.[27] The satisfaction of our desires involves not just a state of mind, but a state of the world—one, in this instance, involving the real production of a real novel. That's why we don't envy the man who is living in a fool's paradise, imagining (say) his wife to be loving and faithful when she's really anything but. In general we want to believe our desires are satisfied only when they *are* satisfied. For what matters is their actual satisfaction, not (or, more precisely, not just) our believing that they are satisfied.

Then again, it's also a familiar thought that the preferences of individuals cannot always be taken at face value; that our well-being is not always served by the satisfaction of our actual preferences.[28] Human irrationality, as I've said, is ubiquitous, and akrasia represents only a small subset of its varieties. Behavioral economists can reel off a tidily tagged and cross-referenced list—preference reversal, anchoring effects, sunk costs, regret, and so forth.[29] Some seem like unhelpful glitches; others (such as regret) are part of the affective texture of our humanity. But the simplest and most pervasive reason that our desires fail to serve our well-being has to do with our informational limitations. I want to swim in the lake, but that's only because I don't know that it has been contaminated with mercury. I reach for the fizzing glass of Drāno, because I think it's Alka-Seltzer. A slew of such examples has given rise to the concept of what James Griffin has called an "informed desire" (or what economists, notably John Harsanyi, call an "informed prefer-ence") account of well-being. Your informed desire is the desire you'd have if, roughly, you had full information and perfect rationality.

The nature of "informed desire" is worth some attention. For per-haps we can agree that the state should endeavor not to remake our souls, or refashion our desires, but only to show us what our true desires are. In this scenario, the state would then defer only to informed, ratio-nal desires. Yes, the rational-desire proponent can say, we fall short of autonomy, as we actually are; yes, we are prey to irrational decisions, as we actually are. But the good society need do nothing more than help us to understand our authentic, "informed" preferences.

I explained earlier that it wouldn't raise the hard problems of soul making if the state changed my beliefs or preferences by providing in-formation but otherwise left my ethical self unaltered. A government is not engaged in soul making when it puts up a sign warning you that a lake is polluted, or launches a campaign advising people of the dan-gers of unprotected sex in an age of HIV/AIDS. As Mill says in *On Liberty*, "Considerations to aid [someone's] judgment . . . may be of-fered to him, even obtruded on him, by others." The capacity for reason is one ground of our right to manage our own lives, and that capacity is properly exercised when relevant information is used to shape our decisions.[30] At the same time, a considerable literature has explored the way in which our preferences shift in response to our changing situa-tion, state actions, and so forth. Just such considerations lead Cass Sunstein, in a marvelously forceful essay titled "Preferences and Poli-tics," to build a case against "subjective welfarism." A concern for au-tonomy, in his view, argues against indulging actual preferences. Among the examples he lists are a decision to purchase cigarettes by someone unaware of the health risks, a decision not to wear a motorcy-cle helmet by someone influenced by peer pressure, and a decision, by a woman, "to adopt a traditional gender role because of the social stigma attached to refusing to do so."[31] As this list may suggest, the notion of "informed preference" has hidden teeth, and they cut very deep indeed.

Some of the complications are adumbrated at the beginnings of the informed-preference approach within the utilitarian tradition, which is in Mill's own work. Where Jeremy Bentham would identify our welfare with the sensation of pleasure, Mill introduced a criterion of competence. "Of two pleasures, if there be one to which all or almost all who have experience of both give a decided preference, irrespective of any feeling of moral obligation to prefer it, that is the more desirable pleasure," he maintained. For Mill, this competence criterion quickly invites considerations of rationality and knowledge:

> Now it is an unquestionable fact that those who are equally acquainted with, and equally capable of appreciating and enjoying, both, do give a most marked preference to the manner of existence which employs their higher faculties. Few human creatures would consent to be changed into any of the lower animals, for a promise of the fullest allowance of a beast's pleasures; no intelligent human being would consent to be a fool, no instructed person would be an ignoramus, no person of feeling and conscience would be selfish and base, even though they should be persuaded that the fool, the dunce, or the rascal is better satisfied with his lot than they are with theirs.[32]

Mill's qualitative notion of higher and lower utilities has been roundly lambasted, but it represents, in kernel form, an account of well-being that was more fully developed by Henry Sidgwick, a few decades later. In the full-information account of well-being Sidgwick described (but did not endorse) in 1874, "a man's future good on the whole is what he would now desire and seek on the whole if all the consequences of all the different lines of conduct open to him were accurately foreseen and adequately realized in imagination at the present point in time."[33] Or, as the poet Carl Dennis writes, "the god who loves you" must find it painful

> . . . to watch you on Friday evenings
> Driving home from the office, content with your week—
> Three fine houses sold to deserving families—
> Knowing as he does exactly what would have happened
> Had you gone to your second choice for college,
> Knowing the roommate you'd have been allotted
> Whose ardent opinions on painting and music
> Would have kindled in you a lifelong passion.
> A life thirty points above the life you're living
> On any scale of satisfaction. And every point
> A thorn in the side of the god who loves you.[34]

Having full information could, then, be taken to include knowing the future consequences of my actions. It might be that if I take a particular train ride, I will meet a munificent stranger who will do wonderful things for me. Or if I enter a certain convenience store at precisely 3:34 next Tuesday afternoon and purchase a lottery ticket, I will win ten million dollars. In retrospect, I'd be awfully glad I did these things— taking that train, buying that ticket—but it would be strange to say that I really desired to. As a lottery enthusiast, what I desired was to buy a ticket with a chance of winning; a ticket that was assured to win simply wasn't in my option set. And since, in expected-utility theory, buying a lottery ticket is a paradigm instance of irrationality, then, if I were more rational, I should simply have relinquished any desire to buy a lottery ticket. In the munificent-stranger scenario, there's simply no meaningful relation between the full-information desire and my actual desires; I had no particular interest in taking that train, or meeting that stranger: there are a vast number of advantageous things that I could contemplate doing, if I could read tomorrow's newspaper today, but they have no relation at all to anything I actually have reason to do. The fact that I would have been glad if I had done something simply doesn't entail that that is what I really wanted to do.

We can stipulate, then, that "full information" doesn't include full knowledge of future contingencies; but perhaps someone with full knowledge of the world and perfect powers of ratiocination would be able to predict all kinds of future ramifications relevant to a decision. The trouble is that such a hypothetical person would be so remote from me that I'd hesitate to draw inferences from his attitudes: I'm not confident that what he would consider an agreeable state of affairs is what I would consider an agreeable state of affairs. Even aside from such peering-far-into-the-future cases, having "informed desires" is just inconsistent with certain very ordinary endeavors. Apply the "informed desire" test to a poker game: I now wish I hadn't folded, and if I had had perfect information I wouldn't have done so. But if I had perfect information, then, whatever it looked like I was doing, I wouldn't really be playing a game of poker. The "challenge model" of human life involves our dexterity in negotiation among risks and uncertainties.

You might want to fine-tune the model, then. Informed desires, on the simplest account, are the desires I would have if I had full information and unimpaired reason, which is to say, if I were someone else—with apologies to Dr. Evil, let's call him "Maxi Me." But perhaps the relevant desires are not the ones that Maxi Me would have but the desires that Maxi Me would benevolently have for actual me. Often, they're likely to be the same: Maxi Me wouldn't enjoy swimming in a lake contaminated with mercury, and he knows that I wouldn't enjoy swimming in a lake I knew to be contaminated with mercury. But where they diverge, the latter, god-who-loves-you perspective seems the more plausible. For imagine someone has offered me the choice between a glass of a fine Puligny Montrachet 2000 and a glass of insipid plonk. To be "fully informed" here, so many would assume, is to have the experienced palate capable of appreciating the Montrachet.[35] Maxi Me might strongly prefer the Montrachet, but if actual me can't tell the difference, it would seem odd to insist that my true or "informed" preference tracks his; there's no reason that a benevolent Maxi Me should want me to plump for his glass. In fact, as we'll see, the informed desire model moves us away from a first-person interpretation of well-being and toward a third-person one: it is the perspective of someone who knows more than you ever could, and wishes your life to go well—the perspective of that god who loves you.[36]

Not an easy job, that, either. We know that lives can be organized around projects—think of Mr. Casaubon and his "key to all mythologies"—that are destined to fail. Our well-being can be affected by all manner of contingencies, including luck. Perhaps I had a "rational aim" to prove Fermat's Last Theorem; but, as it happens, I was pipped at the post by Andrew Wiles. Alas, none of my life's work represents a unique contribution to human knowledge, and, knowing this, I'm filled with an enduring sense of desolation. Perhaps my *grand projet* required subventions from my well-wishers. Should the god who loves me have respected my autonomy by helping me pursue that aim, or have honored my (true but humanly unforeseeable) interests by preventing me from wasting my career?[37]

The biggest problem, though, is of indeterminacy. The "informed desire" account suggests a specific mapping from actual to informed desires, and sometimes we can make sense of this. As I mentioned, economists speak of preferences, so that they can construct ordinal-utility functions from a set of ranked choices: one prefers A to B, and B to C, and so on, and every state of the world has a place in the ranking. Talk of "desire" isn't so neatly bounded. How my bare desire relates to my informed desire—whether the latter can naturally be described as an "informed" version of the same old desire—can depend upon how abstractly the desire is identified. Suppose I have packed my bags for Botswana, in a quest to help combat malnutrition and disease. Someone informs me that the urban poor of Congo need my services more than those of Botswana. I change my itinerary. Now someone else presses me about my ultimate goals, and I come to agree that what I really want is to devote myself to relieving suffering on the planet. In that case, my interlocutor informs me, I should know that factory-farmed pigs represent the largest number of suffering creatures in the world. I cancel my trip to Congo and become an animal-liberation activist. Have my informants reshaped my preferences or merely aided in their fulfillment? What would a fully informed well-wisher want me to want? The question surely admits of no determinate answer; desires can be characterized with various degrees of abstraction, with no obvious stopping point.

Plainly, a desire isn't a function that can just be plugged into a data set: what's in the data set affects my desires. One reason I want to swim in the mercury-tainted lake is that I think it's healthy to be physically active; maybe, however, this will turn out to be false, or (genomic analysis could reveal) false for me. In deciding to go swimming, moreover, I haven't considered all the other possibilities as to how to spend my afternoon. If I do so (as some accounts of "preference autonomy" stipulate), I'll conceive an entirely different desire. Even when we're confining ourselves to preferences, those preferences will be shaped by facts of the world, and, in particular, by which options are attainable. This is, again, a lesson of Elster's work on "adaptive preference formation": our desires are shaped by our sense of what's possible—what we want is contoured by what we think is on offer. So when the state affects what I can get, it often affects what I want.

Recall some of Cass Sunstein's examples of putatively nonautonomous preferences: the fellow who buys cigarettes unaware of the health

risks, the woman who decides "to adopt a traditional gender role because of the social stigma attached to refusing to do so." It's worth
pausing to note how far we've come from the fizzing glass of lye. For
surely we have arrived at soul making through the back door. I just
talked about the indeterminacy of desire descriptions. Consider some
cases that don't seem indeterminate at all: the class of example that led
us to renounce "bare" preferences as a ground of well-being. I want to
drink the Drāno because I think it's Alka-Seltzer. I want to swim in this
lake because I think it's unpolluted. In each case, I can redescribe my
preferences to make their content plain, by spelling out the factual predicate. If I say, "I want to drink that glass of Alka-Seltzer over there," the
natural response isn't *You have no such desire*, or *You don't know what
you want*, but *That's not Alka-Seltzer*. My "erroneous" revealed preference can be redescribed—given a fuller description, we could say—to
make it true. ("I want to drink that glass over there if it is an antacid."
"I want to swim in the lake, so long as it's safe to swim there.") Only
a little less determinately, the humanitarian might say, "I'm going to
start a program to reduce scrofula in Windhoek, Namibia, because I
want to have a real impact on public health in the Third World," and
invite the informed rejoinder, "Then are you sure you don't want to
start a program to reduce AIDS in its adjoining shantytown, Katutura?"
Here, we can plausibly insist, we're not changing her aim, we're just
helping her execute it.

The decision to hew to a traditional gender role does not lend itself
to such redescription. It is not affected by the correction of a few flatly
factual errors. "I want to live as a good wife and mother, if . . ." Well,
if what? To get the woman to change her mind here, you could either
erase the social stigma (which would require erasing other people's,
presumably benighted, commitment to the values it subsists upon) or
you could somehow produce in her a new brazenness, or reflective dis-
regard of that stigma. Either way, you would be engaging in soul making, refashioning ethical projects and ethical identities. Indeed, there
are obvious dangers in ignoring actual preferences in the name of an
"autonomy" that might not be recognizable to its putative beneficiaries.
To return to Brian Barry's famous distinction, we'd need to take care
that "ideal-regarding" concerns are not being passed off as "want-regarding" concerns; and I've expressed my misgivings about overreach-

ing conceptions of autonomy in chapter 2. The hazard is one that T. M. Scanlon identified, of floating too far from what "a person has reason to want and to do."[38] At the very least, we should seek some sort of equilibrium between actual and ostensibly informed desires.

We started with the thought that informed-desire theory might be able to make soul making unnecessary: to make your life go well, we need only be responsive to your informed desires. Now it seems as if informed-desire theory is, if anything, excessively conducive to soul making. But perhaps that shouldn't have been a surprise: for the "information" part of "informed" desire suggests a sharper distinction between facts and values than many people entertain. Even if we think there's an in-principle distinction to be made here (and, as I said in the preface, my hope is to leave open as many of these metaphysical questions as I can), you might think that, in the real world, they are often so interwoven as to be inextricable. As we saw, the issue of whether hewing to traditional gender roles—or, for that matter, writing novels—is a worthwhile thing to do is unlikely to be settled by uncontroversially factual considerations. Griffin makes this explicit, in the course of laying out his own informed-desire account of well-being: "Sometimes desires are defective because we have not got enough, or the right, concepts. Theories need building which will supply new or better concepts, including value concepts."[39]

Now, we can easily imagine lives that we think are scarcely worthwhile, even though the (knowledgeable) fellows who lead them have no complaints, and, in these cases, we might suppose they should be supplied with new value concepts. In particular, in cases where someone's ultimate aims seem defective, it's natural to express our disquiet in identity terms: to wonder whether someone wants to be this or that kind of person.

Imagine a long-lasting, cost-free drug that induces a state of blissful contentment. Take it and you'll lapse into a mild torpor; you'll work enough to secure minimal sustenance—existence is too great a pleasure for you to want to cut it short—but all greater ambitions will have been extinguished. (To sidestep other complications, you may assume that it works only in young adults who haven't yet acquired any dependents. Or, if you prefer, you can imagine a society composed wholly of such bliss cases.) Unlike Nozick's Experience Machine dupes, the people on this drug—call it Bliss—have no desires they have failed to achieve; and they certainly experience deep contentment with their lives. Their capacity for cognitive and instrumental rationality is unimpaired. Why, then, would many of us hesitate to join these happy campers? I suppose we'd feel that they have taken a Rosie Ruiz approach toward life— they've reached the finish line of a metaphorical Boston Marathon, but via a discreditable shortcut. They have little to show by way of self-development, or individuality. Their higher-order and lower-order volitions are aligned, but not through any act of decisive identification.[40] But I think the natural way to account for our disquiet is to insist that a purely want-regarding account of well-being doesn't exhaust what we think the concept entails: there's more to a good life than the satisfaction of whatever desires the person living it happens to have. Such considerations can move us toward what's known (after Derek Parfit) as the "objective-list" account of well-being, or (after Scanlon) a "substantive goods" account. In "What Makes Someone's Life Go Best" Parfit mentions things like "moral goodness, rational activity, the development of one's abilities, having children and being a good parent, knowledge, and the awareness of true beauty," although he is clear that a list of this sort isn't sufficient for such an account. ("What is of value, or is good for someone," he ventures, is "to be engaged in these activities, and to be strongly wanting to do so.")[41] Many discussions of well-being move between an external and an internal perspective—a perspective from which a god who loves you might appraise your life, and a perspective that is yours. Certainly you haven't lived a well-led life, however admirable, if you found it repellent—if you didn't want to secure the substantive goods you did. And, as I've said in chapter 1, to hold that there are objective values in the world doesn't mean that there are objective ways to rank them or trade them off: they don't determine any life in particular. So neither subjective measures of success nor objective measures of success exhaust what we have in mind when we discuss well-being; some equipoise between them is wanted.[42]

Both these dimensions are usually captured in our very highest-order desires. I've said that the ethical evaluation of a life involves a subjective and an objective dimension. In particular, I've said that some things have value to us just because we want them; some things we want because we recognize them to be, in themselves, valuable. If we came to know that novels were without value, we might cease to want to have written one: and the valuelessness of the pursuit would be not a fact about us but one about the world. Very often, subjective considerations track objective ones, and this is particularly so when it comes to those highest-order, life-plan-level desires—what Raz calls "comprehensive goals," what Ronald Dworkin calls our "ambitions," and what Griffin calls "global" desires. And with such desires or goals or ambitions, the basic question is what sort of life one wants to make, which is also to say *what sort of person one wants to be.* Gerald Dworkin, for example, says that higher-order preferences come into play when someone "identifies with the influences that motivate him, assimilates them to himself, views himself as the kind of person who wishes to be moved in particular ways, that these influences are to be identified as 'his.' "[43] This is the language of identity, of social kinds or categories, of considerations that are bound up with those kinds or categories.

I decline Bliss (it would be very natural to say), even though I'm not really committed to any particular goals or projects yet, because I don't choose to be a Bliss Case: this isn't the kind of person I wish to be. The fact that I think of myself as an L means that doing X might be of particular value to me. Conversely, I might refrain from doing X because doing X goes with being an L, and I don't want to be an L. No doubt our pea-hating child, when he grows older, will save himself from his logical merry-go-round and explain what he *really* meant: he doesn't want to join the odious tribe of pea-lovers. It's an unserious example of what can be a deadly serious consideration. Occasionally, people explain why, in extraordinary circumstances, they refrained from killing someone, although they had a strong desire to do so, by saying that they "didn't want to be a murderer." This sounds like a tautology, but it isn't. "Murderer" doesn't quite qualify as a social identity, but it is a social kind, and these people are saying, I didn't want to be this kind of person, didn't want to think of myself as someone in the same category as other murderers (even though the prospective victim deserved to be killed, and I'd be happy to see someone else do the job).

Talk of global desires returns us, then, to the question of our ethical selves—the shaping of our own lives, our identities, and the prospect of ethical success that flows from them. Indeed, Cass Sunstein (who has civic-republican sympathies) argues that a notion of politics founded in a process by which "citizens decide, not what they 'want,' but instead who they are, what their values are, and what those values require" is "a conception of political freedom having deep roots in the American constitutional tradition."[44] And it's that basic conception—of a politics that emerges from a consideration not (just) of what we want but of who we are—that I want to explore.

As I've been saying, it's a reason for caring about things that one thinks of oneself as being a person of a certain kind: what Frankfurt calls "identifying with what one cares about" can be structured by what I've called one's identifications. But this raises a new question. We've been discussing irrationality—the failures of reason and information—mainly as a disjunction between our "naked" (ignorant or akratic) preferences and our "informed" ones. That is, we've been discussing our defections from rationality as obstacles to ethical success, where that success was defined, in part, by our ethical identities. What if our identities themselves harbor irrationality? Can we have rational aims in the service of an irrational identity?

IRRATIONAL IDENTITIES

There are reasons to proceed carefully here. To speak about the rationality of identities, you might suppose, is like speaking about the size of colors, a Rylean category mistake. Doesn't identity flow from feelings like identification, loyalty, a sense of belonging—feelings that don't lend themselves to rational inquiry? But that can't be the whole of it, of course. Insofar as identities can be characterized as having both normative and factual aspects, both can offend against reason: an identity's basic norms might be in conflict with one another; its constitutive factual claims might be in conflict with the truth. These days, people often invoke the fact-value distinction in order to assert its collapse.[45] My own suspicion is that we have been apt to declare its demise too hastily; it wouldn't be the object of so many search-and-destroy missions if it didn't enjoy some lingering vitality. But for my purposes, little depends on where you stand in the debate. I will simply stipulate the commonplace that autonomy and well-being depend upon ideals of rationality (and though I'll be ignoring question-begging accounts that define rationality simply in terms of the maximizing of well-being, I won't dwell on the contested nature of rationality). And so I want to propose a thought experiment that begins with some familiar premises—premises widely shared by secular and scientific souls, in our post-Weberian world—but swiftly overreaches the bounds of autonomist liberalism.

Voyage to Cartesia

Imagine a Gulliverian visit to a regime that, in the name of promoting well-being, inculcates and fosters a creed we may call hard rationalism. The hard rationalists' creed isn't one that is universally shared—they have no time for the notion that rationality is situated or culturally relative—but it is common enough. It is the kind of ideal instrumental rationality enshrined in neoclassical economics and decision theory. The hard rationalists are (to bring in a few touchstones of the literature) sympathetic to Locke's notion that "the *freedom* . . . of man and liberty of acting according to his own will, is grounded on his having reason";[46] they may have some kinship with the classical political philosophers who see the rational search for truth as the thing to be promoted. They also consider themselves liberals, of a sort: they care about personal autonomy, and rationality is an essential part of the kind of autonomy they seek to foster. Here in the republic of Cartesia, reason is seen as the foundation of democracy.

Since the hard rationalists were elected to office, they have introduced many uncontroversial reforms. For example, no accredited school in Cartesia may teach that $2 + 3 = 7$. Nothing to worry about in this. But they extend the principles of scientific rationality further—much further.

Consider an alchemist of yore, someone who had, as his driving ambition, the development of techniques to convert base metal to gold, by means of spells and tabletop chemistry. Hasn't misinformation or cognitive incapacity diminished the value of this life? Wouldn't a concern for his autonomy oblige us to try to show him the error of his ways? Thus the hard rationalists have decided—out of a concern for our autonomy and welfare, mind you—that the inculcation of irrational creeds is to be discouraged. Christians who believe in a God that defies the laws of science ought to be dissuaded from their false convictions: no resurrection, no transubstantiation. Surely, the hard rationalists say, a fellow who organizes his life around an entity that, contrary to his conviction, doesn't exist is not in possession of rational autonomy: we owe it to him to help him see his error. So it goes with religious adherents whose conduct is guided by rewards and punishments that will be meted out in the hereafter. Such a religion, argue Cartesia's governors, functions like a giant Experience Machine: it creates the illusion that this intention or that will produce various states of affairs, when those states don't actually exist.

Now, our hard rationalists happily tolerate a diversity of values, preferences, folkways. In addition to prizing individual liberty and autonomy, they value (up to a point) freedom of association, and, in their naturalistic way, they recognize that partiality is an ingrained aspect of human psychology. So they have no interest in expunging identitarian allegiances as such. There could even be religions that are consistent with their requirements. They have met Unitarians of a certain stripe (the kind whom, as the joke has it, you persecute by burning a question mark on their lawn) who seem to them sufficiently reasonable. Mordecai Kaplan, author of *Judaism as a Civilization* (1934) and founder of the naturalistic creed known as Reconstructionism, once defined Judaism as the folk religion of the Jewish people; the rituals were significant inasmuch as they enshrined certain social values, but he had little time for the supernatural as such. (No doubt I oversimplify.) Richard Braithwaite developed a form of Anglicanism consistent with his own empiricist bent, in which the theological elements ("stories," he called them) were psychological props for the moral demands of a Christian way of life.[47] A form of the faith thus anthropologized—denatured?—will not much trouble our hard rationalist.

It's where identities are grounded in mystifications, in failures of rationality, that intervention is required. For example, when members of a Jewish denomination define themselves as having a literal relation to the Exodus story, the hard rationalist scowls. He points to a scholarly consensus that the ancient Israelites were never in Egypt, that the Exodus story is a farrago of borrowed myths. And surely an identity that is rooted in and partly constituted by a false narrative is itself a form of mystification. Maybe it's not as bad as Experience-Machine-like appeals to the supernatural, but it's still a form of deception. And the government will campaign against these mystifications in the same spirit in which it provides pamphlets and instructional materials concerning healthful dietary practices and the dangers of tobacco.

Indeed, social identities that involve no appeal to the supernatural, and no myth of origins, may still trouble our hard rationalists when these identities are self-undermining. In a variety of cases, an identity has a set of norms associated with it such that, in the actual world, attempting to conform to some subset of those norms undermines one's capacity to conform to others. The result is that its members have projects and ambitions that undermine one another, and, it's plausible to conclude, their lives will go worse than they might have if they had access to a (more) coherent social identity. A project to reform the identity in order to make its norms more harmonious might therefore seem to be in the interest of those people. If informing people of the facts could achieve this reform, then government might choose to do it; but if irrationalities lead citizens not to respond to the facts in this reasonable way, the governors of Cartesia might then consider other mechanisms of reform, if any were available.

Surely, there are many ethnic and racial identities in the modern world that fit this abstract characterization. They are self-undermining; their failures of rationality have been regularly announced to no obvious effect; and there are available mechanisms of reform that could be carried out by governments that would lead people to new, more rational identities. These reforms could thus increase the chances of ethical success among members of the identity group.

Let me depart the shores of Cartesia for a while and sketch in more detail the argument for one case: that of an American racial identity.

Black Like Whom?

Identities give those who have them reasons for action, as I've said, and so people will say to themselves sometimes, "Because I am an L, I should do X." Such an appeal is, in the terms I am proposing, standardly an appeal to a norm associated with that identity. Most social identities, especially of historically subordinated groups, have norms of solidarity: "Because I am an L," an L will say, "I should do this thing for that other L." An identity can be self-undermining, then, if the *social conception* that in part defines the identity pulls, so to speak, in different directions, because it has criteria for ascribing the identity that are inconsistent with the facts. Racial identities in the United States have exactly this feature. Many Americans believe that a person with one African American and one European American parent is an African American, following the so-called "one-drop rule" that prevailed in some legal conceptions of black identity in the period before the abolition of slavery and of the legal institutions of "Jim Crow," America's system of apartheid. While most Americans understand this to mean that some African Americans will "look white," they mostly suppose that this phenomenon is rare in relation to the African American population as a whole. But in fact, it seems that very many—perhaps even a majority—of the Americans who are descended from African slaves "look white," are treated as white, and identify as such.[48] To put the matter as paradoxically as possible: many people who are African American by the one-drop rule are, are regarded as, and regard themselves as, white. Most people in the United States have a social conception of the African American identity that entails that this is not so. So they have a social conception that is inconsistent with the facts.

The result is a norm of solidarity such that African Americans very often have a reason for identity-based generosity to people they believe, on the basis of another part of their social conception, to be white. If they acted on the norm based on the one-drop rule, their identity-based generosity would be regularly directed toward people they regard as whites.

To be sure, it is also part of the social conception of African American identity that there are some people of African American ancestry who were raised as white people, not knowing of their African ancestry; who look like other white people and thus have the skin-privilege associated with whiteness; and are, as a result, not really African American. People who have thought about the matter a little will know that this means that the one-drop rule is not to be taken absolutely, and that, as a result, their notion of what it means to be an African American has fuzzy boundaries. But, because they do not take to heart the inconsistency that I have just described, they regard this as a minor anomaly that makes little practical difference. Nor will the mere provision of information solve the problem. There has been a great circulation of exactly the sort of information that I have been providing among educated Americans in the last few decades and, more particularly, among African Americans. During this same period, however, the sort of Black Nationalism I have identified has become stronger, especially among the middle-class black people who are most likely to have received this information.

Now, there are a number of rebuttals to the picture I've been sketching. Instead of concluding that African Americans, qua African Americans, typically have clashing constitutive convictions, one might conclude, rather, that they don't really abide by the one-drop rule. One could dispute, therefore, that the belief in question is really very important: if they don't really take hypostatic descent literally, perhaps it doesn't much matter that they give it lip service. Or one might conclude that people can possess an identity without sharing a plump and coherent theory of what it involves. One could further object that all groups, including those that command partiality, have fuzzy boundaries.

But suppose we take these men and women at their word. On the one hand, they have a social conception of identity that is at odds with the facts. On the other, they are infused with a sense of racial solidarity, a form of partiality; it is important to them that black people should do well; and making a contribution to that end is one of the aims by which they define the success of their lives. It is the similarity of this sentiment to the sentiment that underlies much patriotism that leads people to call such dispositions "nationalist." Like other nationalists, these people have the thought that they would like their people to do well *because they are their people.* It might be that if African Americans ceased to be (or, at any rate, to think of themselves as being) the victims of unrecompensed injustice, they might mostly cease to identify as African Americans, so that this form of nationalism would cease. But while it exists, the success of many African American lives is thus tied up with the project of racial uplift—a project, as I say, that highlights the inconsistency between one set of beliefs (about the prevalence of passing) and another (about how to ascribe African American identity). Can this identity be rationalized?

Where Rationalizing Goes Wrong

That's just the kind of question they'd ask in Cartesia; but, of course, not everything about Cartesia will strike us as unsympathetic. Our hard rationalists push antismoking campaigns, just as modern liberal states do; they, like us, are inclined to think that smoking is irrational, a detriment to our well-being. The trouble is that the governors of Cartesia don't stop with antismoking campaigns, or, for that matter, helmet and seat-belt laws. Black, Christian, Jew, Muslim: inasmuch as these identities are predicated upon falsehoods, Cartesia has devised programs to discourage or revise them.

Surely it's not absurd to think that the state has an interest in promoting rationality; and surely it's not absurd to think that rationality is a precondition of agency, which is, in turn, the ground of liberty. The state, we can agree, shouldn't automatically defer to the preferences of misinformed or panicked citizens. It must, in a wide range of affairs, act according to its best conception of the truth. And surely our lives go better when our aims are rational; as a rule, aims do not succeed when they're predicated on falsehoods. Our hard rationalist is, indeed, impressed by Griffin's discussion of the good life: "We want to be in touch with a reality outside ourselves. We do not want just to have convincing impressions of having a life of value, of accomplishing something with our lives. We also want to have clear perceptions of the reality about us."[49] *Clear perceptions of the reality about us*: Yes, says the Rationalist, now let me help you with that.

What, then, is wrong with this regime?

There's a cluster of immediate, contingent concerns we should take on board. Start with a mote-and-beam worry—it's the one I mentioned much earlier—about whether we can rely upon the governors to be more rational than the governed. Even if they were, one is inclined to doubt that any actual regime of this sort would treat its citizens with equal respect, and one is inclined to doubt that it would long command democratic support and legitimacy. (These are the sorts of considerations—preserving state legitimacy in the face of disagreement—that make neutralism attractive to Larmore and Nagel.) The governors of Cartesia are simply taking a hard-line stand on too many controversial issues. Which leads to another pair of worries: imagine the warfare that would, in consequence, arise between the state and families (assuming the state doesn't want to take on responsibility for raising children). Such a regime would severely encroach on the liberty of parents. And such conflict is unlikely to be good for the child. (I'll say more about this later on.)

Then there are grounds for metaphysical and epistemological disquiet. How to characterize these putative failures of rationality is controversial, even (or particularly) among those who make a specialty of the subject. Earlier I mentioned the cordite haze enveloping the fact-value distinction. But even without taking a stand on that matter, and even accepting that it's better, *ceteris paribus*, that children not be taught false beliefs, we can acknowledge that few of our scientific theories are immune to revision. Mill himself recognized that large realms of human knowledge lacked the certitude of arithmetic: "The peculiarity of the evidence of mathematical truths is that all the argument is on one side. There are no objections, and no answer to objections. But on every subject in which difference of opinion is possible, the truth depends on a balance to be struck between two sets of conflicting reasons. Even in natural philosophy, there is always some other explanation possible of the same facts. . . . The beliefs which we have most warrant for have no safeguard to rest on, but a standing invitation to the whole world to prove them unfounded."[50] We would be reckless to rescind that standing invitation; we do well to pay obeisance to fallibilism.

The matter of analytic falsehoods raises another problem. Yes, certain beliefs are analytically false: $2 + 3 = 7$, for example; perhaps the doctrine of the Trinity is, too. In these cases, however, it's not clear how you could put them into practice—what it would mean to hold these beliefs, or whether, putting aside your protestations, you really could hold them. Gore Vidal likes to talk about ancient mystery sects whose rites have passed down so many generations that their priests utter incantations in language they no longer understand. The observation is satirical, but there's a good point buried here. Where religious observance involves the affirmation of creeds, what may ultimately matter isn't the epistemic content of the sentences ("I believe in One God, the Father Almighty . . .") but the practice of uttering them. By Protestant habit, we're inclined to describe the devout as believers, rather than practitioners; yet the emphasis is likely misplaced.

The critique of Cartesia could be extended; but, in sum, we could fault our hard rationalist for putting too little value on autonomy's autarchic dimension, and too much on (a controversial interpretation of) its rational dimension. In Cartesia, all forms of irrationality were discouraged. In a modern liberal democracy, only some forms of irrationality may be discouraged. Which are these? Here are some tenets to which many liberals, especially antiperfectionist liberals, would assent. Forms of irrationality that jeopardize the democratic polity (that, for example, straightforwardly interfere with the ability to exercise citizenship) are proper targets of state intervention. Such interventions ought to be disciplined by a concern for freedom of association, for the social forms that give meaning and shape to individual lives, and so we should tread cautiously around forms of irrationality that are linked to identity groups, especially religions. A balance of interests will be struck. Thus though the state should hesitate to campaign against the religious belief that Satan will snatch your soul if you eat too much carob, it may justly decide to campaign against the religious belief that Satan will snatch your soul if you enter the voting booth.

But what kind of rationality-promoting measures, if any, would be justified by a concern for my welfare alone? We've granted that the state can do many things in order to protect the well-being of its citizens: it puts up traffic lights at dangerous intersections; it monitors the quality of drinking water, enforces contracts, and all the rest. And, as we've seen, most liberals think it can promote certain values and foster rationality in order to serve civic ends, those involving the stability and survival of the polity. The question is whether it can promote rationality not for civic ends, but for my own good. We'll want to be sure that we can downshift from the impermissible regime of hard rationalism to a permissible one of more modest and prudent rationalism.

Abhorrent and Self-Undermining Identities

How can we reconcile a respect for people as they are with a concern for people as they might be? How to bring together autonomism and constructionism—the sturdy value of negative liberty with an awareness of how our desires and identifications are shaped? Here we can learn from our earlier discussion of informed preferences, where we concluded that an autonomist political order ought to attend neither to our bare preferences nor to "informed" preferences alone, but to some equilibrium of the two.

There are also lessons to be drawn from Cartesia. The hard rationalists viewed with disfavor religious identities that were bound up with beliefs they considered florid fantasies. They were confident that a state that cared for us would set about the project of soul making entailed by reforming our metaphysical convictions. And they'd have their hands full, too: given our defections from reason, all of us would likely have substantially "irrational" identities, at least by their lights. We found reasons to balk at their confidence. Some were to do with respect for autonomy, and with epistemic humility. But, as I also suggested, contemporary (and historical) religious traditions in many places do not share the concern for doctrinal correctness that characterizes much Christianity, for example, or some modern streams of Islam. It can be argued that many forms of modern Judaism, while committed to certain practices, are theologically quite noncommittal; and, indeed, there was once an Anglican bishop of Woolwich who confessed that being "honest to God" might lead to metaphysical atheism.[51] Yet there are cases where the urge to intervene is not so easily shunted aside; I'll discuss two. The first involves what I'll call abhorrent identities. The second returns us to our previous discussion of self-undermining identities—where the threats to our ethical success derive from the ways in which its norms pull in different directions.

There are identities—an example that suggests itself, not least by its self-awarded label, is the Christian Identity movement—that are constituted in part by profoundly unappetizing commitments. These are different from those of the theocratic communities we considered in chapter 3, which had the character of small despotisms; what's at issue here isn't any direct encroachment upon the self-direction of its members. Members of the Christian Identity movement, a quasi-religious sect in North America with perhaps fifty thousand adherents, hold an amalgam of evaluative and factual commitments (if you'll suffer the distinction) that are deeply at odds with America's moral modernity. They think that Anglo-Saxons and related groups are racially descended from the ancient Israelites; that Jews are the spawn of Cain, and Satanic in nature; that the "mud races" (nonwhites) are subhuman; and so forth. Unless autonomy is weighed at naught, to treat members of the movement as the Chinese government has treated members of the Falun Gong would be insupportable. But neither must we bend over backward to insulate their creed from the burdens that come with being deeply antinomian. There's no cause to worry about the fact that the ordinary curriculum in our public schools, or, for that matter, many features of our civil and criminal code, conflict with, and tend to undermine, the teachings of the movement. On the contrary, this is surely a desirable result. Even people who wish to have no truck with soul making will happily accede, although they would offer another description of what was going on (e.g., teaching the truth, or discouraging immoral conduct, or equipping people for citizenship). What makes this case a little too easy, for my purposes, is that the identity in question is morally, not merely ethically, impaired: a creed that calls for race war and so forth directs us to engage in immorality. Our campaign against it will be in the name of morality, not the ethical flourishing of its members. Christian Identity may be bad for its members. Their lives will be impaired by these beliefs. But we don't take specific action against them for this reason; we generally do so only when they threaten others.[52]

A trickier case is the one I laid out earlier: that of self-undermining identities. (And let me again stress that false beliefs about one's identity do not, in themselves, make it self-undermining.) What if our identities make conflicting claims—are internally contradictory? Many people will accept that the state may foster rationality; many people will accept that the state can seek to promote well-being; almost everyone will agree that hard rationalism oversteps its brief. To what degree may the state legitimately seek to reshape contradictory social identities, thus reforming those whose individual identities are partially defined by them, in the name of the success of their individual lives? (Though I'm discussing the state in relation to identities and social forms, it should be obvious that the state isn't a major actor in these respects. Other elements of what we call "society" are.) In particular, how might the state respond to the irrationalities of race, beyond the mere provision of information?

Here's a relatively trivial example. Current U.S. practices presuppose, by and large, that there is a fact of the matter about everyone as to whether or not she is African American. One is required to fill in forms for all sorts of purposes that fix one's race, and other people—arresting police officers, for example—may be required to do so as well. As a result, many people, who think of themselves as clearly and obviously black or white or something other than either of these in the racial system, are encouraged by this practice in the belief that the racial system is in fact relatively straightforward. Were the government to modify these practices, it would remove at least one tiny strut that gives support to the idea that social conceptions of race are consistent with reality: the fact that the state appears to be able to construct successful practices that assume that social conception. Such a modification could be motivated in many ways (not least by the recognition that the relevant social conceptions *are* rationally defective). But it might, surely, also be motivated by the thought that government action here could help to re-shape—or, anyway, diminish the salience of—racial identities in ways that would lessen their self-conflicting character.

Of course, you can debate whether this is a state intervention or the cessation of one.[53] What's more, it will be correctly observed, at this point, that the policy I am speaking of here is necessary only because the state already collects racial "data." Why not simply say that the state should stay away from all racial classifications? There are benefits that might ensue; but, of course, the result would be to prevent the government from being able to assess the presence of discrimination, and to attempt countermeasures. And, for reasons that Robert C. Post has articulated, antidiscrimination law itself, though it is usually conceived as simply the assertion of the basic liberal tenet of equal treatment, can involve forms of soul making, too.

Soul Making and Stereotypes

I have spent some time considering those arguments for soul making which are meant to respond to our pervasive defections from reason. But the irrationality rationale hardly exhausts the grounds for liberal soul making. Liberal soul making may aim, as we've seen, at the modification of social identities in ways that derive directly from the recognition of their ethical importance.

To view antidiscrimination law in the context of soul making may seem contrary to its guiding spirit. For the usual conception of antidiscrimination law centers on equality, and equality is best understood negatively: equality as a political ideal is a matter of not taking irrelevant distinctions into account. People should be treated differently, so to speak, because there are *grounds* for treating them differently (or at least no grounds for not doing so): egalitarians are people who have strong views about which grounds are and are not permissible. Questions of equality arise largely when treatment is not only disparate but invidiously so. It's one thing to give pink cookies to the girls and blue ones to the boys: another to give the boys expensive toys and the girls cheap trinkets. Now, it used to be taken for granted that it was all right for the state and for private employers and for those who provided public accommodations to make invidious distinctions between blacks and whites, and between men and women. The statutes and the constitutional lawmaking of the last four decades include many attempts to get away from that practice and that assumption.

In particular, antidiscrimination law is aimed at what we might categorize as *public actions.* This term is intended to cover actions taken by state officials in their official capacity—which are clearly subject to norms of nondiscrimination—but also to include actions undertaken by people in the course of hiring and managing employees in large businesses and in admitting people to and ministering to them in public accommodations. It is an interesting question why, in a liberal society, antidiscrimination should be enforced as a legal norm in the sphere of public actions that are not state actions. I think the answer is clear enough: in our world, allowing each of us a fair chance at developing a dignified, autonomous existence requires that we have access to employment and public space, as well as to the rights and privileges of the citizen. If dignity and autonomy are core liberal values, a liberal will want the state to insist on reasonable access to employment and to public space for all. Why limit this insistence to public actions? Because to include other spheres of action within the ambit of antidiscrimination law—to require me not to distinguish between men and women, blacks and whites, in my everyday interactions—would infringe unduly on my capacity to construct my own life. Freedom of expression and of association are central to such self-construction, and requiring me to have dinner parties at which gender or racial identity does not feature as a ground for choosing the guests interferes with these freedoms. Constraining employers, hotel-keepers, and the like by granting us public rights against them does indeed limit their freedom: but it does so in a way that is usually less central to their life projects than the opportunities they would deny us are to ours. (That is why the limitation to public actions is appropriate, though there is reasonable room for debate about exactly what belongs in the category of public action.) Where so constraining an employer does interfere profoundly with individual or collective projects—as requiring the Catholic Church to employ women as priests undoubtedly would—we cannot justify it on these grounds. And since we have, as a result, to adjudicate the claims of individuals against such organizations, we are speaking here of the balancing of opposing interests. It would be a mistake to allow the centrality of a project to my individuality by itself to trump your interests in such cases—do we want the centrality of anti-Semitic hatred to my life to entitle me to keep Jews out of my hotel?—and so we are obliged also, in the end, to address the merits of the projects.

This standard liberal account does not yet seem to entail soul making. But you will already have anticipated one shortcut that would take us there: perhaps *stereotyping* plays a role in our ethical identities and is a remediable defection from rationality. You would find support for this view in some legal opinions; as we'll see, judges sometimes refer to the notion of "irrational prejudice" in this context. And so you might think that when a society takes measures against such stereotyping, as via antidiscrimination law, it would, ipso facto, be remodeling our ethical identities.

But this is too quick. Indeed, it's worth pausing to reflect on the promiscuous use of the word "stereotype" in the legal judgments and argumentation that surround civil rights law. For in the context of American antidiscrimination law, the term "stereotype" covers at least three distinct ideas.

The first is the idea of ascribing a property to an individual on the basis of the belief that it is characteristic of some social group to which she belongs, where there is indeed a statistical correlation between that property and being a member of that group, but where, in fact, she does not have that property. This is the case of the strong woman who presents herself for a job as a firefighter and is told that she will not be considered because "women are not strong enough to be firemen." Here, there is a general fact about the group that is relevant to the employment decision—strength, let us suppose, really is what the case law calls a "bona fide occupational qualification" for a firefighter, and women really are, on average, less strong than men—but this general fact does not bear on the question of Mary's suitability to the task if she is in fact stronger than most women, stronger, in fact, than the weakest male firefighter. Let's call these *statistical stereotypes*.[54]

A second idea invoked by the word "stereotype" is just a false belief about a group. In the context of antidiscrimination, the relevance of such stereotypes—let's call them *simply false stereotypes*—is that public actors may give as their ground for doing something the belief that A has some characteristic, because they believe that all members of a group to which A belongs have, or are very likely to have, that characteristic. And they may do this even when the characteristic is not, in fact, common in the group. The classic examples here are ethnic stereotypes, which lead people, say, not to do business with members of a group because they are purportedly "shifty and dishonest," when, in fact, they are not, or not especially so. Simply false stereotypes burden people for no good reason, too. But to identify the burden may require an inquiry into whether the stereotype is, in fact, simply false.

The third, and, for our purposes, most interesting sense of the word "stereotype" comes up in the case of gender-related norms of dress and behavior. Two examples Robert C. Post has analyzed are *Wilson v. Southwest Airlines*, where an airline was sued for its policy of hiring only "attractive female flight attendants," and *Craft v. Metromedia, Inc.*, where a TV anchorwoman complained that her employer insisted that she wear more "feminine" clothes.[55] In such cases, a stereotype is not a view about how members of the group behave *simpliciter*: it is a view about how they behave grounded in a social consensus about how they *ought* to behave in order to conform appropriately to the norms associated with membership in their group. I shall call this a *normative stereotype*. When employers require female employees to wear dresses and male employees not to do so, they are invoking normative gender stereotypes. (There are obvious connections between statistical and normative stereotypes, of course. Many of the generalizations involved in statistical stereotyping are true because there are normative stereotypes to which people are conforming.)

Now granted these distinctions, we can see that different stereotypes deserve different responses. Both the first two kinds of stereotype involve error: intellectual error, since they involve misunderstanding the facts, with simply false stereotypes; or misunderstanding their relevance, with statistical ones. But there is no reason to suppose that normative stereotypes, as such, must be wrong, or that public actions grounded on them, even where they involve differences in treatment that are judged to be invidious, are to be criticized. (Given the way the clothing market works, the demand, made of a woman, that she wear business attire appropriate to her sex, may well require her to spend more money than does the same demand made of her male colleagues. That makes it invidious, since she is paying a cost in virtue of her gender. Still, it is not obvious that this is a harm that rises to the level of requiring a public right, or the expenditure of public funds, to remedy it.) And yet the courts have, in a variety of cases, taken it upon themselves to intervene in such normative stereotypes. And some of these interventions amount to piecemeal soul making.

This isn't precisely how the judges or the legislators would describe what they were up to, needless to say.[56] Post, in the course of an arresting and persuasive line of argument, has identified what he calls the "dominant conception" of American antidiscrimination law, according to which individuals are to be treated as if they lacked gender, race, and so forth; we are somehow to blind ourselves to these forbidden attributes and perceive only their inherent merit. Post wants us to recognize, on the contrary, that "antidiscrimination law is itself a social practice, which regulates other social practices, because the latter have become for one reason or another controversial. It is because the meaning of categories like race, gender, and beauty have become contested that we use antidiscrimination law to reshape them in ways that reflect the purposes of law."[57] Note that Post's argument is not just about the consequences of the legal decisions in antidiscrimination cases, but about their motivation, as well: his argument is that there's a mismatch between the "dominant conception" we have of what we're doing, and what we really are doing—that the patterns of actual judicial decision making better conform to his account than to the one that judges are apt to invoke. As actually practiced, antidiscrimination law, in this view, does involve a management of "the natures and habits of men's souls," as Plato had it.

Post draws our attention to judicial interpretations of Title VII, where there is some mention of stereotypes, but the focus is not in the first place on normative stereotypes. The Court speaks of "stubborn but irrational prejudice" in *Lam v. University of Hawaii*—suggesting that cognitive problems, simply false or statistical stereotyping, are at issue. In *Donahue v. Shoe Corporation of America*, there is explicit mention of forming "opinions of people on the basis of skin color, religion, national origin, and other superficial features." Similarly, in the ensuing discussion of state antidiscrimination statutes, there is talk of "stereotyped impressions about the characteristics of a class to which the person belongs," which could also mean that the characteristics are incorrectly assigned either to the class (simply false stereotyping) or to the individual (statistical stereotyping).[58]

But there are hints all along that normative stereotyping is also in the offing. When Justice Brennan, in *Price Waterhouse v. Hopkins*, interprets the federal statute as insisting that "sex, race, religion and national origin are not relevant to the selection, evaluation, or compensation of employees," he must mean that they are not relevant *in se*, since they are clearly relevant statistically. And to hold that they are irrelevant *in se* might seem to be to reject normative stereotypes that declare certain jobs suitable or unsuitable for African Americans or for women. Someone who didn't engage in statistical stereotyping and had no false beliefs about the capabilities and character of women or blacks might still believe, by way of a normative stereotype, that each has a proper place that is different from the place of men or of white people.

How do we distinguish between *Wilson* (the case successfully brought by Southwest Airlines flight attendants) and *Craft* (the case unsuccessfully brought by the female TV news anchor)? Here we can say that the practice of offering airline service that is aimed at attracting heterosexual men of conventional tastes by requiring women to "act sexy" for them is demeaning to women in a way or to a degree that requiring a woman news anchor to "maintain professional, businesslike appearances, 'consistent with community standards,' " is not. In fact the standards invoked by the television station KMBC in *Craft* presuppose that women, though governed by different norms of dress, are nevertheless properly to be found in professional, business positions. This isn't to deny that the codes of dress for women in the "conservative" Kansas City market are likely to play a role in limiting the opportunities of businesswomen or reflect a lack of equal respect for them. But they do so to a significantly lesser degree than do the codes requiring airline attendants to engage in "sexy dressing."[59] The social engineering that antidiscrimination law involves is, indeed, piecemeal.

Normative stereotypes—which are close kin to what I've earlier called life-scripts—are central to an understanding of the place of identity and individuality in moral and civic life, in ways we've explored. But not just any normative stereotypes will do. They have to be consistent with the construction of a dignified individuality. To the extent that existing norms, enforced through public action, construct an identity as lacking in dignity, or have built into them the inferiorization of those who bear it, they fail to be so. As Post rightly insists, antidiscrimination law may be concerned with the reshaping of gender norms; it is not concerned with their abolition. The abolition of gender norms would be the abolition of gender and the radical transformation—perhaps beyond human recognition—of sexuality. But their reform could begin to make it less true that our society constructs women as inferior to men. Similarly, when everyday social practices—such as the provision of racially segregated public accommodations or the proscription of interracial relations—project "an inferior or demeaning image on another" (in Charles Taylor's formulation), proscribing such practices can be one way of reforming the social conception of the racial identity *black* with the aim of improving the success of the lives of black people through the reform of their identities. That is soul making par excellence; and for identities that have, historically, been wrongly derogated, such soul making, however piecemeal, can be one of the duties of a state that cares equally for all its citizens.

The example also shows why it's a mistaken to think of soul making as something like brainwashing—to picture soul making as what happens when the state gets into your head. For, of course, the meaning of who I am isn't just in my head; my ethical projects flow from a universe of social facts. Inasmuch as our identities are social things—products of social conceptions and of our treatment by others—a shift in normative stereotype changes who I am. At the same time, it is also open to me to contest the alteration of a social identity: perhaps what it means to be a man has changed, in the course of my lifetime, in ways I deplore. I can then resist the new scripts, the new normative stereotypes: public actions may change the meanings of social identities without eliminating the possibility of dissent and contestation. To have autonomy, surely, is to have the capacity to resist; as liberals, we may not impose a life upon someone against his or her will. But what may we do before people have a will at all?

EDUCATED SOULS

"I think I may say, that of all the men we meet with, nine parts out of ten are what they are, good or evil, useful or not, by their education," Locke wrote. " 'Tis that which makes the great difference in mankind. The little and almost insensible impressions on our tender infancies, have very important and lasting consequences: and there 'tis, as in the foundations of some rivers, where a gentle application of the hand turns the flexible waters into channels, that make them take quite contrary courses, and by this little direction given them at first in the source, they receive different tendencies, and arrive at last at very remote and distant places."[60] We may renounce Locke's hopeful belief in some self-ratifying rationality; we may view the impressionable young as not quite so impressionable as he did. But there is no democratic society that does not take education—the French term *formation* is the argument in a word—with utmost seriousness, and none that does not contend with the prospect of educative soul making. It is a striking fact that, among developed countries, anyway, a program of universal education has indeed become universal.

Liberal-democratic approaches to education have typically involved those two concerns we touched upon at the beginning of this chapter. The first is to do with the good of the individual: preparing a child for an autonomous existence. The second is to do with the good of the polity: a self-perpetuating political order cannot be indifferent to the promulgation of at least some of its constitutive tenets. (It is a version of the dictum laid down by the architect of John Stuart Mill's own education, his father, James: "The end of Education is to render the individual as much as possible an instrument of happiness, first to himself, and next to other beings.")[61]

Still, this by itself does not tell us much about how government should play its part. One must not conclude that, because the state is bound to shape our identities, it should do so purposefully and with the good of each of us in mind, engaging freely in soul making. And neither the thought that some identities are obstacles to individuality nor the thought that they are instruments of self-creation establishes any real boundaries: it is preposterous to suppose that children could be aided—and equally unattractive to suppose that they *should* be aided—to reach adulthood with no social identities at all; but the fact that they will, perforce, have some set of identities underconstrains what we may do in shaping them during childhood. At the same time, it is abundantly clear that some parents view public education as a threatening and disruptive force in their lives. If your aim is to produce children who will hew to the luminous path of truth, then talk about self-creation, or, indeed, individuality is unlikely to put you at your ease. You will think not about the construction of character but about its corruption.

Here are two accounts of liberal education, the first from Bruce Ackerman, and the second from Michael Oakeshott:

> The entire educational system will, if you like, resemble a great sphere. Children land upon the sphere at different points, depending on their primary culture; the task is to help them explore the globe in a way that permits them to glimpse the deeper meanings of the dramas passing on around them. At the end of the journey, however, the now mature citizen has every right to locate himself at the very point from which he began—just as he may also strike out to discover an unoccupied portion of the sphere.[62]

> Each of us is born in a corner of the earth and at a particular moment in historic time, lapped round with locality. But school and university are places apart where a declared learner is emancipated from the limitations of his local circumstances and from the wants he may happen to have acquired, and is moved by intimations of what he has never yet dreamed. . . . They are, then, sheltered places where excellence may be heard because the din of local partialities is no more than a distant rumble.[63]

Despite the political distance between the two authors, both of these accounts are, in deep ways, strikingly consonant with the Millian vision. They eloquently express some widely shared (albeit liberal) ideals of what education should do for us: that it should, as we say, "expand our horizons," that it should expose us to a broader world than the one we already inhabit. And, of course, these accounts emphasize the immediate benefits to the children, who may gain deeper understanding of the "dramas passing on around them," who may be "emancipated from the limitations of . . . local circumstances."

Yet almost any educational system, even one that avowedly relinquishes a civic mission, is going to have to contend with people who feel threatened by its manner or its substance. Take those two descriptions of liberal education. Both sound pluralist, humane, openhearted: and, for some citizens, this is just the problem. If you think you dwell in the City upon a Hill, you may not be pleased to see it reduced to a mere point on "a great sphere"; nor will the promise to reduce "local partialities" to a "distant rumble" necessarily please those whose partialities they are.

Here we should start with the assumption that the role parents play in the raising of children gives them rights, in respect to the shaping of their children's identities, that are a necessary corollary of parental obligations. We do not believe that social reproduction should be carried out as it is in *Brave New World*. We believe that children should be raised primarily in families and that those families should be able to try to induct their children into the mores, identities, and traditions that the adult members of the family take as their own.

Of course, if your only goal were to secure the "reservoir of individuality, the springs of difference" that Horace Kallen identified with ethnic pluralism, you could imagine other means to that end. The state could take over the raising of children and assign them, more or less arbitrarily, to one of a range of "interesting" identities. The resources for self-construction available would depend solely on the imagination and the will of the state and its servants, along with whatever spontaneous inventions would occur among the adults in such a society. This alternative is a pretty far-fetched one. The intimacy of family life; the love of children for parents (and other relatives) and of parents (and other relatives) for children; the sense of a family identity, family traditions:

all these would be lost (along, I might add, with the meaning invested in family feuds). More than this, the state would be endowed with a quite enormous power in the shaping of the citizenry; a power whose potential for abuse is obvious enough.

Once we have left the raising of children to families, we are bound to acknowledge that parental love includes the desire to shape children into identities one cares about, and to teach them identity-related values, in particular, along with the other ethical truths that the child will need to live her life well. Alasdair MacIntyre puts it this way: "We enter human society ... with one or more imputed characters—roles into which we have been drafted—and we have to learn what they are in order to be able to understand how others respond to us and how our responses to them are apt to be construed."[64] A state that, in the name of a child's future autonomy, actively undermined parental choices in that regard—this was, recall, one of the troubles with Cartesia—would be a state constantly at odds with parents: and that would not be good for their children.

These considerations don't override the requirements of political order, but they will inevitably temper them, and the role that education does and should play in the creation of citizens has long been controversial. In a 1909 book that has served as a touchstone of one approach, Ellwood Cubberley, a prominent, progressive American educator, voiced alarm at the recent immigrant wave of "southern and eastern Europeans":

> Illiterate, docile, lacking in self-reliance and initiative, and not possessing the Anglo-Teutonic conception of law, order, and government, their coming has served to dilute our national stock, and to corrupt tremendously our civic life. . . . Our task is to break up these groups or settlements, to assimilate and amalgamate these people as part of the American race, and to implant in their children, so far as can be done, the Anglo-Saxon conception of righteousness, law and order and popular government, and to awaken in them a reverence for our democratic institutions and for those things in our national life which we as a people hold to be of abiding worth.[65]

The passage is a combination of the appalling and the appealing. His recent commentators have little time for the racialist assumptions, the national stereotypes, the fear of ethnic differences—for the notion that civic survival requires the imposition of a unitary Anglo-Saxon identity. On the other hand, as they recognize, the ideal of literate and self-reliant citizens who care about the rule of law and popular government is not a thing to discount. The enduring question is whether we can have the latter without some version of the former.

"A liberal democratic polity does not rest on diversity, but on shared political commitments weighty enough to override competing values," Stephen Macedo writes, and he stresses that "the abstract ideals of liberal justice lay claims of mutual respect on every group in society, whereas the claims of particularity advanced by pluralists create no necessary claim for tolerance or respect."[66] What he calls transformative liberalism suggests that one legitimate function of a liberal state is, and has been, to attenuate the strong, *Blut-und-Boden* identitarian commitments it encounters: to process the surly sources of alternative authority—whether Catholicism or English nativism—and leave something diluted by broader liberal commitments: call it Identity Lite. Historically speaking, this is precisely what the American republic has done, which is what some find so alarming. And yet it is not enough to find a balancing of interests between We the People and We the Peoples; we must also consider the interests of Me the Person, while acknowledging the enmeshment of them all.

No system of compulsory education can sidestep such tensions altogether. Indeed, if it has been common to view preparation for autonomy and citizenship as being at the heart of education in a liberal democracy, it has, in turn, been common to identify as a major source of conflict the tension between the present autonomy of parents and the interests (or, we could say, the future autonomy) of the child. What is in fact in the interest of a child may itself be a crucially contested matter. But even if you flatly identified the interests of the child with the project of "democratic" or "liberal" education, you'd still have to address the question of how to take parental desires into account. As Eamonn Callan points out, parents can make all sorts of bad choices that we'd never dream of interfering with. Suppose, he says, the parents of a musically gifted and engaged child can afford to buy him a piano, or take an expensive vacation, but not both; they decide to take the vacation. However much we might condemn the decision, he says, "scarcely anyone would think the parents were not within their moral right in choosing as they did." We may conclude, he says, that "just because a particular option is educationally bad it does not follow that parents have no right to choose it." As he frames the problem, "the heart of the matter is how to distinguish bad educational options that are within the scope of parents' rights from options that are bad in a way that puts them outside, all the while avoiding both parental despotism and its child-centered inversion."[67]

Now, you might think that the state should intervene against parental preferences only when those preferences would severely diminish a child's well-being. (After all, we don't think parents would be within their moral rights if they chose to malnourish their young.) But our intuitions about when to intervene don't track with magnitude of harm—with how greatly some act would diminish a child's well-being. Suppose the child in question has an enormous musical gift, which brings him and others deep gratification. It may be that the parents' decision (add ancillary stipulations to taste) will enormously diminish his well-being. Our disapproval grows—but most of us still wouldn't think a liberal democracy should coerce them into making a better decision. Conversely, we can imagine plenty of scenarios in which, although a child's well-being would be only modestly diminished, the state could legitimately infringe on parental choice. The parent's wish to have a child educated at a particular school might be defeated if the state refuses to certify the school, perhaps judging it to be educationally inadequate; and the state would be within its rights even if the child would be only a little worse off. Social services will remove an abused or neglected child from its parents: but perhaps the occasional black eye will have diminished the child's present happiness and future prospects far less than the missing piano. When we speak of the well-being of the child as the primary concern, then, the notion of it we have in mind is a satisficing, not a maximizing, one.[68]

Which doesn't tell us much about what children may, and *must*, be provided. Let me return to our piano-deprived prodigy for a moment, and increase the stakes all around. Suppose, on the one hand, that the child's parents belonged to a fundamentalist sect that had, as a core and constitutive commitment, the renunciation of all music. Because they view music as sinful, they have refused to let their child have any further exposure to it, and have expressly demanded that the school accommodate their wishes. The issue of citizen-competence isn't at stake; playing the piano isn't an aspect of that. (And the belief that music is sinful, unlike, say, the belief that voting is sinful, doesn't directly undermine the civic aims of democracy.) A parent's ambition to raise a child of his or her own religious identity is something you'd infringe upon only with extreme reluctance, if at all. Are there any conceivable circumstances in which government officials properly could? Suppose we have reason to think that the child would thereby be deprived of his only real chance of flourishing: perhaps because the child is severely disabled in other respects. Surely it's just a fact that this vocation requires the acquisition of skills starting at an early age; you can't start only upon reaching majority and achieve real proficiency. So it's just possible that there could be circumstances in which, as a last resort, the state would be justified in intervening, maybe even in removing child from his family. Such an action would flow from the determination that the child will otherwise fail to reach a minimal level of well-being.

But states can and do make educational requirements that go well beyond baseline welfare; and conflicts between parental rights and a child's "rights in trust" (in Joel Feinberg's formulation)—or, less tendentiously, conflicts between parents and schools—can be difficult to sort out. That's especially so when those conflicts are organized along identitarian lines.

First, a caveat. I will be moving on, in the next section, to focus on identity-related truth claims, and the focus will seem natural, given the prominence of the "creation science" controversy, and the like. But, as I've suggested earlier, we should resist thinking of conflicts between identity groups as simply conflicts between belief systems. Social practices aren't just sets of propositions; and the significance of an avowal—the recitation of the catechism, say—may lie primarily in its performance rather than in its assertoric force.[69] Just so, much of what we learn in the classroom isn't reducible to the official content of instruction, and identity-based clashes can arise even from pedagogic style.

Let me start with a minor example of such a clash. Suppose an instructor, intent on preparing her students for the demands of liberal democracy, establishes a rule that no discussion is complete until everyone has spoken. The idea is that everyone is of equal worth, and so equally entitled to express his or her opinions and receive respectful attention. The instructor also makes a habit of asking children to explain what other children have said, for a dialogue of equals requires listening as well as speaking. These practices are meant to be ways of communicating equality of respect and the place of discourse and reason in the relations of people who respect one another. (Adherents of "constructivist pedagogy" are particularly partial to this sort of approach.) On this theory, a child who has learned spontaneously to attend to what other children say and who expects a discussion of a question to be one that requires everyone's voice is learning about dignity and respect.

None of this sounds terribly controversial (putting aside, for a moment, the empirical questions about efficacy). But it already raises problems in our ethnically plural society. Not every social group in this country believes that children should be encouraged to speak up: some Chinese American families teach children that proper behavior calls for attentive silence in the presence of adults—and the teacher is an adult. Children know nothing, after all; or, at least, nothing of importance. They are in class to learn. From this perspective, the practices I have just described look guaranteed to produce children who chatter and expect to be listened to; children, in short, who are ill-mannered.[70]

I have said that, though parents have the central role in raising their children, the state can rightly intervene to protect the child's growth to autonomy; if the sorts of practices I have described were necessary for that purpose, they could be warranted by that fact. But the parents do not lose their role because the state's experts have a good-faith disagreement with them about what is best for their children. It would be open to our instructor to defend her pedagogical technique as something more than a sectarian preference: facility with language and its use in social life requires lots of practice; it may be that children who are talked to and reasoned with do better, on average, at cognitive tasks that are broadly useful in modern life. But Chinese Americans have not been having a hard time preparing their children to perform well at the cognitive tasks by which our schools measure their success and failure; and it is not an unreasonable hypothesis that the capacity for careful attention and for sustained intellectual work is connected with being able to sit quietly in the presence of adults. Our instructor could, for her part, explain to parents that her practices place value on listening as well as on speaking: and that both of them are consistent with, for example, insisting that children also learn to work quietly together and alone. In all events, an amicable solution would not seem out of reach; neither party is likely to see the other as a looming peril.

At the other extreme from these practice-based conflicts are concerns about the content of the curriculum, which can get quite heated even when they don't frontally involve identity issues. There are curricular questions, for example, about what weight to place on various topics. How much American history should children in America know? Within that history, should the focus be on individuals or on social processes; on America's failures or her successes? In recent years, some critics have objected to a history curriculum that has too much of Harriet Tubman and not enough of Thomas Jefferson; and they have also objected to a curriculum whose discussion of Thomas Jefferson focuses too much on his betrayal of liberty—in his persistent failure to emancipate his slaves—and not enough on his place as the author of the Declaration of Independence, as liberty's champion. No doubt a focus too lopsided shades off into simple untruth: the real debates here, though, are not about what happened but about what narratives we will embed them in; they are about which of the many true stories we will tell.

From the point of view of democratic politics, these questions aren't terribly daunting. We need to prepare children with the truth and the capacity to acquire more of it. Because—like us, but more so—they cannot absorb the whole truth, in all its complexity, all at once, we must begin with simplified stories; sometimes, even, with what is literally untrue. The obvious model where untruth prepares the way for truth is physics: the easiest way, we think, to prepare children for Einstein and Schrödinger is to teach them Newton and Maxwell first. But Newton and Maxwell did not know about relativity or about the indeterminacy of the fundamental physical laws, and so their physics, which assumes absolute space and deterministic laws, is just not true. And the teaching of history is full of cases where we can delve deeper as we grow older into stories we first heard, in simplified versions, in first grade. Because it is on the way to the truth, or because it is the closest thing to the truth that, at a certain age, they can understand, such misinformation (and misinformation is what it is, strictly speaking) can be seen as aimed at helping children develop toward an autonomy rooted in the best available understanding of the world. The hard cases, of course, are the ones where the controversy is about what the truth is.

CONFLICTS OVER IDENTITY CLAIMS

The greatest controversies about education in democracies, as we know, tend to occur when people feel that their own children are being taught things that are inconsistent with claims that are crucial marks of their own collective identities. I shall call a claim—whether moral or not—that is, in this sort of way, implicated with a certain collective identity an *identity claim*. Much debate over what shall be taught in the schools about identity claims is thus centrally concerned with insisting on the state's recognition of some identities (say, Christian) or its nonrecognition of others (say, lesbian and gay). Now, it will immediately be clear why the notion of raising children to autonomy—with its corollary that we should equip them with the truths they need—does not help much in deciding what should be taught about these particular questions. It does not help because there is substantial social disagreement as to what those truths *are*; and, in the cases where the claims in dispute are identity-related, such disagreements, we can predict, will not be settled by the appointment of commissions of experts to resolve them. "In regard to religion, I do not think it right either oneself to teach, or to allow anyone else to teach one's children, authoritatively, anything whatever that one does not from the bottom of one's heart & by the clearest light of one's reason, believe to be true," Mill wrote in an 1868 letter to a certain Charles Friend;[71] it is a precept that has been taken to heart most zealously by his opponents.

You might think the answer should be to stress the democracy in liberal democracy. Let us have public debate among equals and then vote for what should be taught. But one option, in that public debate, is to declare that on some topics we may require the state to step back and leave the matter to the parents. It is not the case (though this seems often to escape notice) that the only option—even in a majoritarian system)—would be to teach what the majority believes to be true.

Here, by way of an unphilosophical compromise, is one proposal: where identity-related propositions are at stake, parents are permitted to insist that their children not be taught what is contrary to their beliefs; and, in return, the state will be able to insist that the children be told what other citizens believe, in the name of a desire for the sort of mutual knowledge across identities that is a condition for living productively together.

Thus it seems reasonable to teach children about the range of religious traditions in the communities within which they live (indeed, in the world), without requiring them to assent to any of them, so that, to begin with, at least, they will assent only to the religion they have learned at home. This allows the children the knowledge to make identity choices as they themselves grow to autonomy; but it gives parents a special, primary, place in shaping those choices. Only where a parent's choice seems to compromise the possibility of an autonomous adulthood (as would be the case with a refusal, on religious grounds, to allow one's children to learn to read) must the liberal state step in. The proposal is inherently vague—just when have a child's prospects for autonomy been substantially compromised?—and how civic-minded liberals will feel about an inherently vague proposal like this will depend, in part, on how they balance the contending claims; on whether my notion of "good enough" autonomy is good enough for them. But the proposal will not necessarily satisfy all those seeking exemptions either, which I suppose is what makes it a compromise.

Consider the case of *Mozert v. Hawkins County Board of Education*, in which a group of fundamentalists objected to the adoption of the Holt, Rinehart and Winston "basic reading series" in their local elementary school. (The case, which started making its way through the courts in 1983, has been widely analyzed, and its history ably recounted in a book by Stephen Bates.)[72] Some of the parents saw Satanism in stories that involved, say, invisibility or the ability to read minds; others objected to passages that celebrated women for accomplishments outside the home. The U.S. Court of Appeals, in ruling against the plaintiffs, was struck by their intolerance: they had made it clear that the mere exposure of their children to the offending themes—such as magic, feminism, and telepathy—was intolerable, whether or not these things were presented as true. And, indeed, Vicki Frost, the plaintiff who testified at greatest length, said that it would be acceptable for the school to expose her children to the beliefs of other religions or philosophies only if they were identified as erroneous. So my proposal would not satisfy these parents. Indeed, if one took them at their word, one might despair of reaching any lasting compromise with so uncompromising a group.

But when one descends to the messy particulars of the situation as it developed—attends to all the missed opportunities for conciliation and the hardening of positions on both sides—one is struck by how readily the whole battle might have been avoided. The pedagogical theories of the plaintiffs were extreme. Not so their specific demands: that they be allowed to keep their children enrolled in the school but opt out of the reading classes. (Testing could have been conducted to ensure that their children's reading proficiency kept pace with the required standards; and the parents would have accepted the additional burden of providing alternative reading instruction.) The goals of democratic education are advanced only if the illiberal stay in school; and the in-or-out stance of the Hawkins County School Board ill-served that purpose.[73]

By invoking prudential considerations, I don't mean to sentence the civic-minded to a career of reflexive conflict-avoidance: to what might be termed "aversive liberalism"—the sort that aims only to give no offense. The reason that political officials have to exercise caution and discretion in these circumstances is simply that education is compulsory. And, on its face, there is indeed something coercive about a system of universal education. This should worry us—up to a point. A blind man undergoes sight-restoring surgery against his will; that doesn't mean that subsequent decisions based on what he can see are coerced.[74] There *can* be a coercive element in what we blandly term the provision of information, make no mistake, but the element of coercion needn't carry through.

As you'd expect, public schools already maintain a gingerly reticence about the more salient identity claims. In the United States, public-school students will be instructed in arithmetic and science and history, but their teachers will not promulgate views about God's existence or Christ's benevolence; and given the thinness of our "civic religion," this suits most people just fine. Many identity groups that make thicker claims are resigned to being at odds with the official curriculum. Where they are not, the concern for the child's prospective autonomy does have bite. The proposal we've discussed has as a consequence that if intolerance of other identities is built into an identity, or if learning the views of others except as shameful error is one of their norms, we will be seeking, in public education, to reshape those identities so as to exclude this feature. This is liberal soul making, again. Actually existing liberalism, of almost any description, is more than a procedural value: it places a substantive weight on creating a social world in which we each can have a good chance at a life of our own.

It bears repeating that my aim in this chapter has been to venture an account of where soul making fits into a liberal-democratic politics; it has not been to expand or diminish its purview. Because we are persons, our autonomy ought to be respected; because we are encumbered, socially embedded, selves, we will use our autonomy to protect and preserve a wide variety of extraindividual commitments. Finally, because we are human beings, we are frail, and we are *formed*; it is our nature to shape our natures. Earlier I mentioned the seeming paradox that Mill's paramount concern for freedom as noninterference enfolded a concern for governance that had a positive influence on the character of its citizens: what he understood was that the "self" in "self-development" had to be the object of the process before it was its subject—that the cultivation of individuality was the most social thing of all. "What self-culture would be possible without aid from the general sentiment of mankind?" Mill asked in an 1854 essay, "Nature." Soul making is a part of politics, if not in that Platonic sense wherein it is the purpose of politics, then at least in the sense that political decisions must take into account the effects they have on the character of citizens. And so it would be pointless to praise or dispraise soul making in itself, to characterize it as an ally or adversary of individuality: a knife in the hands of an assailant can take a life; a knife in the hands of a surgeon can save one. "The duty of man is the same in respect to his own nature as in respect to the nature of all other things," Mill wrote in the same essay, "namely not to follow but to amend it."[75] The verb "amend"—rather than, say, transform, eradicate, or harness—is a modest one, and properly so. There's a reason that the various discussions in this chapter have concluded with some gesture toward a necessary equilibrium—between our bare and "informed" or "rational" preferences, between a concern for people as they are, and for people as they might be, the identities we have and those we might achieve. In each case, to ignore the first term is tyranny; to give up on the second is defeatism, or complacency. We have other choices.

Chapter Six

～ Rooted Cosmopolitanism

A WORLDWIDE WEB—RUTHLESS COSMOPOLITANS—ETHICAL
PARTIALITY—TWO CONCEPTS OF OBLIGATION—COSMOPOLI-
TAN PATRIOTISM—CONFRONTATION AND CONVERSATION—
RIVALROUS GOODS, RIVALROUS GODS—TRAVELING TALES—
GLOBALIZING HUMAN RIGHTS—COSMOPOLITAN
CONVERSATION

A WORLDWIDE WEB

When my father died, my sisters and I found a hand-
written draft of the final message he had meant to leave us. It began by
reminding us of the history of our two families, his in Ghana and our
mother's in England, which he took to be a summary account of who
we were. But then he wrote, "Remember that you are citizens of the
world." He told us that wherever we chose to live—and, as citizens of
the world, we could surely choose to live anywhere that would have
us—we should endeavor to leave that place "better than you found it."
"Deep inside of me," he went on, "is a great love for mankind and an
abiding desire to see mankind, under God, fulfill its highest destiny."

That notion of leaving a place "better than you found it" was a large
part of what my father understood by citizenship. It wasn't just a matter
of belonging to a community; it was a matter of taking responsibility
with that community for its destiny. As evidenced by his long-term
practical commitment to the United Nations and a host of other international organizations, he felt this responsible solidarity with all humanity. But he was also intensely engaged with many narrower, overlapping communities. He titled the account he wrote of his life, *The
Autobiography of an African Patriot*: and what he meant by this epithet
was not just that he was an African and a patriot of Ghana, but that he
was a patriot of Africa as well. He felt about the continent and its people

what he felt about Ghana and Ghanaians: that they were fellows, that they had a shared destiny. And he felt the same thing, in a more intimate way, about Ashanti, the region of Ghana where he and I were raised, the residuum of the great Asante empire that had dominated our region before its conquest by the British.

Growing up with this father and an English mother, who was both deeply connected to our family in England and fully rooted in Ghana, where she has now lived for half a century, I never found it hard to live with many such loyalties. Our community was Asante, was Ghana, was Africa, but it was also (in no particular order) England, the Methodist Church, the Third World: and, in his final words of love and guidance, my father insisted that it was also all humanity.

Is there sense in the sentiment? Is being a citizen of the world—a "cosmopolitan," in the word's root sense—something one can, or should, aspire to? If we "dip into the future" do we really anticipate "the Parliament of man, the Federation of the world."[1] People have offered reasons for skepticism, and from a range of perspectives. Some deny that the notion, however endearing the "Locksley Hall" rhetoric, can be reconciled with the constitutive role of our local and positional attachments. "Cosmopolitanism," in their view, gives to aery nothing a local habitation and a name: but aery nothing it remains. Others view it not as unattainable but as objectionable; for them it is a distinctively modern mode of deracination—something essentially parasitic upon the tribalisms it disdains, the posturing *de haut en bas* of privilege. Cosmopolitan values, it has been said, are really imperial ones—a parochialism, yet again, puffed up with universalist pretensions; liberalism on safari. And, as we'll see, even for sympathetic souls, cosmopolitanism poses a congeries of paradoxes.

I think there are forms of cosmopolitanism worth defending—forms that survive theoretical and practical scrutiny. But before turning to such theoretical and practical considerations, I want to set out a few historical ones.

Here, personal history is a small inlet to public history. My sisters and I reside in four different countries—I in America, and they in Namibia, Nigeria, and Ghana—but wherever we live, we are connected to Ghana and to England, our family roots, and to other places by love and friendship and experience. And what strikes me about these trajectories—

apart from the fact that they are reproduced in many, many families today—is not the difficulty of these relocations but how easy they have largely been. Indeed, far from being especially modern, our little family experiment actually belongs to one of the oldest patterns of the species.

In every region of the world, throughout recorded history, men and women have traveled great distances—in pursuit of trade, of empire, of knowledge, of converts, of slaves—shaping the minds and the material lives of people in other regions with objects and ideas from far away. Alexander's empire molded the politics but also the sculpture of Egypt and northern India; the Mughals and the Mongols shaped the economies but also the architecture of great swaths of Asia; the Bantu migrations populated half the African continent, bringing language and religion but also ironworking and new forms of agriculture. The effects are clear in religion: Islamic states stretch from Morocco to Indonesia; Christianity is strong on every continent, borne often by missionaries in the wake of empire, while Judaism has traveled to every continent with barely a hint of evangelism; and Buddhism, which long ago migrated from India into much of East and Southeast Asia, can now be found in Europe and Africa and the Americas as well. But it is not just religions that travel: Gujaratis and Sikhs, and people whose ancestors came from many different parts of China or of Africa, live in global diasporas. The traders of the Silk Road changed the style of elite dress in Italy. The Ming china in Swahili graves follows the path of Admiral Cheng Ho, who, as a representative of the Ming court, established relations with a range of East African rulers. And the parade of such examples is endless: the Mande merchants of the Sahel; the English, Dutch, Italian, and Iberian sailors of the Western Age of Adventure; the Polynesian navigators who first populated the Pacific. The nomadic urge is deep within us. The ancestors of the human population outside Africa probably left that continent no more than a mere hundred thousand years or so ago. It has not taken us very long to cover the planet. We have always been a traveling species.

So the interpenetration of societies and forms of life is a very old phenomenon, one that is natural to us (and that has produced, no doubt, much bloodshed and violence and suspicion, as well as much productive and friendly exchange). Over the past few decades, it is true, the ratio of what is settled to what has traveled has changed everywhere.

Ideas, objects, and people from "outside" are now more—and more obviously—present everywhere than they have ever been. Calling this process "globalization," as we often do, is all very well but tells us very little about how it is either novel or significant. For, as I have suggested, you could describe the history of the human species as a process of globalization: the globalization, if you like, of the *longue durée*—in fact, of the longest humanly possible *durée*, that of the period within which we have been fully human.

In our historical myopia, to be sure, we more normally use the term to speak of recent events. We reflect, in the language of globalization, on the way in which CNN and the BBC have come to have audiences around the planet, and on the creation of global products, from Nestlé's powdered milk to Mercedes-Benz cars, from Coca-Cola to Microsoft Windows, from the Beatles to Shakira. Globalization surfaces as the theme of discussions of the internationalization of legal norms—in the sphere of trade through the WTO; in the sphere of human rights, through the treaties that have followed in the wake of the UN's Declaration of Human Rights—and in work on the development of transnational accounting standards in commerce or of systems of cross-national commercial arbitration. Globalization can mean the increasing dominance of English as the language of business or the spread of liberal democracy or the growth of the Internet. And we hear it spoken of both by those who celebrate and by those who deplore the fluidity of capital flows, whose material preconditions lie in the same information technology that has made the Internet possible. Planes and boats and trains, satellites and cables of copper and optic fiber, and the people and things and ideas that travel all of them, are, indeed, bringing us all ever more definitively into a single web. And that web is physical, biological, electronic, artistic, literary, musical, linguistic, juridical, religious, economic, familial.

Our increasing interconnectedness—and our growing awareness of it—has not, of course, made us into denizens of a single community, the proverbial "global village." Everyone knows you cannot have face-to-face relations with six billion people. But you cannot have face-to-face relations with ten million or a million or a hundred thousand people (with your fellow Swazis or Swahilis or Swedes) either; and we humans have long had practice in identifying, in nations, cities, and towns, with groups on this grander scale. Rome, after all, in the years around the birth of Christ, already had a population of nearly a million people; and being a citizen of that city and its empire was, as Saint Paul insisted, a substantial thing. To be *civis Romanus* was to be bound together with other Romans not by mutual knowledge or recognition, but by language, law, and literature. Increasingly, since the eighteenth century, people all around the planet have grown into national affiliations that extend over territories that would take weeks or months to traverse on foot, covering thousands of villages, towns, and cities, millions of people, and, often, dozens of languages, or scores of barely mutually intelligible dialects.

These nations have absorbed some of the central functions of the old Greek πολις: they are the sources of law for their inhabitants, for example, and they define their identities when they travel away from home. It is, I think, not unnatural that we have come to call the public business of these nations "politics." Still, as I have been insisting, nations differ from the πολις so substantially in scale—there is no space large enough to encompass their free citizens in a single gathering—that relations between citizens must, of necessity, be relations between strangers. What accounts, then, for the thick, black line we draw between these strangers and (in a convenient shorthand of Michael Walzer's) "political strangers," those who are not members of our polity?

And so we return to that recently much bruited idea of the cosmopolitan. A cosmopolitan should—etymologically, at least—be someone who thinks that the world is, so to speak, our shared hometown, reproducing something very like the self-conscious oxymoron of the "global village." I am poorly equipped, I fear, to summarize the history of this idea, or perhaps I should say, this word. Cosmopolitanism as an ideal in the West is conventionally regarded as a legacy of Stoicism, a movement of which Zeno of Citium (334–262 B.C.E.)—the Cypriot rather than the Eleatic—is conventionally regarded as the founder. But Zeno seems to have begun within the broad framework laid out by the Cynics, who had been the first to coin the deliberately paradoxical expression χοσμου πολιτης, "citizen of the cosmos." The paradox would have been clear to anyone in the classical Greek world. A citizen—a πολιτης—belongs to a particular πολις: a city to which he or she owes loyalty; the χοσμος for Cynics and for Stoics is the world, not in the sense of the earth, but in the sense of the universe. But for most of their contemporaries, to be a πολιτης of one place was exactly not to be a πολιτης of any other. Talk of citizenship in the χοσμος reflected a rejection of the call of local loyalties—reflected, in fact, the general Cynic hostility to custom and tradition—and so it was more than a mere appeal to a universal human solidarity. It would be as if someone asked you where your home was and you said "anywhere" or "everywhere"—to which it would be natural to reply that, in that case, you did not have a home at all.

Cosmopolitanism might have come to mean the proposal that we create a world-state to govern a world community; but this is not what we nowadays mean by cosmopolitanism, and, significantly, it is not what the Stoics had in mind, either. Marcus Aurelius, one of the most enduring of the later Stoics, writes in the concluding paragraphs of the final, twelfth, book of his *Meditations*: "O man, citizenship of this great world-city has been yours. Whether for five years or fivescore, what is that to you? Whatever the law of that city decrees is fair to one and all alike."[2] Now if anyone had ever been in a position to try to establish a world-government, it would have been Marcus Aurelius. He was, after all, one of the last great emperors of the greatest empire of the classical West. But the world-city he was talking about reflected a sense of spiritual rather than political confraternity—here χοσμος really means universe—because, as one of his many translators once put it, "just as to the Athenian Athens was the 'dear city of Cecrops', to the philosopher the universe is the dear city of God."[3] He took for granted that all states—even Rome—had boundaries on their sovereignty.

In this, he was like most normative political theorists. Not only have such theorists had little to say about what might be owed to outsiders, but they have gone to great lengths to avoid the problem of outsiders altogether. Have you noticed their fondness for islands? Before and after Thomas More, many of the great utopian writers plopped their imaginary societies down on islands (with results ranging from the industrious scientism of Francis Bacon's Bensalem to the sensual surfeit of Henry Neville's *Isle of Pines*); and our geographical preferences follow suit. Ronald Dworkin, in a well-known essay about how we ought to think about equality, presents a hypothetical auction among shipwreck survivors—"the immigrants," he calls them—equipped with "an equal and large number of clamshells" for the task of making a life on a desert island. John Rawls, in *A Theory of Justice*, conjured up no island but did stipulate that the well-ordered society he was theorizing would have the boundaries of "a self-contained national community," whereupon Robert Nozick (by way of critique) gave us a whole archipelago—ten Robinson Crusoes on ten different islands.[4] If island locales are *scènes à faire* in normative political theory, it isn't because normative political theorists are unsociable fellows; it is because the conceit is helpful in thinking about what a well-ordered society might look like. But what's occluded, of course, is exactly the moral status of political strangers. Cosmopolitanism (which has recently gathered its own theorists) takes this to be a serious omission. If the history of the world is as I've described it, then, wherever you live, the matter of outsiders isn't a sociopolitical anomaly—a small, messy chore, like cleaning out the attic, to be dealt with when we have a spare hour or two. No island, you could say, is an island.

That political philosophy has largely neglected questions of national membership is particularly odd given the political history of the West since the Enlightenment. The first modern Western constitutions—the French and the American—were produced in a great ferment of ideas about the rights not just of citizens but of human beings as such: the title of the Declaration of the Rights of Man and Citizen mentions the human first; and the American Declaration of Independence enunciates the fundamental truths from which its politics are to be derived as truths about "all men." (It is worth recalling, as well, that alien suffrage was common in the early republic in local elections.)

The neglect is odder still when we reflect that the moral underpinnings of modern political theory are, as I have insisted, generally consistent with ethical individualism. If there were some reason to think that national communities were themselves ultimate units of concern (and we looked at some such approaches in chapter 3, though not with favor), then the fact that we distinguished between members and nonmembers would, perhaps, be easy enough to justify: for on such a view members and nonmembers would contribute differently, no doubt, to the nation's well-being. On the assumption that all morality begins with persons and not with peoples, however, the making of distinctions between one kind of person and another will always have to be justified:

and it will have to be justified in terms of what it means for individuals, and not for nations or communities of other sorts.[5] Still, if cosmopolitanism, in its universalist aspect, raises challenges for partiality—the "group feelings" that we all have—one could equally say that the existence of group feelings raises problems for cosmopolitanism. So before we ask where cosmopolitanism can take us, we'll want to satisfy ourselves that we can imagine a congenial kind of cosmopolitanism in the first place. Nobody would entertain the cosmopolitan project who couldn't imagine wanting to be a cosmopolitan.

RUTHLESS COSMOPOLITANISM

Although, as I say, I want to defend a form of cosmopolitanism, I can imagine some candidates for the title that are outright repugnant. An ideology can be staunchly supranational and also staunchly illiberal: moral universalism can carry a uniformitarian agenda. Especially in their ruthlessly utopian varieties, universalisms can be malignant indeed. One could speak, then, of *toxic cosmopolitans*, some connected with radical social movements, and some, of course, with reactionary ones: consider what Michael Ignatieff has called the "apocalyptic nihilism" of the September 11 terrorists. It's a commonplace that fundamentalism represents a reaction against modernity (and is, in at least this sense, an outgrowth of modernity); but these men were anything but locals. They were widely traveled, and relatively well educated; more to the point, they were dedicated to a universalist vision of *ummah*—the global Muslim community. It was to this pure and uncompromising ideal, seemingly undiluted by lesser loyalties, that they devoted themselves. Their thinking was planetary (indeed, cosmic), multiethnic, and, with one obvious exception, unconcerned with sublunary human particularity.[6] It was also a photo negative of everything a liberal might hope to find in cosmopolitanism (a measure of tolerance, epistemic modesty, open-mindedness, let's say). But has it no claim to the title? Surely, there is little profit in joining a tug-of-war over a word—in casting out, by definitional fiat, every odious contender. And there are many of them. They include less apocalyptic, and more familiar, strains of uniformitarianism, such as Victorian mission

Christianity or the colonial *mission civilisatrice*, that manifest love for others by attempting to impose their own purportedly superior ways, often by the sword. One sometimes hears a glibly evolutionary account of cosmopolitanism, where it is taken as a Kohlbergian triumph of disinterested reason over beclouded partiality. The phenomenon of toxic cosmopolitanism should, at the very least, help us resist this temptation.

Even when we restrict our attention to those forms of cosmopolitanism that might call themselves liberal, not all are equally embraceable. Marcus Aurelius, especially when played on-screen by Richard Harris with a spirit-gummed beard, represents the creed's more appealing countenance. Yet cosmopolitanism unmodified—taken as a sort of rigorous abjuration of partiality, the discarding of all local loyalties—is a hard sell. It is a position that has little grip upon our hearts. Yet it may have some purchase on our intellects. If persons are of equal worth, as liberals claim, what could justify favoring members of your particular group over others?

Extreme cosmopolitanism entails what Susan Wolf has called "extreme impartialism," which eschews any lesser allegiances than the moral obligations we have to our fellow human beings. William Godwin gave us the locus classicus of this posture in *An Enquiry Concerning Political Justice*, where he wrote, "What magic is there in the pronoun 'my,' that should justify us in overturning the decisions of impartial truth?" and contemplated, with equanimity, the prospect of rescuing the venerable Archbishop Fenelon from a fire and leaving his valet (insofar as his life was less valuable) to burn. "Suppose the valet had been my brother, my father or my benefactor," he continued. "This would not alter the truth of the proposition."[7] A few people seem to find heroism in the moral austerity, and the *bodenlosig* rhetoric, that accompanies such barrel-proof cosmopolitanism; but most of us find the smell of burning friends and relations distinctly off-putting. And the japes and gibes at this form of moral abstractedness are familiar: "Lover of his kind and hater of his kindred," Edmund Burke said of Rousseau. "Telescopic philanthropy" was what Dickens memorably satirized in the character of Mrs. Jellyby, of *Bleak House*. Oblivious to the misery and chaos of her own household as she attends to her grand improving projects overseas, Mrs. Jellyby is described as "a pretty, very diminutive, plump woman of from forty to fifty, with handsome eyes, though they had a curious habit of seeming to look a long way off. As if," we are advised, "they could see nothing nearer than Africa!"[8]

To be fair, the position has its more sympathetic representatives, as when Virginia Woolf, in *Three Guineas*, spoke of "freedom from unreal loyalties": "By freedom from unreal loyalties is meant that you must rid yourself of pride of nationality in the first place; also of religious pride, college pride, school pride, family pride, sex pride and those unreal loyalties that spring from them."[9] Visionary souls have seen such loyalties as the root cause of worldly strife—a case that Tolstoy made with especial vehemence. "Stupid and immoral" was how he described patriotism. "To destroy war, destroy patriotism," he wrote in an 1896 essay, a couple of decades before his country was swept by revolution in the name of a political *internationale*.[10]

But the wishy-washy version of cosmopolitanism I want to defend doesn't seek to destroy patriotism, or separate out "real" from "unreal" loyalties. More important, it isn't exhausted by the appeal to moral universalism. I want, accordingly, to resist the sharp distinction that is sometimes made between "moral" and "cultural" cosmopolitanism, where the former comprises those principles of moral universalism and impartialism, and the latter comprises the values of the world traveler, who takes pleasure in conversation with exotic strangers. The discourse of cosmopolitanism will add to our understanding only when it is informed by both of these ideals: if we care *about* others who are not part of our political order—others who may have commitments and beliefs that are unlike our own—we must have a way to talk *to* them.

A form of cosmopolitanism worth pursuing need not reflexively celebrate human difference; but it cannot be indifferent to the challenge of engaging with it. So, on the one hand, we should distinguish this project from the diversitarianism of the game warden, who ticks off the species in the park, counting each further one a contribution to his assets. On the other hand, we should distinguish it from simple universalism. You wouldn't be a cosmopolitan—or, anyway, you wouldn't share in what was distinctively valuable in cosmopolitanism—if you were a humanitarian who (to invert Marx's slogan) sought to change the world but not to understand it. A tenable cosmopolitanism, in the first instance, must take seriously the value of human life, and the value of particular human lives, the lives people have made for themselves, within the communities that help lend significance to those lives. This prescription captures the challenge. A cosmopolitanism with prospects must reconcile a kind of universalism with the legitimacy of at least some forms of partiality.

ETHICAL PARTIALITY

One might suppose this is easier said than done. In fact, it is easier done than said. We imagine that we know the ways of the beery, blinkered jingoist—all red-flushed cheeks and angry snarl. We may imagine, too, that we know the chilly detachment of the extreme impartialist; the look in Mrs. Jellyby's eyes that tells us she could see "nothing nearer than Africa." Fortunately, these are not our options. My father—for whom there was indeed nothing nearer than Africa—never saw a conflict between his cosmopolitan credo and the patriotism that quickened his spirit and defined his largest ambitions. His generation of independence leaders lived through cycles of hope and disappointment, the wrenching spectacle of high ideals succumbing to low corruption, incompetence, despotism; but, of course, hope persisted. He once published a column in the *Pioneer*, the local newspaper in Kumasi, under the headline "Is Ghana Worth Dying For?"—he meant dying as a political dissident, as an opponent to homegrown tyranny—and I know that his heart's answer was yes. Starting from the days when he was an outspoken member of the opposition in Ghana's parliament, he became all too well acquainted with the inside of Nsawam Prison, and with threats of execution (threats that would be swiftly fulfilled for some of his cellmates). All this is to say that for him, the question "Is Ghana Worth Dying For?" was not an abstraction.[11]

Yet though cosmopolitan patriotism may be untroubling in practice, liberalism has been mightily troubled by it in theory. Isn't patriotism, or any form of partiality, a defection from moral universalism? A few philosophers have sought to defend the partialists from their universalist critics—or, rather more to the point, the universalists from their partialist critics—by claiming that the partialist, fine fellow though he is, is merely a misunderstood universalist. In particular, these philosophers insist that so-called special obligations—what's owed to certain

people in virtue of some shared relationship or attribute—can be disar-
ticulated into moral considerations of a general order. Depending on
the circumstance, they might explain away the *appearance* of special
obligation by reference to a principle of reciprocity or fairness, to the
duties that we owe in virtue of benefits we have received. Perhaps special
obligations arise from some implicit contractarian arrangement, which
can be parsed in terms of tacit promises and reasonable expectations.
Perhaps (consistent with the slogan "Think globally, act locally") these
special obligations are justified by considerations of efficiency in doing
good. Perhaps the obligations flow only from the choice to have entered
or remained a part of some association. In truth, none of these attempts
at reduction have a grip on us comparable to what they seek to reduce.[12]
You always feel as you would if someone gave you a twenty-dollar bill
as change for a five: the generosity is touching but you wonder about
the accounting.

And so special obligations—or what are variously dubbed associative
duties or special responsibilities—pose difficulties for moral theory.
Not only can they be regarded as an unjust burden (on those who must
discharge them), but they seem to confer an unjust advantage (on those
who benefit).[13] Samuel Scheffler, who, in the course of several wonder-
fully perspicacious essays, has done as much as anyone to frame the
debate, dubs this the "distributive objection"; and he suggests that the
liberal's trouble with partiality isn't an anomaly but a symptom of
something deeper. His conclusion is that liberalism contains a tension
among three values, those of autonomy (that is, some core concern
for liberty), loyalty (that is, associational life, in all its richness, and
responsibilities), and moral equality (that is, the notion that persons
are of equal worth, or, anyway, due equal respect). "Associative duties,"
Scheffler says, "do not merely permit the assignment of priority to the
interests of one's associates; they require it." And he issues a challenge:
"If all people are of equal value and importance, then what is it about
my relation to my associates that makes it not merely permissible but
obligatory for me to give their interests priority over the interests of
other people?" In his view, "It remains to be seen whether the question
can be given a satisfactory answer."[14]

There is, of course, an easy Berlinian riposte. Start with some graceful
hand waving about incommensurability; declare that nothing could

reconcile these great goods; and (with a tip of the trilby) commend liberal pluralism for living with the contradictions. That this riposte is familiar and expected does not make it false. Still, we can do better. The right answer, I believe, is that it's the wrong question.

Spouses and Blouses

One way to dissolve the problem—an approach that I want to reject, but that deserves consideration—eschews reductionism but insists that an obligation can be both special and universal. Let's agree that friendship is a universal good. The fact that a friendship depends upon a special relation between those involved—so advocates of this approach would argue—no more violates the precepts of moral equality or impersonal morality than does the special responsibility of a doctor to attend to people who are sick.[15] For that matter, it would be a trivial exercise to preface the strictures of partiality with the universal quantifier: for all persons, priority of concern should go to close friends. A doting father, charged with violating moral equality, could thus reply that he'd favor *anyone* who was in the position of being his son; the Kiwanis loyalist would favor anyone who was in the position of being a Kiwanis Club member. (Notice that the obligation-generating nature of special relationships is taken as basic, not epiphenomenal: that's why this isn't a species of the reductionism we sniffed at earlier.) Andrew Mason—in the course of defending something like this approach—says the nature of a deed can depend on the doer; and that's clearly right.[16] It is the difference between adulterous and connubial congress. It is why a CEO might hesitate to send his executive assistant to play catch with his son. What's universal is being nice to one's friends, not being nice to your friend Mary: but the first sponsors the second. On the view we're considering, every act of partiality is, in just this way, the instantiation of a general rule, or, anyway, a general moral good.

Recall Scheffler's challenge: "If all people are of equal value and importance, then what is it about my relation to my associates that makes it not merely permissible but obligatory for me to give their interests priority over the interests of other people?" Here, the rejoinder would be that you wouldn't be giving their interests priority over the interests of other people *in the same position*. What you're responsive to, ultimately, are universal edicts that govern obligations toward those with whom you have some particular relation. This can be no more troubling to the tenet of moral equality than the fact that, at a four-way stop sign, you ceded the right of way to the motorist who arrived before you did. What you did for him is what you'd do for anyone who happened to be in his position. Or so the argument would run.

Whether or not you find this approach plausible, it's helpful to spell out why it fails. Imagine someone who is true to his school because he believes (perhaps having been tutored by Anthony Powell or Brian Wilson) in the rule that one should be true to one's school. That's the sort of objective partiality we've been considering; yet surely there's no real school spirit there. What's missing is the look and feel of genuine partiality. By contrast, imagine someone who is true to Montgomery Bell Academy because, as a proud alumnus, he thinks it deserves his loyalty: this isn't something he has to reflect on; it's something he feels, and something, in his view, that anybody who had the privilege of attending Montgomery Bell Academy ought to feel.

What's wrong with our first alumnus—that is, what's wrong with grounding our partiality, our sense of special responsibility, in an understanding of a general (albeit partialist) principle? Loyalists aren't loyalists because they honor loyalty in the abstract, and are transferring it to the particulars at hand, as the fourteenth Lord Berners is said to have dyed the pigeons of Faringdon House out of a general love for pastel hues. You don't value your wife because you value wives generally, and this one *happens* to be yours. "A man who took good care of his children, because he recognized that he was responsible for their existence and that no one else would look after them if he did not, might still lack the motivation that a good father would have," Scanlon nicely observes. "The lack of affect is a sign of the fact that the person I have described fails to see the good in being a parent—fails to see having children and caring for them as a way in which it is desirable to live. Without this evaluative element, mere affect would be meaningless."[17] Consider, by way of contrast, the motorist who, at the four-way stop sign by State and Main, cedes the right of way to a white Buick that arrived at the intersection first. Here, the motorist is following the general rules of the road, and this particular car just happens to have arrived first at this particular intersection. Actual existing partiality admits of no *happens to.* Broadly speaking, then, the problem with universalizing accounts of partiality is simply that they seem remote from the attitude and emotion—the *evaluative affect,* let's say—of someone with special responsibilities.

There is, to be sure, a truth buried within the effort to universalize partiality. We can recognize and approve partialist sentiment in others; we can be horrified at its absence. We can admire loyalty that we don't share; the notion of "honor among thieves" can make sense to someone who isn't a thief. We do hold the relationships people have with their spouses to be valuable, and applaud Penelope's faithfulness to Ulysses. But none of this is why, in the end, you value *your* relationship with *your* spouse. Which points to the peculiar character of the good in question. *Friends* and *wealth* are both things we could hold to be intrinsically good; but they're goods of categorically different kinds. You may not mind whether you have this million dollars or that million dollars; but you value your friend not as a token of the type *friend* but as this particular person with whom you have a highly particularized relationship.[18] A radical egalitarian might give his money to the poor, but he can't give his friends to the friendless. Particularist goods, even when they exemplify a good that is objective or universal, have this peculiar characteristic of being, so to speak, nontransferable. And, in ways we'll examine, partiality is typically concerned with such particularist goods.

Now, a skeptic could claim that all this is beside the point—that, after all, one could venture the same things about garments. To say that someone wants a blouse doesn't mean that a blouse is of any use to her as a general thing; only blouses that fit are of value to her. Shall we speak loftily about the particularistic value of blouses? This line of objection is the insurance adjuster's, and what makes this claim of particularism specious is that *any* blouse of a certain specification would do. When it comes to your spouse, by contrast, you will accept no substitutes.[19] And once we are concerned with particularist goods—or, for that matter, with what I'll be calling project-dependent values—Scheffler's "distributive objection" starts to lose its force; these are things that, by their nature, cannot be distributed.

Hovering over talk of moral equality seems to be the analogy of resource equality, the allocation of goods in limited supply: equal respect as the equal (or, anyway, just) apportionment of clamshells. In those terms, we might be tempted to say, of the currency of human-kind-ness,[20] that once you have paid the tax morality requires, you may spend the rest as you please, as your associational commitments and personal projects will impel you to. But the metaphor confuses. If what we're concerned with are particularist goods, we will not make sense of them through clamshells. We might find that we can talk about what we owe to others as persons—*suum cuique tribunes*, in the Roman formula-tion—without even using the word "equality."[21]

The Domain of Moral Equality

And here's where the opposition between associative duties and moral equality (in the sense of equitable treatment) really does dissolve. For it is a category mistake to hold that persons are bound by moral equality in the first place. Liberalism, in most accounts, is indeed con-cerned with moral equality: the state is to display equal respect toward its citizens. Where we go wrong is to suppose that *individuals* should be subject to the same constraint. Social justice may require impartial-ity—or evenhandedness, or fairness, or (under some construction) "neutrality." But social justice is not an attribute of individuals. An individual can no more be required to be impartial among his fellow creatures than he can be obligated to administer his own currency sys-tem. Here we find the "logic of congruence" at its most grotesque. If the invocation of moral equality, in this context, involves an illicit trans-position from politics to persons, a related error—which appears in both the realm of the personal and that of the political—is to assume that "equal" means "identical." As I insisted in the previous chapter, disparate treatment raises problems for equality only when the dispa-rate treatment is not only based on morally irrelevant features but in-vidious. Yes, as persons, we are obliged to give others what we owe them as fellow human beings; yet these dictates of morality (under most plausible conceptions of morality) vastly underdetermine the range of things that we care about.

The relation between normative theories and actual, empirical human norms—our moral common sense—is a complicated affair, which I won't try to explore. Needless to say, we often reject a moral theory because it makes recommendations that don't track with actual existing human norms. ("It can't be wrong / When it feels so right" is how the matter is formulated in the philosophy of Debbie Boone.)[22] And there really is a substantial amount of convergence among humanity about what's bad: all societies have sanctions against murder, theft, and so forth. The trouble is, agreement at this level doesn't guarantee very much; societies that endorse particular acts that we'd describe as murder or theft don't always do so under that description.[23] What's more, we know that "moral common sense" can be seriously defective. Indeed, two major strains of our moral modernity flow from feminist and antiracist campaigns; and here there is a crevasse between ordinary liberal morality and the norms that have obtained among the vast majority of human beings throughout the history of our species. Surely, part of what gives extreme impartialism whatever flinty glamour it has these days is the salience of the civil-rights paradigm of discrimination. Rawls's notion of "reflective equilibrium"—to be arrived at through the adjustment of theory to intuition, and intuition to theory—is meant to bridge the crevasse. Still, it has been a characteristic error to overlearn the hard-won lessons of political equality. Solidarity worries us because we take its obverse face to be exclusion; but should we? The difference between treating others better than you must because you like them and treating others worse than you might because you dislike them is one that only an economist could fail to see. Racism, for example, typically involves giving people less than they are owed, failing to acknowledge their due as fellow human beings; to succumb to racism is to fall short of our obligation to "take seriously and weigh appropriately the fact that they are persons in deliberating about what to do" (as Darwall glosses "recognition respect").[24] Yet I can give you your due and still treat my friend better.

The civil-rights paradigm—I say all this by way of diagnosis—directs us to think about impartiality as the absence of wrongful bias.[25] Often the duties of our office require impartiality; "public actions," as I used the term in chapter 5, may be rightly constrained by the concerns of equitable treatment. But there are distinctions to be made, and we're all accustomed to making them. We readily distinguish a local hardware-store owner who has put his son in charge of managing the shop from the political official—or the head of a publicly held company—who has exploited his position to enrich members of his family. To put the matter paradoxically: impartiality is a strictly position-dependent obligation. What is a virtue in a referee is not a virtue in a prize-fighter's wife.

Let me summarize my worries about "moral equality." First, I urged that the model of distributive justice was a poor fit with particularist goods. *My friend Mary* is not simply an instantiation of the general good represented by *friendship*; she's not like one first-class stamp on a roll of first-class stamps. Second, I maintained that equality wasn't what morality demanded of us as individuals; it denotes a regulative ideal for political, not personal, conduct. We go wrong when we conflate personal and political ideals, and, in particular, when we assume that, because there are connections between the two, they are the same.

Which brings us to the next term of the challenge: that special obligations are, indeed, *obligations*. It's one thing to say that you're permitted to give way to partiality, that the political ideal of moral equality doesn't automatically rule it out. It's another thing to say you *must*. What is the nature of this particular *must*?

Two Concepts of Obligation

A principal source of confusion here arises from all those do-the-right-thing words: "duties," "responsibilities," "obligations." They present two kinds of reasons for action as one. At various points in this book (as advertised in the preface) I've been following Ronald Dworkin in marking a distinction between morality, which has to do with what we owe to others, and ethics, which has to do with what kind of life it is good for us to lead. Ethical considerations are responsive to what Williams calls our "ground projects," our individual conception of what kind of person we seek to be. This is a broad bundle, and it subsumes a variant definition of the ethical that Avishai Margalit (building on Michael Walzer and others) offers, one whose tighter focus will be especially useful here. Here, the distinction between the ethical and the moral corresponds to "thick" relations—which invoke a community founded in a shared past or "collective memory"—and "thin" relations, which we have with strangers, and which are stipulatively entailed by a shared humanity. Margalit has recently suggested that "ought" in the ethical context is used in something like the sense of the "medical ought": the assertion "you ought to take your medicine," he notes, is "relative to the assumption that you want to be healthy."[26] (No such rider attaches to the moral ought, since morality is what persons, qua persons, owe to persons, qua persons.) Margalit's notion of the ethical helpfully amplifies a crucial aspect of Dworkin's: our projects—and, with them, our sense of what it is to live well—involve creating a life out of materials and circumstances that we have been given; this involves developing an identity, enmeshed in larger, collective narratives but not exhausted by them. It involves social forms—attorney, bird-watcher—that, as Raz says, make certain activities and projects possible. It involves, equally, a sense of belonging, of being situated within a larger narrative or narratives. With all this in mind, I want to see what happens when we distinguish between the moral ought and the ethical ought.

In chapter 2, we saw how idealizations were typically guided by some purpose, some set of interests. We could tell a story about someone that was all about causation and constraint, and another story that was all about freedom and choice; and which story it made sense to tell depended upon what we were interested in—what we were trying to explain, to make sense of, to accomplish. (By way of a crude example: retributive justice concerns itself with agency; distributive justice concerns itself with structure. The first attends to our choices; the second to our option set. The first speaks of decision; the second speaks of circumstances.) The central idealization of liberal theory is, of course, the "moral person," who, in virtue of being a human being, has various obligations to other human beings. The interests that conjure up the moral person are those of social justice—which is to say, of the well-ordered *society*, the just *state*, the ideal of liberal *governance*. The realm of the ethical, by contrast, encompasses what you must do as an embedded self with thick relations to others. The interests that entrain the "ethical self" are those of specific, encumbered human beings who are members of particular communities. To create a life, I've said, is to create a life out of the materials that history has given you. An identity is always articulated through concepts (and practices) made available to you by religion, society, school, and state, mediated by family, peers, friends. Bear in mind, too, that the sort of ethical identities that

Margalit focuses on do not exhaust the factors relevant to making a good life. Some aspects of your individual identity set, or what I've been calling your individuality, are brand-name collective identities and some are anything but: Male, Methodist, Scrabble Enthusiast, Aramaic Scholar, son of this man and this woman—all the scarcely countable coordinates that specify *you*. Ethical concerns and constraints arise from my individuality; moral ones arise from my personhood. Ethical ones govern how I behave toward people with whom I have a thick relationship—and tend to be more demanding the thicker that relationship is.

Whether the story you tell of your life is one of constraint or one of freedom relates, as I say, to the purpose of your story. So you might take it to be a fool's errand to reconcile the putative tensions between loyalty and impartiality, between the claims of my ties and relationships and the claims of universalism. Surely, an idealization that undergirds political theory need not take in all the relational differentia that are crucial when the project is what kind of life is a good one for me to live. Rather than integrating the two accounts, that is, you might suppose we'd do better to honor the disjunction—to say, for some purposes, I am a Person, and for others, I am a particular identitarian bundle swaddled in relational facts.[27] In particular, you might suppose that—as with the registers of structure and agency—it is useful to hive off the two vocabularies in connection with two separate projects: the political task of creating a well-ordered society and the personal task of leading a good life.

Well, we can do so—but only up to a point. What makes the realm of "soul making" so vexed and so fascinating is precisely that it represents the intersection between these two projects, and thus between these two normative registers. And the same, ultimately, is true of rooted cosmopolitanism: it is a composite project, a negotiation between disparate tasks. Generally speaking, associative duties can be categorized as *ethical* rather than moral.[28] They involve duties to yourself (in Dworkin's terms), insofar as they reflect your commitment to living a certain kind of life; they involve duties to an ethical community (in Margalit's terms), insofar as they reflect your participation in them, the fact that you enjoy thick relations with certain people through your identities. As with the classic—and vaguely congruent—Hegelian distinction between *Sittlichkeit* and *Moralität*, this response to the challenge of reconciling loyalty and impersonal morality requires a mixed theory of value: one that has space for both project-dependent and objective principles; for obligations that are moral and universal and for obligations that are ethical and relative to our thick relations, to our projects—to our identities.[29]

To say that the ethical can't be assimilated to the moral, though, is not to say that the two are strangers to each other. Routine acts of supererogation, once other people have reason to take them for granted and have come to depend on them, can engender moral responsibilities.[30] In this way, an "ethical ought" may entrain a "moral ought"; moral obligations can play catch-up with ethical ones. In the forest of our obligations, it can be hard to distinguish bough from vine.

Let me try to head off two misinterpretations this discussion is bound to invite. One is to imagine a neat hierarchy wherein moral obligations must be, so to speak, lexically satisfied before we attend to ethical entreaties. (Advocates of "moderate patriotism" have urged something of the sort: special obligations are fine, so long as the demands of morality are met.)[31] A second temptation is to identify the contrast between the moral and the ethical with that between the compulsory and the optional.

Moral obligations must discipline ethical ones. Yet this is not to say that the obligations of universal morality must *always* get priority to ethical obligations—to others or to ourselves. Granted, certain ethical obligations would be simply ruled out by moral concerns of significant magnitude (there's *something* to the assumption of hierarchy); but such a rule is too rough-and-ready to guide us in finer-grained examples. Suppose you have the opportunity to achieve some project of tremendous importance to you, but to seize the opportunity requires breaking a promise. Say you've just heard about an architecture competition, and you know that a design you've labored on for years would be certain to win, so you race to get your balsa-wood model to the competition officials before the deadline—perforce breaking a promise (a lunch date, say) and the speed limit in order to do so. Only the most unattractive sort of moralism would automatically reproach you for your decision.[32] So there will be complicated trade-offs between these different normative registers, between what we have reason to do as abstract moral agents and as the particular people we are: which is to say, between what we have moral reason to do and what we have reason to do, all things—the ethical now included—considered. This messiness makes the line between the moral and the ethical less bright and tight than a purist might like; but then few normative theories offer anything like algorithms for action (and those, like Benthamite utilitarianism, that do, often have preposterous consequences). Here, as often in normative theory, it is as well to remember the sound admonition Aristotle offered at the beginnings of the subject: in ethics we are "speaking about things which are true only for the most part."

You can see how the second temptation—assimilating the ethical to the voluntary—arises. You can't opt out of the human race, whereas associational duties normally involve metaphysically contingent features of who you are.[33] Metaphysically contingent doesn't mean optional, however. It is tempting to distinguish these cases by insisting that your participation in ethical relationships is voluntary. Margalit suggests something like that. "There is no obligation, in my view, to be engaged in ethical relations," he says. "It remains an option to lead a polite solitary life with no engagements and no commitments of the sort involved in ethical life." The picture of choice can be misleading. As he acknowledges, many ethical engagements "are forced on us in much the same way that family relations are."[34] Opting out is not always feasible, or even possible: many relational identities are far from voluntary. George Eliot's Will Ladislaw, asked to explain his "preference" for his beloved, explodes, "I never had a preference for her, any more than I had a preference for breathing."[35] Indeed, we do not choose to fall in love, any more than we choose the circumstances into which we are born. You do not choose to be a son or daughter; a Serb or a Bosnian; a Korean or an Mbuti. (The great Russian cellist Gregor Piatigorsky insisted the same was true of his profession: "Nobody can really choose music as a profession," he used to say. "It chooses you." That is why we speak of "vocations": they call to us; we don't summon them.) In all sorts of ways, as we've seen, our identities are neither wholly scripted for us nor wholly scripted by us.

All the same, the fact that you did not choose to be your mother's son does not mean you have no special responsibilities as a result. Unlike moral strictures, special responsibilities of this sort are fulfilled in degree. *Thou shalt not kill* is a test you take pass-fail. *Honor thy father and thy mother* admits of gradations. When we speak of a good American, or a good Catholic—or, indeed, a good son—the "good" qualifies the identitarian project: it is an ethical, not a moral, predicate. One could, consistent with the demands of morality, be an OK American, a mediocre Catholic, a so-so son.

What's increasingly clear, I hope, is that we're omitting information when we employ the term "obligation" indifferently to designate moral and ethical oughts. Moral judgments provide reasons for action. But ethical ones provide reasons, too—just reasons of a different order, because they are relative to an agent's identity set, to our individuality. They bear on what kind of person we are, or wish to be. All of which invites the thought that there is a zone of "ought," of ethical obligation, that is intermediate between the wholly required and the wholly supererogatory.[36] Kant, in the *Critique of Judgment*, said that in making aesthetic judgments "one solicits assent from everyone else."[37] You might suppose there's a similar distinction to be drawn here: where morality requires compliance, ethics calls for it.

Let me suggest another way of marking the difference between two forms of obligation, the moral and the ethical. Even if defection from what morality requires were rampant in some society, the requirements of morality would be undiminished. Societies ought not to engage in genocide but avidly do so. What's right and wrong, morally, doesn't depend upon the vagaries of our motivations. (This point is not to be confused with the entirely separate question, central to debates over moral internalism, about whether moral judgments, once you have accepted them, are in themselves action-guiding.) By contrast, the realm of the ethical *is* motivationally sensitive. In some matrilineal societies, for instance, you have a strong sense of special obligation toward the offspring of your uncle on the distaff side. Thus in the Akan region of Ghana the relevant relational term—*nua*—doesn't distinguish between your siblings and your maternal cousins; when you say someone is your sister or brother, you have to go on to specify "same mother, same father."[38] If, because of various shifts in the mores of family structure, this ceased to be so, the ethical obligations would cease to be what they were. (And, as socially entrenched as kinship structure would appear to be, there have been just such familial reconfigurations around Africa's "matrilineal belt," just as the privileging of the paternal line has diminished in many American families.) The arena of thick relations—of special obligations—is motivationally sensitive in just this way: it depends upon specific norms that determine the ethical significance of various relational facts.[39] Conduct that is shaped by ethical concerns—by our membership in an ethical community, which is to say, by aspects of our collective identities—is part of what gives content to those ethical relations, that ethical community, that identity. Ethical obligation, that is, is internal to the identity. Who you are is constituted, in part, by what you care about; to cease to care about those things would be to cease to be the sort of person you are. Since an ethical community is constituted in part by special responsibilities that obtain among its members, if nobody felt such special responsibilities, there would be no such community, no such demands.[40] In the realm of the ethical, you can *only* get an "ought" from an "is."

So far I have simply described a space where partiality seems to be situated; I have not said why partiality might be of value. In fact, the most powerful defense of partiality is the simplest: for human beings, relationships are an important good—I would be inclined to say they were objectively valuable—and many (noninstrumental) relationships, as Scheffler rightly insists, require partiality. These relationships are constituted, in part, by the sense of special caring between those involved, and couldn't exist "unless they are seen as providing reasons for unequal treatment."[41] The pronoun "my" *is* magical, and we'd be inclined to view someone wholly unsusceptible to its magic as a monster, or, possibly, a utilitarian. A little earlier, I complained about the idea that treating people equally—in the sense of adhering to the ideal of equal respect—means treating people the same. I went on to say that the political doctrine that the state should show equal concern toward its citizens has been mistaken for a moral imperative that persons should show equal concern to one another. For, of course, we do not relate to others only as "persons"; we relate to them as people—as siblings, cousins, friends, teammates, colleagues, fellow Kiwanis Club members, and so forth. In the terms I've been introducing, the requirements of "thin" moral relations—what we owe to persons—do not rule out (though they may bound) the existence of "thick" ethical relations. The social nature of our projects, our self-understandings through identity groups, underpins the thick ethical relations we have with certain others, and explains why our treatment of people, above the baseline moral dictum of *suum cuique tribunes*, varies with who they are. And because we are a social species, such relations are objectively good. (In these cases, we can say that a relationship of this sort is *a good for you* and also objectively enshrines a good.)

Suppose you're with me so far. It's good to have social ties, we can all agree; and relationships that matter provide reasons for partiality, for unequal treatment. Our identities, our identifications, make some ties matter to us, and give rise to ethical communities. But a defense of partiality—of special responsibilities, associative duties—is only a necessary condition for a defense of national identities; it is far from a sufficient one. After all, nations, those "imagined communities," in Benedict Anderson's classic formulation, can seem awfully big, and awfully arbitrary. It could still be that special responsibilities make sense within truly thick relations (with lovers, family, friends) but not within the imaginary fraternity we have with our conationals. Even if you accept that some ethical relations, some ethical communities, provide reasons for partiality, you could still wonder whether nations are among them.

COSMOPOLITAN PATRIOTISM

In a recent satirical fable, the writer George Saunders assayed the subject of "fluid-nations," citizenship of which depends not on geographical contiguity but on "values, loyalties, and/or habitual patterns of behavior" that traverse geo-national borders. Among such fluid-nations are People Who Say They Hate Television but Admit to Watching It Now and Then, Just to Relax; Elderly Persons Whose First Thought Upon Hearing of a Death Is Relief That They Are Still Alive, Followed by Guilt for Having Had That First Feeling; and Makes Excellent Strudel. His fictive social scientists in the field of Patriotic Studies have, in the course of their researches, arrived at some notable findings. For example, an analysis of World War II statistics showed that, in the clash between American and German soldiers, fellow citizens of the fluid-nation Men Who Fish did not hesitate to kill each other. On the other hand, we're told, Individuals Reluctant to Kill for an Abstraction did show deficits in geo-national patriotism:

> Results indicated that citizens of Individuals Reluctant to Kill for an Abstraction scored, on average, thirty-nine points lower on the National-Allegiance Criterion than did members of the control group. . . . Shown photographs of members of an opposing geo-nation, and asked, "What sort of person do you believe this person to be?," citizens of Individuals Reluctant to Kill for an Abstraction were sixty-four per cent more likely to choose the response "Don't know, would have to meet them first." Given the opportunity to poke with a rubber baton a citizen of a geo-nation traditionally opposed to their geo-nation (an individual who was at that time taunting them with a slogan from a list of Provocative Slogans), citizens of Individuals Reluctant to Kill for an Abstraction were found to be seventy-one per cent less likely to poke than were members of the control group.[42]

Saunders is having sport, in part, with the patent arbitrariness of the ways human beings sort themselves out, the absurdity of categorical chauvinisms. For one evident abstraction is, of course, the nation itself. What gives the satire its force is that actual full-blooded nations do feel different from these notional categories. But should they? Are they entitled to the claims they make upon our evaluative affect?

As I've suggested, a defense of partiality that proceeds from the paradigm of friendship or family cannot, without modification, be invoked in defense of national partiality. It is one thing to make the case for partiality involving those with whom we have face-to-face social connections: that relations of love and friendship are a deep and universal human good surely goes without saying (not that this stopped me from saying it). But nationalism posits a relation among strangers. Indeed, in its historical ascent, nationalism, which is often contrasted with individualism, can equally seem to be a spawn of individualism. One thing that distinguishes national identities from the other ascribed identities with which they sometimes compete (your child, your spouse, your vassal, and other such relational identities) is that *fellow national* is a "category of equivalent persons," sustained by impersonal mediating institutions, as the sociologist Craig Calhoun has argued.[43] The partiality of the nationalist may be thicker than water, but it is thinner than blood.

It's important to remember how abstract a thing the nation really is. National partiality is, of course, what the concept of cosmopolitanism is usually assumed to oppose, and yet the connection between the two is more complicated than this. Nationalism itself has much in common with its putative antithesis, cosmopolitanism: for nationalism, too, exhorts quite a loftily abstract level of allegiance—a vast, encompassing project that extends far beyond ourselves and our families. (For Ghanaians of my father's generation, national feeling was a hard-won achievement, one enabled by political principle and dispassion: though it did not supplant the special obligations one had with respect to one's *ethnie*, matriclan, and family, it did, in some sense, demote them.) That's what makes the contrast between cosmopolitanism and nationalism so vexed. Nations, if they aren't universal enough for the universalist, certainly aren't local enough for the localist. To cast it in the terms of the preceding discussion, if special responsibilities are thought to be worrying because they represent an abridgment of moral universalism, cosmopolitanism is thought to be worrying because it represents an abridgment of special responsibilities. But what's troublesome about cosmopolitanism—that it sometimes puts the abstract demands of a categorical identity (in this case, a shared humanity) above our rooted, *Blut-und-Boden* loyalties—is just what's troublesome about nationalism. If national allegiances are reasons for actions, they will sometimes interfere with the reasons presented by more local, and "thicker," allegiances. (Recall Sartre's famous story, in "Existentialism as Humanism," of the student who, during the Second World War, must wrestle with an agonizing dilemma: his brother has been killed by the Nazis, and he is all his mother has left. Shall he fight to free France, even though his mother would be devastated to lose him? Which takes priority, mother or motherland?)

Indeed, the usual complaints that nationalists hurl at cosmopolitans are complaints that have been hurled at nationalists, and with greater justice: nationalism, too, has been charged with effacing local partialities and solidarities, with promulgating norms that undermine local traditions and customs—with being a force for homogeneity. Upholding differences among groups, I said in chapter 4, typically entails the erasure of differences within groups. (If cosmopolitans are never fully cosmopolitan, the locals are never fully local.) As Friedrich Meinecke observed a century ago, "Cosmopolitanism and nationalism stood side by side in a close, living relationship for a long time."[44] Certainly liberal advocates of each have often been, as it were, intellectual compatriots.

In a recent, eloquent defense of cosmopolitanism, Martha Nussbaum writes:

> We should recognize humanity whenever it occurs, and give its fundamental ingredients, reason and moral capacity, our first allegiance and respect. . . .
>
> The idea of the world citizen is in this way the ancestor and the source of Kant's idea of the "kingdom of ends," and has a similar function in inspiring and regulating moral and political conduct. One should always behave so as to treat with equal respect the dignity of reason and moral choice in every human being.

At the same time, Nussbaum says that, for cosmopolitans, "it is right to give the local an additional measure of concern." In her view, "the primary reason a cosmopolitan should have for this is not that the local is better per se, but rather that this is the only sensible way to do good."[45] Thus speaks the liberal cosmopolitan.

Compare this with Giuseppe Mazzini, the great prophet of Italian nationalism, urging his nationalist creed upon the workers of Italy:

> Your first duties—first as regards importance—are, as I have already told you, towards Humanity. You are *men* before you are either citizens or fathers. If you do not embrace the whole human family in your affection; if you do not bear witness to your belief in the Unity of that family, . . . if, wheresoever a fellow-creature suffers, or the dignity of human nature is violated by falsehood or tyranny—you are not ready, if able, to aid the unhappy, and do not feel called upon to combat, if able, for the redemption of the betrayed and oppressed—you violate your law of life, you comprehend not that Religion which will be the guide and blessing of the future.
>
> But what can each of you, singly, *do* for the moral improvement and progress of Humanity? . . . The individual is too insignificant, and Humanity too vast. The mariner of Brittany prays to God as he puts to sea; "*Help me, my God! my boat is so small and Thy ocean so wide!*" And this prayer is the true expression of the condition of each one of you, until you find the means of infinitely multiplying your forces and powers of action. This means was provided for you by God when He gave you a country.[46]

We do not go too far to say these are, in their fundamental suppositions, the same creed: localism is an instrument to achieve universal ideals, universal goals. This sort of Goldilocks defense of the nation—as a way station between the two extremes, one too big, one too small—appeals both to the putative cosmopolitan and to the putative nationalist, united in their shared humanism. As Mazzini goes on to insist, "In labouring for our own country on the right principle, we labour for Humanity. Our country is the fulcrum of the lever we have to wield for the common good." Thus speaks the liberal nationalist.

Mazzini's heartfelt humanism is hardly anomalous even among those who have most treasured the particularity of local custom. In an often-quoted passage from *Reflections on the Revolution in France*, Burke wrote: "To be attached to the subdivision, to love the little platoon we belong to in society, is the first principle (the germ, as it were) of public affections. It is the first link in the series by which we proceed towards a love to our country and to mankind." Far from being hostile to cosmopolitanism, the argument posits the culminating value of universalism, that overarching love of humanity; that's how love of the little platoon is justified, as a first step along the path.[47]

For reasons that will now be familiar, of course, we cannot be content with such merely instrumental accounts of national sentiment. Yes, to be a citizen of the world is to be concerned for your fellow citizens, and, as Nussbaum says, the way you live that concern is often just by doing things for people in particular places. A citizen of the world can make the world better by making some local place better, even though that place need not be the place of her literal or original citizenship. This is why, when my father told us we were citizens of the world, he went on to tell us that we should work, for that reason, for the good of the places where—whether for the moment or for a lifetime—we had pitched our tents. Still, given my father's sense of loyalty to Ghana, to the Asante, and to his matriclan, among other ties, he would have expected others to be loyal to their national, ethnic, and familial identities: and such loyalty could not be a coolly cerebral decision, an impartial calculation as to how one would best make the world a better place. (He would have had pity for Mrs. Jellyby's neglected young daughter, who is driven to exclaim, "I wish Africa was dead!") On the contrary, he knew that many of these sorts of relationships could not exist without a feeling of special obligation. He would have his children be cosmopolitan, but—in both senses—*partial* cosmopolitans.

Needless to say, the nation is hardly unique in involving "a category of equivalent persons." Most collective identities connect us to strangers, people whom we will never meet: fellow Catholics, fellow lesbians, fellow mathematicians, fellow Angelinos. If, as I say, you come to interpret and shape your sense of yourself, and your life, through such identifications, the conduct of perfect strangers may inspire in you feelings of pride or shame. These identifications will help determine your projects, and help provide reasons for action. Who we are, as any viable cosmopolitanism must acknowledge, helps determine what we care about. To adopt the national project (and we should acknowledge the complexity of such projects; as I say, Ghana, as a project, had much to do with the postcolonial hopes of independence) is, in some measure, to lead a certain kind of life. *Imagined*, as Benedict Anderson would insist, doesn't mean unreal: nothing could be more powerful than the human imagination. Indeed, it's a notable fact that you can experience a sense of special responsibility toward nationals who are not conationals. Consider Lord Byron, sailing to Greece to participate in a rebellion against the Turks. Or even the (very) complicated ethnic sympathies of a colonial figure like T. E. Lawrence, whom we know, after all, not as Lawrence of England, but as Lawrence of Arabia. Or the foreigners, the International Brigade, who, alongside the republicans, fought the Falangists during the Spanish Civil War: here, a fight for universal principles—a fight against fascism—usually came to entail more local forms of identification. But there's no better example of the phenomenon than the Corsican we know as Napoleon—born Nabulio—who, before he became the embodiment of French empire, had been a vehemently anti-French patriot of his island nation. The identifications that give rise to our ethical concerns aren't simply inherited; one's national loyalties aren't determined solely by the geography of one's nativity.

You could accept this catechism, of course, and still suppose that those things we have come, contingently, to value (not in that we have "chosen" to value them, but in that we could, consistent with our moral obligations, not do so), matter less than those that are morally incumbent upon us. In Nussbaum's view, "The accident of where one is born is just that, an accident; any human being might have been born in any nation," and so such differences shouldn't "erect barriers between us and our fellow human beings." But here the notion of "accident" is overtaxed. The quality of being metaphysically necessary to who we are (e.g., date of birth, sex, and parentage, at least in one widely accepted account of personal identity) doesn't track with moral salience.[48] The fact that I am my mother's son is metaphysically contingent to her and metaphysically necessary to me: but nobody would claim any corresponding asymmetry in the special responsibilities that obtain between us. Even putting the topic of personal identity aside, we can agree that many of the things we care most about in life are the result of accident—we can wonder, with Carl Dennis, what might have happened had we taken a different trivial-seeming decision at some point in our lives. By accident I acquire a family; by accident I acquire a profound commitment to this or that social or political agenda. By accident, I am who I am.

The power of project-dependent values, then, can't be gainsaid, least of all when the project is national. Urging the unique force of nationalism, Benedict Anderson, whose *Imagined Communities* remains one of our most eloquent retheorizations of the nation, asks, "Who will willingly die for Comecon"—the old Eastern European Council for Mutual Economic Assistance—"or the EEC?" You see his point. Supranational economic organizations don't seem to involve the shared memories, the thick narratives, that nations (or families, or religions) do. They don't furnish *identities*. Their sway is purely formal; a matter of contract and treaty. If nobody will *give* his life for these organizations, it might have something to do with the fact that nobody *makes* his life out of them. But the rhetorical question—"Who would willingly die?"—would be misapplied if it were meant to single out nationalism from the various upstart contenders. Recall that, before the researchers intervened, the Rattlers were arming themselves with rocks for a raid against their rivals. A dismaying number of urban dwellers have died in intergang warfare—dying *as a* member of the Crips, say; killing *as a* member of the Bloods—and among them are strangers killed by strangers for wearing the wrong colors. These assailants are true to their tribe—and that tribe, we can safely conclude, does not consist of Individuals Reluctant to Kill for an Abstraction.[49]

Still, the matter of national citizenship does raise a number of persistent issues, especially in the context of international concerns. Nussbaum, defending cosmopolitanism *against* patriotism, argues that in "conceding that a morally arbitrary boundary such as the boundary of the nation has a deep and formative role in our deliberations, we seem to deprive ourselves of any principled way of arguing to citizens that they should in fact join hands" across the "boundaries of ethnicity, class, gender and race."[50] I can say what I think is wrong here only if I insist on the distinction between state and nation. Their conflation is a perfectly natural one for a modern person—even after Rwanda, Sri Lanka, Amritsar, Bosnia, Azerbaijan. But the yoking of nation and state in the Enlightenment was intended to bring the arbitrary boundaries of states into conformity with the "natural" ethnoterritorial boundaries of nations; the idea, of course, was that the boundaries of one could be arbitrary, while the boundaries of the other were not.

Not that I want to endorse this essentially Herderian way of thinking; I'm inclined to doubt that nations ever preexist states. A nation—here is a loose and unphilosophical definition—is an "imagined community" of traditions or ancestry running beyond the scale of the face-to-face and seeking political expression for itself. But all the nations I can think of that are not coterminous with states are the legacy of older state arrangements—as Asante is in what has become Ghana; as the Serbian and Croatian nations are in what used to be Yugoslavia.[51] I want, in fact, to distinguish the nation and the state to make a point entirely opposite to Herder's; namely, that if anything is arbitrary, it is not the state but the nation. Since human beings live in political orders narrower than the species, and since it is within those political orders that questions of public right and wrong are largely argued out and decided, the fact of being a fellow citizen—someone who is a member of the same order—is not, with respect to our normative commitments, arbitrary at all.[52]

The nation *is* arbitrary, but not in the sense that we can discard it in our normative reflections. It is arbitrary in the root sense of that term; because its importance in our lives is, in the *Oxford English Dictionary*'s lapidary formulation, "dependent upon will or pleasure." Nations often matter more to people than do states: mono-ethnic Serbia makes more sense to some than multicultural Bosnia; a Hutu (or a Tutsi) Rwanda makes more sense to others than a peaceful shared citizenship of Tutsi and Hutu; only when Britain or France became nations as well as states did ordinary citizens come to care much about being French or British.[53] But notice that the reason nations matter is that they matter to *individuals*. When nations matter ethically, they do so, in the first instance, for the same reason that football and opera matter: as things cared about by autonomous agents, whose autonomous desires we ought to acknowledge and take account of even if we cannot always accede to them. This isn't to adopt a voluntarist account of national identity (or, indeed, a voluntarist account of opera loving). It's just to stress that here we are in the realm of project-dependent values. If nationals are bound together, it is, as I have already said, on the Roman model, by language, law, and literature, and if they share an experience of events, it is not in propria persona, but through their shared exposure to narrations of those events: in folktale and novel and movie, in newspapers and magazines, on radio and television, in the national histories taught in modern national schools. Narrative was central to earlier forms of political identity, too: the Homeric poems for the Greek city-states; the Augustan poetry of Virgil (but also of Horace) for a cultivated Roman elite; the epic of Sundiata for Malinke societies in West Africa; the Vulgate for medieval Christendom; the story of Shaka for the Zulu nation. If there is something distinctive about the new, national, stories, perhaps it is this: that they bind citizens not in a shared relation to gods, kings, and heroes, but as fellow participants, "equivalent persons" in a common story. Modern political communities, that is, are bound together through representations in which the community itself is an actor; and what binds each of us to the community—and thus to each other—is our participation, through our national identity, in that action. Our modern solidarity derives from stories in which we participate through synecdoche.

States, on the other hand, have intrinsic moral value: they matter not because people care about them but because they regulate our lives through forms of coercion that will always require moral justification. State institutions matter because they are both necessary to so many modern human purposes and because they have so great a potential for abuse. As Hobbes famously saw, the state, to do its job, has to have a monopoly of certain forms of authorized coercion; and the exercise of that authority cries out for (but often does not deserve) justification even in places, like so many postcolonial societies, where many people have no positive feeling for the state at all. Cosmopolitans, then, need not claim that the state is morally arbitrary in the way that I have suggested the nation is. There are many reasons to think that living in political communities narrower than the species is better for us than would be our engulfment in a single world-state: a Cosmopolis of which we cosmopolitans would be not figurative but literal citizens.

It is because humans live best on a smaller scale that liberal cosmopolitans should acknowledge the ethical salience of not just the state but the county, the town, the street, the business, the craft, the profession, the family *as* communities, as circles among the many circles narrower than the human horizon that are appropriate spheres of moral concern. They should, in short, endorse the right of others to live in democratic states, with rich possibilities of association within and across their borders, states of which they can be patriotic citizens. And, as cosmopolitans, they can claim that right for themselves.

To contemplate cosmopolitanism of this variety is to contemplate the *task* of cosmopolitanism, which is debate and conversation across nations. Within a legitimate polity, we can decree that all shall drive on the right; that torture shall be forbidden; that carbon emissions shall be restricted. (Within legitimate polities, there are also ways in which people may contest such decrees.) Political philosophy has, of course, had a great deal to say about how such a polity should be ordered, about what justice or legitimacy requires. But once we are speaking not within but among polities, we cannot rely upon decrees and injunctions. We must rely on the ability to listen and to talk to people whose commitments, beliefs, and projects may seem distant from our own.

CONFRONTATION AND CONVERSATION

Early on in Laurence Sterne's *A Sentimental Journey*, the narrator reports the observations of an "old French officer":

Le POUR, *et le* CONTRE *se trouvent en chaque nation*; there is a balance, said he, of good and bad every where; and nothing but the knowing it is so can emancipate one half of the world from the prepossessions which it holds against the other—that the advantage of travel, as it regarded the *sçavoir vivre*, was by seeing a great deal of men and manners; it taught us mutual toleration; and mutual toleration, concluded he, making me a bow, taught us mutual love.[54]

Here is an English writer of the old canon writing in English but also French about a journey to France at a time when it was at war with England; which should remind us of the easy cosmopolitanism that existed among educated men and women in Europe before the nineteenth century. Cosmopolitanism of this sort begins by urging that we should know others, with their differences, and believes that this will lead us to toleration, perhaps even to "mutual love."

This way of making the argument raises an immediate problem. For it starts with an acknowledgment that good and bad exist in each place. And if that is so, won't treating people in other places as fellow citizens require us, indeed, to love the good but also to seek to eradicate the bad? Why should a liberal cosmopolitan love the French as they are, rather than helping them to become better? Why not take advantage, at the same time, of the ways in which they can improve us? Of course, we can learn from other kinds of people and from other societies, just as they can learn from us. But if we do that, we shall inevitably move toward a world of greater uniformity. Differences will remain, naturally, but they will remain precisely in the spheres that are morally indifferent: cosmopolitanism about these spheres will be fine, but surely only because they are, from a moral point of view, of secondary importance. Here is a respect for difference that remains committed to the existence of universal standards.

But there is another way to go. That is to argue against universal standards—the Good, with a capital G—and to defend difference because there is no Archimedean point outside the world of contesting localities from which to adjudicate. This has its less attractive exponents: ASEAN despots who defend the intolerance of their regimes against Amnesty International by arguing that human rights campaigns are just another colonial attempt to impose Western norms upon "Asian values"; or those who defend the infibulation ("Pharaonic circumcision") of female offspring as an expression of "African values."

But it also has its more engaging defenders: who want to keep a space for forms of life threatened by the economic and political hegemony of the industrialized world. (We have heard from some of these defenders in chapter 4.)

Thinking about these debates can help us to distinguish two ways in which we might justify tolerance for illiberal practices that are grounded in local traditions. Most people feel very differently about male and female "circumcision." The circumcision of male infants has, so far as I know, very little to be said for it as a medical procedure; and even if it did, it is a form of irreversible bodily alteration that might, on general liberal grounds, best be left to men to decide on for themselves.[55] Something similar might be said for the piercing of the earlobes of infant girls. Yet, surely, attempts to impose this view on the billions of people who practice one or the other would be an unjustified invasion of societies where these practices are tied to a sense of "identity." It is here that the two possible lines of response come apart.

One line is, as I say, to repudiate the universalism whose sway I have largely been taking for granted. Liberalism is just *our* local framework; Confucianism and many African traditional religions provide others, each of which is, as they say, "equally valid." This will allow us to permit male circumcision, but only at the cost of allowing female infibulation as well. It will be no surprise, by now, that I have very little sympathy with this line of approach. It requires us to define hermetically sealed worlds, closed off from one another, within which everyone is trapped into a moral consensus, inaccessible to arguments from outside. It abjures moral universalism from the very Archimedean point it repudiates. And it deals poorly with the reality of internal dissent: what are we to say of the African women who are opposed to infibulation? Or of Indonesians who have struggled to speak freely? I would rather argue that the harm done by involuntary male circumcision, say, was too small to offset the value that it derives from the wider meanings in which it is embedded. That would allow us to distinguish it from infibulation and Indonesian limitations on free expression, because these latter, however well rooted in local traditions, are too burdensome to be justified by their contributions to the meanings of particular African or Southeast Asian identities.

My complaint about antiuniversalism is that it protects difference at the cost of partitioning each community into a moral world of its own. And so you might suppose that such an approach has simply made itself irrelevant to the project of cosmopolitanism. After all, a simple celebration of roots does not represent a confrontation with cosmopolitanism, only an alternative to it. But there *is* an antiuniversalist approach—one made familiar by Richard Rorty—that seems genuinely engaged by the project of liberal cosmopolitanism. Indeed, if we can speak of that seeming oxymoron, a thoroughly particularist cosmopolitanism, Rorty has made the best case for it.

The case begins with what he calls "ironism," which combines the acknowledgment of the historical contingency of our own central beliefs and desires—what he dubs our "final vocabulary"—with "radical and continuing doubts" about our own starting points. This ironism is a pretty regular feature of the contemporary academy, though it is also as well to remember that the world is full of people (inside the academy as well as outside) whose doubts, if any, about the grounding of their own moral positions are far from manifest. Ironism is grounded in the experience of being "impressed by other vocabularies . . . taken as final by people or books" one has encountered, and the conviction that nothing in his own final vocabulary can either "underwrite or dissolve" these doubts, because *his* vocabulary is no closer to reality than anyone else's.[56] It arises, then, from the sort of cross-national encounters with which liberal cosmopolitanism, as Sterne's French officer articulates it, begins. Ironism isn't for homebodies.

Skeptical antiuniversalism of this sort is not, of course, just Rorty's: a host of skeptics have, in recent decades, declared themselves in opposition to "Enlightenment humanism." The humanism they have in mind—with its notion of a human essence, a human nature that grounds the universality of human rights—has come to seem to many simply preposterous. But the argument made by its opponents has not always managed to avoid muddle. Critiques of Enlightenment along these lines—critiques that combine antirealism in metaphysics and skepticism in epistemology—have been combined with a critique whose foundations are, so to speak, *plus universaliste que le roi.* Often, that is, attacks on "Enlightenment humanism" have been attacks not on the universality of Enlightenment pretensions but on the Eurocentrism of their real bases. But, of course, Hume's or Kant's or Hegel's inability to imagine that an African could achieve anything in the sphere of "arts and letters" is objectionable not because it is humanist or universalist but because it is neither. What has motivated this recent antiuniversalism has been, in large part, a conviction that past universalism was a projection of European values and interests. This is a critique best expressed by the statement that the actually existing Enlightenment was insufficiently Enlightened; it is not an argument that Enlightenment was the wrong project.

To be sure, skeptics of the older humanism have enlisted pragmatic consideration, too. At the end of his essay "Justice as a Larger Loyalty," Rorty writes: "I think that discarding the residual rationalism that we inherit from the Enlightenment is advisable for many reasons. Some of these are theoretical and of interest only to philosophy professors. . . . Others are more practical. One practical reason is that getting rid of rationalistic rhetoric would permit the West to approach the non-West in the role of someone with an instructive story to tell, rather than in the role of someone purporting to be making better use of a universal human capacity."[57]

The "universal human capacity" in question is "reason": Rorty wants "Western" interlocutors, in their dialogue with the "non-West," not to try to demonstrate that their use of the universal capacity of reason has revealed more truths and a better way to live, but to suggest instead that among our "shared beliefs and desires there may be enough resources to permit agreement on how to coexist without violence."[58] That, then, is a proposal for what, as I say, might seem a pleasing paradox: an antiuniversalist cosmopolitanism. I shall return to it after sketching a version I find more congenial.

If we want to hold on to the idea that the ethnocentrism of the Enlightenment was wrong, but still sympathize with the radical and continuing doubts of the ironists, we must find, I think, a different response from Rorty's to the cosmopolitan experience of being "impressed by other vocabularies." I prefer to speak *with* the Enlightenment: to think of dialogue—and I don't mean just the dialogue across nations that cosmopolitans favor—as a shared search for truth and justice.

People from other parts of the world, we can all agree, attract our moral attention; through them we see the "balance of good and bad" in a particular position, and our sympathy is engaged. In the past, in a humanist narrative, this would have been glossed as the discovery of our common humanity, and these responses to others could have been defended as a source of insight into that human nature. "Yes, they are different and we rejoice in that: but we can rejoice in it, in the end, only because it is *human* difference." (Strains of "Ode an die Freude" in the background here: "Alle Menschen werden Brüder . . ." und so weiter.) This—I agree with the critic of Enlightenment humanism here—is the wrong conclusion.

To find the right one, let me begin by filling in the caricature of the view that we have both rejected. On that older view, there was an objective human nature: there were objective needs and interests, grounded in both our animal and our rational natures, and it was in these common natures that our common human rights were somehow based. The task one faced, then, in addressing a society other than one's own—in addressing a people whose moral views were Other—was to point them to that common nature and show how it grounded these moral claims. Principles were universal: what was local was their application. This was a form of moral realism: the view that the universe, not human sentiment, determines what is right and good. And for the moral realist, of course, if the universe is on my side, it will naturally be opposed to those Others who disagree with me.

Many problems were identified over the years with this project. One was that it appeared to commit what G. E. Moore dubbed the "naturalistic fallacy," the mistake Hume purportedly discovered of trying to derive an "ought" from an "is," confusing facts and values, the True and the Good. After two centuries of Humean philosophy we are now (as I've once or twice had occasion to remark) being urged from many philosophical directions to give up the fact-value opposition and accept some form of moral realism. Moral facts, on these views, are in as good shape as facts about the birds and the bees. Rorty seems to want to go the other way, here, giving up the idea that the universe determines what the facts are, so that values are in no worse shape than facts. This is a philosopher's debate that I have a stake in; and about this I think he is wrong. But the debates over realism about the True and the Good carry no special weight in the context of a dialogue between Rorty's "West" and "non-West," or, to be slightly more concrete, between "human rights" and "Asian values." For, if the naturalistic fallacy is a mistake, then the old humanist argument is a bad foundation for belief in human rights, *even within the West.*

The problem I want to raise for dialogue across societies arises even if moral realism is correct. And if the position I am caricaturing as the older humanism had ever seriously faced other societies, it would have had to contend with this very untheoretical problem.

I happen to believe that there is such a thing as a universal human biology, that there is a biological human nature. I would say, for example, that it is shaped by the more than 99 percent of our genes that we all share, by the fact that our closest common ancestor may have lived a little more than a hundred thousand years ago. Such central events as the old triad of "birth, copulation and death"—"all the facts when you come to brass tacks," as T. S. Eliot has it—are, in obvious ways, reflections of that biology. So I don't think what's wrong with the older argument is the appeal to a human essence.

The problem that becomes clear in real cases is that the many interests that people have in virtue of our shared biology do not function outside their symbolic contexts. We give birth not to organisms but to kin; we copulate not with other bodies but with lovers and spouses; and the end of the organic life has a meaning that depends crucially not only on questions of fact (is there a life beyond?) but also on questions of value (do we have, in our society, the notion of a life that is, in some sense completed?). A shared biology, a natural human essence, does not give us, in the relevant sense, a shared ethical nature. And once you enter into a genuine dialogue with people who hold views other than your own about these matters, you are going to discover that there is no non-question-begging way of settling on the basic facts, whether moral or nonmoral, from which to begin the discussion. There are no guaranteed foundations. It does no good here to say, with the old-school moral realist, that whether we can persuade people of the correctness of our view of the good for them is a separate issue from whether our view is correct. I, too, think that is right; but that is, so far, just a theoretical question, an issue for philosophers.

In real life, judgments about right and wrong are intimately tied up with metaphysical and religious belief and with beliefs about the natural order. And these are matters about which agreement may be difficult to achieve. (It's hard to persuade people that there are, on the one hand, no electrons or, on the other, no witches.) Real dialogue will quickly get stymied in these circumstances because interlocutors who disagree at *this* level are likely to treat each other's claims as "merely hypothetical" and are thus not likely to engage with them seriously.

The result is that if we in fact take up dialogue across substantial gaps of belief, experience, imagination, or desire, we will end up unable to find real agreements at the level of principle; and, more than this, we shall often end up failing to agree not just about principle—about what we ought to believe—but about what is to be done. Practically speaking, we need not resolve disagreements of principle about why we should save this child from drowning if, in fact, we agree that the child must be saved. But what if you believe that the child is meant to die because an ancestor has called her, and I do not?

I want to suggest that there was something wrong with the original picture of how dialogue should be grounded. It was based on the idea that we must find points of agreement at the level of principle: here is human nature; here is what human nature dictates. What we learn from efforts at actual intercultural dialogue—what we learn from travel, but also from poems or novels or films from other places—is that we can identify points of agreement that are much more local and contingent than this. We can agree, in fact, with many moments of judgment, even if we do not share the framework within which those judgments are made, even if we cannot identify a framework, even if there are no principles articulated at all. And, to the extent that we have problems finding our way into narratives or neighborhoods, such problems can occur just as easily with narratives and neighborhoods around the corner as they do with those from far away.

Our ironist does not notice this, I think, because he supposes that debates within the West are different from debates across a Western/non-Western divide. And that is because he believes—as Rorty's provocative avowal of "ethnocentrism" suggests—that something called "Western culture" does for conversations within the West what the universe was supposed to do for my humanist. In Rorty's view, something called "Western culture," historically contingent as it may be, is what we all share; it is the sea we navigate together, the air we all breathe. I do not believe in the homogeneity of this cold Western air, or in its difference at every point from the air of the "warm South."

After my admonitions in chapter 4, you will not be surprised that I have managed to write of these issues without using the word "culture," except (as in the last few sentences) by way of citation. Indeed, I've come to think that in these sorts of explanations, culture, like the luminiferous ether of nineteenth-century physics, doesn't do much work. I don't say the word "culture" should be banned from our lexicon; I do not claim it is always entirely without utility. But, as we've seen, its weedlike profusion can sometimes crowd out analysis. Treating international difference, between what Rorty calls "the West" and "the non-West," as an especially profound kind of something called "cultural difference" is, in my view, a characteristically modern mistake. When I reread *A Sentimental Journey* not long ago, it struck me as a much stranger book than any African novel I have read recently: it was harder work; it needed more footnotes; there were more sentences I had to read twice. The sexual politics of Sterne's casual libertinage (the libertinage, I should remind you, of a priest of the Church of England) is stranger to me than anything in Lady Murasaki's gender politics. How does it help, in these circumstances, to speak of Western culture as something that undergirds "our" response to Sterne, or of Japanese culture as a barrier to "our" grasping Murasaki Shikibu?

It would be a long task to think through why we have come to invoke "culture" as the name for the gap between us here and them there. But we should acknowledge how much that gap is the product of a disciplinary artifact. Anthropology, our source of narratives of otherness, has a professional bias toward difference. Who would want to go out for a year of fieldwork "in the bush" in order to return with the news that "they" do so many things just as we do? We don't hear about cross-cultural sameness for the same reason we don't hear about all those noncarcinogenic substances in our environment: sameness is the null result.[59] I spoke a little while ago about "dialogue across societies," and perhaps you thought this was just a periphrastic way of invoking cross-*cultural* dialogue. But if it is true that there are difficulties in what we think of as cross-cultural dialogue, they are often no more and no less substantial than those of dialogues within societies.

RIVALROUS GOODS, RIVALROUS GODS

The conflation of diversity and disagreement is, to be sure, a common error. In fact, though, arguments tend to be the most intense, and numerous, among people who share a lot of their ideational and normative tenets. You will have few disagreements with your cat. Confronted with someone remote from us in his or her idiom and assumptions, we're more likely to react with plain incomprehension than with disagreement. (That's just a basic fact about ethnography. Why are these Nuer cavorting with this cucumber? You need to know more to have an opinion.) And there are fruitful kinds of disagreement that you can have only if you share all sorts of previous founding assumptions. There's a sense in which the economists Joseph Stiglitz and Andrei Shleifer have far more to quarrel about—far more by way of substantive disagreement—than do Stiglitz and the poet Jorie Graham, who, in turn, have more to quarrel about than Stiglitz and Kenge, one of the Mbuti pygmies Colin Turnbull writes about in *The Forest People.* And the area of dispute between our two American macroeconomists will involve not merely technical questions but, indeed, substantive questions of "value," which, in this context, might include how much certain considerations—distributive justice, transparency, nonpaternalism, etc.—matter. Nor is this merely the narcissism of small differences. (In order to disagree with me about whether an antirealist semantics is appropriate for the indicative conditional, you have to agree with lots of prior propositions, including the notion that it's worth having opinions about the matter at all.) To boil it down to a slogan: Disagreement presupposes the cognitive option of agreement.[60]

It should perhaps go without saying that the existence of conflict—geopolitical tension—doesn't track with moral or metaphysical difference, either. For the most part, conflict between national powers doesn't arise from clashing conceptions of the good. On the contrary, conflict arises when both have identified the same thing as good; and where it is, in the economic argot, a "rivalrous good" (something that cannot be shared by two parties at the same time: a port, an oil field, a piece of fertile territory).[61] The fact that both Palestinians and Israelis—in particular, that both observant Muslims and observant Jews—have a special relation to Jerusalem, to the Temple Mount, has been a reliable source of conflict. Cosmopolitan education, Martha Nussbaum says, should help students "to recognize humanity wherever they encounter it, undeterred by traits that are strange to them," and "learn enough about the different to recognize common aims, aspirations, and values, and enough about these common ends to see how variously they are instantiated in the many cultures and their histories." Again, I think this is a commendable ideal; but it would be a mistake to think that harmony among peoples could thereby be achieved. Proximity, spiritual or otherwise, is as conducive to antagonism as it is to amity. Giacomo Leopardi, in his *Pensieri*, says that "a certain wise man, when someone said to him, 'I love you,' replied, 'Why not, if you are not of my religion, or a relative of mine, or a neighbor, or someone who looks after me?' "[62]

Traveling Tales

The cosmopolitanism I want to defend is not the name for a dialogue among static closed cultures, each of which is internally homogenous and different from all the others; not a celebration of the beauty of a collection of closed boxes. What I want to make plausible is, instead, a form of universalism that is sensitive to the ways in which historical context may shape the significance of a practice. At the same time, I want to elaborate on the notion that we often don't need robust theoretical agreement in order to secure shared practices.

The humanism I have caricatured was right in thinking that what we humans share is important. It was wrong about the contours of what we share. Far from relying on a common understanding of our common human nature or a common articulation (through principles) of a moral sphere, we often respond to the situations of others with shared judgments about particular cases. We in our settings are able to find many moments when we share with people from different settings a sense that something has gone right or gone wrong. It isn't principle that brings the missionary doctor and the distressed mother together at the hospital bedside of a child with cholera: it is a shared concern for this particular child. And you do not need to be a missionary or an ethnographer to discover such moments: it happens also when we read.

What we find in the epic or novel, which is always a message in a bottle from some other position, even if it was written and published last week in your hometown, derives not from a theoretical understanding of us as having a commonly understood common nature—not, then, from an understanding that we (we readers and writers) all share—but from an invitation to respond in imagination to narratively constructed situations. In short, what makes the cosmopolitan experience possible for us, whether as readers or as travelers, is not that we share beliefs and values because of our common capacity for reason: in the novel, at least, it is not "reason" but a different human capacity that grounds our sharing: namely, the grasp of a narrative logic that allows us to construct the world to which our imaginations respond. That capacity is to be found up the Amazon, the Mississippi, the Congo, the Indus, and the Yellow rivers, just as it is found on the banks of the Avon and the Dordogne. In chapter 1, I mentioned that a number of philosophers had found reason to emphasize that we make sense of our lives through narrative, that we see our actions and experiences as part of a story. And the basic human capacity to grasp stories, even strange stories, is also what links us, powerfully, to others, even strange others.

I am insisting on agreement about particulars rather than about universals and on the role of the narrative imagination—our response to a sequence of particulars—because they are neglected elements in our accounts of how we respond to people who are different from ourselves. I do not deny that agreement about universals occurs, too. And the gift, and grasp, of narrative is not the only thing we share. Here is a point, in fact, where our philosopher's disagreement about rationalism makes a difference: for "rationalistic rhetoric" claims that in all encounters human beings are struggling with similar mental apparatus to understand a single world. Not only do I believe, unlike Rorty, that this is just how things are; I believe, despite Rorty, that thinking this way helps in disagreements with others, whether those others are down the street today or across oceans or centuries from ourselves. Rorty supposes that the rationalist is bound to think that "we" are right and "they" are wrong: but if there is one world only, then it is also possible that *they* might be right. We can learn from each other's stories only if we share both human capacities and a single world: relativism about either is a reason not to converse but to fall silent.

Cosmopolitanism imagines a world in which people and novels and music and films and philosophies travel between places where they are understood differently, because people are different and welcome to their difference. Cosmopolitanism can work because there can be common conversations about these shared ideas and objects. But what makes the conversations possible is not always shared "culture"; not even, as the older humanists imagined, universal principles or values (though, as I say, people from far away can discover that their principles meet); nor yet shared understanding (though people with very different experiences can end up agreeing about the darnedest things). What works in encounters with other human beings across gaps of space, time, and experience is enormously various. For stories—epic poems as well as modern forms like novels and films, for example—it is the capacity to follow a narrative and conjure a world: and, it turns out, there are people everywhere more than willing to do this. This is the moral epistemology that makes cosmopolitanism possible.

The agenda of liberal cosmopolitanism focuses on conversations among places: but the case for those conversations applies for conversations among cities, regions, classes, genders, races, sexualities, across all the dimensions of difference. For we do learn something about humanity in responding to the worlds people conjure with words in the narrative framework of the folktale, or with images in the frame of film: we learn about the extraordinary diversity of human responses to our world and the myriad points of intersection of those various responses. If there is a critique of the Enlightenment to be made, it is not that the *philosophes* believed in human nature, or the universality of reason: it is rather that they were so dismally unimaginative about the range of what we have in common.

The position I have arrived at may seem to be uneasily placed between the impulses I have dubbed universalistic and antiuniversalistic. I have said that what two people or two societies have in common as a basis for dialogue will generally include an odd hodgepodge of particular and general: narrative imagination, the capacity for love and reason, some principles, judgments about the rightness and wrongness of particular cases, the appreciation of certain objects. But that dodges such key questions as whether there really are Asian values that differ from Western values, for example, in placing a lesser moral weight on individuality than on the collective. What's at issue isn't whether what we can share is various—it is—but whether or not it includes respect for certain fundamental moral values, among them, in particular, the fundamental human rights.

And, to insist on a point, I am not concerned only with whether we all have these rights—I believe we do ... but then I *would*, since, to the extent that there is something called the West, I am pretty firmly intellectually ensconced in it. I *am* concerned with what I called the practical question of whether we can expect everybody in the world (or at any rate almost everybody, once they give us a reasonable degree of attention) to come around to *agreeing* that we have those rights.

This is, of course, too large a question to answer here: and it is, in a certain sense, a question whose answer is developing before our eyes. We are watching a world in which people are facing each other with different ideas about what matters in human life, and influences are traveling, through the media and popular culture and evangelism and, no doubt, in many other ways. But in order to think clearly about what is at stake here, we must be clear about what picture of rights we are endorsing.

Globalizing Human Rights

Human rights as they actually exist are, above all, creatures of something like law: they are the results of agreements promulgated by states, agreements that set rule-governed constraints on the actions of states and individuals, sometimes requiring action, sometimes forbidding it. They are used by officials to justify actions both within and across states, and they are called upon by citizens of many states claiming protection from abuse. The wide diversity of people who call upon them includes, to be sure, a substantial diversity of opinion on matters metaphysical—on religion in particular—and even if there is a single truth to be had about these matters, it is not one that we shall all come to soon.

The major advantage of instruments that are not framed as the working out of a metaphysical tradition is, obviously, that people from different metaphysical traditions can accept them. The major disadvantage is that without some grounding—metaphysical or not—it is hard to see why they should have any power or effect. The mere making of declarations that one should behave this way or that does not in general lead people to act in conformity with them, especially in the absence of mechanisms of enforcement. Granted the fact that they are so weakly philosophically grounded, there is a puzzle about what gives human rights instruments their power.

As Michael Ignatieff has observed in a thoughtful discussion of the matter, "human rights has gone global by going local." People around the world, working in different religious and juridical traditions, have nevertheless found reasons to support various human rights instruments because those instruments embody protections that they both want and need. "Human rights is the only universally available moral vernacular that validates the claims of women and children against the oppression they experience in patriarchal and tribal societies; it is the only vernacular that enables dependent persons to perceive themselves as moral agents and to act against practices—arranged marriages, purdah, civic disenfranchisement, genital mutilation, domestic slavery, and so on—that are ratified by the weight and authority of their cultures," Ignatieff writes. "These agents seek out human rights protection precisely because it legitimizes their protests against oppression."[63] The moral individualism of human-rights discourse, as he insists, is what enables it to play this role, and so we cannot say that the notion of human rights is metaphysically *naked*; but it is, or should be, scantily clad, conceptually speaking.[64] Certainly, we do not need to agree that we are all created in the image of God, or that we have natural rights that flow from our human essence, to agree that we do not want to be tortured by government officials, that we do not want to be subjected to arbitrary arrest, or have our lives, families, and property forfeited.

Still, it must be acknowledged that talk of human rights has long had a tendency to overflow its banks. You could see this tendency even in the Universal Declaration of Human Rights (UDHR), which the United Nations proclaimed in 1948, and it has been much in evidence since. The concern here is not that human rights are a Western parochialism; much of the UDHR is devoted to repudiating "traditional" Western values, including various forms of discrimination. No doubt some human-rights claims will be rejected, especially outside the nations of the developed world, when they are controversial, presuming too "thick" a conception of the human good. But sometimes we go wrong, too, when we use the glory term "human rights" to refer to objectives that aren't remotely controversial. Everybody can agree that it's a bad thing to starve to death. But (as I shall suggest in a moment) there's good reason to use "human rights" to designate something like side-constraints or conditions on the achievement of social goods, rather than those goods in themselves.[65] By contrast, the UDHR noticeably helps itself to both. To say, with the UDHR, that everyone has a right to education (to be compulsory through elementary school), and that higher education shall be equally available to all, according to merit, and that everyone has the right to ample food, clothing, medical care, and social services is to say—what? That these are terribly important things. And so they are. To say these things shouldn't be called rights isn't to say they're less important than rights; often they're *more* important. But they aren't things that an impoverished state, however well meaning, can simply provide. Unlike, say, a prohibition on torture, their realization depends on resources, not just on political will; they cannot simply be decreed. To think of human rights as side-constraints, as Robert Nozick did, is to say that if you have a right to X, then no one may deprive you of it. "Individuals have rights," he says, on the first page of *Anarchy, State and Utopia*, "and there are things no person or group may do to them (without violating their rights)." Side-constraints, then, are boundaries that it is always morally wrong to cross. We may pursue all sorts of goals, both moral and personal, but, on this view, we may do so only in ways that avoid violating the rights of others. Criticism of this idea has focused on Nozick's view that the constraints in question are infinitely stringent; for him, they are boundaries we must respect no matter what. And it is, indeed, more plausible to suppose that human rights may sometimes be abridged not only because there are circumstances where rights conflict and we must chose between them, but also because sufficiently substantial considerations of cost may sometimes be enough to outweigh a right. Take something as seemingly fundamental as freedom of expression ("through any media and regardless of frontiers," in the rhetoric of the UDHR). Suppose that abridging your freedom of expression significantly reduced the chances of an outbreak of rioting that would cause much damage to life and property. Here rights conflict. Or suppose that the problem is only that, because many people would be gravely offended, protecting your speech in these circumstances would be extraordinarily expensive. Here a right conflicts with considerations of cost.[66] Still, once we conceive of human rights as constraints on the pursuit of social ends, we should not include among them demands that states cannot meet. That is why negative rights to do something—where other people have the obligation not to hinder me if I do choose to do it—are so prominent in the basic human rights instruments: abstaining from action is almost always possible.

Now human rights are rights you have not just against states but against all other people: my right to life is not a right only against the government. So in committing ourselves to human rights in international law, we are requiring states not just to respect them, but also to attempt to enforce respect for these rights on the part of those they govern. Even if the right in question is a negative right, protecting it will require more of a state than that it abstain from infringing it itself. And this can already take states beyond the realm of what they have the resources to do. In a society in which marriages are thought of as arrangements between families, where the choice or even the consent of the woman is not required, merely passing a law requiring that marriages require consent will not protect the rights of women. And many governments may rightly judge that they simply do not have the legitimacy to enforce such a law (they may not be able, for example, to get their police to take it seriously); and, even if they can, the financial costs of effective enforcement might leave them unable to carry out their other obligations.

You could extend the claims of human rights beyond the realm of negative rights. You could say, for example, that states ought affirmatively to guarantee certain basic needs—for nutrition and for nurture in infancy, say—either by requiring others to provide them (as when we require parents to sustain their children) or by providing them themselves (as when governments guarantee a minimum level of welfare, so long as they have the resources to do so). But such extensions increase the risk, already present, as we saw, in the case of negative rights, that we will be announcing that people have an entitlement that cannot in fact be met; which amounts, in effect, to declaring that a state has a duty to do what it cannot in fact do. Such pronouncements not only offend against the fundamental moral requirement that "ought implies can"; in doing so, they discredit the regime of human rights.

None of this is to deny the importance of international agreements establishing (or, if you like, recording) norms other than human rights: the World Health Organization and UNAIDS make declarations and policies for combating AIDS; UNESCO selects World Heritage Properties and nations pay money into the World Heritage Fund to provide resources for their protection; UNICEF promotes breastfeeding and clean water; and there are many international accounting conventions and Internet protocols that are sustained directly neither by governments nor by intergovernmental organizations. Who could be against any of this? All I am insisting is that not every good needs to be explained in the language of human rights, a language that makes most sense if it is kept within bounds.

Mission creep is not the only thing that bedevils talk of human rights. Consider the problem of indeterminacy. The predicate "arbitrary"—as when one seeks to prohibit arbitrary arrest, or arbitrary interference with privacy, family, home—typically gets a vigorous workout in the formal language of human rights, but what counts as "arbitrary" is irreducibly a matter of judgment. And so it is with what constitutes "degrading" treatment; in various patriarchal societies, measures that we might consider part of the subjugation of women are justified, sincerely, as measures to protect women's dignity. (Many members of these societies would hold that the woman whose genitals have not been properly "feminized" by surgery, or whose visage can be gazed upon without barrier by lascivious men, has been subjected to degrading treatment.) Such practices are frequently "thickly" embedded, fraught with social significances. We saw earlier that different societies evince greater agreement about the bad than about the good; but, as I also noted, people think of their acts "under descriptions," and public actors seldom intend (or, at any rate, admit they intend) opprobrious deeds under opprobrious descriptions.

In raising these few perplexities, I have taken only a brief glimpse into a vast and crowded armory. On the subject of rights, you will find a great deal of conceptual ammunition for any position you wish to take. The basic dilemma is a familiar one. A conception of rights that's highly determinate in its application may not be thin enough to win widespread agreement; a conception of rights that's thin enough to win widespread agreement risks indeterminacy or impotence.

And yet the impressive thing about human rights, it seems to me, is how effectively they have functioned despite all their manifest limitations and obscurities. Yes, the promulgation of human rights, by international institutions, hardly guarantees assent—and even assent hardly guarantees anything in particular. The miracle is how well we've done without such guarantees. The substance of these rights will indeed always be contested and interpreted; but that doesn't mean they aren't useful instruments for drawing attention to the many ways in which people are brutal to one another. Like Ignatieff, I prefer to see human rights as a language for deliberation, or argument, or some other form of conversation.

And it is conversation, not mere conversion, that we should seek; we must be open to the prospect of gaining insight from our interlocutors. Let me take one example out of many. As Joseph Chan and others have remarked, the Confucian tradition holds it important that children take care of their elderly parents; from this perspective, the elderly would seem to have a right to our care similar to the claim that young children have on our nurture.[67] Certainly, in the wake of what happened in Paris during a recent heat wave that coincided with *le grand depart*—when thousands of elderly residents died alone in their apartments (some of whose children, according to news reports, declined to cut short their holidays to collect the bodies)—one wonders whether our "Western" attitude toward the care of the elderly isn't in need of reform. Now I have already expressed skepticism about the extension of such positive rights—which the right to care from your children surely is—so I offer this not as an example of a proposal I endorse, but as an example of a place where the flow of insight seems to be not from Us to Them, but in Our direction.

Though we've often been served notice that other societies, or their self-appointed spokesmen, resist talk of human rights—mistrusting them as a distinctively Western imposition, as excessively "individualist"—we should also be alert to the ways in which human rights, especially in their thinner conceptions, have managed to root themselves in a wide variety of social contexts. In effect, the reason why we do not need to ground human rights in any particular metaphysics is that many of them are already grounded in many metaphysics and can already derive sustenance from those many sources. A simple example, which I've used before, comes from the traditions of Asante, where I grew up. Free Asante citizens—both men and women—in the period before the state was conquered by Britain as well as since, are preoccupied with notions of personal dignity, with respect and self-respect. Treating others with the respect that is their due is central to Asante social life, as is a reciprocal anxiety about loss of respect, shame, and disgrace. Just as European liberalism—and democratic sentiment— grew by extending to every man and (then) woman the dignity that feudal society offered only to the aristocracy, and thus presupposes, in some sense, aspects of that feudal understanding of dignity,[68] so modern Ghanaian thinking about politics depends, in part, on the prior grasp of concepts such as *animuonyam* (respect). Well-known Akan proverbs make it clear that, in the past, respect was precisely not something that belonged to everybody: *Agya Kra ne Agya Kwakyerēmē, emu biara mu nni animuonyam.* (Father Soul and Father Slave Kyerēmē, neither is respected; that is, whatever you call him, a slave is still a slave.) But just as *dignitas*, which was once, by definition, the property of an elite, has grown into human dignity, which is the property of every man and woman, so *animuonyam* can be the basis of the respect for all others that lies at the heart of a commitment to human rights.

The struggle is familiar in the Roman context as well. In the sixth poem of the first of the two books of conversational verse we now call Horace's Satires, the poet—himself the son of a father who had once been a slave—addresses Maecenas, the richest and noblest of the private patrons of the arts in Augustan Rome. Despite the fine example of Maecenas, who, as Horace puts it, "says it's no matter who your parents are, so long as you're worthy,"[69] the poet complains that most Romans take the opposite view.

> Thus he who does solemnly swear to his citizens to take care of the city,
> The empire, and Italy, and the sanctuaries of the gods,
> Forces every mortal to pay attention, and to ask
> From what father he may be descended, whether he is base because of the
> obscurity of his mother.[70]

Quo patre sit natus, num ignota matre inhonestus: Horace underlines
the way in which identities that are liberating for some—the noble ancestry that helps to make Maecenas's public life so rewarding—feed on
the onerousness of complementary identities (as slaves, freedmen, the
"lowborn") for others. But he is also arguing that real nobility—the
poem is entitled "De vera nobilitate"—is what Maecenas takes it to be:
a quality independent of conventional indices of social rank. Horace's
point is not, however, just that someone like himself, a freedman's son,
can, as an empirical matter, be "honestus." It is also that social status
of this sort is not a legitimate parameter: the measure of one's life does
not depend on whether or not one comes from a "good family." Similar
arguments can be, and have been, waged in different conceptual idioms.

When it comes to those cases where the different traditions part, a
richer metaphysical grounding would not help us. For when someone
argues—in the name of Confucian values or Maoism or Hinduism or
Islam—that the human-rights tradition is overly individualist and so
certain individual rights have a lesser weight than community interests,
the return to first principles will simply take us from one terrain of
disagreement to another where there seems no reason to expect greater
hope of resolution.

Cass Sunstein has defended what he calls "incompletely theorized
agreements" in the context of American constitutional law.[71] I would
like to defend a similar freedom from the demand for high doctrine in
the development of the internal practices of human-rights law. We
should be able to defend our treaties by arguing that they offer people
protections against governments that most of their citizens desire, and
that are important enough that they also want other peoples, through
their governments, to help sustain them. Once we seek to defend these
rights in this pragmatic way, we can appeal to a highly diverse set of
arguments: perhaps some rights—to freedom of expression, for example—are not only necessary for dignity and the maintenance of respect
but also helpful in the development of economies and the stabilization
of polities. And all of these are things that are wanted by most people
everywhere. Sunstein's account of "incompletely theorized agreement"
goes together with a proposal for a certain kind of judicial modesty:
and, as I say, we do not go wrong if we resist designating everything we
should devoutly hope for a "fundamental human right."

To make this pragmatic point—to argue for basic rights in a way that is receptive to a metaphysical ecumenism, responsive to the moral vocabularies we find on the ground—is not to hold, as some have suggested, that the foundation of the legitimacy of human rights is the consent of a majority of our species. After all, our most fundamental rights restrain majorities, and their consent to the system that embodies those restraints does not entail their consent to the rights themselves— otherwise there would be no need of them. (As Louis Menand has memorably observed, "Coercion is natural; freedom is artificial.")[72] If consent is an empirical notion, then most Americans do not consent to many rights that they actually have: for example, their right to marry even if they are condemned for capital crimes. The remarkable currency that human-rights discourse has gained around the world demonstrates that it speaks to people in a diversity of positions and traditions; this chord of resonating agreement explains why we can find global support for the human rights system. One reason for articulating these ideas in international documents, which are widely circulated and advertised, is just to draw attention to that core of agreement, however narrow, and to help to give it practical force. We needn't be unduly troubled by the fact that metaphysical debate is unlikely to yield consensus, because human rights can, and therefore should, be sustained without metaphysical consensus.

COSMOPOLITAN CONVERSATION

The roots of the cosmopolitanism I am defending are liberal: and they are responsive to liberalism's insistence on human dignity. It has never been easy to say what this entails, and, indeed, it seems to me that exploring what it might mean is liberalism's historic project. But we have already learned some lessons about what a life of dignity requires in the modern world. So let me return to the themes with which this book began. I would insist, again, that the individual whose self-creation is being valued here is not, in the justly censorious sense of the term, individualist. Nothing I have said is inconsistent with the recognition of the many ways in which we human beings are naturally and inevitably social. First, because we are incapable of developing on our own, because we need human nurture, moral and intellectual education, practice with language, if we are to develop into full persons. This is a sociality of mutual dependence. Second, because we desire relationship with others: friends, lovers, parents, children, the wider family, colleagues, neighbors. This is sociality as an end. And third, because many other things we value—literature, and the arts, the whole world of culture; education; money; and, in the modern world, food and housing—depend essentially on society for their production. This is instrumental sociality. But I have already discussed all the reasons why this picture recognizes the social construction of the individual self.

This picture, as we saw, acknowledges that identity is at the heart of human life: liberalism, in ways I've explored in chapter 3, takes this picture seriously, and tries to construct a state and society that take account of the ethics of identity without losing sight of the values of personal autonomy. But the cosmopolitan impulse is central to this view, too, because it sees a world of cultural and social variety as a precondition for the self-creation that is at the heart of a meaningful human life. Let me be clear. Cosmopolitanism values human variety for what it makes possible for human agency, and some kinds of cultural variety constrain more than they enable. The cosmopolitan's high appraisal of variety flows, for reasons I gave in chapter 4, from the human choices it enables, but variety is not something we value no matter what. (This is one reason why I think it is not helpful to see cosmopolitanism as expressing an aesthetic ideal.) There are other values. You can have an enormous amount of diversity between societies, even if they are all, in some sense, democratic.[73] But the fundamental idea that every society should respect human dignity and personal autonomy is more basic than the cosmopolitan love of variety; indeed, as I say, it is the autonomy that variety enables that is its fundamental justification. Cosmopolitans do not ask other people to maintain the diversity of the species at the price of their individual autonomy. We can't require others to provide us with a cultural museum to tour through or to visit on satellite television's endless virtual safari; nor can we demand an assortment of Shangri-las to enlarge the range of our own options for identity. The options we need in order for our choices to be substantial must be freely sustained, as must the human variety whose existence is, for the cosmopolitan, an endless source of insight and pleasure. In theory, so I've argued, a whole society could come to be centered on a single set of values without coercion. I might be skeptical about the virtues of such a homogenized society as a place for myself to live (even if the values it was centered on were in some sense mine). I would think it might risk many cultural and economic and moral perils, because it might require in the end a kind of closing oneself off from the rest of the world. But those in such a society would no doubt have things to say in response—or might refuse to discuss the matter with me at all—and, in the end, they might well find their considerations weightier than mine. Freely chosen homogeneity, then, raises no problems for me: in the end, I would say, Good luck to them. But, as I have said, there is no ground for thinking that people are rushing toward homogeneity; and, in fact, in a world more respectful of human dignity and personal autonomy such movement toward homogeneity as there is would probably slow down.

Skepticism about the genuinely cosmopolitan character of the view I have been defending may flow in part from the thought that it seems so much a creature of Europe and its liberal tradition.[74] So it may be well to insist, in closing, that my own attachment to these ideas comes, as much as anything, from my father, who grew up in Asante, at a time when the independence of its moral climate from that of European Enlightenment was extremely obvious. Now, it would be preposterous to claim that he came to his cosmopolitanism or his faith in human rights and the rule of law unaffected by European traditions. But it would be equally untenable to deny that the view he arrived at had roots in Asante (indeed, as one travels the world, reviewing the liberal nationalisms of South Asia and Africa in the mid–twentieth century, one is impressed not only by their similarities but also by their local inflections). Two things, in particular, strike me about the local character of the source of my father's increasing commitment to individual rights: first, that it grew out of experience of illiberal government; second, that it depended on a sense of his own dignity and the dignity of his fellow citizens that was the product of Asante conceptions.

The first point—about experience—is crucial to the case for liberalism. The historical experience of the dangers of intolerance—religious intolerance in Europe in the seventeenth century, for example, for

Locke; racial intolerance in the colonial context, for Gandhi (or for African independence leaders like my father)—often underlies the common liberal skepticism about state intervention in the lives of individuals. My father saw the colonial state's abuses of his fellows (and himself) and, in particular, the refusal to pay them the respect that was their due. As a lawyer and a member of the opposition, he traveled Ghana in the years after independence defending people whose rights were being abused by the postcolonial state. The political tradition of liberalism flows from these experiences of illiberal government. That liberal restraint on government recommends itself to people rooted in so many different traditions shows its grasp of a truth about human beings and about modern politics. Just as the centrality of murderous religious warfare in the period leading up to Locke's *Treatises* placed religious toleration at the core of Locke's understanding of the liberalism he defended, so the persecution of political dissenters by postcolonial despots has made protection of political dissent central to the liberalism of those who resist postcolonial states in Africa. (My father worried little about the state's entanglement with religion; once, I remember, as we sat in front of the television in the late evening, my father sang along with the national hymn, which was played some evenings as an alternative to the more secular national anthem, to end the day. "This would be a much better national anthem," he said to me. And I replied, ever the good liberal, "But the anthem has the advantage that you don't have to believe in God to sing it sincerely." "No one in Ghana is silly enough not to believe in God," my father replied.[75] I now think he was right not to be worried about the entanglement: there was no history of religious intolerance in Ghana of the sort that makes necessary the separation of church and state; a genial ecumenism had been the norm at least until the arrival of American TV evangelism.) But more important yet to my father's concern with individual human dignity was its roots in the preoccupation that I said free Asante citizens—both men and women—have with notions of respect and self-respect. *Dignitas*, as understood by Cicero, reflects much that was similar between republican Roman ideology and the views of the *animuonyam*-prizing nineteenth-century Asante elite; it was, I think, as an Asante that my father recognized and admired Cicero, not as a British subject.

Although I've argued for the importance of stories, you shouldn't let my own storytelling convince you that the prospects for a liberal cosmopolitanism are as rosy as I am making them out to be. Pessimists can cite a dismal litany to the contrary. Still, it's hard to ignore the conceptual currency that the fundamental human rights have enjoyed among millions of ordinary people around the world. Inasmuch as we are, already, fellow citizens of a world, we do not have to wait for institutional change to exercise our common citizenship: to engage in dialogue with others around the world about the questions great and small that we must solve together, about the many projects in which we can learn from each other, is already to live as fellow citizens, the way Marcus Aurelius and Laurence Sterne's French officer did. I have been arguing that there is a great range among the starting points we have for these conversations, the shared points of entry from which we can proceed. This is as true of conversations between Confucians from Shanghai and Pentecostals from Peoria as it is for conversations between people who differ in class and gender, or profession, or along a whole range of dimensions of identity. From these conversations we can be led to common action—for our shared environment, for human rights, for the simple enjoyment of comity. And such comity is as likely to prevail among those who revere different totems as among those who revere the same ones.

If this book has a totem, it is, of course, John Stuart Mill, and we should not be surprised to find that he himself has pithily expressed the cosmopolitan ideal: "To human beings, who, as hitherto educated, can scarcely cultivate even a good quality without running it into a fault, it is indispensable to be perpetually comparing their own notions and customs with the experience and example of persons in different circumstances from themselves: and there is no nation which does not need to borrow from others, not merely particular arts or practices, but essential points of character in which its own type is inferior."[76] Mill would join us, then, in rejecting a form of humanism that requires us to put our differences aside; the cosmopolitan believes, with him, that sometimes it is the differences we bring to the table that make it rewarding to interact at all. But he would also concede, as we should, that what we share can be important, too, though the cosmopolitan will insist that what we share with others is not always ethnonational in character: sometimes it will just be that you and I both like to fish or (with apologies to George Saunders) make excellent strudel. Perhaps we have read and admired Goethe in translation, or responded with the same sense of wonder to a postcard of Angkor Wat or the Parthenon, or believe, as lawyers with very different trainings, in the ideal of the rule of law. This is, perhaps, the anglophone voice of cosmopolitanism. But, in the cosmopolitan spirit, let me end with a similar thought from my father's tradition. *Kuro korō mu nni nyansa*, the proverb says: In a single πολις there is no wisdom.[77]

Acknowledgments

~

I HAVE DISCUSSED the ethics of identity with students and colleagues in many fields—anthropology, literary studies, history, law, sociology, political science, and, of course, philosophy—and on three continents. And so I have had the privilege of learning from responses (not all of them meant to be helpful!) to lectures in places as various as Basel, Berkeley, Berlin, Cambridge, Cape Town, Frankfurt, London, New York, Oxford, Paris, and Rio de Janeiro, as well as from university audiences in many other places in the United States. I apologize that I cannot recall every name and occasion (not least, I am sure, because many who have pushed my thinking along made contributions that I didn't absorb until long after our conversations); and rather than attempt a necessarily incomplete list of all occasions that I can recall, I must ask most of those from whom I have learned to recognize themselves in this general acknowledgment. I have also, of course, learned a great deal from the many literatures that abut the issues I have taken up, and I have tried to record these specific debts in endnotes.

Still, I do recall especially valuable conversations over the years— some brief, some very extended—with Elizabeth Anderson, Susan Babbitt, Richard Bernstein, Homi Bhabha, Jacquie Bhabha, Vincent Crapanzano, Ronald Dworkin, Amy Gutmann, David Hollinger, Mark Johnston, Tom Kelly, Philip Kitcher, Mahmood Mamdani, Tom Nagel, Alexander Nehamas, Robert Nozick, Martha Nussbaum, Susan Moller Okin, Lucius Outlaw, Philip Pettit, David Rieff, Tim Scanlon, Amartya Sen, Jesse Sheidlower, Tommie Shelby, Robert Silvers, and Charles Taylor. For much of the decade of the 1990s I was a member of a "Pentimento" reading group in Cambridge, Massachusetts (so named for a coffee shop where we once met) that included at various times Larry Blum, Jorge Garcia, Martha Minow, David Wilkins, and David Wong, among others, from all of whom I learned a great deal. I was much helped by many questioners at a seminar at NYU Law School run by Ronnie Dworkin and Tom Nagel in the fall of 1997, and by the respondents to the two sets of Tanner Lectures I gave at UC San Diego, in 1994, and in Cambridge, England, in 2001. No doubt my longest-running intellectual (and personal) debt is to Skip Gates, who befriended a philosophy student at Cambridge, a quarter-century ago, and persuaded him to take an interest in matters beyond the foundations of probabilistic semantics. As I have been finishing this book, I have benefited from the collegiality of Chris Eisgruber, Steve Macedo, Josh Ober, and Peter Singer, at the Center for Human Values, here at Princeton, and from the discussions of the Center's graduate student and visiting faculty fellows: our almost weekly seminars have often contained insights that I have been able to put to use. Among students, I owe a special debt to the members of two seminars at NYU Law school, where I began to think and write more specifically about individuality in the fall of 1998; to many students in Afro-American Studies at Harvard, with whom I discussed questions of identity between 1991 and 2002; to a graduate seminar at Princeton on "neutrality" in the spring of 2002; and to two classes of Princeton freshmen, who enlivened a seminar on "individuality as an ideal" in the falls of 2002 and 2003.

A close-to-final manuscript of this book received very helpful comments from my colleague Chris Eisgruber, whose profound legal knowledge and long-term interest in questions of religion and the American Constitution helped me enormously; and from three readers for Princeton University Press. Two of them have asked to remain anonymous, so I must thank them without naming them: but the third, Jacob Levy, I am delighted to be able to thank by name, especially since his comments were such a generous combination of correction and encouragement. I should also like to thank Ian Malcolm of Princeton University Press for organizing these referees and helping me to think about how to respond to them. Also at the Press, Lauren Lepow was a graceful and gracious copyeditor and I would like to thank Frank Mahood for his elegant design. My penultimate thanks must go to the Philosophy Department of the University at Buffalo, SUNY, who allowed me to give the complete argument of this book its first outing as the 2004 George F. Hourani Lectures.

Ideas, I think, are not best thought of as possessed or even originated by individuals, and, no doubt, many of those who aided me were passing on, as I am, thoughts that began with others. One can, however, originate formulations and combinations of ideas, a style of expressing them, a path through the issues: that is what it is to be a book's true author. But I cannot claim to be even in that sense the whole author of this book, since every page is inflected by the myriad careful comments, contributions, and criticisms of my partner, Henry Finder: the name on the title page is mine, and I take responsibility for the book and its claims, but it is ours, I think, as substantially as Mill claimed *On Liberty* to be a joint production with Harriet Taylor. (The comparison of this book with that one ends there: but a cat may look at a king!) Harriet Taylor did not live to see the book's publication, and so we cannot say whether she would have accepted Mill's assertion that it was the working out of views they held in common. In his generosity, Henry insists (as perhaps Harriet would have) that his assistance was merely editorial. But I know that I would have my name on a different and much inferior book without him. If I had been dedicating this book to him in Latin, I would have had to struggle as to whether to write his name in the dative ("to or for," as I was taught) or the ablative ("by, with, or from"). It is surely fitting that a book insisting that one's individuality can be expressed in projects deeply shared should be the practical expression of what it preaches.

Notes

⌒

Preface

1. I think it is a little unfortunate that the term "individualism," which has, in ordinary usage, a whiff of unsociability about it, should have come to be the technical philosophical label for this position. So it is perhaps worth saying at the start that individualism of this sort is the basis for an extensive concern for others. (After all, if individuals matter, then it matters what you do to them.) That individualism of some sort is widely assumed is reflected in the pervasiveness of attempts to show why the state should recommend itself to individuals in a "state of nature." (This is not meant as a precise formulation; precision would require further discussion, for example, of what it is to say that something matters.)

2. The first political party to use the term "liberal" (or, more precisely, its cognate in Spanish) were the "Liberales" in early nineteenth-century Spain. By 1827, Robert Southey has the word in English to describe political positions in "The Devil's Walk," whose stanzas 28 and 29 (spoken in the voice of one of Satan's "daughters") run:

> You will not think, great Cosmocrat!
> That I spend my time in fooling;
> Many irons, my Sire, have we in the fire,
> And I must leave none of them cooling;
> For you must know state-councils here
> Are held which I bear rule in.
> When my liberal notions
> Produce mischievous motions,
> There's many a man of good intent,
> In either house of Parliament,
> Whom I shall find a tool in;
> And I have hopeful pupils too,
> Who all this while are schooling.
>
> Fine progress they make in our liberal opinions,
> My Utilitarians,
> My all sorts of —inians

And all sorts of —arians,
My all sorts of —ists,
And my Prigs and my Whigs,
Who have all sorts of twists,
Trained in the very way, I know,
Father, you would have them go;
High and low,
Wise and foolish, great and small,
March-of-Intellect Boys all.

See the hypertext edition at http://www.rc.umd.edu/editions/shelley/devil/1dwcover
.html.

3. These elections were, of course, by a small "electorate" of rulers of towns, states, and other units of the Reich. But the first American elections were on a decidedly limited franchise, too. If democracy means an electoral system with basically full adult franchise, then democracy is a latecomer in liberal practice. Indeed, key liberals were skeptical of democracy: Mill (who, in his *Considerations on Representative Government*, proposed a system of "plural voting," in which greater voting power would go to the better educated) was worried throughout *On Liberty* about the tyranny of the majority; and, of course, the U.S. Constitution wasn't democratic, for it didn't give the franchise to all adult citizens. (Arguably, this process was completed only when the voting age was lowered to eighteen, which happened less than half a century ago.) But I do not mean to express skepticism about democracy in this sense or to suggest that it does not follow from core liberal ideas. Respect for others as free and equal requires a means of expressing everyone's political equality by providing everyone with equal roles in selecting the government. In the end, something like democracy will probably come out of the liberal tradition. All I want to insist on is that the connection between liberalism and democracy needs to be argued.

4. T. M. Scanlon, *What We Owe to Each Other* (Cambridge: Harvard University Press, 1998), 172; Bernard Williams, *Ethics and the Limits of Philosophy* (Cambridge: Harvard University Press, 1985), 6 and 174; "Translators' Preface," in Henri Bergson, *The Two Sources of Morality and Religion*, trans. R. Ashley Audra and Cloudesley Brereton, with the assistance of W. Horsfall Carter (New York: Doubleday, 1935); Ronald Dworkin, *Sovereign Virtue: The Theory and Practice of Equality* (Cambridge: Harvard University Press, 2000), 485 n. 1. There are similarities here with the Kantian distinction between *Rechtspflichten* and *Tugendpflichten*, or, elsewhere, between *officia perfecta* and *officia imperfecta*. Note, however, that Dworkin's definition allows that the ethical might subsume the moral. It might be best to lead a life in which you treat others as they should be treated.

5. Peter Railton, "Pluralism, Determinacy, and Dilemma," *Ethics* 102, no. 4 (July 1992): 722. See also Michael Blake, "Rights for People, Not for Cultures," *Civilization* 7, no. 4 (August–September 2000): 50–53. "The ambiguity in valuing diversity lies, on one level, in whether it means valuing people of distinct backgrounds or valuing the diver-

sity of backgrounds itself," Blake writes. "The first notion—that people ought to be respected as equals regardless of their ethnicity, race, gender, and other distinguishing traits—is today a part of any plausible political philosophy. But it hardly follows that we must value and preserve diversity itself, in the abstract; we have, I think, no reason to regret that the world does not contain twice as many cultures as it does" (52). I'll return to this matter in chapter 4.

6. For a cautionary discussion of such pitfalls, see Richard Handler, "Is 'Identity' a Useful Cross-Cultural Concept?" in *Commemorations: The Politics of National Identity*, ed. John R. Gillis (Princeton: Princeton University Press, 1994), 27–40.

Chapter One The Ethics of Individuality

1. References to Mill's works will be by title, followed by volume and page number in *The Collected Works of John Stuart Mill*, ed. John M. Robson (Toronto: University of Toronto Press, 1963–91), vols. 1–33—henceforth *CWM*. Here, I'm quoting from *The Autobiography of John Stuart Mill*, *CWM* 1:33, 35. Mill also makes it clear that his education was not a matter of knowledge passively acquired. "Most boys or youths who have had much knowledge drilled into them, have their mental capacities not strengthened but overlaid by it. They are crammed with mere facts, and with the opinions or phrases of other people, and these are accepted as a substitute for the power to form opinions of their own: and thus the sons of eminent fathers, who have spared no pains in their education, so often grow up mere parroters of what they have learnt, incapable of using their minds except in the furrows traced for them. Mine, however, was not an education of cram. My father never permitted anything which I learnt to degenerate into a mere exercise of memory." Mill, *Autobiography, CWM* 1:21.

2. Mill, *The Earlier Letters, 1812–1848, CWM* 12:30.

3. Mill, *Autobiography, CWM* 1:139.

4. Ibid., 259.

5. Mill, *On Liberty, CWM* 18:261.

6. Ibid., 267.

7. There are those who believe that Mill was always a consistent utilitarian, and who think, therefore, that he must, at bottom, be arguing for some connection between individuality and utility. But there is no general argument in *On Liberty* for such a connection, and Mill speaks here and elsewhere for individuality in ways that are plausible without such a connection. Even if you do assume a connection, it's not clear that the utility function would be doing any work, given that Mill's conception of happiness seems to have encompassed individuality. To possess and exercise the capacity to choose freely isn't valuable simply because it leads to happiness; rather, it seems to be part of what Mill had in mind by happiness. These issues receive careful attention in Fred Berger, *Happiness, Justice, and Freedom: The Moral and Political Philosophy of John Stuart Mill* (Berkeley and Los Angeles: University of California Press, 1984); John Gray,

Mill on Liberty: A Defence (London: Routledge and Kegan Paul, 1983); and Richard J. Arneson, "Mill versus Paternalism," *Ethics* 90 (July 1980): 470–98. And see n. 45 below.

8. Mill elaborates: "The human faculties of perception, judgement, discriminative feeling, mental activity, and even moral preference, are exercised only in making a choice. He who does anything because it is the custom makes no choice." A little later, "character" becomes a value term: "A person whose desires and impulses are his own— are the expression of his own nature, as it has been developed and modified by his own culture—is said to have a character. One whose desires and impulses are not his own, has no character, no more than a steam-engine has a character." Mill, *On Liberty, CWM* 18:262, 264.

9. Ibid., 270. Mill dates his emphasis on the training of the human being, rather than the "ordering of outward circumstances," to the shifting of his thoughts after the winter of 1826, when "I, for the first time, gave its proper place, among the prime necessities of human well-being, to the internal culture of the individual." Mill, *Autobiography, CWM* 1:147.

10. See Lawrence Haworth's attentive discussion, identifying three ways in which autonomy can be associated with Millian individuality: "Sense 1: if we think of autonomy as a *capacity*, then to have individuality is to have developed that capacity so that it is a realized personality trait. Sense 2: if we think of autonomy as a mode of life, as in 'living autonomously,' then individuality (the developed personality trait) is a necessary condition for autonomy. Sense 3: when we say of someone that 'he is autonomous' we may have in mind that his capacity for autonomy is developed; in such contexts being autonomous and having individuality are synonymous." Lawrence Haworth, *Autonomy: An Essay in Philosophical Psychology and Ethics* (New Haven: Yale University Press, 1986), 166. Cf. Arneson, "Mill versus Paternalism," 477.

11. In urging the appeal of individuality, Mill has recourse to a battery of considerations. Some are aesthetic (by cultivating what is individual, "human beings become a noble and beautiful object of contemplation," *On Liberty, CWM* 18:266); some are semi-Carlylean (great heroes and geniuses will arise from the muck of mediocrity); and some considerations flow from the straitening effects of custom (the tendency "to maim by compression, like a Chinese lady's foot, every part of human nature which stands out prominently, and tends to make the person markedly dissimilar in outline to commonplace humanity," ibid., 271).

12. Mill, *A System of Logic, CWM* 8:842–43.

13. John Rawls, *A Theory of Justice* (Cambridge: Harvard University Press, 1971), 408. Here he makes explicit reference to Josiah Royce's *The Philosophy of Loyalty*, where it is used to "characterize the coherent, systematic purposes of the individual, what makes him a conscious, unified moral person" (in Rawls's gloss). I'll return to the subject of goals and rationality in chapter 5.

14. J. L. Mackie, "Can There Be a Right-Based Moral Theory?" in *Ethical Theory* 2: Theories about How We Should Live, ed. James Rachels (Oxford: Oxford University Press, 1998), 136; Daniel A. Bell, *Communitarianism and Its Critics* (New York: Oxford University Press, 1993), 6; Michael Slote, *Goods and Virtues* (Oxford: Oxford University

Press, 1983), 43–47. Slote's focus is on the use of "plans of life" in recent contributions to liberal philosophy, notably those of David Richards, Charles Fried, and John Cooper.

15. In *Principles of Political Economy*, *CWM* 3:953–54, Mill writes that an "exception to the doctrine that individuals are the best judges of their own interest, is when an individual attempts to decide irrevocably now, what will be best for his interest at some future and distant time. The presumption in favour of individual judgment is only legitimate, where the judgment is grounded on actual, and especially on present, personal experience; not where it is formed antecedently to experience, and not suffered to be reversed even after experience has condemned it. When persons have bound themselves by a contract, not simply to do some one thing, but to continue doing something for ever or for a prolonged period, without any power of revoking the engagement, the presumption which their perseverance in that course of conduct would otherwise raise in favour of its being advantageous to them, does not exist; and any such presumption which can be grounded on their having voluntarily entered into the contract, perhaps at an early age, and without any real knowledge of what they undertook, is commonly next to null. The practical maxim of leaving contracts free is not applicable without great limitations in case of engagement in perpetuity; and the law should be extremely jealous of such engagements; should refuse its sanction to them, when the obligations they impose are such as the contracting party cannot be a competent judge of; if it ever does sanction them, it should take every possible security for their being contracted with foresight and deliberation; and in compensation for not permitting the parties themselves to revoke their engagement, should grant them a release from it, on a sufficient case being made out before an impartial authority. These considerations are eminently applicable to marriage, the most important of all cases of engagement for life."

16. Charles Dickens, *Dombey and Son* (New York: Oxford University Press, 1991), 139.

17. To be sure, in the course of his love affair with Mrs. Taylor, Mill assayed all sorts of plans, and one of them called for the two to elope and exile themselves, brazening out the ostracism that would result. He would resign himself to being (as he wrote to Harriet in 1835) "obscure & insignificant." This did not go down well with her, and at moments she questioned his own "planfulness": "The most horrible feeling I ever know is when for moments the fear comes over me that *nothing* which you say of yourself is to be absolutely relied on—that you are not sure even of your strongest feelings," she wrote to Mill in September 1833. Bruce Mazlish, *James and John Stuart Mill: Father and Son in the Nineteenth Century* (New York: Basic Books, 1975), 289.

18. As Mill is careful to stipulate: "[I]t would be absurd to pretend that people ought to live as if nothing whatever had been known in the world before they came into it; as if experience had as yet done nothing towards showing that one mode of existence, or of conduct, is preferable to another. Nobody denies that people should be so taught and trained in youth, as to know and benefit by the ascertained results of human experience. . . . The traditions and customs of other people are, to a certain extent, evidence of what their experience has taught them; presumptive evidence, and as such, have a claim to this deference." Chapter 3 of *On Liberty*, *CWM* 18:262.

19. Kazuo Ishiguro, *The Remains of the Day* (New York: Knopf, 1989), 199.

20. Ibid., 228.

21. Ibid., 245. A measure of Ishiguro's stylistic subtlety is that this last sentence ends with a split infinitive, which would have been avoided by the kind of person Mr. Stevens aspires to be.

22. Or so Caroline Fox reproduces it in her *Memories of Old Friends*, ed. Horace N. Pym, 2nd ed. (London, 1882); quoted in Charles Larrabee Street, *Individualism and Individuality in the Philosophy of John Stuart Mill* (Milwaukee: Morehouse Publishing, 1926), 41. We can stipulate, on Mill's behalf, that the "highest thing" might be chosen from a set with many members.

23. Mill, *Utilitarianism, CWM* 10:212.

24. Ishiguro, *Remains*, 210.

25. Ibid., 185–86. Mill, it must be said, would not have been wholly out of sympathy with Mr. Stevens's skepticism. "As soon as any idea of equality enters the head of an uneducated English working man, his head is turned by it," Mill wrote. "When he ceases to be servile, he becomes insolent." Mill, *Principles of Political Economy, CWM* 2:109.

26. Mill, *System of Logic, CWM* 8:942.

27. Harriet Taylor, Michael St. John Packe tells us, had at one point hoped to be a journalist, a published commentator, like her sometime friend Harriet Martineau. But early in her relationship with Mill, she decided to shelve her own career and focus on promoting his, expressing herself "through her effect on him," as Packe writes. "It was Mill, not she, who was to be the writer; his, not her, development that was important to the world." Michael St. John Packe, *The Life of John Stuart Mill* (New York: Macmillan, 1954), 140. Despite the element of subordination, though, her role as coach and critic was the polar opposite of the servitor's determined equanimity.

28. Some might object that a failure of genuine autonomy (a notion I'll explore in the next chapter) led to this mishap: had he exercised his faculties for critical evaluation more strenuously, he would have been less susceptible to the bad luck of working for a fool. But (as we'll see), some forms of intellectual outsourcing are universal and inevitable, and it can be unreasonable to hold us accountable for assessments we are not competent to make. (Imagine two X-ray crystallographers who take jobs based on their proximity to their homes. One makes a great contribution to human knowledge, because she happens to be working with a team of highly successful molecular biochemists; the other makes very little contribution at all.) Of course, Ishiguro's narrative is powered by the mismatch between the starchy certitudes of Stevens's mind and the actual facts of the world, and we may leave it an open question, for the moment, whether Stevens's life, or any life so beset, is an example of human flourishing or human failure.

29. Thomas E. Hill, "Servility and Self-Respect," in *Autonomy and Self-Respect* (Cambridge: Cambridge University Press, 1991).

30. Ground projects are "a nexus of projects which largely give meaning to life," as glossed in Bernard Williams, "Persons, Character, and Morality," in *Moral Luck* (Cambridge: Cambridge University Press, 1981), 13.

31. Published 1967; first recorded on the Frank Sinatra album *My Way* (Warner Bros., February 13, 1969), track 6. Words and music by Giles Thibault, Jacques Revaux, and Claude François (originally as "Comme d'Habitude"), English lyrics by Paul Anka. There may be a small parable of globalization in the fact that Claude François was Egyptian-born and Anka was of Lebanese parentage; and some might draw conclusions about the differences between French and Anglo-Saxon concerns from the fact that the original French lyrics are about the routines of an empty love affair.

32. Even this is a little too quick: there can be, as we'll see in chapter 6, two kinds of obligation.

33. Oscar Wilde, *The Soul of Man under Socialism and Selected Critical Prose*, ed. Linda Dowling (New York: Penguin, 2001), 134. Wilde also had, to be sure, a Nietzschean mode, with which he is more widely associated, prizing self-invention above all.

34. "I am the last person to undervalue the self-regarding virtues; they are only second in importance, if even second, to the social," Mill writes in chapter 4 of *On Liberty, CWM* 18:277. Notice that these sets of virtues can evidently be ranked, even if uncertainly.

35. Bernard Williams, "The Truth in Relativism," in *Moral Luck*.

36. I'll be saying much more about the notion in chapter 3; but I should spell out that here I'm using "identity" in a sense that has gained currency only in the postwar era. There's a much older philosophical discourse on "personal identity," of course, centering on the continuity of an individual over time.

37. As my colleague Mark Johnston pointed out to me, not all living-as involves identities in this way: a closeted homosexual lives as a straight person but does not have a straight identity (or, in the nice example he offered me, the spy Kim Philby lived as a British civil servant, though what he really was—a loyal servant of the Soviet government—meant that this was not his true identity). So, as I say, I am not claiming that talk of someone's "living as an X" always introduces an identity of X. Clarification of the issues here must await the discussion of (what I call) "identification" in the section of chapter 3 titled "The Structure of Social Identities."

38. Ishiguro, *Remains*, 199.

39. These are labels of convenience: not everyone who invokes authenticity uses it this way, and one of the profoundest critics of what I am calling the "existentialist" view is Nietzsche.

40. Mill, *System of Logic, CWM* 8:840.

41. Michel Foucault, *Ethics: Subjectivity and Truth* (New York: The New Press, 1998), 262.

42. Charles Taylor, *The Ethics of Authenticity* (Cambridge: Harvard University Press, 1991), 40. I should note that my stipulative use of "authenticity" is different from Taylor's use of the term, which is meant to take in both the models of discovery and of self-creation.

43. Friedrich Nietzsche, *The Gay Science*, ed. and trans. Walter Kaufmann (New York: Vintage, 1974), 232.

44. Charles Taylor, *Multiculturalism: Examining the Politics of Recognition*, ed. Amy Gutmann (Princeton: Princeton University Press, 1994), 32.

45. Mill continues: "This it is which makes any mind, of well-developed feelings, work with, and not against, the outward motives to care for others, afforded by what I have called the external sanctions; and when those sanctions are wanting, or act in an opposite direction, constitutes in itself a powerful internal binding force, in proportion to the sensitiveness and thoughtfulness of the character; since few but those whose mind is a moral blank, could bear to lay out their course of life on the plan of paying no regard to others except so far as their own private interest compels." *Utilitarianism*, *CWM* 10:233. Elsewhere in *Utilitarianism*, he urges that "education and opinion, which have so vast a power over human character, should so use that power as to establish in the mind of every individual an indissoluble association between his own happiness and the good of the whole." Ibid., 218. Even before the failure of self-cultivation, "selfishness" was, Mill held, "the principal cause which makes life unsatisfactory," and he inveighed against the notion that there is "an inherent necessity that any human being should be a selfish egotist, devoid of every feeling or care but those which centre in his own miserable individuality." Ibid.,215–16. On this issue, see also the discussions in Wendy Donner, *The Liberal Self: John Stuart Mill's Moral and Political Philosophy* (Ithaca: Cornell University Press, 1992), 180, and in Alan Ryan, *The Philosophy of John Stuart Mill*, rev. ed. (Basingstoke: Macmillan, 1987), 200. The salience of the social is another point of affinity that Mill would have had with Wilhelm von Humboldt, whom Charles Taylor aptly describes as both individualist and holist. Immediately after the passage of his that Mill quoted in the opening of the third chapter of *On Liberty*, Humboldt wrote, "It is through a social union, therefore, based on the internal wants and capacities of its members, that each is enabled to participate in the rich collective resources of all the others. . . . The effectiveness of all such relations [of friendship, "ordinary love"] as instruments of cultivation, entirely depends on the extent to which the members can succeed in combining their personal independence with the intimacy of the association; for whilst, without this intimacy, one individual cannot sufficiently possess, as it were, the nature of the others, independence is no less essential, in order that each, in being possessed, may be transformed in his own unique way. . . . This individual vigor, then, and manifold diversity, combine themselves in originality. . . . Just as this individuality springs naturally from freedom of action, and the greatest diversity in agents, it tends in turn directly to produce them." Wilhelm von Humboldt, *On the Limits of State Action*, ed. J. W. Burrows (Cambridge: Cambridge University Press, 1969), 17.

46. John Gray—in his insightful early work *Mill on Liberty: A Defence*—notes that both the model of discovery and that of choice or creation play a role in Mill's conception of autonomy. So it would be misleading to ask whether autonomous choice is the criterion of the "higher pleasures" or the instrument of them. "[T]his distinction between a criterial and an evidential view of the relations between autonomy and the higher pleasures fails to capture the spirit of Mill's view of the matter," he writes. "There can be no doubt that Mill does take choice-making to be itself a necessary ingredient

of happiness and of any higher pleasure: it is a necessary condition of a pleasure being a higher pleasure that it consist in activities that have been chosen after experience of an appropriate range of alternatives. But the sufficient condition of a pleasure's being a higher pleasure is that it expresses the individual nature of the man whose pleasure it is, and this, for the man himself as for others, is a matter of discovery and not of choice. Mill's position here is a complex one. On the one hand, like Aristotle, he affirmed that men were the makers of their own character. On the other hand, there is no doubt that Mill held to the Romantic belief that each has a quiddity or essence which awaits his discovery and which, if he is lucky, he may express in any one of a small number of styles of life. Mill seems, in his complex way, to be treating choice-making as itself partially constitutive of a happy human life and as instrumental to it." Gray, *Defence*, 73.

47. Given Mill's tendency to exalt variety, it's noteworthy that he was inclined to doubt that there was "really any distinction between the highest masculine and the highest feminine character," as he wrote in a letter to Thomas Carlyle (October 1833): "But the women, of all I have known, who possessed the highest measure of what are considered feminine qualities, have combined with them more of the highest *masculine* qualities than I have ever seen in any but one or two men, & those one or two men were also in many respects almost women. I suspect it is the second-rate people of the two sexes that are unlike—the first-rate are alike in both." *The Earlier Letters, 1812– 1848, CWM* 12:184.

48. Of course, it's not just our own life that we narrativize in this way: we do the same to the lives of others. After Lincoln died, Mill wrote to John Elliot Cairns (the author of the abolitionist tract *Slave Power*): "What I now principally feel is that the death of Lincoln, like that of Socrates, is a worthy end to a noble life, and puts the seal of universal remembrance upon his worth. He has now a place among the great names of history, and one could have wished nothing better for him personally than to die almost, or quite unconsciously, in perhaps the happiest moment of his life. How one rejoices that he lived to know of Lee's surrender." Mill to Cairnes, May 28, 1865, *The Late Letters, 1849–1873, CWM* 16:1057.

49. Taylor, *Authenticity*, 47. Alasdair MacIntyre, *After Virtue: A Study in Moral Theory*, 2nd ed. (Notre Dame: University of Notre Dame Press, 1984), 212, 207–8.

50. And sometimes characters in fictional narratives muse about how they draw upon fictional narratives. "Never in my life had I confessed so much or received so many confessions," Humbert Humbert recalls of his feigned intimacies with Lolita's mother, whom he is about to wed. "The sincerity and artlessness with which she discussed what she called her 'love-life,' from first necking to connubial catch-as-catch-can, were, ethically, in striking contrast with my glib compositions, but technically the two sets were congeneric since both were affected by the same stuff (soap operas, psychoanalysis and cheap novelettes) upon which I drew for my characters and she for her mode of expression." Vladimir Nabokov, *Lolita* (New York: Vintage, 1997), 80.

51. To possess virtue requires "a life that can be conceived and evaluated as a whole," says Alasdair MacIntyre, in his *After Virtue*, 205. We may, of course, reject the demand

for a unified self as too stringent, remote from the loose, baggy, and somewhat aleatory nature of life as some of us experience it. Joseph Raz gets it about right when he observes: "An autonomous life is neither necessarily planned nor is it necessarily unified. There is, however, a grain of truth in the view that autonomy gives life a unity. The autonomous person has or is gradually developing a conception of himself, and his actions are sensitive to his past. A person who has projects is sensitive to his past in at least two respects. He must be aware of having the pursuits he has, and he must be aware of his progress in them." Raz, *The Morality of Freedom* (Oxford: Oxford University Press, 1986), 385.

52. Ian Hacking, "Making Up People," in *Reconstructing Individualism: Autonomy, Individuality, and the Self in Western Thought*, ed. Thomas C. Heller, Morton Sosna, and David E. Wellbery (Stanford: Stanford University Press, 1986), 222–36.

53. This isn't to say that cleverness isn't a social product; it obviously is. You couldn't be clever if you grew up like Caspar Hauser. Nor it is to say that the social significance of cleverness isn't the result of social practices, attitudes, and shared beliefs.

54. The "career" concept is fascinatingly traced in Richard Sennett, *The Corrosion of Character* (New York: Norton, 1998).

55. *Utilitarianism, CWM* 10:231.

56. See, e.g., Robert M. Adams, "Common Projects and Moral Virtue," *Midwest Studies in Philosophy* 13 (1988): 297–307; Nancy Sherman, "The Virtues of Common Pursuit," *Philosophy and Phenomenological Research* 53, no. 2 (June 1993): 277–99; and Michael Bratman, "Shared Cooperative Activities," *Philosophical Review* 101, no. 2 (April 1992): 327–41, and "Shared Intention," *Ethics* 104 (1993): 97–113; and Margaret Gilbert, *Living Together* (Lanham, MD: Rowman and Littlefield, 1996).

57. Mill, *Autobiography, CWM* 1:251.

58. See Wendy Donner's persuasive charting of the theme of development in Mill, in her *Liberal Self.*

59. *Considerations on Representative Government, CWM* 19:390; and see Donner, *Liberal Self,* 126.

60. See, for example, Bhikhu Parekh, *Rethinking Multiculturalism* (Cambridge: Harvard University Press, 2000), 44, and Martha Nussbaum, "A Plea for Difficulty," in Susan Moller Okin, *Is Multiculturalism Bad for Women?*, ed. Joshua Cohen, Matthew Howard, and Martha C. Nussbaum (Princeton: Princeton University Press, 1999), 111. (We may put aside, for the nonce, the familiar objection that the putative neutralists aren't neutral, by this exacting standard.) I'll return to this matter in chapter 2, in the section titled "Autonomy as Intolerance."

61. Isaiah Berlin, "Two Concepts of Liberty" in *Four Essays on Liberty* (Oxford: Oxford University Press, 1969), 118–72.

62. Of course, Berlin didn't say it *had* to go awry. My "*pace*" here is meant only to acknowledge his anxiety that it might go awry.

63. Mill, *On Liberty, CWM* 18:267. In his 1983 *Defence* (in contrast to his later position), Gray argued that "Mill's conception of the good life may be perfectionist in the sense that it ranks lives which are in large measure self-chosen over those that are

customary, but this is a procedural perfectionism rather than a full theory of the good life. In weighting autonomy and security heavily in any scheme of human welfare, and giving priority to autonomy once certain conditions have been established, Mill does work with what Rawls has termed a thin theory of the good—a minimalist conception of human welfare expressed in terms of a theory of vital interests or primary goods." Gray, *Defence*, 88.

64. In *Principles of Political Economy, CWM* 3:803–4, he advances a principle of expediency: "There is a multitude of cases in which governments, with general approbation, assume powers and execute functions for which no reason can be assigned except the simple one, that they conduce to general convenience. We may take as an example, the function (which is a monopoly too) of coining money. This is assumed for no more recondite purpose than that of saving to individuals the trouble, delay, and expense of weighing and assaying. No one, however, even of those most jealous of state interference, has objected to this as an improper exercise of the powers of government. Prescribing a set of standard weights and measures is another instance. Paving, lighting, and cleansing the streets and thoroughfares, is another; whether done by the general government, or, as is more usual, and generally more advisable, by a municipal authority. Making or improving harbours, building lighthouses, making surveys in order to have accurate maps and charts, raising dykes to keep the sea out, and embankments to keep rivers in, are cases in point." And a little later: "Examples might be indefinitely multiplied without intruding on any disputed ground. But enough has been said to show that the admitted functions of government embrace a much wider field than can easily be included within the ring-fence of any restrictive definition, and that it is hardly possible to find any ground of justification common to them all, except the comprehensive one of general expediency; nor to limit the interference of government by any universal rule, save the simple and vague one, that it should never be admitted but when the case of expediency is strong."

65. Mill, *On Liberty, CWM* 18:270.

66. In *A System of Logic*, Mill even identified something he called "the Art of Life," which, he said, had "three departments": "Morality, Prudence or Policy, and Aesthetics; the Right, the Expedient, and the Beautiful or Noble, in human conduct and works. To this art (which, in the main, is unfortunately still to be created), all other arts are subordinate; since its principles are those which must determine whether the special aim of any particular art is worthy and desirable, and what is its place in the scale of desirable things. Every art is thus a joint result of laws of nature disclosed by science, and of the general principles of what has been called Teleology, or the Doctrine of Ends." *System of Logic, CWM* 8:949. Charles Larrabee Street (in Street, *Individualism*, 49) comments, "And yet at other times Mill saw clearly enough that there was a certain incommensurability among values. His famous admission of qualitative distinction between pleasures, damaging as it was to his own system, is an indication of this." The diagnosis adumbrates Berlin's, though Street's book appeared in 1926.

67. Matthew Arnold, *Culture and Anarchy*, ed. Samuel Lipman (New Haven: Yale University Press, 1994), 36.

68. Rawls, *A Theory of Justice*, 424.

69. Amartya Sen, *Inequality Reexamined* (Cambridge: Harvard University Press, 1992), xi.

70. These issues are extensively discussed in Joel Feinberg's *Harm to Others* (New York: Oxford University Press, 1984).

71. *On Liberty*, *CWM* 18:283. Here, Mill makes it clear that his version of utilitarianism recognizes incommensurability. Amartya Sen reads a "vector view of utility" in such passages: see Sen, "Plural Utility," *Proceedings of the Aristotelian Society* 81 (1982): 196–97.

72. Mill held that the state should require and subsidize education, but not provide it, probably because in his day, state education essentially meant sectarian education, under the tutelage of the established church. See John Kleinig, *Paternalism* (Totowa: Rowman & Allanheld, 1984), 34.

73. See Raz, *Morality of Freedom*, 400, 410, 414, 415–16.

74. Mill, *Utilitarianism*, *CWM* 10:256. And see Donner, *Liberal Self*, 164.

75. Mill, *Principles of Political Economy*, *CWM* 3:937. It may be worth quoting his position here more fully: "It is evident, even at first sight, that the authoritative form of government intervention has a much more limited sphere of legitimate action than the other. It requires a much stronger necessity to justify it in any case; while there are large departments of human life from which it must be unreservedly and imperiously excluded. Whatever theory we adopt respecting the foundation of the social union, and under whatever political institutions we live, there is a circle around every individual human being which no government, be it that of one, of a few, or of the many, ought to be permitted to overstep: there is a part of the life of every person who has come to years of discretion, within which the individuality of that person ought to reign uncontrolled either by any other individual or by the public collectively. That there is, or ought to be, some space in human existence thus entrenched around, and sacred from authoritative intrusion, no one who professes the smallest regard to human freedom or dignity will call in question: the point to be determined is, where the limit should be placed; how large a province of human life this reserved territory should include. I apprehend that it ought to include all that part which concerns only the life, whether inward or outward, of the individual, and does not affect the interests of others, or affects them only through the moral influence of example. With respect to the domain of the inward consciousness, the thoughts and feelings, and as much of external conduct as is personal only, involving no consequences, none at least of a painful or injurious kind, to other people: I hold that it is allowable in all, and in the more thoughtful and cultivated often a duty, to assert and promulgate, with all the force they are capable of, their opinion of what is good or bad, admirable or contemptible, but not to compel others to conform to that opinion; whether the force used is that of extra-legal coercion, or exerts itself by means of the law." *Principles of Political Economy*, *CWM* 3:937–38.

76. *CWM* 5:634. See discussions in Gray, *Defence*, 64, and Street, *Individualism*, 50.

77. *On Liberty, CWM* 18:291. On the other hand, Mill also wrote that there are "conditions of society in which a vigorous despotism is in itself the best mode of government for training the people in what is specifically wanting to render them capable of a higher civilization." Mill, *Considerations on Representative Government,* in *CWM* 19:567. At such moments, we hear not the liberal but the chief examiner of India House, the paragovernmental body in charge of British India and his employer for four decades. For a reading of Mill that focuses on these imperial strains, see Uday Singh Mehta, *Liberalism and Empire* (Chicago: University of Chicago Press, 1999), 97–106. There's an interesting paradox here: following Comte, he worries that a high degree of individuality is inconsistent with a high degree of civilization; so that societies that qualify for political autonomy are precisely those that have, in some measure, sacrificed personal autonomy.

78. Mill, *Principles of Political Economy, CWM* 3:937.

79. *On Liberty, CWM* 18:277. Cf. the thoughtful discussion of Mill on the self-regarding/other-regarding distinction in Kleinig, *Paternalism,* 32–37.

80. *On Liberty, CWM* 18:305.

81. Mill, *Autobiography, CWM* 1:213.

82. Ibid., 249.

83. Packe, *The Life,* 405.

84. Letter to Arthur Hardy, May 14, 1859, quoted in Ibid., 409.

85. *Autobiography, CWM* 1:251.

86. John Stuart Mill and Harriet Taylor, *Essays on Sex Equality,* ed. Alice S. Rossi (Chicago: University of Chicago Press, 1970), 236; quoted in Mazlish, *James and John,* 342.

Chapter Two Autonomy and Its Critics

1. I quote the passage as translated by Richard Pevear and Larissa Volokhonsky, *Anna Karenina* (New York: Viking, 2000), 6–7. (The actual paper Stepan would have read, they suggest, was *The Voice,* edited by a certain A. Kraevsky.)

2. Gerald Dworkin, *The Theory and Practice of Autonomy* (Cambridge: Cambridge University Press, 1988), 38.

3. Joel Feinberg, *Harm to Self* (New York: Oxford University Press, 1986), 32 and 380 n. 11. See also David Riesman and Nathan Glazer, "The Meaning of Opinion," *Public Opinion Quarterly* 12, no. 4 (Winter 1948–49): 638–39, where Stepan is cited as an example of the "other-directed" people who are "possessed of a relatively high level of information about politics and a stock of opinions like a well-furnished wine-cellar, but lacking in any genuine affect about opinions which would lead them to discriminate between those opinions which have meaning in today's world from those which are mere opinionatedness."

4. Haworth, *Autonomy,* 7.

5. Robert Young, "Autonomy and 'the Inner Self,' " *American Philosophical Quarterly* 17, no. 1 (January 1980): 36. So much for Isaiah Berlin's point that it is not only a society that harbors plural and incommensurable values: "Values may easily clash within the breast of a single individual." There's good reason to be suspicious of the notion of a life that is a "unified order," even as an ideal.

6. Stanley Benn, "Freedom, Autonomy, and the Concept of the Person," *Proceedings of the Aristotelian Society* 76 (1975–76): 129. See also the wide-ranging discussion of autonomy, authenticity, and autarky in the context of "liberal soulcraft," in Peter Digeser, *Our Politics, Our Selves* (Princeton: Princeton University Press, 1995), 166–95.

7. For example, Gray, *Defence*, 74; and William E. Connelly, *The Terms of Political Discourse*, 2nd ed. (Princeton: Princeton University Press, 1983), 150–51.

8. David Johnston, *The Idea of a Liberal Theory: A Critique and Reconstruction* (Princeton: Princeton University Press, 1996), 102.

9. Raz, *Morality of Freedom*, 370, 371.

10. Ibid., 381–82.

11. "Self-creation and the creation of values discussed here are not uniquely connected with the ideal of personal autonomy. They represent a necessary feature of practical reasoning. . . . The ideal of autonomy picks on these features and demands that they be expanded. It requires that self-creation must proceed, in part, through choice among an adequate range of options; that the agent must be aware of his options and of the meaning of his choices; and that he must be independent of coercion and manipulation by others. The ideal of autonomy, if you like, makes a virtue out of necessity." Ibid., 390.

12. George Sher, *Beyond Neutrality: Perfectionism and Politics* (Cambridge: Cambridge University Press, 1997), 50. Again, inasmuch as reasons are defined as guides to action, reason-responsive behavior is pretty much a condition of basic human rationality.

13. Conventional religious history might complicate that picture: on the one hand, the autonomy of the individual conscience seems to have been at least one strain in Protestantism; on the other hand, Luther and Calvin, who burned heretics freely, were scarcely exemplars of tolerance. "Any liberal argument that invokes autonomy as a general rule of public action in effect takes sides in the ongoing struggle between reason and faith, reflection and tradition," Galston maintains, in *Liberal Pluralism: The Implications of Value Pluralism for Political Theory and Practice* (Cambridge: Cambridge University Press, 2002), 25; but it's perhaps not so obvious *which* side. For further reflections on these two themes in liberal thought, see Jacob T. Levy's superb "Liberalism's Divide after Socialism—and Before," *Social Philosophy and Policy* 20, no. 1 (Winter 2003): 278–97.

14. John Gray, *Isaiah Berlin* (Princeton: Princeton University Press, 1996), 32–33.

15. Susan Mendus, *Toleration and the Limits of Liberalism* (Basingstoke: Macmillan, 1989), 108; Charles E. Larmore, *Patterns of Moral Complexity* (Cambridge: Cambridge University Press, 1987), 129; Chandran Kukathas, "Are There Any Cultural Rights?" *Political Theory* 20, no. 1 (February 1992): 120; Parekh, *Rethinking Multiculturalism*, 44.

16. Lawrence Haworth convincingly argues that substantive independence is not a precondition for autonomy: "A cloistered nun who devotes her life to Christ and whose days follow a set pattern has made herself substantively dependent. If the decision to enter cloistered life was a serious and personal one and if moreover it is renewed from time to time, her substantive dependence need not be taken as a sign that she lacks personal autonomy. The question of autonomy here refers to whether the life she leads is her own. . . . That is to say that the independence that makes one autonomous is procedural, not substantive." Haworth, *Autonomy*, 20. But when people cite lives of religious devotion as inconsistent with autonomism, it's not always clear which feature of those lives is relevant: the actual texture of the life governed by self-denying ordinances or the metaphysical and ethical commitments of religious self-abnegation. Obviously an autonomous existence need not be an unencumbered one. Everyone would agree that a "fully autonomous liberal individual" can be married; can encumber him- or herself with all sorts of obligations and duties that come with having a family, working as a corporate comptroller, being chairman of the City Opera. Viewed from one perspective, this person's life is a cascade of "detrimental reliance" torts waiting to happen: there are tens of thousands of things that he must and must not do, on pain of civil, criminal, or social sanction. Almost every hour of his conscious life is accounted for, controlled by one obligation or another, because his family, his coworkers, his colleagues in this or that civil association are all depending upon him in various tightly specified ways. But nobody could imagine that a life of such constraint is inconsistent with liberal autonomy.

17. "Democratic Character and Community: The Logic of Congruence?" *Journal of Political Philosophy* 2, no. 1 (1994): 67–97. See also introduction to *Civil Society and Government*, ed. Nancy L. Rosenblum and Robert C. Post (Princeton: Princeton University Press, 2001): "The claim is that the internal lives of associations should mirror public norms of equality, nondiscrimination, due process, and so on. . . . Taken too far, however, this logic of moral education . . . invites state institutions to colonize social life in the name of progressive public ideals."

18. John Gray, *Two Faces of Liberalism* (New York: The New Press, 2000), 56.

19. Ibid., 99.

20. Gray, *Isaiah Berlin*, 152. It is a curious gloss on Berlin, who wrote of "the ideal of freedom to choose ends without claiming eternal validity for them" as connected to "the pluralism of values." Isaiah Berlin, "Two Concepts of Liberty," in *Four Essays*, 172.

21. See Brian Barry's critique in *Culture and Equality* (Cambridge: Harvard University Press, 2001), 133.

22. Gray, *Two Faces*, 103.

23. Ibid., 13, 14.

24. Michael Walzer, "On Involuntary Associations," in *Freedom of Association*, ed. Amy Gutmann (Princeton: Princeton University Press, 1998), 70. Charles Taylor, *Sources of the Self: The Making of the Modern Identity* (Cambridge: Harvard University Press, 1989), 36, 27. Michael Sandel, *Liberalism and the Limits of Justice* (Cambridge: Cambridge University Press, 1982), 179. Bell, *Communitarianism*, 37. These concerns lead

others to try to supplant talk of "autonomy" with different argot. Thus Loren Lomasky, in his *Persons, Rights, and the Moral Community* (New York: Oxford University Press, 1987), prefers the notion of "project pursuers." Lomasky writes, "A person's commitments may be unarticulated and not at all the product of conscious deliberation culminating in a moment of supreme decision. They may rather be something that he has gradually and imperceptibly come to assume over time." Indeed, many projects of ours are "ingested with one's mother's milk, become by imperceptible degrees more firmly fixed over time within one's volitionary makeup, and never trotted out to be cross-examined at the bar of reason" (42, 44). But it would be natural to take this just as guidance for how we should *interpret* autonomy.

25. Sandel, *Limits*, 179.

26. Tolstoy, *Anna Karenina*, 7.

27. Ibid.

28. Ibid., 15.

29. Arguing that our theories of meaning must take into account the "division of linguistic labor," Putnam, in a much discussed essay, noted that he couldn't tell an elm from a beech tree; when he used the word "elm," its meaning was provided by the existence of expert users—a "special subclass of speakers." Hilary Putnam, "The Meaning of 'Meaning,' " in *Mind, Language, and Reality: Philosophical Papers*, vol. 2 (Cambridge: Cambridge University Press, 1975).

30. For accounts of how people acquire their political opinions and identities, see Donald Green, Bradley Palmquist, and Eric Schickler, *Partisan Hearts and Minds: Political Parties and the Social Identities of Voters* (New Haven: Yale University Press, 2002); and Paul M. Sniderman, "Taking Sides: A Fixed Choice Theory of Political Reasoning," in *Elements of Reason: Cognition, Choice, and the Bounds of Rationality*, ed. Arthur Lupia, Mathew D. McCubbins, and Samuel L. Popkin (Cambridge: Cambridge University Press, 2000), 67–84. For an account of the attenuated consciousness typical of daily life, see, e.g., John Bargh and Tanya L. Chartrand, "The Unbearable Automaticity of Being," *American Psychologist* 54 (July 1999): 462–79. In Bargh's account, essentially, an internal Mr. Stevens deals with a great proportion of our activities. "Conscious direction of behavior is important, but it takes place a small minority of the time," Bargh says. Bargh has aptly called this "thought lite," citing Dan Gilbert who says it involves "one-third less effort than regular thinking," except, of course, that it *is* regular thinking. So the political philosopher Daniel A. Bell is quite right to say (in Bell, *Communitarianism*, 32) that "the normal mode of existence is that of unreflectively acting in a way specified by the practices of one's social world." Social practices of this sort "include ways of sitting, standing, dressing, pronouncing, walking, greeting, playing sports, and more generally encountering objects and people." But, of course, he enlists such considerations by way of a critique of the liberal rhetoric of planning and the conscious exercise of practical reason: "When acting in a way specified by social practices, we need not have plans and goals, let alone the long-range life-plans that, say, Rawls would suppose." This is no more than half right; the fact that (say) running a marathon involves innumerable activities we would be hard-pressed to describe as conscious deci-

sions doesn't mean that our wish to race and win the marathon couldn't be described in terms of plans and goals.

31. Raz, *Morality of Freedom*, 373.

32. A variety of congruent examples are presented and analyzed in chapter 10 of Alfred R. Mele, *Autonomous Agents* (New York: Oxford University Press, 1995). And cf. the four cases discussed in Raz, *Morality of Freedom*, 15.

33. Cf. the discussion in Andrew Mason, "Autonomy, Liberalism and State Neutrality," *Philosophical Quarterly* 40 (October 1990): 436. As Colin Bird points out, political freedom, for Mill, "requires merely that individuals enjoy adequate opportunities to live autonomous, self-directed lives should they wish to do so. Nowhere does Mill suggest that those who fail to take that opportunity are politically unfree." Colin Bird, *The Myth of Liberal Individualism* (Cambridge: Cambridge University Press, 1999), 133.

34. *Utilitarianism, CWM* 10:231–32. At times here, Mill can sound like a curious blend of Sandel and B. F. Skinner: "If we now suppose this feeling of unity to be taught as a religion, and the whole force of education, of institutions, and of opinion, directed, as it once was in the case of religion, to make every person grow up from infancy surrounded on all sides both by the profession and the practice of it, I think that no one, who can realise this conception, will feel any misgiving about the sufficiency of the ultimate sanction for the Happiness Morality."

35. Raz, *Morality of Freedom*, 373. The difficulty of measuring gradients of liberty was conveyed by Berlin's cautious metaphor: "The extent of a man's negative freedom is, as it were, a function of what doors, and how many, are open to him; upon what prospects they open; and how open they are. This formula must not be pressed too far, for not all doors are of equal importance, inasmuch as the paths on which they open vary in the opportunities they offer. Consequently, the problem of how an over-all increase of liberty in particular circumstances is to be secured, and how it is to be distributed (especially in situations, and this is almost invariably the case, in which the opening of one door leads to the lifting of other barriers and the lowering of still others), how, in a word, the maximization of opportunities is in any concrete case to be achieved, can be an agonizing problem, not to be solved by any hard-and-fast rule." Isaiah Berlin, introduction to *Four Essays*, xlviii–xlix.

36. Samuel Scheffler, "Responsibility, Reactive Attitudes, and Liberalism in Philosophy and Politics," *Philosophy and Public Affairs* 21, no. 4 (Autumn 1992): 309.

37. Dworkin, *Theory and Practice of Autonomy*, 62–81.

38. Charles Taylor, "To Follow a Rule," in *Philosophical Arguments* (Cambridge: Harvard University Press, 1995), 168, 173.

39. Ibid., 168, 170, 178.

40. James Tully, "Wittgenstein and Political Philosophy: Understanding Practices of Critical Reflection," *Political Theory* 17, no. 2 (May 1989): 193, 195. Taylor has also been criticized by way of *tu quoque*. Thus Jeremy Waldron: "The very idea of individuality and autonomy, [Taylor] argues, is a social artifact, a way of thinking about and managing the self that is sustained in a particular social and historical context. I am sure that he is right about that. But we must not assume, simply because individuality is an

artifact, that the social structures that are said to produce it are necessarily natural. Certainly there is nothing natural about communitarian, ethnic, or nationalist ideas." Jeremy Waldron, "Minority Cultures and the Cosmopolitan Alternative," *University of Michigan Journal of Law Reform* 25 (1992): 780–81.

41. See my "Tolerable Falsehoods," in *Consequences of Theory*, ed. Jonathan Arac and Barbara Johnson (Baltimore: Johns Hopkins University Press, 1991), 63–90.

42. Immanuel Kant, *Groundwork of the Metaphysic of Morals*, trans. H. J. Paton (New York: Harper & Row, 1964), 118. A great deal has been written on the influence on Kant of scientific models of explanation, especially Newtonian physics; see, for example, Michael Friedman, *Kant and the Exact Sciences* (Cambridge: Harvard University Press, 1992).

43. Kant, *Groundwork*, 126.

44. Richard Wright, *Native Son* (New York: HarperCollins, 1998). Louis Menand points out these conflicting interpretations in "Richard Wright: The Hammer and the Nail," in *American Studies* (New York: Farrar Straus & Giroux, 2002), 83–85. "Two years before Wright formally broke with the Communist Party," Menand notes, "he had already turned in Marx for Nietzsche."

45. In close juxtaposition, Mill's *A System of Logic* presents both the ideal of the self-choosing person and the regularities that inform his character. Mill writes: "[I]f we examine closely, we shall find that this feeling, of our being able to modify our own character if we wish, is itself the feeling of moral freedom which we are conscious of. A person feels morally free who feels that his habits or his temptations are not his masters, but he theirs; who, even in yielding to them, knows that he could resist; that were he desirous of altogether throwing them off, there would not be required for that purpose a stronger desire than he knows himself to be capable of feeling." *System of Logic*, CWM 8:841. In his chapter calling for a science of ethology, he writes: "[A]ll modes of feeling and conduct met with among mankind have causes which produce them; and in the propositions which assign those causes will be found the explanation of the empirical laws, and the limiting principle of our reliance on them. Human beings do not all feel and act alike in the same circumstances; but it is possible to determine what makes one person, in a given position, feel or act in one way, another in another; how any given mode of feeling and conduct, compatible with the general laws (physical and mental) of human nature, has been, or may be, formed. In other words, mankind may not have one universal character, but there exist universal laws of the Formation of Character . . . it is by these laws, combined with the facts of each particular case, that the whole of the phenomena of human action and feeling are produced." *System of Logic*, CWM 8:864.

46. Kant, *Groundwork*, 128.

47. Jürgen Habermas, *Knowledge and Human Interests*, trans. Jeremy J. Shapiro (London: Heinemann, 1972), 135, 176. Without belaboring the shortcomings here, I would mention that the distinction between a "practical" interest in mutual understanding and a "technical" interest in control is far from clear, for example; nor is it clear how these differences in interest "constitute" a field of inquiry (though I seek to contribute

to the answer to this question later); or that we should seek to understand differences between domains of knowledge at the perilous level of abstraction at which natural, social, and critical knowledge are supposed to be differentiated.

48. Here again I'd direct attention to the diagnosis ventured in Charles Taylor, "Cross-Purposes: The Liberal-Communitarian Debate," in *Philosophical Arguments*. Discussing the contrast between "unencumbered" and "situated" selves, Taylor notes, "It could be used to argue that because a totally unencumbered self is a human impossibility, the extreme atomist model of society is a chimera. Or one could argue that both (relatively) unencumbered and situated selves are possibilities, as would be also (relatively) atomist and holist societies, but that the viable combinations between these two levels are restricted: a highly collectivist society would be hard to combine with an unencumbered identity, or a highly individualist life form would be impossible where selves are thickly situated" (182). I've focused on what I consider the more fruitful and plausible interpretation, which has to do with different representations of the same social reality. But it's also the case that structure is easier to see from a distance. And that's one reason that various critics of autonomism represent it as a contrast between the West and the Rest. It's a position that comes down to this: we have subjects and they have structures. But of course no society has a lock on agency, on rational choice making; and no society has a lock on social matrices.

49. We sometimes offer (external) explanations rather than reasons for our actions—as when someone explains his own indolence by saying he's clinically depressed (or, in other cultures, by saying that a spell has been cast on him). It's a very different thing when the explanation is offered by another. The loss of personhood under these interpretive circumstances is memorably captured in Jonathan Franzen's portrait of Gary Lambert, unhappy husband of Caroline, in *The Corrections*. "He'd had the sense, moments earlier, that Caroline was on the verge of accusing him of being 'depressed,' and he was afraid that if the idea that he was depressed gained currency, he would forfeit the right to his opinions. He would forfeit his moral certainties; every word he spoke would become a symptom of disease; he would never again win an argument." Franzen, *The Corrections* (New York: Farrar, Straus and Giroux), 161.

Chapter Three The Demands of Identity

1. Muzafer Sherif, O. J. Harvey, B. Jack White, William R. Hood, and Carolyn W. Sherif, *The Robbers Cave Experiment: Intergroup Conflict and Cooperation* (Middletown: Wesleyan University Press, 1988; originally published by the Institute of Group Relations, the University of Oklahoma, 1961).

2. Tellingly, when the Eagles, playing on the baseball diamond, first heard the Rattlers, a group of whose existence they'd learned only a day or two previously, one of them made a remark about "those nigger campers." Ibid., 95. What was obviously a salient social distinction for them came immediately to mind as an all-purpose designation for the outgroup. (Later on, "communist" became a term of derogation.)

3. Ibid., 111.

4. Ibid., 116.

5. Donald Horowitz, *Ethnic Groups in Conflict* (Berkeley and Los Angeles: University of California Press, 1985), 179.

6. Jean-Loup Amselle, *Mestizo Logics: Anthropology of Identity in Africa and Elsewhere*, trans. Claudia Royal (Stanford: Stanford University Press, 1998), 33. Horowitz, *Ethnic Groups*, 69.

7. The usage of "identity," in this sense, is usually traced to Erik Erikson; in, e.g., "Identity and the Life Cycle," *Psychological Issues* 1 (1959); but he often evoked by the term something quite private, an "inner" sort of psychological wholeness. In a 1956 essay, though, Erikson speaks of a relation between a "person's conception of himself and his community's conception of him." He was, in various ways, taking up themes that had been explored by some of his immediate forebears. In 1922, Max Weber, in *Wirtschaft und Gesellschaft*, described *Gemeinsamkeit*, ethnic identity, as deriving from a sense of a common past, but he added, "On the other hand it is primarily the political community, no matter how artificially organized, that inspires the belief in common ethnicity." *Economy and Society: An Outline of Interpretive Sociology*, ed. Claus Wittich and Guenther Roth (Berkeley and Los Angeles: University of California Press, 1979). Erikson claims that he began to employ "identity" and "identity crisis" in the 1930s, and that "they seemed naturally grounded in the experience of emigration, immigration, and Americanization." Erik H. Erikson, " 'Identity Crisis' in Autobiographical Perspective," in *Life History and the Historical Moment* (New York: Norton, 1975), 43; and see Adam Kuper, *Culture: The Anthropologists' Account* (Cambridge: Harvard University Press, 1999), 237. Still, Erikson tended to use the term where others might have used "self," or "ego." The distinctive notion of a "social identity" is first used extensively in the writings of Alvin W. Gouldner in the 1950s. (I am grateful to Jesse Sheidlower for his lexical erudition.)

8. Hacking, "Making Up People." As he would be the first to acknowledge, this insight is already present in what sociologists call "labeling theory." See Mary McIntosh, "The Homosexual Role," in *Forms of Desire: Sexual Orientation and the Social Constructionist Controversy*, ed. Edward Stein (New York: Routledge, 1988), 25–42.

9. Hacking "Making Up People," 236.

10. See especially section 23 of G.E.M. Anscombe, *Intention* (Oxford: Basil Blackwell, 1972), 37–41; and her "Under a Description," *Nous* 13 (1979): 219–33, insisting, inter alia, that the different descriptions of a given action don't, of course, designate different actions.

11. "His movement is quick and forward, a little too precise, a little too rapid. He comes toward the patrons with a step a little too quick. He bends forward a little too eagerly, his eyes express an interest too solicitous for the order of the customer." Jean-Paul Sartre, *Being and Nothingness*, trans. Hazel E. Barnes, as cited in Hacking, "Making Up People," 231. And, Hacking observes, "As with almost every way in which it is possible to be a person, it is possible to be a *garçon de café* only at a certain time, in a certain place, in a certain social setting. The feudal serf putting food on my lady's table

can no more choose to be a *garçon de café* than he can choose to be lord of the manor. But the impossibility is evidently of a different kind" (231).

12. I first offered an account of this form in my essay in Kwame Anthony Appiah and Amy Gutmann, *Color Conscious: The Political Morality of Race* (Princeton: Princeton University Press, 1998). The discussion of identity develops the account given there.

13. Groups will generally have more than one label, so that part of what one learns in coming to understand an identity is a way of assigning members to the group and a label associated with it. Thus one has, so to speak, an individual concept associated with the group, which is one's own set of criteria of ascription.

14. Such narratives, as with ethnic identities, often involve literal descent, but they need not. A lesbian may regard, as an identitarian forebear, Gertrude Stein (who, perhaps aptly, remarked, "What good are roots if you can't take them with you?").

15. Imagine, though, an identity group that was recognized by nobody outside the group: something like a supersecret Masonic Lodge, or a community of wizards that lived among us. Here the treatment-as-L has counterfactual valence: if we knew some people were wizards, we *would* treat them differently. As with the Robbers Cave experiment, identities emerge through opposition. A group who lived on an island without knowledge of the outside world would not have a shared identity. (This point is well made in the classic *Ethnic Groups and Boundaries* [New York: Little, Brown and Co., 1969] by the Norwegian anthropologist Fredrik Barth.)

16. Nor is the making of racial distinctions always morally suspect. In the medical realm, benevolent profiling isn't uncommon: a doctor may recommend that a patient with Ashkenazi ancestry be tested for Tay-Sachs, an African American for sickle-cell anemia. Here the at-risk populations are largely coextensive with a socially salient identity. (Though we need to remember that sickling is not restricted to African Americans, and that a person of Ashkenazi and African American ancestry might end up counting as black rather than Jewish.) Still, though these traits may supervene upon the identities, they're not constitutive of them. A disposition to this or that disorder has no real ethical salience for the relevant identity group: if, through some prenatal treatment, the disorders vanished from the human population, these identities would not be appreciably altered. (By contrast, there could be identity groups that *were* defined in terms of a pathology—cancer survivors or alcoholics, say.) The case of social subordination and race is more complicated: a history of disadvantage, and its present-day sequelae, surely *is* part of the content of an African American identity. For that matter, you needn't subscribe to Sartre's controversial analysis in *Anti-Semite and Jew* to recognize that a self-affirmative Jewish identity cannot easily be detached from a history of persecution.

17. That will seem uncontroversial in the case of sexual identity. But it may also be the nature of preferences—even for stamp collecting—that you don't conceive them as something you control: you don't will yourself to be interested in stamps. (Unless, perhaps, someone you love—your child, say—is already a stamp-collector!)

18. Societal cultures—the term is Will Kymlicka's—are characterized by territorial concentration, institutional structure, and internal social integration.

19. The First Amendment speaks only of what laws *Congress* shall make; the American Founders knew that some of the states that came together to form the union did, in fact, have established religions. So I am really drawing on the current understanding of religious toleration, as embodied in historically recent interpretations of the First Amendment, not on the original understandings of it.

20. A characteristic formulation is Bhikhu Parekh's: "[T]he liberal is in theory committed to equal respect for persons. Since human beings are culturally embedded, respect for them entails respect for their cultures and ways of life." See Bhikhu Parekh, "Superior People: The Narrowness of Liberalism from Mill to Rawls," *Times Literary Supplement*, February 25, 1994, 13. I shall be arguing that the enthymematic argument in this sentence is too quick. And Raz, too—in his *Ethics in the Public Domain* (Oxford: Oxford University Press, 1995), 174—has affirmed the "equal standing" of "stable and viable cultural communities."

21. "The more important human groupings"—that is, "encompassing groups"—"need to be based on shared history, and on criteria of nonvoluntaristic (at or least not wholly contractarian) membership to have the value they have," Avishai Margalit and Joseph Raz argue in "National Self-Determination," *Journal of Philosophy* 87, no. 9 (September 1990): 456. And John Gray places a similar emphasis on the ascriptive, nonvoluntary nature of such differing ways of life. "Today, as throughout human history, human identities are primarily ascriptive, not elective. For nearly everyone, belonging to a community is a matter of fate, not choice. . . . Any political ideal that neglects these realities can only be pernicious in its consequences." In his view, we have blinked at the true challenges posed by Difference: "In recent liberal writings, the fact of pluralism refers to a diversity of personal ideals whose place is in the realm of voluntary association. The background idea here is that of the autonomous individual selecting a particular style of life. This type of diversity resembles the diversity of ethnic cuisines that can be found in some cities. . . . But the fact of pluralism is not the trivial and banal truth that individuals hold to different personal ideals. It is the coexistence of different ways of life. Conventional liberal thought contrives to misunderstand this fact, because it takes for granted a consensus on liberal values." Gray, *Two Faces*, 121, 13.

22. Note that the cultural sovereignty that Kukathas upholds isn't founded on cultural rights, which he avowedly rejects, but on the paramount importance of the freedom of association, and on a severely restrictive vision of the liberal state.

23. For an excellent discussion of the Ottoman millet system, see Michael Walzer, *On Toleration* (New Haven: Yale University Press, 1999).

24. Galston, *Liberal Pluralism*, 22. Even Raz worries that liberal autonomism could be too demanding: "If what I will call for brevity's sake 'multicultural measures' are to be taken only with regard to cultural groups that embrace and pursue the right degree of toleration and freedom toward both their own measures and others, then none will qualify. . . . But we will not qualify either. . . . We are homophobic and racist, indifferent to the poor and disadvantaged at least as much, though not necessarily in the same ways, as all those cultural groups for the sake of whose members multicultural measures

are adopted." Joseph Raz, "How Perfect Should One Be? And Whose Culture Is?" in Okin, *Is Multiculturalism Bad for Women?*, 96.

25. Kukathas, "Cultural Rights?" 105–39, and Chandran Kukathas, "Liberalism and Multiculturalism: The Politics of Indifference," *Political Theory* 26, no. 5 (October 1998): 686–99. Kukathas, who identifies himself as a liberal individualist, also subscribes to the general prohibition of coercion and slavery. What he recommends is a "politics of indifference": while minorities would be able, within certain broad parameters, to regulate their conduct as they preferred, the state would be unburdened by any further obligation to provide assistance or support.

26. Kukathas, "Cultural Rights?" 126.

27. Avishai Margalit and Moshe Habertal—in their "Liberalism and the Right to Culture," *Social Research* 64 (1994): 491–510—stipulate that a cultural community cannot abridge the right to exit, on the "pretext that if people begin to leave, then the culture will be destroyed." But, as Jacob T. Levy points out, this isn't necessarily a pretext: small communities may indeed be threatened by such exit. One consideration or the other must be sacrificed. For that matter, recall Ursula LeGuin's classic short story "The Ones Who Walk Away from Omelas"—that ethicist's delight—about a nearly perfect society that apparently depends on the suffering of one unfortunate child who is kept locked in a dark basement. See Ursula LeGuin, *The Wind's Twelve Quarters* (New York: Harper & Row, 1975).

28. Amy Gutmann, in her *Identity in Democracy* (Princeton: Princeton University Press, 2003), a book I regrettably encountered too late to take full advantage of, helpfully distinguishes among cultural, voluntary, ascriptive, and religious identity groups, and has a keen eye for the different ways in which "exit" might apply to each. See her discussion of a Canadian case in which members of a Hutterite church colony (where all personal property belongs to the church) were expelled for renouncing its beliefs, and so deprived of all their belongings. Gutmann suggests that a right to exit must be effective, not merely formal: "only an effective right to exit voluntary groups is consistent with valuing them so greatly as to defend a right to free association." The Pueblo case raises issues of sexual discrimination, as well, in that the children of men, but not women, who marry outside the group are given tribal membership. See Kymlicka, *Multicultural Citizenship* (Oxford: Oxford University Press, 1995), 233; and Gutmann, *Identity*, 45–47.

29. Leslie Green, "Internal Minorities and Their Rights," in *The Rights of Minority Cultures*, ed. Will Kymlicka (Oxford: Oxford University Press, 1995), 266–67.

30. See Levy's clear-eyed study *The Multiculturalism of Fear* (New York: Oxford University Press, 2000), 112. Further to this point, Albert O. Hirschman—in *Exit, Voice, and Loyalty* (Cambridge: Harvard University Press, 1970), 76—writes, "exit is ordinarily unthinkable, though not always wholly impossible, from such primordial human groupings as family, tribe, church, and state," and, in a footnote, goes on: "There is no intention here to associate absence of exit with 'primitiveness.' Edmund Leach has noted that many so-called primitive tribes are far from being closed societies. In his classic study *Political Systems of Highland Burma* (1954) he traced in detail the way in

which members of one social system (*gumsha*) will periodically move to another (*gum-lao*) and back again. Exit may be more effectively ruled out in a so-called advanced open society than among the tribes studied by Leach." He also notes that "with exit either impossible or unthinkable, provision is generally made in these organizations for expelling or excommunicating the individual member in certain circumstances."

31. Kymlicka, *Multicultural Citizenship*, 41, 42. The particular examples that Kymlicka explores are group-libel laws (with respect to the Rushdie affair) and land-in-trust (with respect to Canadian indigenes). His conclusion, in chapter 5 of *Multicultural Citizenship*, is that we should reject external protections that are also internal restrictions. But here, too, it's clear that the lurking issue for Kymlicka is really legitimacy— what a state must do to be a legitimate authority among constituent nationalities.

32. Michael J. Perry, *Love and Power: The Role of Religion and Morality in American Politics* (New York: Oxford University Press, 1991).

33. John Rawls, "The Idea of Public Reason Revisited," in *John Rawls: Collected Papers*, ed. Samuel Freeman (Cambridge: Harvard University Press, 1999), 574, 611. And far from showing distaste for religious argument, Rawls has explicitly commended the religious vocabulary of Martin Luther King, Jr., and of the earlier abolitionists—as, for that matter, of Abraham Lincoln's religious declarations of Thanksgiving—as serving the ultimate interests of public reason. Ibid., 593 n. 54.

34. Kymlicka, *Multicultural Citizenship*, 113, 111.

35. *Church of Lukumi Babalu Aye v. City of Hialeah* (1993).

36. Government discretion in providing monetary support for religious institutions, and in promoting religious displays, was significantly enlarged in such post–Warren Court decisions as *Widmar v. Vincent* (1981), *Mueller v. Allen* (1983). *Marsh v. Chambers* (1983), *Lynch v. Donnelly* (1984), *Bowen v. Kendrick* (1988), and, in some measure, *County of Allegheny v. ACLU* (1989); the position of religious officials in the exercise of state power has been fortified in such cases as *McDaniel v. Paty* (1978) and *Witters v. Department of Services* (1986).

37. Critics have raised other objections to the appeal to individual autonomy in judicial opinions, namely, that they conflate avocational preferences with matters of deep commitment. See Michael Sandel's discussion of *Thornton v. Caldor* in his *Democracy's Discontents* (Cambridge: Harvard University Press, 1996), 67–68.

38. Stephen L. Carter, *The Culture of Disbelief* (New York: Basic Books, 1993), 142. This Madisonian rationale raises two main areas for concern. One has to do with the highly defeasible nature of such consequentialist defenses. Then, too, the effect of so designating the rationale may be to narrow the freedoms it supports. Once a purpose is assigned, the domain of the right can be narrowly demarcated to serve that purpose, as much jurisprudence of free speech—the second subject of the First Amendment— has amply demonstrated. If the designated purpose of freedom of expression is (say) to promote the truth, then literature and speech that, in the judgment of the courts, has no such plausible claim may be stripped of protection. An instrumental defense of religious freedom might invite similar constriction. In the domain of speech, instrumental rationales have led to a hierarchy of speech categories, in which, for example,

political speech has been adjudged worthy of a great deal of legal protection, and commercial speech adjudged worthy of much less. An instrumentalist account like Carter's, if taken seriously, would conduce to similar results: forms of corporate worship that play a useful political role by challenging secular norms ought to receive greater deference than those that do not. "If, as I have been arguing, religions are at their most useful when they serve as democratic intermediaries and preach resistance, then it is at precisely that moment . . . when the religious tradition most diverges from the mainstream, that protection is both most needed and most deserved," Carter writes, in *Disbelief*, 1993), 132. Needed, for sure—but how do we determine that the Scientologist really *deserves* more protection than the Presbyterian complainant in *Kurland v. Caldor*? Our worries about the scope and fortitude of such instrumental rationales will be underscored by Carter's admission that "[n]o religion always challenges the state's imposed meanings, and few do it very often" (Carter, *Disbelief*, 273). I leave it for historians to debate whether American churches have, in the past century or two, served more often as agents of state order or as sites of genuine resistance to political power.

39. The rationale opens another avenue of inquiry, which I shall pursue later. Are religious groups different? If not all religious organizations perform the function of challenging state authority, not all organizations that do perform that function are religious. Why grant religious groups rights and privileges over other forms of civil organization that may have an equal or greater claim to performing this valuable service? In Carter's view, "the process of the quest for meaning, the group search for sense and value that is central to the religious task as I have defined it . . . is more likely than other competing sources of authority to turn up alternative meanings precisely because of religion's focus on the ultimate." This may be so, but it is a generalization for which we might substitute our particular judgments about this or that example. The "subversive church" thesis calls to mind Ferdinand Mount's well-known "subversive family" thesis, which holds that the family has, through history, undermined the hegemony of the state through *its* assertions of a rival autonomy. But this is only to begin a list of competitors for the title of value-subversion. Many have variously praised or condemned the university for playing just this role. And, of course, nonreligious creeds like Rudolph Steiner's anthroposophy, ethical humanism, Objectivism, Ethical Culture, and various of the so-called recovery movements have also provided alternative sources of meaning for millions of people. At the very least, religion has no monopoly on the claim of contesting the moral authority of the state.

40. In this spirit, Carter advises that "[g]iven its starting point and its methodology, creationism is as rational an explanation as any other." It runs into trouble only because its starting point and methodology "reflect an essential axiom—literal inerrancy—that is not widely shared. In this sense, the wrongness of creationism becomes a matter of power: yes, it is wrong because proved wrong, but it is proved wrong only in a particular epistemological universe." Thus the war over creation science is "ultimately over epistemology, not religion"; and it is not between truth and falsity, either, but "between competing systems of discerning truth." For at the end of the day, Carter suggests, only might makes right: "We win because you lose. We have the power and you don't. On

such distinctions, all too often, is the modern notion of truth premised." Carter, *Disbelief*, 175–76, 182. Of course, one may doubt whether the fundamentalist supporters of creation science will appreciate Carter's stout defense of their rationality, for it smacks of the relativism they find most offensive about "secular humanism." One cannot take another person's view seriously as a competitor for the truth about the one world we all share by allowing that it proceeds by way of a different epistemology. For that puts aside the question whether it is a sound epistemology, a good way of getting at the truth. I think a case can be made that Carter has just found another way not to take the substance of these religious views seriously. It's just that it happens to be a way that gets them more of what they want.

41. The community of Jehovah's Witnesses is divided on this issue, however, and there is an organization—Associated Jehovah's Witnesses for Reform on Blood—that argues that the current policy is neither coherent nor biblically warranted. See http://www.ajwrb.org. Jehovah's Witness teaching on this matter begins with Lev. 3:17. "It shall be a perpetual statute for your generations throughout all your dwellings, that ye eat neither fat nor blood."

42. Carter, *Disbelief*, 221; Michael McConnell, "God Is Dead and We Have Killed Him: Freedom of Religion in the Post-Modern Age," *Brigham Young University Law Review* 163 (Winter 1993): 181.

43. Carter, *Disbelief*, 5.

44. Whatever your philosophical or religious commitments, the blood transfusion cases are likely to raise hard issues. (I leave alone the obvious potential conflicts: the devout patient who must forgo lifesaving treatment or risk his everlasting soul, attended by a differently devout doctor who must make every effort to preserve his life or risk her own everlasting soul.) From a deontological perspective, the central issue may be one of individual autonomy. Issues of consent will then loom large; autonomy claims carry less weight when jurors consider the medically unnecessary death of young children whose parents are Christian Scientists. On humanitarian grounds, we might—if we think the patient's view will be stable and enduring (and creedal association may offer probative evidence for this)—hesitate to condemn someone to a life made desolate by the apprehension of an eternity in hell. So liberal secularism will, in the hardest cases, yield no univocal answers, either.

45. Greenawalt, "Five Questions about Religion Judges Are Afraid to Ask," in *Obligations of Citizenship and Demands of Faith*, ed. Nancy L. Rosenblum (Princeton: Princeton University Press, 2000), 199.

46. As Otto von Bismarck is supposed to have said, "Wer weiß, wie Gesetze und Würste zustande kommen, der kann nachts nicht mehr ruhig schlafen." Even if a piece of legislation or an official pronouncement comes with a formal statement of intent, we have no very good grounds for supposing it to be dispositive: imagine if the state of Virginia had reintroduced its antimiscegenation laws, after they were struck down in *Loving v. Virginia* as an impermissible institution of white supremacy, with a grand introduction declaring that the aim of the new law was to provide equal protection to all races. This would hardly satisfy us that the law was now neutral.

47. Judges, of course, like many other officials, regularly exercise discretion. Where the reason for a failure to exercise available discretion to the advantage of a certain person is hostility to that person in virtue of her identity, the act is not neutral: for, absent the bias, she would have been treated better. That's because the range of grounds for exercising discretion is limited and bias is an impermissible ground.

48. The notion of "disparate impact" was introduced in *Griggs v. Duke Power Company*, 401 U.S. 424 (1971). Chief Justice Burger, writing for the Court, said, "[G]ood intent or absence of discriminatory intent does not redeem employment procedures or testing mechanisms that operate as 'built-in headwinds' for minority groups and are unrelated to measuring job capability."

49. One doesn't typically think of left-handed persons as forming an identity group, but suppose there were a strong Sinistral Identity movement. So long as the rationale for putting door handles on the left of doors was not to penalize left-handedness *in se*, and the cost of accommodating the Sinistrals was high, the policy would not raise issues of bias.

50. Thomas Nagel, "Moral Conflict and Political Legitimacy," *Philosophy and Public Affairs* 16 (Summer 1987): 215–40. I'll formulate the point in what follows in terms of there being *a* reason. Even if we offer many reasons, which taken together support a policy, their conjunction can be treated as a single reason.

51. So it's true they are worse off—in the sense of having been coerced into doing something they believe to be wrong—because they have an unreasonable belief. Of course, if the unreasonable belief were the defining essence of their religion, we could not distinguish between the fact of their being Witnesses and the fact of their believing that blood transfusions lead to damnation. So if an identity were defined by an unreasonable belief that was relevant to a matter of policy in this sort of way, we would be unable to treat them neutrally by my test (or by Nagel's). See my discussion of "abhorrent identities" in chapter 5. That we cannot achieve neutrality in every possible circumstance does not, of course, impugn it as an aim in the many circumstances where it *is* possible.

52. David A. Strauss, "Discriminatory Intent and the Taming of Brown," *University of Chicago Law Review* 56 (1989): 956–60.

53. *Thomas v. Review Board of the Indiana Employment Security Division* (1980), 450 U.S. 707, 101 S.Ct. 1425, 67 L.Ed.2d 624. To establish that Thomas's free exercise had been burdened, Burger relied on a gloss on *Everson*: "More than 30 years ago, the Court held that a person may not be compelled to choose between the exercise of a First Amendment right and participation in an otherwise available public program."

54. It can be true (to recur to my first point) that you would have fared better if P, and not if P and Q (where "P" is "you were not a Jehovah's Witness" and "Q" is "you were an atheist"; perhaps, if Thomas hadn't been a Jehovah's Witness, he'd have been a Baptist, and Baptists are well regarded in Indiana).

55. As I say, I believe it is not; and, like Chief Justice Burger, I think that it is obvious that this does not amount to establishment.

56. The argument might run as follows. To the extent that we are equals as citizens, the state owes us equal consideration. Insofar as resources—including not only economic but also symbolic and other resources—are made available by the state, they should be made available equally. Perhaps a state that identified with heterosexuals as such, providing them with material resources (such as tax benefits for couples) or symbolic goods (such as the recognition of their partnerships) or practical benefits (such as the laws governing the division of property in the unhappy event of separation) and denied them to homosexuals would be failing to treat people of different sexualities with the required equality. Distinguishing in law between parents and childless couples, on the other hand, granted that the having and raising of children is something in which there is a proper public interest, would not be open to the same objection, provided, of course, that there was some reasonable relationship between the distinctions made and the effects sought; and that is true even though "parent" is surely an important social identity, as I have defined that term.

57. Recognition is not the same as accommodation, we should be clear. A U.S. court that grants free-exercise exemptions does not see itself in the business of fostering that particular creed. Accommodation is meant to facilitate free exercise; recognition can come close to "establishment." Still, to confer an exemption is to confer recognition, too.

58. Taylor, *Multiculturalism*, 36. An earlier version of my discussion here appears in this volume as one of several responses to Taylor's seminal paper. Cf. Axel Honneth, *The Struggle for Recognition* (Cambridge: MIT Press, 1995).

59. Taylor, *Multiculturalism*, 53.

60. There is an immense scholarly literature on the politics of language and language policy, but nobody interested in the subject should ignore the empirically and analytically impressive studies by the political scientist David D. Laitin, including *Identity in Formation: The Russian-Speaking Populations in the Near Abroad* (Ithaca: Cornell University Press, 1998); *Language Repertoires and State Construction in Africa* (Cambridge: Cambridge University Press, 1992); and *Politics, Language, and Thought: The Somali Experience* (Chicago: University of Chicago Press, 1977).

61. The identities whose recognition Taylor discusses are largely what we can call "collective social identities": religion, gender, ethnicity, race, sexuality. This list is somewhat heterogeneous: such collective identities matter to their bearers and to others in very different ways. Religion, for example, unlike all the others, entails attachments to creeds or commitment to practices. Gender and sexuality, unlike the rest, are both grounded in the sexual body; both are differently experienced at different places and times: still, everywhere that I know of, gender identity proposes norms of behavior, of dress, of character. And, of course, gender and sexuality are, despite these abstract similarities, in many ways profoundly different. In our society, for example, passing as a woman or a man is hard, passing as straight (or gay) is relatively easy. There are other collective identities—disabled people, for example—that have sought recognition, modeling themselves sometimes on racial minorities (with whom they share the experience of discrimination and insult), or (as with deaf people) on ethnic groups. And

there are castes, in South Asia; and clans on every continent; and classes, with enormously varying degrees of class-consciousness, all over the industrialized world. But the major collective identities that demand recognition in North America currently go under the rubrics of religion, gender, ethnicity (or nationality), race, and sexuality; and that they matter to us for reasons so heterogeneous should, I think, make us want to be careful not to assume that what goes for one goes for the others.

62. Taylor, *Multiculturalism*, 31.

63. Irony is not the Bohemian's only problem. As we saw in chapter 1, this notion of authenticity has built into it a series of errors of philosophical anthropology. It is, first of all, wrong in failing to see what Taylor—or, indeed, George Herbert Mead—so clearly recognized, namely, the way in which the self is, as Taylor says, dialogically constituted. The rhetoric of authenticity proposes not only that I have a way of being that is all my own, but that in developing it I must fight against the family, organized religion, society, the school, the state—all the forces of convention. This is wrong, however, not only because I develop a conception of my own identity in dialogue with other people's understandings of who I am (Taylor's point), but also because my identity is crucially constituted through concepts and practices made available to me by religion, society, school, and state, and mediated to varying degrees by the family. Dialogue shapes the identity I develop as I grow up: but the very material out of which I form it is provided, in part, by my society, by what Taylor calls its language in "a broad sense," including the language of art, of gesture, and so forth. I shall borrow and extend Taylor's term "monological" here to describe views of authenticity that make these connected errors.

64. Dworkin, *Sovereign Virtue*, 260.

65. Ibid., 261.

66. Sherif, *Robbers Cave*, 179.

Chapter Four The Trouble with Culture

1. For anorexia, see Mervat Nasser, *Culture and Weight Consciousness* (New York: Routledge, 1997). For zydeco, see Dick Shurman, "New Orleans, Louisiana, and Zydeco," in *The New Blackwell Guide to Recorded Blues*, ed. John Cowley and Paul Oliver (Cambridge, Mass.: Blackwell Publishers, 1996).

2. Mary Waters, *Ethnic Options* (Berkeley and Los Angeles: University of California Press, 1990).

3. Geoffrey Nunberg, "Lingo Jingo: English Only and the New Nativism," *American Prospect*, no. 33 (July–August 1997): 40–47.

4. See Stephen Macedo, "Transformative Constitutionalism and the Case of Religion: Defending the Moderate Hegemony of Liberalism," *Political Theory* 26, no. 1 (February 1998): 56–89.

5. Marshall Sahlins, "Goodbye to Tristes Tropes: Ethnography in the Context of Modern World History," *Journal of Modern History* 65 (1993): 3–4.

6. Herder, to whom the word owes its currency, is thought to have borrowed Cicero's metaphor of philosophy as self-cultivation ("cultura autem animi philosophia est").

7. Edward Burnett Tylor, *Primitive Culture* (London: John Murray, 1871), 1. Adam Kuper provides a lively and compelling *tour d'horizon* in his *Culture: The Anthropologists' Account.*

8. "With more of these goods men can generally be assured of greater success in carrying out their intentions and in advancing their ends, whatever these ends may be." Thus people in the original position know they want more rather than less of the primary goods. Rawls, *A Theory of Justice*, 92–93.

9. Kymlicka, *Liberalism, Community, and Culture* (Oxford: Oxford University Press, 1991), 167. Or, in a later formulation: "Put simply, freedom involves making choices amongst various options, and our societal culture not only provides these options, but also makes them meaningful to us." Kymlicka, *Multicultural Citizenship*, 83.

10. Ronald Dworkin, *A Matter of Principle* (Cambridge: Harvard University Press, 1985), 232–33.

11. Margalit and Raz, "Self-Determination," 449; and see Kymlicka, *Multicultural Citizenship*, 89.

12. Berlin, "Two Concepts of Liberty," in *Four Essays*, 132.

13. Kymlicka, *Multicultural Citizenship*, 26; Iris Marion Young, *Inclusion and Democracy* (New York: Oxford University Press, 2000).

14. In a strategy whose limitations we discussed in the previous chapter, the state is to give these communities *external rights* (rights against the cultural impositions of outsiders), while minimizing *internal constraints*—that is, they should limit the degree to which these communities constrain the autonomy of their individual members, although there will inevitably be trade-offs between the desideratum of cultural survival and individual freedoms. Jeremy Waldron notes that a similar notion of culture has been entrenched and promulgated in measures such as Article 27, International Covenant on Civil and Political Rights: "In those States in which ethnic, religious or linguistic minorities exist, persons belonging to such minorities shall not be denied the right, in community with the other members of their group, to enjoy their own culture, to profess and practise their own religion, or to use their own language." He further observes, "A recent United Nations report rejected the view that Article 27 is nothing but a nondiscrimination provision: it insisted that special measures for minority cultures . . . are required and that such measures are as important as nondiscrimination in defending fundamental human rights in this area. . . . They also may involve the recognition that minority cultures are entitled to protect themselves by placing limits on the incursion of outsiders and limits on their own members' choices about career, family, lifestyle, and exit." Waldron, "Cosmopolitan Alternative," 758.

15. Kymlicka, *Finding Our Way: Rethinking Ethnocultural Relations in Canada* (New York: Oxford University Press, 1998), 44.

16. Kymlicka, *Multicultural Citizenship*, 84.

17. Similar questions arise when Raz—in his *Ethics in the Public Domain*, 174—affirms the "equal standing" of "stable and viable cultural communities." First, of course, one

would want to question the logic by which the concept of equal standing is extended from the individual to the collectivity. But the attempt to restrict the domain of multicultural measures isn't entirely helpful, either. Once again, this way of speaking incurs the Reverse–Robin Hood reductio. If a cultural community is stable and viable, one might wonder, why does it need state recognition? And if it isn't, why does it deserve it?

18. "The prosperity of the culture is important to the well-being of its members," Margalit and Raz say ("Self-Determination," 449). "If the culture is decaying . . . the options and opportunities open to its members will shrink, become less attractive, and their pursuit less likely to be successful." At a guess, what underlies such talk of cultural decay is something to do with the relation between autonomy and the division of labor. If autonomy requires choice among life plans, then societies with high levels of division of labor will offer more and deeper choices. (Again, differences of "culture" seem to be coextensive with differences of affluence.) It may be, then, that cultural "decay" is merely a proxy for material deprivation, for a less-evolved system of the cognitive/cultural division of labor.

19. John Tomasi, "Kymlicka, Liberalism, and Respect for Cultural Minorities," *Ethics* 105, no. 3 (April 1995): 590.

20. Ibid., 589.

21. Raz, *Ethics in the Public Domain*, 177.

22. Margalit and Raz, "Self-Determination," 444.

23. Taylor, "Irreducibly Social Goods," in his *Philosophical Arguments*, 142. It is not obvious that such a notion of "social goods" is inconsistent with ethical individualism. For compare Raz's very similar formulation of "collective goods." These are inherent public goods, to be distinguished from contingent public goods. Clean water is a contingent public good, important so long as individuals lack control over their own water supply. By contrast, Raz says, "It is a public good, and inherently so, that this society is a tolerant society, that it is an educated society, that it is infused with a sense of respect for human beings, etc." Raz argues that a belief in such inherent goods is compatible with humanism, with ethical individualism, and, in particular, with a prior commitment to personal autonomy.

24. Margalit and Raz, "Self-Determination," 449–61.

25. Taylor, "Irreducibly Social Goods," 136.

26. In "Cross-Purposes," Taylor writes about the tendency to confuse two senses of the "good": "In the broad sense, it means anything valuable we seek; in the narrower sense, it refers to life plans or ways of life so valued" (194).

27. James Griffin, *Well-Being: Its Meaning, Measurement, and Moral Importance* (Oxford: Oxford University Press, 1986), 387–88.

28. Taylor, "Irreducibly Social Goods," 137.

29. Horowitz, *Ethnic Groups*, 176–77. And see the English-language newspaper *Dawn*, March 6, 1995: "Sindhis live in the perpetual fear of being turned into Red Indians by the never ending migration into [the] urban part of the province from not only up country but also from India, Bangladesh, Burma, Iran, Afghanistan and many such places."

30. Dworkin, *A Matter of Principle*, 233.

31. Kymlicka, *Multicultural Citizenship*, 104, 100.

32. Ibid., 104.

33. Charles Moore, "Time for a More Liberal and 'Racist' Immigration Policy," *Spectator*, October 19, 1991. I am not alone in wondering what the scare-quotes are doing in Moore's title.

34. See my "Immigrants and Refugees: Individualism and the Moral Status of Strangers," forthcoming in the *Arguments of the Philosophers* volume on the work of Michael Dummett.

35. Taylor, *Multiculturalism*, 58–59.

36. Ibid., 41, 40.

37. Earlier, the author explains that he "began field work in Quebec in 1977 with the intention of constructing a cultural account of Québécois nationalist ideology," searching out the symbols and meanings by which Québécois identity was expressed. It was a task he had to abandon: "I no longer claim to be able either to present an account of 'the' culture or to demonstrate its integration, but will focus instead on cultural objectification in relation to the interpenetration of discourses—that is, on attempts to construct bounded cultural objects—*a process that paradoxically demonstrates the absence of such objects*." Richard Handler, *Nationalism and the Politics of Culture in Quebec* (Madison: University of Wisconsin Press, 1988), 39, 27.

38. See my *In My Father's House* (New York: Oxford University Press, 1992), 77, 178; David Laitin, *Hegemony and Culture: Politics and Religious Change among the Yoruba* (Chicago: University of Chicago Press, 1986), 7–8; Johannes Fabian, *Language and Colonial Power* (Cambridge: Cambridge University Press, 1986), 42–43. And see also Iver Peterson, "The Mire of Tribe Recognition," *New York Times*, December 28, 2002.

39. Kymlicka, *Multicultural Citizenship*, 104.

40. Margalit and Raz, "Self-Determination," 445.

41. In particular, this is a point I've made about attempts to render race as a mere historical artifact: cf. *In My Father's House*, 32.

42. Walter Benn Michaels, *Our America: Nativism, Modernism, and Pluralism* (Durham: Duke University Press, 1996), 181–82. Elsewhere he writes: "Cultural identity in the '20s required . . . the anticipation of culture by race: to be a Navajo you have to do Navajo things, but you can't really count as doing Navajo things unless you are already a Navajo." And so: "Accounts of cultural identity that do any work require a racial component. For insofar as our culture remains nothing more than what we do and believe, it is impotently descriptive. The fact, in other words, that something belongs to our culture cannot count as a motive for our doing it since, if it does belong to our culture, we already do it and if we don't do it (if we've stopped or haven't yet started doing it), it doesn't belong to our culture. (It makes no sense, for example, to claim that we shouldn't teach Shakespeare because he isn't part of our culture since to teach him will immediately make him part of our culture, but it also makes no sense to claim that we should teach him because he is part of our culture since, if we stop teaching him, he won't be any longer.) It is only if we think that our culture is not whatever

beliefs and practices we actually happen to have but is instead the beliefs and practices that should properly go with the sort of people we happen to be that the fact of something belonging to our culture can count as a reason for doing it. But to think this is to appeal to something that must be beyond culture and that cannot be derived from culture because our sense of which culture is properly ours must be derived from it. This has been the function of race. . . . The modern concept of culture is not, in other words, a critique of racism; it is a form of racism. . . . To put the point as bluntly as possible, 'cultural pluralism' is an oxymoron: its commitment to culture is contradicted by its commitment to pluralism. . . . Cultural pluralism is thus committed in principle to identity essentialism, which is to say that in cultural pluralism, culture does not constitute identity, it reflects, or more precisely, expresses it." Michaels, *Our America*, 125, 128–29. I agree with most of this, except the identification of descent-based with race-based identities and the equation of race-based thinking with racism.

43. Raz, *Ethics in the Public Domain*, 178–79. What such state "imprimatur" entails is left unclear; there are some, such as the critical race theorist Mari Matsuda, who go so far as to suggest that the state endorses what it permits. See Matsuda, "Public Response to Racist Speech: Considering the Victim's Story," in Mari Matsuda, Charles R. Lawrence, III, et al., *Words That Wound: Critical Race Theory, Assaultive Speech, and the First Amendment* (Boulder, CO: Westview Press, 1993), 17–51.

44. They grant that "groups and their cultures may be pernicious, based on the denigration and persecution of other groups," but, of course, that is likely to be true, to some extent, of all cultures. Margalit and Raz, "Self-Determination," 449.

45. Jon Elster, *Political Psychology* (Cambridge: Cambridge University Press, 1993), 80.

46. Kymlicka, *Multicultural Citizenship*, 100. See, e.g., Jean Bethke Elshtain, "Homosexual Politics: The Paradox of Gay Liberation," *Salmagundi*, nos. 58–59 (Fall 1982–Winter 1983): 252–80. Liberation movements among India's Dalits ("untouchables") typically involve defection from Hindutva, which sometimes involves a switch of ethicoreligious allegiance to some form of Buddhism (as among followers of B. R. Ambedkar), or to Christianity.

47. Hobbes, *De Cive* (1651), chapter 3, paragraph 31; Mill, *On Liberty*, CWM 18:270.

48. See Taylor, "Cross-Purposes," 185. There are other precursors, to be sure. As Samuel Fleischacker observes, the celebration of diversity goes back to the Enlightenment, the "rejection of its Christian predecessor's universalism," and, he further remarks on Leibniz's "Principle of Variety," "according to which God will necessarily create a world as full of different things as rationally possible, because there can be no sufficient reason for creating less than the most complete possible world and no sufficient reason for creating any two items of the complete world exactly alike." Samuel Fleischacker, *The Ethics of Culture* (Ithaca: Cornell University Press, 1994), 208, 210.

49. Chapter 3 of *On Liberty*, CWM 18:274–75.

50. Basil Mitchell, *Law, Morality, and Religion in a Secular Society* (Oxford: Oxford University Press, 1965, 1970), citing, inter alia, P. F. Strawson, "Social Morality and Individual Ideal," reprinted in Strawson, *Freedom and Resentment* (London: Methuen, 1974).

51. Mill, *On Liberty*, CWM 18:272.

52. The spectacle of liberal theorists—Parekh is joined in this by Martha Nussbaum and others—aggrieved on John Knox's behalf is a curious one. To begin with, Mill, though he did not work with anything like the post-Rawlsian concept of neutrality, made the remark in the context of a treatise opposing state tyranny and the restriction of unpopular views. The form of respect Mill was hesitant to grant Knox was (in Darwall's terms) "appraisal respect." And the appraisal seems entirely justified. Given Mill's Scottish origins, he would have been quite familiar with Knox's legacy, which was, in no small part, one of murderous intolerance. Preaching in Perth, in the spring of 1559, Knox whipped up mobs ("brethren," he called them in a private letter, in contrast to his later expedient disavowals) who then sacked and pillaged Catholic churches and monasteries. He regularly argued that every Protestant was within his rights to massacre every Catholic: "idolaters" must "die the death" at the hands of the "people of God." His "Brief Exhortation to England" was the exhortation to expel the "dregs of Popery." He reacted gleefully when Cardinal Beaton was stabbed to death ("These things we write merrily," he recounted in his *History of the Reformation in Scotland*). He drew up a "Confession of Faith" sanctioning the attending of mass with the death penalty. And when Mary Stewart's secretary David Riccio was stabbed to death by a band of men in front of her—the result of a purely political intrigue orchestrated by her husband— Knox declared that "the act was most just and worthy of all praise." This is to say nothing of his most famous work, *The First Blast of the Trumpet Against the Monstrous Regiment of Women* (1558). ("To promote a woman to bear rule, superiority, dominion, or empire above any realm, nation, or city, is repugnant to nature; contumely to God, a thing most contrary to his revealed will and approved ordinance; and finally, it is the subversion of good order, of all equity and justice.") No viable form of liberalism can require that we be indifferent between a Knox and a Pericles, or, anyway, between what each would have represented to Mill.

53. Mill, *On Liberty*, CWM 18:224. As Uday Mehta and others have been quick to point out, even as Mill urges autonomy only for members of a "civilized community," he also regards savage communities with a wistful eye, for the bygone age of heroism and individuality he thinks they still enjoy. Mehta notes that Mill was evidently of two minds on this matter. For in *Considerations on Representative Government*, Mill says that "progress" refers to the heightening of "mental activity, enterprise, and courage," and is associated with "originality and invention." CWM 19:386. Mehta, *Liberalism and Empire*, 101–2, 103.

54. "Despotism is a legitimate mode of government in dealing with barbarians, provided the end be their improvement, and the means justified by actually effecting that end. Liberty, as a principle, has no application to any state of things anterior to the time when mankind have become capable of being improved by free and equal discussion. Until then, there is nothing for them but implicit obedience to an Akbar or a Charlemagne, if they are so fortunate as to find one." Mill, *On Liberty*, CWM 18:224.

55. Mill goes on to say, "It is curious, withal, that the earliest known civilization was, we have the strongest reason to believe, a negro civilization. The original Egyptians are

inferred, from the evidence of their sculptures, to have been a negro race: it was from negroes, therefore, that the Greeks learnt their first lessons in civilization. . . . But I again renounce all advantage from facts: were the whites born ever so superior in intelligence to the blacks, and competent by nature to instruct and advise them, it would not be the less monstrous to assert that they had therefore a right either to subdue them by force, or circumvent them by superior skill; to throw upon them the toils and hardships of life, reserving for themselves, under the misapplied name of work, its agreeable excitements." From "The Negro Question," *Fraser's Magazine* in January 1850 (*CWM* 21:93); Carlyle had published his "discourse" the previous year, and he reprinted his piece in 1853, under the slightly revised title "Occasional Discourse on the Nigger Question."

56. From an article titled "The Contest in America," which he published in *Fraser's Magazine* in January 1862 (*CWM* 21:138), and which helped bolster support among British Liberals for the Union. Here he scoffed at the notion that the South, in its decision to secede, had a political will to be respected: "First, it is necessary to ask, Have the slaves been consulted? Has their will been counted as any part in the estimate of collective volition? . . . Remember, *we* consider them to be human beings, entitled to human rights." (The term "human rights," as opposed to "natural rights" or the "rights of man," would acquire wide currency only after the Second World War.)

57. Difference-exalting postmodernists sometimes summon, as an exemplar, Edmund Burke, in particular the Burke who denounced the practices of the British in India. Yet Burke's argument, too, made appeal to the notion that the Indians were, in certain respects, like the British, not least in the deeply hierarchical nature of their society. Indeed, his speeches on the subject of the East Indian dominion were rife with European comparanda: "If I were to take the whole aggregate of our possessions there, I should compare it, as the nearest parallel I can find, with the empire of Germany. Our immediate possessions I should compare with the Austrian dominions,—and they would not suffer in the comparison. The nabob of Oude might stand for the king of Prussia; the nabob of Arcot I would compare, as superior in territory and equal in revenue, to the elector of Saxony. Cheyt Sing, the rajah of Benares, might well rank with the prince of Hesse, at least; and the rajah of Tanjore (though hardly equal in extent of dominion, superior in revenue), to the elector of Bavaria. The polygars and the northern zemindars, and other great chiefs, might well class with the rest of the princes, dukes, counts, marquises, and bishops, in the empire; all of whom I mention to honour, and surely without disparagement to any or all of those most respectable princes and grandees." Edmund Burke, *The Speeches of the Right Honourable Edmund Burke, in the House of Commons, and Westminster Hall* (London: Longman, Hurst, Rees, Orme, & Brown, 1816), 2:416. This is from his speech on Fox's East India Bill (which can be found, too, in volume 4 of Edmund Burke, *Select Works of Edmund Burke, and Miscellaneous Writings*, ed. E. J. Payne and Francis Canavan [Indianapolis, IN: Liberty Fund, 1999]).

58. Bernard Williams, introduction to *Concepts and Categories: Philosophical Essays by Isaiah Berlin*, ed. Henry Hardy (New York: Viking, 1979), xvii. Williams goes on to caution that there "are logical, psychological, and sociological limits on what range of

values an individual can seriously respect in one life, or one society respect in the lives of various of its citizens."

59. Isaiah Berlin finds this rationale in Mill, although it is possible to feel that, like the greedy master of an Easter egg hunt, or a shady police detective, he has not only found it but planted it as well: "If anyone were to argue that a given, actual or attainable social arrangement yielded enough happiness—that given the virtually impassible limits on the nature of men and their environments . . . it were better to concentrate on the best that we have, since change would, in all empirical likelihood, lead to lowering of general happiness, and should therefore be avoided, we may be sure that Mill would have rejected this argument out of hand. He was committed to the answer that we can never tell (until we have tried) where greater truth or happiness (or any other form of experience) may lie. Finality is therefore in principle impossible: all solutions must be tentative and provisional." Berlin, "John Stuart Mill and the Ends of Life," in *Four Essays*, 182. Needless to say, Berlin is here not only glossing an ancestor but stating a view that has come to be identified with Berlin himself as much as anyone. The argument is attractive, but it does not compel agreement. David Johnston, for one, objects that the actual price of such experimentation might be higher than we think, ruining people's lives and the lives of their children. Perhaps the claim is that the overall social consequences of experimentation will be good; but, as Johnston notes, "its force still really depends on whether one thinks the long-run tendencies of human affairs lead toward improvement or toward decline. In a century that has seen total war and totalitarian despotism, the correct view of this long-run tendency is not clear." David Johnston, *The Idea of a Liberal Theory: A Critique and Reconstruction* (Princeton: Princeton University Press, 1996), 92. The point is merely that we shouldn't necessarily content ourselves with an *ipse dixit* defense of experimentation.

60. I am grateful to Gabriela Carone for helping me to see this point more clearly.

61. Steven Wall distinguishes between comprehensive and peripheral options. A comprehensive option might be to lead a Christian life; a peripheral one, in his example, would be to choose this or that church. Wall thinks that if one has "access to a large number of significantly different options but none of them are options that he could imagine himself wholeheartedly engaging in, then he does not have a sufficiently wide range to be autonomous," and, in a footnote, bravely confronts the problem of someone with extravagant demands, someone who believes he or she "must have the option of being a slave-owner, an Olympic sprinter or the spouse of a glamorous movie star." Indeed, if all other options hold no savor for them, then that's what they need to be autonomous, Wall concludes. But this can't be right. Autonomy involves the rational prerequisites of making choices among (per Raz) "acceptable options"—the choice can't be among morally repugnant possibilities—but to deny that the frustrated dreamer enjoyed autonomy amounts to an ideal of compulsory happiness. There's also a confusion of what "option" amounts to here, for project pursuers. To have the option of pursuing a destiny (marrying a movie star, say) isn't the same as being able simply to elect that destiny. Nobody, in any recognizable society, is *guaranteed* a destiny. (Save for trivial, self-securable ones. But most involve the participation of other people.) Also,

some are zero-sum, exclusive: if you wanted to be Miss America 2000, it follows that you wanted nobody else to be. If you want to be CEO of the company, the fulfillment of your desire requires the frustration of other people's desires, assuming you're not the only one with this ambition. So there's some ambiguity surrounding the term "option." Wall resolves it by weakening the satisfaction condition: "the option requirement will often be satisfied in degrees." Steven Wall, *Liberalism, Perfectionism, and Restraint* (Cambridge: Cambridge University Press, 1998), 140–43.

62. At one point, Gerald Dworkin refers to Charles Ainslie's chicken experiment: you peck on the white key to prevent having to choose between lesser and greater rewards you got by pecking, or refraining from pecking, on the red key. "If one wants to be the kind of person who makes decisions and accepts the responsibility for them, or who chooses and develops a life-plan, then choices are valued not for what they produce nor for what they are in themselves, but as constitutive of a certain ideal of a good life. What makes a life ours is that it is shaped by our choices, is selected from alternatives, and therefore choice is valued as a necessary part of a larger complex. But, again, this would at most support the view that, with respect to a certain range of choices, it is desirable to have some options. . . . In the realm of choices, as in all others, we must conclude—enough is enough." Dworkin, *Theory and Practice of Autonomy*, 76, 80–81. And see Barry Schwartz, *The Paradox of Choice* (New York: Ecco Press, 2004).

63. Except under certain special circumstances, e.g., where A contains every value B does *and* some value it doesn't. But nobody could infer this of any actual community.

64. Galston, *Liberal Pluralism*, 60.

65. Monomania is meant to be a place of internal homogeneity (one still conducive to human flourishing); but you could challenge that description. The presence of a diversity of homogeneous groups makes it an option for people who are currently in one group to migrate to (or just learn from) others. Provided Monomania also allowed such migration among locations, as it would have to if each one was to sustain its character, the fact that the diversity was external rather than internal would not stop it enriching the options, and thus the autonomy, of the individuals in each distinct and relatively homogeneous πολις. But then you could argue that Monomania was a place of internal diversity after all.

66. John Tomlinson observes: "It is difficult to object to global homogenisation (supposing, of course, that this is occurring) without falling back on the simple intuition that it is a good thing that there is variety in culture. But then we have to ask, a good thing for whom? Who is to enjoy the range of cultural difference? It is not difficult to see how this preference for variety might become that of the Western global-cultural tourist as much as the concerned anthropologist. There are probably much stronger arguments for the uniformity of cultures in the broad sense, where uniformity implies, for example, maximizing of health care, nutritional technology, housing provision, education, and so on across all cultures. Clearly there are other major issues of value here which relate to the cultural processes of modernity itself. Not all objections to 'cultural imperialism'—'homogeneity' being a good example—are grounded unambiguously in what the left would call the critique of domination. To risk labouring the point, we

need to ask, 'who speaks?' " Tomlinson, *Cultural Imperialism* (Baltimore: Johns Hopkins University Press, 1991), 98.

67. Montesquieu, *The Spirit of the Laws*, ed. Anne Cohler, Basia Miller, and Harold Stone (Cambridge: Cambridge University Press, 1989), 310.

68. David Ingram, *Group Rights: Reconciling Equality and Difference* (Lawrence: University of Kansas Press, 2000), 257. The castigation of individualism, of course, represents a considerable swerve from Mill. But then the diagnosis is bizarre: what ailed the Ik wasn't Western culture, individualist or no, but crippling deprivation, the result of a government action that forced these hunter-gatherers from their land and compelled them to become farmers, an activity with which they had no experience. To talk about the Ik, many of whom were starving to death, as if they had been ruined by watching too many Hollywood blockbusters, suggests a peculiar cultural narcissism. For another critique of the biodiversity trope, see Blake, "Rights for People, Not for Cultures."

69. "Once a culture becomes one among several, within a closely integrated political and economic system, practices that used to shape opportunities may come to restrict them," Raz says. "And they may conflict with aspirations legitimately encouraged by the larger society within which members of that community live. It is a mistake to think that multicultural measures can counteract these facts. Nor should they try. They should not aim to preserve the pristine purity of different cultural groups. They should aim to enable them to adjust and change to a new form of existence within a larger community." Raz, *Ethics in the Public Domain*, 99.

70. Galston, *Liberal Pluralism*, 64.

71. Tomlinson, *Cultural Imperialism*, 67.

72. Stephen Macedo, *Diversity and Distrust: Civic Education in a Multicultural Democracy* (Cambridge: Harvard University Press, 2000), 2. And perfectionists tend to have a sharply bounded appreciation of diversity, too. Thus Steven Wall writes, "On an autonomy-based account of political morality, diversity is valuable to the extent that it contributes to human flourishing. On this account, there is no good reason to preserve ways of life that impeded human flourishing simply because their continued existence would contribute to a more diverse world." Indeed, he suggests that a political morality "that refuses to take diversity to be a good in and of itself reveals its commitment to humanism—the notion that it is the flourishing of human beings that matters." Wall, *Liberalism, Perfectionism, and Restraint*, 181, 182.

Chapter Five Soul Making

1. *Considerations on Representative Government*, CWM 19:390, cited in chapter 1, n. 58. Mill continues, "The first question in respect to any political institutions is how far they tend to foster in the members of the community the various desirable qualities ... moral, intellectual, and active."

2. Plato's characterization is variously rendered. In Jowett's translation of *Laws I*, the Athenian stranger concludes: "And this knowledge of the natures and habits of

men's souls will be of the greatest use in that art which has the management of them; and that art, if I am not mistaken, is politics." For the resurgence of republicanism, see, especially, the work of Quentin Skinner and Philip Pettit. The liberal perfectionism I have in mind is associated with the work of Joseph Raz, Thomas Hurka, George Sher, and Steven Wall, among others. More controversially described as perfectionist is the "Aristotelian social democracy" that Martha Nussbaum and Amartya Sen have proposed: one centered not on the just distribution of resources, as in Rawls, but on the provision of capabilities (to a certain threshold) to all citizens. There may even be Rawlsian routes to the perfectionism he notably disavowed: his *Theory of Justice*, as we saw, referred approvingly to what he called the Aristotelian Principle, the notion that, "other things being equal, human beings enjoy the exercise of their realized capacities, and this enjoyment increases the more the capacity is realized, or the greater its complexity."

3. Popper wrote, "One of the crucial points in Spinoza's political theory is the impossibility of knowing and of controlling what other people think. He defines 'tyranny' as the attempt to achieve the impossible, and to exercise power where it cannot be exercised. Spinoza, it must be remembered, was not exactly a liberal; he did not believe in institutional controls of power, but thought that a prince has a right to exercise his powers up to their actual limit. Yet what Spinoza calls 'tyranny', and declares to be in conflict with reason, is treated quite innocently by holistic planners as a 'scientific' problem, the 'problem of transforming men'." Karl R. Popper, chapter 24 of *The Poverty of Historicism* (London: Routledge and Kegan Paul, 1974), 90. In *Liberalism* (1911), L. T. Hobhouse writes, "there is the sphere of what is called personal liberty—a sphere most difficult to define, but the arena of the fiercest strife of passion and the deepest feelings of mankind. At the basis lies liberty of thought—freedom from inquisition into opinions that a man forms in his own mind—the inner citadel where, if anywhere, the individual must rule." L. T. Hobhouse, *Liberalism and Other Writings*, ed. James Meadowcroft (Cambridge: Cambridge University Press, 1994), 13.

4. "Et sic ex quatuor praedictis potest colligi definitio legis, quae nihil est aliud quam quaedam rationis ordinatio ad bonum commune, ab eo qui curam communitatis habet, promulgata." *Summa Theologiae* Iᵃ–IIae q. 90 a. 4 ad 1.

5. Someone who holds this view can think that infringing upon this sphere is sometimes legitimate: for example, to protect the equal right of others to the satisfaction of their desires. So the presumption is that there is a prima facie duty not to infringe upon people's desires, not an absolute and unrebuttable claim to the desires one has.

6. John Passmore, in *The Perfectibility of Man* (New York: Scribner's, 1970), 20, provides an etymological précis: "[T]he Greek word *teleios*, commonly translated as perfect, is etymologically related to *telos* (end)—the relationship between perfect and the achievement of an end is, as it were, written into it. The English word 'perfect', however, ultimately derives, by way of Middle English, from the Latin word *perficere*, the roots of which, in turn, are *facere*, to make, and a prefix *per* suggesting 'thoroughly'. The perfect, that is, is etymologically definable as the 'thoroughly made', the 'completed.' . . . Perfection is thus cut loose from any connexion with an end." A few caveats as to

its contemporary usage. Although perfectionism holds, contra Rawls, that the government may promote the good, it isn't the view that everybody should lead the same sort of life: Mill's perfectionism arose from his concern with individuality as self-development, and his view that a political arrangement should foster such self-development. Promotion, moreover, doesn't mean maximizing. Perfectionists can deny that human flourishing is something that can be maximized; the view is consistent with value pluralism. A clear and concise account of how little perfectionism, as such, commits you to can be found in Wall, *Liberalism, Perfectionism, and Restraint*, 7–25. Since, as we'll see, any plausible account of well-being involves more than purely subjective considerations, the view that government should promote the well-being of its citizens (and do so for its own sake) would count as perfectionist.

7. One form is the liberalism of the nightwatchman state, or what adherents like to call "classical liberalism." (That characterization can be disputed; see Emma Rothschild's *Economic Sentiments: Adam Smith, Condorcet, and the Enlightenment* [Cambridge: Harvard University Press, 2001] for an argument that Adam Smith was actually closer to modern big-L Liberalism than to "classical liberalism.") But not every version of negative liberalism involves an especially minimal state: some negative liberals think that the prerequisites of negative liberty (such as reasonable health) justify a quite extensive state role. I should also say that the form of negative liberalism I am interested in is a liberalism of principle. It assumes government can be trustworthy and transparent. This is no doubt, to put it gently, a utopian assumption, and there is a liberal tradition that is based not in the arguments I am considering but in that mistrust. It is the liberalism of Madison, who sought to construct a constitution of both checks and balances in which no power could accumulate too easily anywhere. Madison conceived of a rich civil society that would enmesh us all in so many networks of interest that none of them could ever monopolize our concerns and thus become the basis for a permanent dominant majority. Madison helped to design a political system that was meant to sustain a wide diversity of thick social identities without government involvement in soul making. I have some sympathy with these arguments, but I am not going to concern myself with them here. For there are those who would not allow the government to carry out these functions even if it could be trusted, and it is their arguments I am interested in.

8. As I mentioned in n. 6. Further to the point, James Griffin writes, "one does not have to be a monist to be a perfectionist. One can accept a plurality of values, not just because for one person there are irreducibly many different values but also because for different persons there are irreducibly different ideal forms of life. Different forms of life (the artist, the researcher, the politician, the private citizen tending his garden), to the extent that they are good, might instantiate one or other of these ideals." Griffin, *Well-Being*, 59. And Raz—in *The Morality of Freedom*, 399—argues that his commitment to autonomy entails a commitment to pluralism: "[V]aluing autonomy leads to the endorsement of moral pluralism," 399. Of course, to say that human flourishing may assume a multiplicity of forms doesn't mean any form at all will do. As I say,

perfectionists do have views about what constitutes human flourishing; they don't think that my life is well led simply if I think it is. But neither does anyone else.

9. Thomas Hill Green, *Prolegomena to Ethics*, ed. A. C. Bradley (1883; reprint, Bristol: Thoemmes Press, 1997), 295.

10. Mill continues, "Putting these two propositions into a shape more special to their present application; human beings are only secure from evil at the hands of others in proportion as they have the power of being, and are, self-*protecting*; and they only achieve a high degree of success in their struggle with Nature in proportion as they are self-*dependent*, relying on what they themselves can do, either separately or in concert, rather than on what others do for them." *Considerations on Representative Government*, *CWM* 19:404.

11. Mill, famously, addressed the argument that self-regarding conduct had other-regarding consequences—the notion that if someone "deteriorates his bodily or mental faculties, he not only brings evil upon all who depended upon him for any portion of their happiness, but disqualifies himself from rendering the services which he owes to his fellow-creatures generally," and so forth. Chapter 4 of *On Liberty*, *CWM* 18:280. Only consequences that "violate a distinct and assignable obligation," he responds, justify interference. Suffice it to say that he identified a problem; he did not solve it. Raz, as we saw in chapter 1, is able to show that the harm principle can be rather expansively applied, as to cases where we harm someone by diminishing her life chances; again, I think one may legitimately worry that such a conception is *overly* expansive.

12. Egalitarians may wonder why the Sikh (an example I previously mentioned in chapter 3) should qualify for an exemption, and not the secularist who has an equally strong preference for helmet-free cycling. The case is made with customary verve and clarity by Brian Barry, *Culture and Equality*, 44–49. "[W]e must insist on the crucial difference between a denial of equal opportunity to some group (for example, a law forbidding Sikhs to ride motorcycles) and a choice some people make out of that from a set of equal opportunities (for example, a choice not to ride a motorcycle) as a result of certain beliefs," Barry writes. "Those who believe that, even with a crash helmet, riding a motorcycle is too dangerous to be a rational undertaking are (in exactly the same, misleading, sense) 'precluded' from riding one. We all constantly impose restrictions on ourselves in choosing among the options that are legally available to us according to our beliefs about what is right, polite, decent, prudent, professionally appropriate, and so on. Atheists are entitled to feel offended at the idea that the only restraints on self-gratification derive from religious belief" (45). To return to my earlier discussion of free-exercise cases, there are two customary responses to this line of thought. The conventional liberal autonomist can take the fact that the preference is a religious or para-religious custom simply as evidence that it is particularly strongly held. (The fact of Sikh identity would be an informational proxy, attesting to the intensity of the preference.) And the communitarian will denounce the assimilation of identitarian traits to consumer choices: if your head wrap is entailed by your identity, it is not something you "choose."

13. And the existence of the political order is justified by the good it brings to individuals: ethical individualism is obviously consistent with talk of social good. An antiperfectionist effort to promote civic virtue—as with a measure that would make voting compulsory—might be held to be at odds with autonomy or individuality, to be sure. It isn't just perfectionists who are open to such charges.

14. Stephen Macedo, *Liberal Virtues* (Oxford: Clarendon Press, 1991), 129. (In his account, these virtues are, with breeder-reactor efficiency, both necessary to and created by a liberal regime; but he acknowledges that, without supplementation, shortfalls may occur.) A thoroughgoing antiperfectionist could maintain that these things are just citizen skills, no different in kind from knowing how to manipulate the lever in a voting booth: but this isn't a terribly appealing description, and for good reason. Recall Raz's discussion of contingent and inherent public goods, in *The Morality of Freedom*, 198–99. "It is a public good, and inherently so, that this society is a tolerant society, that it is an educated society, that it is infused with a sense of respect for human beings, etc. Living in a society with these characteristics is generally of benefit to individuals." Again, inherent public goods—what Raz calls "collective goods"—are still goods to individuals, consistent with ethical individualism; they do not qualify as the "irreducibly social goods" that Taylor posits. Obviously, it would be open to an antiperfectionist to accept that such character traits are good in themselves, but insist that she was promoting them only for consequential reasons. Perfectionism is distinguished by its rationale, not its prescriptions. Imagine a political theorist for whom the only real value was the enduring maximization of the government's coffers. Careful empirical considerations might lead this theorist to endorse every objective feature of liberal democracy, even though he didn't care a fig for liberty, equality, or even human flourishing. Democrats are not just people who favor democratic political arrangements; they are people who do so for democratic reasons. What's at issue is whether these reasons entrain a conception of the good, an ideal of human flourishing, that political authorities may promote.

15. Amy Gutmann, *Democratic Education* (Princeton: Princeton University Press, 1987), 46.

16. There are, of course, traditions that suppose that we may have, in some sense, more than one life. It would be an interesting question to explore for such traditions what difference it makes that one is supposed to have a sequence of lives. Since in some such traditions—those of Hinduism, for example—the shape of later lives reflects facts about earlier ones, there is a clear sense in which one has responsibility for happenings in later lives; so that sequences of lives have the sort of ethical connectedness that single lives do in the view I am exploring. But these sequences differ substantially from a single human life, as we now conceive of it, because, since memory does not carry across lives, there is no narrative of the whole sequence that plays a role in each member of the sequence; whereas a person living a single life has a sense of each phase of her life as fitting into a single story. (This is one of the many reasons that the loss of memory is so distressing in Alzheimer's.) So even if there are ethical connections across lives, they figure very differently from the connections within them. Disagreement about whether we do in fact live more than one life, in some sense, exemplifies the kind of

metaphysical divergence between traditions that I discuss toward the end of chapter 6 in the section "Rivalrous Goods, Rivalrous Gods."

17. Dworkin defines ambitions in the sense I mean: "Someone's ambitions include all his tastes, preferences, and convictions as well as his overall plan of life: his ambitions furnish his reasons or motives for making one choice rather than another." Dworkin, *Sovereign Virtue*, 322. Other terms have been developed to refer to such overarching interests, including "comprehensive goals" and "global desires," and I'll be making use of these later.

18. In Raz's view, "a person's well-being depends to a large extent on success in socially defined and determined pursuits and activities." In particular, our "comprehensive goals" may exemplify or be based on "social forms." He writes: "The existence of many options consists in part in the existence of certain social conditions. One cannot have an option to be a barrister, a surgeon, or a psychiatrist in a society where those professions, and the institutions their existence presupposes, do not exist . . . the same is true of the options of being an architect or of getting married. It is true that one need not live in a society at all to design buildings regularly, or to cohabit with another person. But doing so is not the same as being an architect or being married. An architect is one who belongs to a socially recognized profession." And, later, "Activities which do not appear to acquire their character from social forms in fact do so. Bird watching seems to be what any sighted person in the vicinity of birds can do. And so he can, except that that would not make him into a bird watcher. He can be that only in a society where this, or at least some other animal tracking activities, are recognized as leisure activities, and which furthermore shares certain attitudes toward natural life generally." Raz, *Morality of Freedom*, 309, 205, 311. Note how this connects to his interpretation of the "harm principle." If to harm someone is to diminish his autonomy, and his autonomy is buttressed by, inter alia, social forms, the harm principle becomes a rather low hurdle— surely too low a hurdle. It's worth emphasizing that all kinds of state actions can have all kinds of unintended consequences, some identitarian in nature.

19. Alexander Hamilton, John Jay, and James Madison, *The Federalist: A Commentary on the Constitution of the United States* (New York: Random House, Modern Library, 1941), 335 (No. 51).

20. Harry Frankfurt, "Freedom of the Will and the Concept of a Person," in *The Importance of What We Care About: Philosophical Essays* (New York: Cambridge University Press, 1988), 19.

21. Frankfurt, "The Importance of What We Care About," in Frankfurt, *The Importance of What We Care About*, 83, 91.

22. See Michael Stocker, *Plural and Conflicting Values* (Oxford: Clarendon Press), 211–37, and Thomas E. Hill, "Weakness of Will and Character," in *Autonomy and Self-Respect*, 118–37; David Pears, *Motivated Irrationality* (Oxford: Clarendon Press, 1983). The literature on akrasia is vast, and there are accounts arguing that akrasia, if it is a coherent concept, is merely a response to plural and incommensurable values. Still, my use of it here is close to the common sense of our folk psychology.

23. Rom. 7:19 (King James Bible).

24. Jon Elster has done more than anyone to explore the ramifications of "self-binding," in such books as *Ulysses Unbound* (Cambridge: Cambridge University Press, 2000) and *Strong Feelings* (Cambridge: MIT Press, 2000). For a thoughtful exploration of how liberal democracies might deal with people of seriously defective rationality, see Judith Lynn Failer, *Who Qualifies for Rights? Homelessness, Mental Illness, and Civil Commitment* (Ithaca: Cornell University Press, 2002).

25. Objections can be raised even to the Self-Management card. Mill was, for good reasons, suspicious of binding contracts that make us comply with the decisions of our earlier selves. In the passage from *Principles of Political Economy* (1848), book 5, chapter 2, that I quoted in chapter 1, n. 14, Mill argued that an "exception to the doctrine that individuals are the best judges of their own interest, is when an individual attempts to decide irrevocably now, what will be best for his interest at some future and distant time." I've been assuming that my higher-order desires are stable, but what if they change? Does the assent of my previous self—or the prospective assent of my later self—really justify ignoring my current desires? "Don't do something you'll regret later" might sound like a plausible edict, but it would create a tyranny of the later self. I may know, to a dead certainty, that I'll regret something, but still have reason to do it. We're familiar with the human tendency to discount future utility; but the discounting of past utility is even more severe. It may be a matter of indifference to me today, and of regret to me tomorrow, that I ate that cherry pie yesterday; but it could still have been a monstrous infringement of my preferences to stop me at the time. Let's say that a doctor tells an ailing eighty-year-old that if only he'd lived a life of great abstemiousness, he'd have another ten years of good health. The octogenarian, now on his deathbed, may devoutly wish he'd done so: he values those decades of culinary pleasures at nothing, and if he could, he'd retrospectively sentence his younger self to decades of thin gruel. But what of it? My future self commands no absolute authority over my current one, and the inconsistencies of our preferences, even if predictable, aren't signs of irrationality. Again, it could be that, in some "Shawshank Redemption" scenario, I'm about to serve forty years in prison. Given my extreme claustrophobia, I know that those years will be pure hell, and I am contemplating suicide. A friend points out that if I get out in forty years, I'll feel glad I persisted, and will probably last another good three or four years. I know he's right. But what weight should I give that? My eighty-year-old self doesn't face four decades of hell; only I do.

26. Of course, to have given Freud morphine, against his wishes (which were clearly expressed, stable, and reflective), would have infringed on his autonomy: even a thoroughgoing hedonist might worry that the consequent distress would survive the morphine infusion. If you're not a hedonist, you might (1) consider autonomy to be a part of someone's well-being; or you might (2) think that autonomy and well-being were in conflict, and that there was no compelling reason to favor the latter over the former. In any event, there's plenty of evidence that physical suffering doesn't negate the possibility of well-being. Here's a more challenging example than that of Freud's final days: I'm told of an unexpected result that emerged in a study of juvenile cancer patients undergoing radiation and bone-marrow grafts. Using a standard questionnaire, the

researcher asked them to assess their well-being, including their quality of life, their physical capability, and so forth. What puzzled him was that the patients, though debilitated and subjected to the most grueling treatments, rated themselves higher than did a group of perfectly healthy kids from the neighborhood. The grueling treatment, plainly, provided the former with a heartening sense of purpose, lacking in their listless, mopey (but healthy) peers. The patients were suffering to a purpose, they clearly felt. But what if they weren't, and the experimental protocol proved ineffective? As Sen points out in his essay on "plural utilities," we feel sorry for the man living in a fool's paradise; but when he is disabused, we feel even sorrier for him. "The *fact* of the desire fulfillment and the awareness of it can be *both* relevant," he says. Sen, "Plural Utility," 203. (It would, in general, not be an act of kindness to tell someone that his late wife had secretly been another man's mistress.) Yet as soon as researchers discovered that the experimental treatment was ineffective, they obviously would have had a moral obligation to inform their patients and discontinue the treatment immediately.

27. Nozick, *Anarchy, State, and Utopia* (New York: Basic Books, 1974), 42–43. That the desire isn't reducible to an experience doesn't mean there isn't an experiential requirement. The situation has, accordingly, been parsed in terms of first-order and second-order desires; perhaps the first-order desire was to feel as if one had written a novel, and the second-order desire was that the satisfaction of the first-order desire was justified by the objective completion of the task. Let me make this plausible. Sir Walter Scott, by his own account, once wrote a novel, *The Bride of Lammermoor*, in such a laudanum-addled state that when he received the proofs he found he remembered none of the characters and none of the plot. Push this to a further extreme, and imagine a novelist who has no clear memory of writing a novel, which is then published, according to an arrangement he no longer recalls, under a pseudonym. It's successful, but, as it happens, it never comes to his attention. (He therefore has no false beliefs about the book, because he has no beliefs about it at all.) It's the opposite of the Experience Machine problem: here someone has successfully published a novel but does not have the belief that he did.

28. Cass Sunstein provides a wide-ranging working out of this thought in his "Preferences and Politics," *Philosophy and Public Affairs* 20, no. 3 (1991), about which I'll say more presently.

29. For some useful overviews of the literature, see Gerd Gigerenzer, *Calculated Risks* (New York: Simon & Schuster, 2002); *Heuristics and Biases*, ed. Thomas Gilovich, Dale Griffin, and Daniel Kahneman (Cambridge: Cambridge University Press, 2002); and Massimo Piattelli-Palmarini, *Inevitable Illusions* (New York: John Wiley & Sons, 1994). Some of our cognitive failures have to do not with the world, or conflicting desires, but with our failure to predict our own emotional states. In the psychological literature, for example, there has lately been much talk about "affective forecasting," and the biases to which people succumb in trying to predict what will make them happy.

30. Mill, *On Liberty*, CWM 18:274. The provision of *mis*information, on the other hand, interferes with the carrying out of our projects; and where it interferes with the success of those projects, it is especially objectionable on that ground.

31. Sunstein, "Preferences," 12.

32. Mill, *Utilitarianism, CWM* 10:211.

33. Sidgwick, *The Method of Ethics* (Indianapolis: Hackett, 1981), 111.

34. Carl Dennis, *Practical Gods* (New York: Penguin, 2001), 72.

35. A rebuttable assumption, to be sure. Indeed, it would be open to a first-person informed-preference theorist to shunt aside counterexamples that involve divergent *tastes*. Maybe there's a psychologically possible world in which you love organ music, and another in which you love chamber music, but none in which you love both. Now we wouldn't be able to say which kind of music "Maxi Me" should favor. And what this shows is that taste formation isn't best understood in terms of full information. Pop music marketers distinguish between songs that people rate highly on a first hearing, and songs that they come to love only after (say) eight or nine hearings (but perhaps become heartily sick of after seventy hearings). Whatever accounts for these tastes, it doesn't seem to be epistemic in nature. Repeated exposure to something can have causal effects that aren't, and shouldn't be, attributed to "full information." So you might say that, when it comes to such aesthetic choices, an informed desire account should defer to my actual desires. (For enthusiasts of value pluralism, as will be clear, such problems are ubiquitous.)

36. This consideration is in line with Scanlon's skepticism about whether "well-being" does much work in first-person (as opposed to third-person) accounts. In a nutshell, Scanlon says that if I want, and have reason to want, something (to save Venice, perhaps), we don't add anything to insist that in wanting it I also have opinions about how it affects my well-being; I want it in itself. Scanlon, *What We Owe to Each Other*, 134–35. By contrast, the god who loves you wishes your campaign to succeed because he cares about your well-being.

37. There's a problem with cases involving omniscient benefactors: why don't they just tell you what will happen? Scanlon—in ibid., 135—has offered a similar case: "Suppose, for example, that I have good reason to pursue a career as an artist, or as a labor organizer, even though this may lead to a lower level of well-being for me overall because of the difficulty and discomfort that this life involves. Suppose also that I cannot do this without help from some friends or family members. Do they have reason to help me even though they are not thereby promoting my well-being? It seems to me that they may." But there are reasons our intuitions are less than crystal clear in this instance: How can we, mere mortals, be confident that your well-being will be diminished? Do you really have good reason, all things considered, to lead a life that will diminish your well-being—does your decision represent some cognitive incapacity or underrating of future hardship? And, finally, of course, what's meant by well-being, and is it likely to be enhanced by your renouncing a pretty comprehensive goal?

38. "It may be *likely* that a person has reason to want those things for which he or she would have an informed desire, but this is by no means certain," Scanlon writes in ibid., 115. So that, though not all of our preferences merit automatic respect, we mustn't value bare desire fulfillment at nothing: public officials should be hesitant to assume they know our wants better than we do, or they may incur the worst abuses of "positive

liberty" that Berlin warned about. See his specific cautions, about the invocation of people's "true" wants, in "Two Concepts of Liberty," in *Four Essays*, 133–34. I'll explore the specter of overweening rationalism further in the next section.

39. Griffin, *Well-Being*, 12–13.

40. Ronald Dworkin, in *Sovereign Virtue*, 272, invokes his "challenge model" to argue against protecting people from "choosing wasteful or bad lives" by means of "educational constraints and devices that remove bad options from people's view and imagination." (And see Wall, *Liberalism, Perfectionism, and Restraint*, 224–25.) But to make that judgment requires some appreciation of substantive goods; and, of course, the bliss-case existence represents the repudiation of the challenge model.

41. Derek Parfit, "What Makes Someone's Life Go Best," in his *Reasons and Persons* (Oxford: Oxford University Press, 1986), 499. (Critics sometimes object to "objective list" measures because they're too narrow, too one-size-fits-all: but the lists are typically so broadly categorical that they're not very determining at all.) James Griffin, in *Well-Being*, though he disavows the objective-list account, offers a catalog of the "ends of life," which he calls "the truth buried in perfectionism," and which has something of the character of an objective list.

42. Parfit seems sympathetic to such a hybrid between a hedonic and an objective-good account: your life has value if and only if you both engage in objectively valuable activities and want to do so. And Scanlon, for one, thinks that the very notion of "well-being" does work only in that third-person context; from a first-person perspective, he proposes that we will get what we want if we speak of our success in our "rational aims." But insofar as informed-desire accounts introduce idealized agents, they often tacitly adopt such a third-person perspective. Of course, a benevolent observer must be sensitive to our actual wants: "be all you can be" is not a dictate of rationality. As Richard Arneson plausibly says, "A rational person with full information and after careful deliberation might well prefer a life with less accomplishment and less pain to a life of more accomplishment and more pain. This choice would not be a misguided choice to toss away one's good." Arneson, "Perfectionism and Politics," *Ethics* 111, no. 1 (October 2000): 54.

43. Gerald Dworkin, "The Concept of Autonomy," in *The Inner Citadel*, ed. John Christman (New York: Oxford University Press, 1989), 60.

44. Sunstein, "Preferences," 13; though he's speaking of the society writ large, not factions within it.

45. Among the collapsers, moreover, it is possible to identify two different parties, distinguished by their emphases: those who mainly wish to expose the value-ladenness of the putatively factual, and those who mainly wish to insist upon the facticity of value. It's perhaps worth pointing out that you can't show that the distinction has collapsed by showing that, say, science involves both facts and values. The Anscombean notion of relative bruteness is helpful here. Even many moral realists have no problem making an in-kind distinction between a brute fact (water is H_2O) and a "moral" fact (so-and-so is a brave man); the description of a man's brave acts is brute relative to the specification of him as a brave man.

46. John Locke, *Two Treatises of Government*, chapter 6, section 63.

47. Richard Braithwaite, "An Empiricist's View of the Nature of Religious Belief," in *The Philosophy of Religion*, ed. Basil Mitchell (Oxford: Oxford University Press, 1971), 72–91.

48. This was drawn to my attention by Brent Staples in a Du Bois Lecture in early April 2001, and will, no doubt, be discussed in the book that will be based on those lectures. He was kind enough to refer me to Robert P. Stuckert, "African Ancestry of the White American Population," *Ohio Journal of Science* 58, no. 3 (May 1958): 155. The article describes its statistical model and the sorts of data against which it was tested, and concludes: "The data presented in this study indicate that the popular belief in the non African background of white persons is invalid. Over twenty-eight million white persons are descendants of persons of African origin." And that was half a century ago.

49. Griffin, *Well-Being*, 136.

50. Mill, *On Liberty, CWM* 18:244.

51. John Robinson, *Honest to God* (London: John Knox Press, 1963).

52. Sometimes those threatened others are their own children, and the way in which they are threatened is by being turned into people with impaired identities. As we shall be discussing later, children cannot have their ethical identities respected when they are not yet in possession of them. So this wouldn't be an exception to the general idea that we don't interfere in the ethical identities of people who have them.

53. This, by the way, is another good example of why it's hard to distinguish, even in principle, between neutrality of justification and neutrality of consequences. Classificatory practices do not necessarily aim at promulgating the identities promulgated: but they do not therefore qualify as only consequentially nonneutral. After all, they take a controversial conception as an accepted fact, and in this their justification is nonneutral. As we saw earlier, each identity that a society sustains in this way is changed by the very fact of government recognition. "Hispanic" in the United States exists as a social identity that includes Mexican Americans, Puerto Ricans, and immigrants from a dozen or so Spanish-speaking countries of Latin America and the Caribbean, in part (admittedly a small part) because of the U.S. government's acknowledgment of those people as a collectivity. Many state acts have taken place since the creation of the identity that are (in some sense) aimed at shaping the identities, and thus the ethical prospects, of Hispanics; among them, for example, the provision of bilingual education programs for adults that allow them to maintain a language-based identity while being integrated into American society.

54. "Rational" discrimination—or what Kenneth Arrow and Edmund Phelps have analyzed as "statistical discrimination"—occurs when a firm discriminates for rational (i.e., profit-maximizing) reasons: for example, in order to economize on information costs. Contrary to certain conservative claims that the free market will, by itself, erode discrimination, then, Phelps and others maintain that, in a range of cases, state intervention may be necessary. As a rule, public action toward an individual based on a statistical stereotype, when she is, in fact, atypical of her group, burdens her for no good reason. The economically minded will object that if you have to consider even

members of groups who are characteristically not suitable for certain positions, there may be higher search costs in filling them than there would be if you were allowed to rule them out in advance. If the costs were astronomically higher or if they somehow burdened some employers more than others—because, for example, much of their competition was from companies working in regimes without antidiscrimination law— then there might, indeed, be a cause for subsidy here. But there seems no very good reason why the costs to the business should trump the costs to the qualified but unrep- resentative member of her group. Rights, whether public in general or civil in particular, always have costs, and they are not always borne by the state. It strikes me as a fortiori true that the cost to business should not automatically trump the cost to the potential employee, if the reason there are few qualified members of the group is historical injus- tice or present discrimination.

55. 517 F. Supp 292 (N.D. Tex. 1981) and 766 F.2Á (8th Cir. 1985); as discussed in Robert C. Post et al., *Prejudicial Appearances: The Logic of American Antidiscrimination Law* (Durham: Duke University Press, 2001), 30–31. My discussion here is drawn, in part, from my "Stereotypes and the Shaping of Identity," a response to his paper, which also appears in this volume.

56. Nor would we necessarily wish them to. See Thomas C. Grey, "Cover Blindness," in Post et al., *Prejudicial*, 85–97.

57. Post et al., *Prejudicial*, 22.

58. Ibid., 16–17; 13, citing *Mueller v. C.A. Muer Corp.*, a Michigan case.

59. Post et al., *Prejudicial*, 30–33. Once we accept this Postian picture of American antidiscrimination law, judges and legislatures and citizens would have to take up the question of which forms of invidiously disparate public action require remedy. We cannot prudently attempt to deal with all of them, making it a crime, for example, to be less courteous to black than to white guests at hotels. I think there is an obvious way to focus such discussions. It is to ask how central a form of public action is to main- taining sexual or racial inequality. Since racism and sexism are systematic and pat- terned, not mere accidental agglomerations of individualized prejudices, this is a rea- sonable question. And I think that those judges who have found it unreasonable to require employers to allow men to wear their hair long, for example, could rightly have given as their rationale the fact that such employers' preferences simply play too small a role in shaping gender in ways that disadvantage women. Similarly, requiring More- house College to enroll more white students would not reduce racial inequality in America, while integrating the elite schools that had historically excluded black people certainly was an important step in that direction.

60. John Locke, *Some Thoughts Concerning Education*, ed. James Axtell (Cambridge: Cambridge University Press, 1968), 112. A valuable discussion of Lockean individuality can be found in Uday Singh Mehta, *The Anxiety of Freedom* (Ithaca: Cornell University Press, 1992), 119–67.

61. *James Mill on Education*, ed. W. H. Burston (Cambridge: Cambridge University Press, 1969), 41.

62. Bruce Ackerman, *Social Justice in the Liberal State* (New Haven: Yale University Press, 1981), 159.

63. Michael Oakeshott, *The Voice of Liberal Learning: Michael Oakeshott on Education*, ed. Timothy Fuller (New Haven: Yale University Press, 1989), 24.

64. MacIntyre, *After Virtue*, 201.

65. Ellwood P. Cubberley, *Changing Conceptions of Education* (Boston: Houghton Mifflin, 1909), 15–16. And see discussions of this in Macedo, *Diversity and Distrust*, 91, and Eamonn Callan, *Creating Citizens* (Oxford: Clarendon Press, 1997), 172.

66. Macedo, *Diversity and Distrust*, 134. "The task of building a common political culture is work that must be done, if not by public schools as we know them, then somehow." One can go too far in this direction; he faults Dewey for doing so. (His prudential conclusion: "We should tolerate the intolerant, as along as they do not genuinely threaten the survival of free institutions, but we need not bend over backward to make life easy for them.")

67. Callan, *Creating Citizens*, 145, 146.

68. That is, the state legitimately intervenes where a minimal, or a "good enough," level of care isn't provided. And you could hold to a satisficing requirement even if you thought the maximizing conception was (perhaps because of value incommensurability) incoherent. There are other complicating considerations here: education, unlike piano playing, is mandatory; the school is an institution that is outside the immediate domestic sphere; failing to maximize another's well-being is not the same as doing harm, or diminishing his current well-being.

69. "Ethnic" challenges to public education are not always motivated by curricular issues per se: the Old Order Amish, in *Wisconsin v. Yoder*, argued that compulsory education beyond the eighth grade would undermine their way of life, regardless of what their children were taught: being forced to spend the time in the classroom, rather than at the farm, was the problem. In that case, the Supreme Court held, "It is one thing to say that compulsory education for a year or two beyond the eighth grade may be necessary when its goal is the preparation of the child for life in modern society as the majority live, but it is quite another if the goal of education be viewed as the preparation of the child for life in the separated agrarian community that is the keystone of the Amish faith." Essentially, they treated the Old Order Amish (and members of the Conservative Amish Mennonite Church, who were fellow plaintiffs) as if they were Native Americans on a reservation—not *quite* citizens of the United States, but existing as benign pockets of Otherness within it.

70. Perhaps I should add that I know of no major court case in which instructional style has been the subject of First Amendment–style scrutiny—where a religious petitioner, say, has held it to be an "undue" burden. Then again, it might be difficult to summon empirical support for constructivist pedagogy: certainly, a certain amount of "situationist" research suggests that classroom conduct is classroom specific and doesn't necessarily travel beyond that context.

71. Mill continues, "It seems to me that to act otherwise on any pretext whatever is little if at all short of a crime against one's children, against one's fellow creatures in

general, & against abstract truth in whatever form it appears most sacred to one's eyes." *The Later Letters, 1849–1873, CWM* 16:1468.

72. Stephen Bates, *Battleground: One Mother's Crusade, the Religious Right, and the Struggle for Control of Our Classrooms* (New York: Simon and Schuster, 1993).

73. Cf. Macedo, "Transformative Constitutionalism," 73: "Since a liberal public morality is always (more or less) in a state of coming-into-being, we should accommodate dissenters when doing so helps draw them into the public moral order: when it helps transform a modus vivendi into a deeper set of shared principled commitments. Will the refusal to accommodate religious complaints about public schooling drive religious families out of public schools and into Christian schools? If so (and assuming that public schools are important agents of liberal socialization, at least by virtue of mixing people of different backgrounds), then we have a powerful pragmatic argument for accommodation."

In the *Mozert* example, one is also struck by how *American* the complaint was: however monist and intolerant their rhetoric, they had also imbibed much of the American civic creed. One would be hard-pressed to imagine citizens in most other modern societies hoping for as much autonomy, in the matter of schooling, as the *Mozert* plaintiffs considered their due.

74. As noted in Mele, *Autonomous Agents*, 185. For a helpful analysis of arguments for paternalism from "subsequent consent," or from "anticipated consent," see Kleinig, *Paternalism*, 55–67.

75. Mill, "Nature," in *Three Essays on Religion, CWM* 10:396.

Chapter Six Rooted Cosmopolitanism

1.

For I dipt into the future, far as human eye could see,

Saw the Vision of the world, and all the wonder that would be;

 Saw the heavens fill with commerce, argosies of magic sails,

Pilots of the purple twilight dropping down with costly bales; . . .

 Till the war-drum throbb'd no longer, and the battle-flags were furl'd

In the Parliament of man, the Federation of the world.

         Alfred, Lord Tennyson, "Locksley Hall" (1842).

2. Marcus Aurelius, *Meditations*, trans. with an introduction by Maxwell Staniforth (New York: Penguin, 1964), 188.

3. Staniforth, introduction to the *Meditations*, 18. It might be objected that Staniforth is a rather Christianizing reader of Marcus Aurelius; but then Western Christianity is a rather Stoicized religion.

4. Dworkin, "What Is Equality? Part 2: Equality of Resources," *Philosophy and Public Affairs* 10, no. 4 (Autumn 1981): 283–345; reprinted with slight changes as chapter 2 in *Sovereign Virtue*; Rawls, *A Theory of Justice*, 457; Nozick, *Anarchy, State, and Utopia*, 185. Nozick's Crusoes become aware of one another only after having prospered to various

degrees; the conceit of the island incubator is a means of exploring the connection between social cooperation and the Rawlsian problem of distributive social justice.

5. Despite this theoretical individualism, "common-sense moral thought" supposes, as Charles Beitz has observed, both "that a government may legitimately restrict immigration in order to protect the stability and cohesion of domestic political life," and "that a government may give greater weight in redistributing income to improving the welfare of the domestic poor than to improving that of the poor elsewhere—even if the domestic poor are already better off than the foreign poor." To make these suppositions consistent with individualism, we should have to show that these principles (each of which expresses partiality for the citizen over the outsider) are somehow justifiable in terms of the way they work out for individuals. Beitz is not alone in thinking that that burden of justification is not easily met. Charles R. Beitz, "Cosmopolitan Ideals and National Sentiment," *Journal of Philosophy* 80, no. 10 (October 1983): 592. As Beitz's writings demonstrate, political theorists have begun to challenge the historical marginality of these issues. Some of this work will be discussed in what follows. But questions of the obligations of states to the foreign poor have been the focus of much attention since Henry Shue's *Basic Rights: Subsistence, Affluence, and American Foreign Policy* (Princeton: Princeton University Press, 1980), to give only one prominent example, while Michael Walzer's justly well regarded *Spheres of Justice* (New York: Basic Books, 1983) prompted a lively literature on the political morality of membership. And Charles Beitz and Thomas Pogge have carried on eloquent campaigns for many years for ways of thinking of international justice that are responsive to individualism, universalism, and equality. Or in Pogge's terms, universality (meaning that individuals are all equal units of concern) and generality (meaning that they are equal units of concern for everyone). Thomas W. Pogge, "Cosmopolitanism and Sovereignty," *Ethics* 103 (October 1992): 48–49.

6. One might want to disqualify creeds that divide the world between infidels and believers, or, for that matter, between Christians and heathen; and yet people can convert (and, often at the point of a sword, many have done so) to Islam, or Christianity, and so what side of the line you're on depends on a feature you can do something about.

7. See Susan Wolf, "Morality and Impartiality," *Philosophical Perspectives* 6 (1992): 243–59; and William Godwin, *Enquiry: Concerning Political Justice and Its Influence on Morals and Happiness* (Toronto: University of Toronto Press, 1946), 1:128.

8. Charles Dickens, *Bleak House* (Oxford: Oxford University Press, 1996), 47.

9. "Directly the seducers come with their seductions to bribe you into captivity, tear up the parchments; refuse to fill up the forms," she continues. This freedom, she suggests, is the distinct province of "the daughters of educated men." Virginia Woolf, *Three Guineas* (New York: Harcourt, 1938), 80, 78. It has not gone unremarked that Woolf, writing in the late 1930s, seems to have been convinced of the moral equivalence between the looming evils abroad and the settled ones at home—she deplored equally "the whole inequity of dictatorship, whether in Oxford or Cambridge, in Whitehall or Downing Street, against Jews or against women, in England, or in Germany, in Italy or

in Spain" (103). And she insisted that a woman in England was, politically, an outsider: " 'Our country,' she will say, 'throughout the greater part of its history has treated me as a slave. . . . Therefore if you insist upon fighting to protect me or 'our' country, let it be understood, soberly and rationally between us, that you are fighting to gratify a sex instinct which I cannot share; to procure benefits in which I have not shared and probably will not share; but not to gratify my instincts, or to protect myself or my country. For the outsider will say, 'in fact, as a woman, I have no country. As a woman, I want no country. As a woman, my country is the whole world' " (109). Here one collective identity is repudiated in the name of another, that of her sex or, anyway, a disinherited political class coextensive with her sex.

10. "Patriotism or Peace?" in *Tolstoy's Writings on Civil Disobedience and Nonviolence* (New York: New American Library, 1968), 75, 107. Marxist-Leninism had a curiously ambivalent relation to cosmopolitanism. The texts the Bolshevik revolutionaries studied were, in the main, hostile to nationalism: "The working man has no fatherland," Marx and Engels wrote, and, of course, the movement they spawned took the *Internationale* to be more than an anthem; at the same time, though, Marx shunned the cosmopolitan as an effluent of capitalism. Notoriously, Stalin's anti-Jewish campaigns, culminating in the "Doctor's Plot," regularly decried "rootless cosmopolitans" who nursed "antipatriotic views."

11. This question was first put to him in 1962 by J. B. Danquah, who was the leader of the major opposition party in Nkrumah's Ghana, and who later died as a political prisoner, of medical neglect. See Joseph Appiah, *Joe Appiah: The Autobiography of an African Patriot* (New York: Praeger, 1990), 266. My father was jailed by three separate regimes; although there were never any charges or any trials, the ostensible rationale was that his imprisonment was some sort of measure against sedition. In Ghana's parliament in the early sixties, for example, he had a tendency to take issue with the increasingly despotic policies of President Kwame Nkrumah. More than a decade and a half later, he found himself in Cell No. 12 of Nsawam Prison; one of his cellmates was a long-ago departed head of state, Akwasi Afrifa, who, along with several others, was soon taken away and executed; my father, despite various threats, was spared, but, as he appreciated, it could easily have been otherwise. He could have avoided arrest: either by avoiding politically perilous speech, or by heeding the members of the security apparatus who warned him ahead of time to leave the country. He declined, of course: departure was ruled out by own sense of Ghanaian patriotism—an allegiance, let's recall, to a political unit created by the union of the Gold Coast Colony and British Togoland in 1956, but bound up, for him, with the project of forming a postcolonial liberal democracy.

12. For some representative arguments along these lines, focusing on the issue of patriotic partiality in the allocation of public resources, see Christopher Heath Wellman, "Relational Facts in Liberal Political Theory: Is There Magic in the Pronoun 'My'?" *Ethics* 110 (April 2000): 537–62 (making, inter alia, a reference-group argument: a country should preferentially assist its citizens because inequality among people in the same society is more invidious than inequality among people who "have never

heard of one another"); Andrew Mason, "Special Obligations to Compatriots," *Ethics* 107 (April 1997): 427–47 (arguing, inter alia, that such obligations stem from the generalizable value of citizenship); Richard W. Miller, "Cosmopolitan Respect and Patriotic Concern," *Philosophy and Public Affairs* 27, no. 3 (Summer 1998): 202–24 (arguing that a state must preferentially assist its own citizens to ensure its legitimacy, especially among the needy). For a vigorous and cogent critique of a wide range of reductionist accounts, see A. John Simmons, "Associative Political Obligations," *Ethics* 106, no. 2 (January 1996): 247–73. I should be clear about my own position here: reductionist accounts could conceivably succeed on their own terms (identifying moral reasons for acting that coincide with partialist—in most of these instances, patriotic—sentiment), but they don't capture the phenomenon that's to be captured, what I'll be calling the evaluative affect of partiality. These reductionist accounts are like health claims for chocolate: they may "justify" the practice of eating it, but, accurate or not, they aren't why anybody does so.

13. I will ignore the distinctions that some political theorists have drawn between "duty" and "obligation." In addition to those essays cited above, the putative clash between national and moral allegiances is explored in Stephen Nathanson, "In Defense of 'Moderate Patriotism,' " *Ethics* 99 (April 1989): 535–52; David Miller, *On Nationalism* (Oxford: Oxford University Press, 1995); Martha Nussbaum, "Patriotism and Cosmopolitanism," in *For Love of Country: Debating the Limits of Patriotism*, ed. Joshua Cohen (Boston: Beacon Press, 1996), and the many short responses to her essay in that volume; Samuel Scheffler, *Boundaries and Allegiances: Problems of Justice and Responsibility in Liberal Thought* (New York: Oxford University Press, 2001); and in a number of essays in *The Morality of Nationalism*, ed. Robert McKim and Jeff McMahon (New York: Oxford University Press, 1997).

14. Scheffler, "Liberalism, Nationalism and Egalitarianism," in *Boundaries*, 79.

15. Advocates of this approach might also invoke Amartya Sen's discussion of "positional objectivity" (where the point of departure is the observation that many claims— e.g., "the sun and the moon look similar in size"—are both position-dependent and objective). Among the positional parameters Sen mentions are someone's knowledge of particular concepts; perhaps a person's special ties should be counted among those positional parameters, too. Amartya Sen, "Positional Objectivity," *Philosophy and Public Affairs* 22, no. 2 (Spring 1993): 126–45.

16. Mason, "Special Obligations to Compatriots," 446. The possibility Mason asks us to entertain is that the desirability of an action may sometimes relate to who did it: "For example, when someone stands in need of help and a friend provides it, not only are the person's needs met but there has also been a realization of the good of friendship." Mutatis mutandis with the case of citizenship: "[W]hen one citizen comes to the aid of another because they are fellow citizens, not only has a needy person been taken care of but also there has been a realization of the good of citizenship." Mason's general account is meant to be consonant with Joseph Raz's argument—in "Liberating Duties," *Law and Philosophy* 8 (1989): 3–21—that the special duties that obtain between two friends are justified by the intrinsic value, the moral good, of friendship *tout court.*

17. Scanlon, *What We Owe to Each Other*, 174. Similarly, Scanlon says, it would be odd to say you valued your children because they were valuable. Allen Wood has traced something like this line of argument to Hegel's critique of Kantian *Moralität*. A related position has been defended by Bernard Williams. In his often-cited discussion, there's a group of people who are drowning after a shipwreck, and a man, who can rescue only one, chooses his wife. If we say that the husband had first determined that his action was morally permissible, we furnish him, in Williams's famous phrase, with "one thought too many." For "it might have been hoped by some (for instance, by his wife) that his motivating thought, fully spelled out, would be the thought that it was his wife, not that it was his wife and that in situations of this kind it is permissible to save one's wife." Williams, "Persons, Character, and Morality," in *Moral Luck*, 13. Consonant arguments have been made by, inter alia, Lawrence Blum, *Friendship, Altruism, and Morality* (London: Routledge, 1982), and Slote, *Goods and Virtues*. For an excellent overview of the arguments here, and a defense of Kant against this strain of interpretation, see Henry Allison, *Kant's Theory of Freedom* (New York: Cambridge University Press, 1990), 180–98.

18. True, a person may be in pursuit of *a* spouse, or *a* friend; and here we properly employ the indefinite article. But that doesn't quite capture all that is to be captured: for example, who qualifies as a congenial spouse. Likewise, we can abstractly wish for opportunity; but the kinds of opportunity that we value are highly specific, shaped by our particular ambitions.

19. Even with a garment, however, you can imagine how truly particularist value can arise, in the currency of "sentimental value." Somewhere, there is an aging baby boomer inconsolable after the theft of a garment: "That was the very blouse I wore to Woodstock—never washed since Janis Joplin was sick on it!" Sentimental value is the thing that drops out of the insurance adjuster's analysis.

20. Perhaps it's worth noting that "kind"—both the adjective and the noun—is etymologically related to Old English words for family and suggests a "family feeling."

21. For some vigorous challenges to conventional liberal arguments as to why equality matters, see Harry Frankfurt, "Equality as a Moral Ideal," in *The Importance of What We Care About*, 134–58, proposing a satisficing rather than egalitarian approach to the distribution of wealth; Elizabeth Anderson, "What Is the Point of Equality?" *Ethics* 109, no. 2 (January 1999): 287–337, proposing that relationships of equality, rather than equality of wealth or resources, are what should matter to liberals; and John Kane's marvelously provocative intervention, "Justice, Impartiality, and Equality: Why the Concept of Justice Does Not Presume Equality," *Political Theory* 24, no. 3 (August 1996): 375–93, arguing precisely for "giving each their due," where our due depends not upon the principle of equality but upon equivalence—"that is, on the Aristotelian doctrine of proportionality."

22. "You Light Up My Life," words and music by Joe Brooks (New York: Big Hill Music Corp., 1979).

23. Judith Jarvis Thomson says the reason torturing a baby is wrong is not that any reasonable system of morality says so; a system of moral rules must start with the fact

that we all find torturing a baby to be wrong. Thomson, *The Realm of Rights* (Cambridge: Harvard University Press, 1990), 30 n. 19; quoted in Scanlon, *What We Owe to Each Other*, 391. Her example is deliberately uncontroversial. Everyone will agree that torturing a baby—under that description—is wrong. But *under that description* isn't a trivial qualifier. Maybe you believe, with the elders of your tribe, that your child has been possessed by evil spirits, and that you are "torturing" it in order to drive them away and save its life, rather as Western doctors routinely inflict pain in the course of their efforts to make us better. One could rejoin that, in this case, the word "torture" isn't apposite—but such attempts at definitional deflection usually lead to boggy terrain. Here's a harder-to-dodge example: consider an inquisitor who tortures a man in order to get him to confess his heretical beliefs, but sincerely wants him to confess in order to save his everlasting soul. Here we'd surely have to agree that he was intentionally inflicting torture, even if his ultimate aim was the betterment of the victim.

24. Stephen L. Darwall, "Two Kinds of Respect," *Ethics* 88, no. 1 (October 1977): 38.

25. An adage among some black Americans raises this concern rather pointedly: "When white folks say 'justice,' they mean 'just us.' " Extreme, thoroughgoing cosmopolitans raise this very objection to conceptions of social justice that are confined to one particular society: in their view, "just us"—unless it is just us human beings—is never a morally permissible demarcation.

26. Margalit, *The Ethics of Memory* (Cambridge: Harvard University Press, 2002), 7, 8. The relevant nomenclatural distinction between thick and thin, of course, runs from Ryle to Geertz to Walzer.

27. This use of "relational facts" comes from Miller, *On Nationalism*; cf. Wellman, "Relational Facts."

28. What if you acknowledge your membership in an association but don't regard it as a good? (This question won't always arise: in a range of instances, you should define the "association" in question such that you can't be a member without taking it to be good. But that's not automatically so.) Exit, of course, may not be an option. (In the mordant Yiddish folk saying: "If you ever forget you're a Jew, a goy will remind you.") Still, if you don't wish to be a good member of that association, you will get by with what you can get away with, comply with the rules but do no more. We can think worse of you—can regard you as a lazy member of the association, apathetic, lacking in civic virtue—without thinking that you are immoral.

29. Can we acknowledge both what we owe to persons as persons and what we owe to particular people who have particular connections to us? Alasdair MacIntyre, in his much-discussed paper "Is Patriotism a Virtue?" raises the question of how cosmopolitanism—in his terms, a "morality of liberal impersonality"—can ground itself; he is inclined to think it is a parochialism with airs, and much the worse for it. MacIntyre argues for a kind of moral localism—eschewing morality as such, for the particular morality of a particular social order; abjuring the vantage point of the abstract rational agent, rather than of this or that "peasant or farmer or quarterback"—and (here's the rub) does so from the Archimedean position his argument denies. For his thesis concerns not my attitude toward my country, but the attitude "we" should have toward

the transnational phenomenon called "patriotism." Cosmopolitanism does not suffer this particular form of incoherence. See Alasdair MacIntyre, "Is Patriotism a Virtue?" The Lindley Lecture, Lawrence, Kansas, 1984, 9, 18. Thomas Hurka, arguing for the irrelevance of the "embedded self" thesis to the debate about national partiality, makes the point forcefully: "Any such universalist claims, no less than those of impartialist morality, issue from a standpoint that the particularist says is not available—namely, one abstracted from any particular social identity and addressed to all humans or all members of cultures as such." Hurka, "The Justification of National Partiality," in McKim and McMahon, *Morality of Nationalism*, 143. And see Scheffler, "Conceptions of Cosmopolitanism," in *Boundaries*, 119, pointing out that MacIntyre here endorses the same disjunction between equality and the existence of "underived special responsibility" that leads to extreme-impartialist cosmopolitanism.

30. Scanlon, in *What We Owe to Each Other*, 174, writes: "[T]he values of friendship and parenthood are not independent of the narrower morality of 'what we owe to each other.' . . . they are both shaped by it and shape it in turn. They are shaped by it insofar as they are relations with others who must be recognized as persons with moral standing that is independent of this relationship; they shape it because they represent important forms of human good which any set of principles that no one could reasonably reject must make room for. But being a good friend or parent involves understanding and responding to values that go beyond this central form of morality."

31. See, for example, Nathanson, "In Defense of 'Moderate Patriotism,' " 538. "[W]e can hold that patriotism is a virtue so long as the actions it encourages are not themselves immoral. So long as devotion and loyalty to one's country do not lead to immoral actions, then patriotism can be quite laudable."

32. You might object that the promisee would, if she knew about the situation, certainly accede to your decision to break your promise, so, by the logic of "anticipated consent" or "subsequent consent," you weren't properly guilty of promise breaking. (Recall the unpicked-up, unpaid-for birthday cake in Raymond Carver's story "A Small, Good Thing"—a cake whose intended recipient was hit by a car, unbeknownst to the furious baker.) But you can't assume that. Perhaps the promise was to somebody who deeply disapproved of your having chosen a career in architecture; perhaps you'd broken a lunch appointment with a rival architect, who would prefer you not enter the competition. (Perhaps, in fact, she picked the date knowing you'd forgotten the deadline.)

33. I'll return to this matter later; suffice it to say that we should proceed carefully here. Being your parent's offspring isn't—at least on one plausible view—metaphysically contingent and normally comes with special obligations. Similarly, being a male or female is a necessary feature of your metaphysical identity, and special duties might relate to your sex. A more fantastical example: imagine an association that arose among people born on a specific date—perhaps it is the birth date of a society's Beloved Leader—and that acquired ethical salience for its members. Being born at a certain time is generally considered a necessary feature of your personal, i.e., metaphysical, identity. A focus on whether features are contingent or not is misplaced. For one thing, in these instances, the social identity supervenes upon these necessary features of our

metaphysical identity but is not exhausted by them; these traits are not sufficient to establish the special duties.

34. Margalit, *The Ethics of Memory*, 106.

35. George Eliot, *Middlemarch* (New York: Oxford University Press, 1985), 835.

36. No doubt there's a further scale in which being a good mother is of greater value than being a good Manchester United fan.

37. Immanuel Kant, *The Critique of the Power of Judgment*, trans. Paul Guyer and Eric Matthews (Cambridge: Cambridge University Press, 2000), 121.

38. I hope it goes without saying that the fact that norms are community-dependent in this way doesn't entail ethical relativism: that an Akan male has these obligations isn't "true for" the Akan; it is true *about* the Akan. Obviously, there are general concerns at stake in this example, namely, the raising of children: one thing that kinship systems of this sort do is solve coordination problems. As with conventions about whether you drive on the left or on the right, what matters is that everyone in a community is following the same rules.

39. Dedicated reductionists—see Wellman, "Relational Facts"—can point out that what I owe to my sister might vary with all sorts of other factors (how we've treated each other, whether we were raised together, and so forth), and so the "relational fact" of "sisterhood" can't be basic. But that doesn't cut much ice: nonreductive partialists don't have to hold that abstractly described relational facts make indefeasible demands; they can hold that this or that historically specific relation makes (defeasible) demands. At the same time, it would be open to the nonreductive partialist to categorize that specific relation in general terms: you owe your sister something extra, unless there are good reasons that you don't—reasons that might include special circumstances or misbehavior on her part.

40. Compare Charles Taylor on Hegel's concept of *Sittlichkeit*: "The crucial characteristic of *Sittlichkeit* is that it enjoins us to bring about what already is. This is a paradoxical way of putting it, but in fact the common life which is the basis of my *sittlich* obligations is already there in existence. It is in virtue of its being an ongoing affair that I have these obligations; and my fulfillment of these obligations is what sustains it and keeps it in being. Hence in *Sittlichkeit* there is no gap between what ought to be and what is, between Sollen and Sein." Charles Taylor, *Hegel and Modern Society* (Cambridge: Cambridge University Press, 1979), 83.

41. Scheffler, "Conceptions of Cosmopolitanism," in *Boundaries*, 121. And see his "Relationships and Responsibilities," in *Boundaries*, 97–110.

42. George Saunders, "A Survey of the Literature," *The New Yorker*, September 22, 2003, 118.

43. Craig Calhoun, "Nationalism and Ethnicity," *Annual Review of Sociology* 19 (1993): 230; and Calhoun, *Nationalism* (Minneapolis: University of Minnesota Press, 197), 42–44. As he notes, religious identities long had this form.

44. Friedrich Meinecke, *Cosmopolitanism and the National State*, trans. Robert B. Kimber (Princeton: Princeton University Press, 1970), 94. Originally published in 1908 as *Weltbürgertum und Nationalstaat: Studien zur Genesis des deutschen Nationalstaats*.

Meinecke is discussing Fichte at this point; but he has expressed the same claim in various ways by this point in discussions of Humboldt, Novalis, and Schlegel.

45. Nussbaum, "Patriotism and Cosmopolitanism," 7–8, 135–36.

46. Mazzini continues, "as when, even as a wise overseer of labour distributes the various branches of employment according to the different capacities of the workmen, he divided Humanity into distinct groups or nuclei upon the face of the earth, thus creating the germ of nationalities." *An Essay on the Duties of Man Addressed to Workingmen* (New York: Funk & Wagnalls, 1898), 57–58.

47. Burke, *Reflections on the Revolution in France*, ed. J.C.D. Clark (Stanford: Stanford University Press, 2001), 202. There's an old Arab proverb that seems to state Burke's point by negation: "I against my brother. My brother and I against my cousin. My cousin, my brother, and I against the world." Notice the absence of any intermediate form of social organization between clan and cosmos, which may reflect the historical weakness of national allegiances in the Arab world.

48. Nussbaum, "Patriotism and Cosmopolitanism," 7. See my article "But Would That Still Be Me? Notes on Gender, 'Race,' Ethnicity as Sources of Identity," *Journal of Philosophy* 87, no. 10 (October 1990): 493–99. And see n. 33 above.

49. What makes Saunders's conceit a satire is that his examples of categorical kinship don't involve the self-conscious form of identification we associate with national membership—they don't even involve the social forms that undergird activities like (to use one of Raz's instances) bird-watching. Then again, it would be easy to imagine a form of collective identity arising from a trait that currently bore none. If some regime sought to persecute left-handers—even people who merely displayed a tendency toward left-handedness—one would expect very soon a sense of fraternity among the sinistral.

50. Nussbaum, "Patriotism and Cosmopolitanism," 14.

51. I do not mean that every nation that is not a state was once a state in the past. I mean rather that a national identity is generated in a people in response to states, rather than being something that by itself generates a desire for statehood. In other words, sharing a language, customs, or practices does not automatically generate a desire for the political expression of that commonality through a single state. American nationalism begins as a response to the British state from a people of remarkably diverse origins, whose leaders nevertheless imagined they were fundamentally Englishmen abroad. Palestinian nationalism, to offer another example, is the product of the experiences of non-Jewish Arabs at the hands of Ottoman, British, and Israeli states that have treated them differentially from other people residing in that part of the eastern Mediterranean littoral. It is not the product simply of shared language because there were no sharp gradients of dialect in the Arabic at the boundaries (wherever you take them to be) of Palestine; it is not the product of shared religion, since Palestinians can be Druze or follow one of several varieties of Christianity or Islam. That the concept of an Arab Jew—or a Jewish Arab—now sounds paradoxical is one of the consequences of a political process, not a fact of nature. Similarly, Pakistani nationalism was created by the differential treatment by British and Indian states of Muslims in the Indian subcontinent; and much of the nationalism of Africa, the Middle East, and Latin

America is a response to colonial states that preexisted any sense of national identity. None of which is to deny the reality of any of the national identities produced by these political histories.

52. For an illuminating account of "range-limited" principles of justice—the sense in which, say, New Zealand institutions of justice are "for" New Zealanders, as opposed to the French—see Jeremy Waldron, "Special Ties and Natural Duties," *Philosophy and Public Affairs* 22 (1993): 3—30. Waldron's arguments—which would pretty much apply to any administrative cartography, any jurisdictional grid—support the notion that state-bounded institutions can, without arbitrariness, "apply" distinctively to the polity's members.

53. See, e.g., Linda Colley, *Britons: Forging the Nation, 1707–1837* (New Haven: Yale University Press, 1992); Eugen Weber, *Peasants into Frenchmen* (Palo Alto: Stanford University Press, 1976).

54. Laurence Sterne, *A Sentimental Journey* (Oxford: Oxford University Press, 1968), 62–63.

55. In my experience, whenever one says this in places where the practice is common, people (usually men) tell one that male circumcision reduces the frequency of some disease or other, for example, human papillomavirus infection. This seems likely to be true, according to the more than a dozen doctors at the International Agency for Research on Cancer Multicenter Cervical Cancer Study Group, who published a recent article titled "Male Circumcision, Penile Human Papillomavirus Infection, and Cervical Cancer in Female Partners" in the *New England Journal of Medicine* 346 (April 11, 2002): 1105–12. But that settles the matter only if there are no corresponding disadvantages to being circumcised; and only if these medical advantages are substantial enough to outweigh any disadvantages and could not be achieved in other ways (for example, by good hygiene). And, of course, these recent claims certainly don't establish that the practice was reasonable when it originated, since they weren't known then.

56. Richard Rorty, "Justice as a Larger Loyalty" in *Cosmopolitics*, ed. Phengh Cheah and Bruce Robbins (Minneapolis: University of Minnesota Press, 1998), 73.

57. Ibid., 57.

58. Ibid., 55.

59. One purpose for which "culture" is often deployed is the defense of "cultural autonomy." For example, the political theorist Anthony Smith speaks of cultural autonomy as a matter of "full control by representatives of the ethnic community over every aspect of its cultural life." Anthony Smith as cited in Tomlinson, *Cultural Imperialism*, 96. It's a shaky notion. John Tomlinson, in a fine discussion, raises questions about the very language of cultural autonomy. We know what it is for an individual to be autonomous—or, more precisely, to have potential degrees of autonomy. And we can easily speak this way of institutions acting for collectivities. But for "cultural autonomy" to make sense, Tomlinson argues, "[c]ultures would need to be things that could be free of external control and things that could be said to act, that is, to be agents. Typical discussions of 'cultural autonomy' tend to gloss over this issue." And trying to flesh out what cultural autonomy would entail, along the lines of Anthony Smith's proposal,

only makes this more apparent. For, Tomlinson notes, we lose the holistic conception of culture as soon as we introduce the apparatus of these representatives, who may not speak "for the culture" as a whole: "Representatives of a cultural community may oppose cultural imports while other members of the community welcome them: we are returned to the individual level of analysis with all its problems. What is at stake is the sense in which a culture in the holistic sense may be said to be capable of autonomy. And the real problem here is that cultures in this sense cannot be seen as agents. Cultures don't 'act' even in the rather abstract sense in which social institutions like government act. Cultures in this sense are simply descriptions of *how people act* in communities in particular historical situations." Individual "cultural representatives" may agitate in UNESCO; we should all attend to the mistreatment of aboriginal peoples. "But what doesn't speak, doesn't act, and therefore can't be said to have autonomy," Tomlinson observes, "is the culture itself." Tomlinson, *Cultural Imperialism*, 96–97.

60. You might want to say that there's a difference in magnitude between the *Lebenswelt* of the Mbuti and that of the marketing executive at Standard Brands, as compared to those of our contending academics, say. But we should resist saying there are *more* disagreements; again, where we cannot compare, we cannot count.

61. I'm taking lexical liberties here: in standard economic usage, those parties are *individuals*, and so a shirt counts as a rivalrous good, whereas a port would not be. But in the context of national conflict, I think the notion can usefully be collectivized.

62. Nussbaum, "Patriotism and Cosmopolitanism," 9. Leopardi goes on to remark, "Our hatred of those who are like us is greater towards those who are most like us." Giacomo Leopardi, *Thoughts*, trans. J. G. Nichols (London: Hesperus Press, 2003), 38.

63. Michael Ignatieff, *Human Rights as Politics and Idolatry* (Princeton: Princeton University Press, 2001), 7, 68. The discussion of human rights in this chapter incorporates parts of my commentary on his 2000 Tanner Lectures, included in that volume.

64. Whether particular laws that have the form of "collective rights"—that assign rights to groups—in fact conduce to the greater welfare of individuals is an empirical matter. Where they do, they would be justified, precisely by the effect they have on individuals. But I would be disinclined to dub strictures that are formally collective "human rights."

65. See L. W. Sumner's fine discussion in "The Analysis of Rights," in *The Moral Foundation of Rights* (Oxford: Clarendon Press, 1987), especially 15–31.

66. In most respects, the United States has a singularly expansive free-expression regime, and yet even here, freedom of expression is tightly corseted, and legitimately so. The First Amendment does not protect a contract killer's verbal contract; it does not protect a fraudulent or defamatory claim; it does not protect expression that is a means of pursuing a tortious or criminal action. Then there's a matter of venue—of *where* this right is to be enjoyed. A student cannot say whatever he wants whenever he wants in a classroom; an employee has no First Amendment rights to expression in a private-sector workplace; a shopper at Macy's cannot display a placard touting the prices at Bloomingdale's. Even in places that look more like a "public forum," you'll find that signage is limited by zoning restrictions and the like. So this freedom,

while real and important, doesn't fully apply in the places where you spend much of your life.

67. See Joseph Chan, "A Confucian Perspective on Human Rights for Contemporary China," in *The East Asian Challenge for Human Rights*, ed. Joanne R. Bauer and Daniel A. Bell (Cambridge: Cambridge University Press, 1999), 212–37; and Joseph Chan, "The Asian Challenge to Universal Human Rights: A Philosophical Appraisal," in *Human Rights and International Relations in the Asia-Pacific Region*, ed. James T. H. Tang (New York: St. Martin's Press, 1995). Should this desideratum be deemed a "right"? Though it is framed as a positive obligation, it could probably be framed as a constraint. Note that this right, unlike most of those enumerated in the UDHR, has to do with the relation between two people, not between a person and the state (though the state may become involved as an enforcer of the right). But to say, for example, that a child has the right not to be neglected is not to say that the child has the right not to starve: if a child's parents are themselves starving, and, despite their efforts, are unable to keep their child from starving, they are not guilty of neglect. Here the fulfillment of the obligation is not resource-dependent. (Recall Mill: "Duty is a thing which may be exacted from a person, as one exacts a debt. Unless we think that it may be exacted from him, we do not call it his duty." *CWM* 10:246.) A right of the elderly to care would have to be understood similarly; and it, too, might have to be traded off against other rights, including those of our children.

68. The democratization of "dignity" can appear paradoxical. As an attribute of status, it would seem to be an ordinal predicate, like "glory." How, then, can it be given to everyone? Of what use is an attribute you acquire in virtue of just being born? To compress and caricature a great deal of political history, one can really point to two contrary strains of such moral egalitarianism. Historians of the French Revolution have described how Jacobinism sought to transpose the thick predicates of family relations to the *citoyens* of the new order. In place of the bad old aristocracy, a new brotherhood of man would emerge. A similar rhetorical move was central to Leninism, where status titles were supplanted by the ubiquitous appellation *tovarich*—friend, usually translated "comrade." In these radical traditions, leveling occurs through demotion: the king is kin, the count a comrade. In modern liberal thought, by contrast, your comrade is a count. Here the move—though it similarly democratizes a thick and positional attribute of premodern ethics—has been to promote everyone to a privileged status. And one can argue that the political morality that stems from cutting everyone down to size will tend to look different from one that stems from hoisting everybody up. It is easier to call for *sacrifice* from friends and family than from exalted strangers—easier to subordinate the preferences of individuals to the putative needs of the collectivity. At the same time, the notion of dignity is helpful in articulating certain forms of assault and humiliation—of "dignitary affront"—that citizens may suffer as a result of public action.

69.

Cum referre negas quali sit quisque parente
natus, dum ingenuus, . . .

Quintus Horatius Flaccus, Sermones 1.6.7–8.

Horace's choice of the word "ingenuus" here leaves it open to us to interpret him as holding that the only obstacle to being a friend of Maecenas's is not being of free birth. For "ingenuus" can mean either "having the characteristics of a freeborn person" or just "freeborn." This is, of course, an ambiguity that it shares with analogous English words such as "gentlemanly" or "classy."

70.

sic qui promittit civis, urbem sibi curae,

imperium fore et Italiam, delubra deorum,

quo patre sit natus, num ignota matre inhonestus,

omnis mortalis curare et quaerere cogit.   Sermones, 1.6.34–37.

71. Cass R. Sunstein, "Incompletely Theorized Agreements," *Harvard Law Review* 108 (1995): 1733–72.

72. He continues, "Freedoms are socially engineered spaces where parties engaged in specified pursuits enjoy protection from parties who would otherwise naturally seek to interfere in those pursuits. One person's freedom is therefore always another person's restriction: we would not have even the concept of freedom if the reality of coercion were not already present." Louis Menand, "The Limits of Academic Freedom," in *The Future of Academic Freedom* (Chicago: University of Chicago Press, 1996), 1.

73. There is no reason to think that every society needs to implement the idea of popular choice in the same way; so different democratic institutions in different societies are consistent with the basic respect for autonomy, too.

74. I should explicitly record my opposition to the view that this origin in any way discredits these ideas, either for non-Europeans or, for that matter, for Europeans. The issues I want to explore have to do with the ways in which these views can be rooted in different traditions. I am not interested in the nativist project of arguing for these principles in the name of authentically Asante (or African) roots. The issues raised in the following paragraphs are thus historical, not justificatory.

75. My father's thought clearly wasn't that there weren't any atheists in Ghana but that their views didn't matter. Locke, of course, agreed: "[T]hose are not at all to be tolerated who deny the being of a God. Promises, covenants, and oaths, which are the bonds of human society, can have no hold upon an atheist. The taking away of God, though but even in thought, dissolves all." "A Letter Concerning Toleration," in *Political Writings of John Locke*, ed. David Wootton (New York: Mentor, 1993), 426.

76. Mill, *Principles of Political Economy, CWM* 3:594.

77. *Kuro* is usually translated as "town" or "hometown": but towns were relatively self-governing in the Asante past, so πολις looks like a translation that gets the right sense.

Index

~

Taha, Mahmoud Mohamed, 125

Taylor, Charles: on authenticity, 100, 105, 283n.42, 305n.63; on autonomy as a social artifact, 54, 293–94n.40; on being a good vs. being a locus of goods, 128, 307n.26; on collective identities, 107–8; on cultural preservation, 133; on culture as a social good, 127–30, 307n.23; on habitus, 54; on Hegel's on *Sittlichkeit*, 334n.40; on Herder, 106; on Humboldt, 284n.45; on identities as dialogically shaped, 108, 305n.63; on identity, 18–19, 20; on language, 20; on liberalism-communitarianism debates, 59; on the monological fallacy, 107, 305n.63; on the Québécois, 133, 135; on recognition, 71, 100–101, 103, 105, 304–5n.61; on self-giving heroism, 129–30, 148; on social goods, 318n.14; understanding our lives in terms of narratives, 22; on unencumbered vs. situated selves, 295n.48; on webs of interlocution, 45

Taylor, Harriet Hardy, 3, 8, 33–34, 281n.17, 282n.27

temperance legislation, 84

Temple Mount, 255–56

Tennyson, Alfred, Lord: "Locksley Hall," 214, 327n.1

Thatcher, Margaret, 132

thick vs. thin relations, 230–31, 232–33, 236–37

Thomas v. Review Board, 96–99, 303nn.53 and 55

Thompson, Judith Jarvis, 331–32n.23

Thornton v. Caldor, 85

tolerance: autonomy as intolerance, 40–45, 290n.13; vs. autonomy/reason, 41, 85, 290n.13; via cosmopolitanism, 247; historical experience of intolerance, 269–70; of illiberal practices grounded in local traditions, 248; Macedo on, 203, 326n.66; vs. respect for culture,

139. *See also* religious tolerance/freedom

Tolstoy, Leo, 222; *Anna Karenina*, 36, 47–48, 289n.3

Tomasi, John, 124

Tomlinson, John, 153, 313n.66, 336–37n.59

travel/interconnectedness, 215–17

tribalism, 152

Trilling, Lionel, 106

Trollope, Anthony, 8

the True vs. the Good, 251–52

Tully, James, 54

Turnbull, Colin, 150, 255

Tylor, Sir Edward Burnett, 119–20, 125

UDHR. *See* Universal Declaration of Human Rights

ummah (global Muslim community), 220

UNAIDS, 263

UNESCO, 263

UNICEF, 263

uniformitarianism, 220–21

Universal Declaration of Human Rights (UDHR; United Nations), 216, 260, 338n.67

universalism: antiuniversalist cosmopolitanism, 250, 258–59; vs. cosmopolitanism, 220, 222–24, 247–50; and diversity, 145; as ethnocentric, 248–49, 253–54; universalist cosmopolitanism, 219–20, 222, 241, 256, 258–59, 328n.5

utopias, island, 218–19

values: countability of, 148, 313n.63; fact-value distinction, xvi–xvii, 181, 188, 323n.45; project-dependent, 147–48, 227, 233, 243, 245; value pluralism, 43–45, 153, 291n.20, 316n.6; Western vs. Asian, 247, 251–52, 258–59

Vidal, Gore, 188

Virgil, 245

volitions, second-order, 166–67

voting, value of, 161

Vulgate, 245